Created and Directed by Hans Höfer

INSIGHT GUIDES

Spain

Executive Editor: Andrew Eames
Project Editor: Kathleen Wheaton
Photography by Joseph Viesti and others

Editorial Director: Brian Bell

HOUGHTON MIFFLIN COMPANY

APA PUBLICATIONS

Spain

Second Edition (2nd Reprint)
© 1995 APA PUBLICATIONS (HK) LTD
All Rights Reserved
Printed in Singapore by Höfer Press Pte. Ltd

Distributed in the United States by:	Distributed in Canada by:	Distributed in the UK & Ireland by:	Worldwide distribution enquiries:
Houghton Mifflin Company	**Thomas Allen & Son**	**GeoCenter International UK Ltd**	**Höfer Communications Pte Ltd**
222 Berkeley Street	390 Steelcase Road East	The Viables Center, Harrow Way	38 Joo Koon Road
Boston, Massachusetts 02116-3764	Markham, Ontario L3R 1G2	Basingstoke, Hampshire RG22 4BJ	Singapore 2262
ISBN: 0-395-68235-5	ISBN: 0-395-68235-5	ISBN: 9-62421-046-2	ISBN: 9-62421-046-2

ABOUT THIS BOOK

There can be few countries in the world which have seen as much recent change as Spain. In the years since General Franco's dictatorship ended, the nation has established true democracy and has welcomed back one of the most enlightened royal families of Europe. Having been on the fringes of the continent, the country is now back at the heart of the European Community; Barcelona hosted the 1992 Olympic Games with great style and Seville staged the Expo'92 World Fair. The economy leapt forward in the late 1980s and faltered with the European recession in the early 1990s; tourism has burgeoned – and that too has changed from the original emphasis on coastal resorts to a new interest in remote villages, rugged sierras, wildlife and the wide open spaces of the interior. Madrid has seen much change, and now boasts some of the world's finest art collections.

New Ingredients

This book has evolved dramatically to keep pace with all those changes. The original *Insight Guide: Spain* became something of a classic, winning the coveted Vega Inclan award from the Spanish Ministry of Tourism in 1987, the year of its first publication. This totally new edition has taken that original book as its foundation and has added essential new chapters which take account of all the recent events and the impact which those events have had on the Spanish outlook on life. It has also added a section on the ever-popular Canary Islands and massively expanded and renewed its comprehensive Travel Tips at the back of the book. In addition, there are new chapters on wildlife, on cafés and on Madrid's social life. All of the regional chapters have been revised, and the Madrid and Barcelona sections in particular have been totally reworked.

All this would not have been possible without the help of the wide network of contacts in Spain that Apa Publications recruited while creating a further seven Insight Guides and 10 Insight Pocket Guides to Spanish islands, regions and cities. After having produced all these regional works, this network of contacts was superbly placed to update the original book, under the guidance of London-based Executive Editor **Andrew Eames**, himself the editor of several of the individual titles.

Thanks are therefore due to **Lucinda Evans** in Madrid for rewriting the Madrid chapter, charting the events and achievements of Spain's big year, 1992, and putting together new pieces on cafés and Madrid life; to **Vicky Hayward**, for revising the Toledo and Escorial chapters; to **David Baird** in southern Spain for taking on updates both in this area and in the west; to **Roger Williams** for bringing eastern Spain up to date, and finally to **Muriel Feiner** for checking the essays and revising Travel Tips, as well as providing valuable language consultancy. Newcomer **Eric Robbins**, author of a book on Spain's wildlife, wrote the new chapter on that subject in this book.

Extra pictures for this edition were provided by New York-based photographer and Spain veteran **Bill Wassman,** and Spain-based **Dominique Dallet**.

The quality of this new edition of *Insight Guide: Spain* is very much the product of the excellence of the original book. The original project editor, **Kathleen Wheaton**, a native

Eames

Wheaton

Feiner

Evans

Wassman

Californian, first went to Spain in 1977 to spend a year at the University of Salamanca. Wheaton returned to Spain in 1980 and taught English in Madrid and San Sebastian. She is now back in New York where she has been on the editorial staff of the *New Yorker*, and has translated children's books while writing fiction of her own. In addition to recruiting the original journalists and photographers, Wheaton wrote the pieces on Castile and Extremadura, early Iberian history, castles, and Madrid.

Credit for the lion's share of the history section goes to **David Unger**, a New York-based poet, writer, and translator.

Ruth MacKay wrote the chapter on contemporary Spain as well as sections on Toledo, El Escorial, Navarre and Aragón. She has been a journalist in Madrid since 1977.

The People chapter was contributed by **Vega McVeagh**, a correspondent of Efe (Spain's state news agency) and the daughter of Americans who settled in Madrid.

New Yorker **Lisa Beebe** wrote the chapters in the section on Southern Spain.

Robert Crowe is a Southern Californian whose roots are in Zaragoza, Spain. He contributed this book's chapter on Valencia. Also originally from California, **Gil Carbajal** wrote the piece on the Spanish region he escapes to at every opportunity: the Balearic Islands. He has lived in Madrid since 1975.

Author of the chapters on Barcelona and Catalonia, **George Semler**, is a New Englander who is now settled in Barcelona, where he works as a journalist, translator, and editor.

John Smith is a seasoned *Insight Guide* contributor. Presently an editorial consultant in Paris, he revisited the Basque and Cantabrian regions of Spain for chapters on those areas, and also applied his background in Spanish art history to the feature on painting. **Francisco Conde**, another Texas native, and son of Galician emigrants, is now an AP correspondent in Madrid. Conde covered Galicia in this guide.

Julian Gray, who wrote about flamenco, is a lecturer on guitar history at the Peabody Conservatory in Baltimore. **Muriel Feiner** became hooked on bullfighting during a college trip to Spain; she now lives in Madrid where she is married to a bullfighter.

Visual Excellence

As always with Insight Guides, top-class photography is a distinguishing characteristic of this book. New York-based photographer **Joe Viesti** is well represented. Readers of Insight Guides will be familiar with Viesti's work in the *Crossing America, Texas, New York State, Italy* and *Canada* titles. Other contributors who deserve special mention include **José Martín**, who supplied the splendid painting reproductions and archival pictures as well as original photography of Madrid, Castile, and Galicia.

Popular Photography columnist **Carl Purcell** produced angles on Madrid and the Spanish south. Other contributors include **Fiona MacGregor, Robin Townsend, Rita Kümmel, Gaetano Barone, Jean Kugler,** and **John** and **Dallas Heaton**.

The finishing touches to this revised edition come from **Carole Mansur**, who completed the proof-reading and the new index.

Unger   *MacKay*   *Semler*   *Smith*   *Viesti*

History & People

Features

Maps

TRAVEL TIPS

INTRODUCTION

REGION BY REGION

Each section contains information on hotels, restaurants, attractions, museums, shopping, etc.

Compiled by Muriel Feiner

*For detailed information
see page 337*

Spain. To the ancient Greeks, it was the land where Hercules' golden apples grew; to the Arabs, it was the ground floor of heaven; to writers such as George Orwell and Ernest Hemingway, it was an arena where history skittered between heroic feats and tragedy, and bullfighters flirted with death in the work of an afternoon. Few other places so dramatically stimulate the imagination.

Yet despite the steady traffic to and from her coastal resorts, Spain has remained in the eyes of outsiders a mysterious, half-mythical country. The Spaniards who are best-known to the world are fictional characters: Don Juan, Don Quixote and Carmen. Fiestas and flamenco are alluring not only for their flamboyance but for their undeniable exoticism, with influences from outside Europe.

Spain's isolation from the rest of Europe began with her peninsular geography and is underscored by history: 700 years of Moorish occupation were followed by a powerful empire that colonised the New World, the failure of which led via civil war to the oppressive regime of General Franco. But as the traveller who sets out across Spain will discover, hundreds of years of solitude have created a country that is anything but homogeneous. Spaniards have traditionally spoken of their land as *Las Españas*; a notion of plurality embracing four languages and seven dialects and climates ranging from the subtropical south, sweet with its carob and hibiscus, to the emerald north, with its gorse and heather and plunging fjords.

Your trip will have a couple of constants. One is light: the sunshine northern Europeans flock to bask in, the burnished red-gold that suffuses whole cities, the lunar contrasts of sun and shadow, the light El Greco, Velázquez and Picasso saw and painted by. The other is a tremendous vitality, ubiquitous as the light, which is observed in cafés and strolling Sunday evening crowds, in haughty urbanites and exuberant festival dancers, or in the dignified courtesy of a stranger on a country road, who offers to share his lunch and enquires after your family.

Of all the Spains you encounter on your Spanish sojourn, surely the most striking and intoxicating is the "new Spain" of post-Francoism: proud parent of a young democracy, ambitious new member of the European Community, a Spain that in the course of a couple of decades has become an outrageous artist, uncensored journalist, idealistic politician, stage for world events and voracious consumer of news and culture. This new Spain is joyfully dispelling a few of the darker old myths, and has given a celebratory glow to the landscapes that await you.

Preceding pages: Stone huts in the Picos de Europa; Costa village; the white town of Casares in Andalusia; windmills in Consuegra, La Mancha. **Left**, La Mancha farmer.

IBERIA: BEGINNINGS

The land now covered by Spain and Portugal is a portion of the former Hercynian continent, which broke apart at Gibraltar sometime before the last Ice Age. Today the southern tip of the peninsula is 8 miles (13 km) from North Africa, but stands somewhat aloof from the main mass of Europe, jutting out into the Atlantic as far west as Ireland, and separated from the rest of the continent by the Pyrenees, whose average height of 5,000 ft (1,500 metres) exceeds that of the Alps. Among western European countries Spain is second only to France in size, or equal to an area slightly larger than California. Most of her 36 million people live in a few densely populated cities, and her long reaches of unfarmed, uninhabited terrain enhance a sense of vastness and solitude. In Spain people tend to speak of Europe as if it were somewhere else.

Climates: Within this self-contained fragment of land, two geographical facts have helped shape her history: the presence of mountains and the absence of rivers.

After Switzerland, Spain is Europe's most mountainous country: the average altitude of the peninsula is around 2,000 ft (600 metres). Mountains serve as a barrier to both Atlantic and Mediterranean air currents, dividing Spain into distinct climatic regions.

The peninsula was named Iberia – Land of Rivers – by tribes who crossed over from North Africa. To those desert people, Spanish rivers might have looked noteworthy, although in fact only two – the Ebro and the Guadalquivir – are reliably full enough to be useful in navigation and irrigation. The Moors, who settled along the banks of the Guadalquivir, praised it to heaven, causing Alexandre Dumas to write indignantly, in 1846: "French writers, never having seen it at all, believed the Arabs. True, Spanish writers could have revealed the less picturesque truth, but since it is the only river in their country large enough to take a boat, why should they decry it? When we got there we found that between the flat and uninteresting banks rolled a mass, not of water but

Preceding pages: A 16th-century map of Iberia. **Left**, tending flocks in Aragón.

of liquid mud with the colour and consistency, if not the taste, of milk chocolate."

Chopped up by high, jagged mountains and lacking any unifying waterways, it was perhaps inevitable that Spain developed as a handful of linguistic and cultural shards; a land "without a backbone", in the words of philosopher Ortega y Gasset. Yet while Iberia's landscape encouraged internal fragmentation and isolation, her position at the mouth of the Mediterranean made her a natural destination for a series of migrants, colonisers and traders.

Continental drifters: Weapons and charred bones from hunters' camps show that Neanderthal Man arrived in Spain as far back as

picted animals found on the floor of the caves imply that the paintings served a ritual purpose, a sympathetic magic to make the hunting good. But their vividness and baffling technical perfection have made them the first chapter in the history of Spanish art. Other cave paintings, showing lively stick figures using bows and arrows, have been found near Valencia. These pictures, dating from between 10,000 and 5,000 years ago, are similar to African paintings of the era, and presage the powerful influence that continent would have over Spanish culture during the next several thousand years.

Great waves of immigration occurred around 3000 BC, when the Iberians crossed

half a million years ago, following herds of European elephants as they migrated south. The earliest human remains have been uncovered on the *meseta*, not far from present-day Madrid in Soria. Neanderthal settlements, 200,000 years old, have been found at Gibraltar, leading archaeologists to argue that at least some of the earliest Spaniards were African.

Of the abundant prehistoric remains in Spain, the most remarkable are the caves of Altamira on the northern Atlantic coast. There, Stone Age artists painted bison, stags, horses and wild boars on the stone ceilings some 14,000 years ago. Bones of the de-

the Strait of Gibraltar and the Ligurians descended the Pyrenees from Italy. In 900 BC, the Celts moved into Spain from France and Britain, then as now fleeing the northern winters and seeking sun.

The word Celto-Iberian, a generic term used to describe all of these groups, does not mean that they intermingled much. Today's fair-haired northern Spaniard, and the slighter, dark-eyed southerner, are present reminders of ancient Spanish tribalism. Territory especially belonging to the Celts included Galicia and Portugal and the northeastern portions of the *meseta*, where numerous forts, or *castros*, have been unearthed. In general, the Celts were known as violent, rustic shepherds who made good mercenaries. Their varied contributions to succeeding civilisations on the peninsula included iron and trousers.

The Iberians flourished in the south. They lived in walled cities, buried their dead in elaborate tombs, and began exploiting the rich copper deposits around Almería. These people have been characterised as peaceful farmers, who were much more receptive to foreigners and foreign ways than their inland neighbours. Nevertheless, the Greek geographer Strabo found common traits among all the isolated bands living on the peninsula: hospitality, grand manners, arrogance, indifference to privation and hatred of outside interference in their community affairs. Over the centuries, historians have continued to hold up Strabo's description as a good thumbnail sketch of the Spanish temperament even today.

El Dorado: The Iberian skill in metallurgy attracted the attention of trading peoples from all over the eastern Mediterranean; it is thought that early Spanish metalwork taught the world to perceive gold as valuable. In 1100 BC, Phoenician traders discovered Spain's mineral wealth and set up ports of call along the coast, notably at Gadir (Cádiz), which soon became their most prosperous city. The Phoenicians brought the art of fish-salting, the Punic alphabet and music from Tyre to Spain; they left Cádiz so laden that their ships' barrels and anchors were said to be of solid silver.

Another seafaring nation anxious for trade, the Greeks, chanced upon Spain when a Greek ship was carried by a storm to Tartessos, a city which stood somewhere near Málaga. At the time, Tartessos had scarcely been touched by Phoenicians, and the Greeks returned home "with a profit greater than any Greeks before their day", according to one contemporary chronicler. They began colonising Iberia in the 7th century BC, at Ampurias (Gerona) and Mainke in the south.

The Greeks added another layer of civilisation to the already cosmopolitan coast. Their contributions to the native culture in-

cluded olives, wine and a stirring passion for bulls, as well as a strong influence on art. The Lady of Elche, a haughty stone statue of an Iberian princess, is Spain's beloved example of the fusion of imported Greek and native Iberian style.

Cádiz became a melting pot of Greeks, Phoenicians and native Iberians, and by the 6th century BC had a reputation as a rich and sinful place, with tall (three-storey) buildings, many millionaires and provocative, castanet-clicking dancers. Tartessos, according to the Greeks, was a city so refined that its laws were written in verse.

Spain eventually worked her way into Greek mythology: the golden apples of the

Hesperides were said to grow there, and it was one of the labours of Hercules to gather them. Some historians have identified Tartessos as the Tarshish of the Bible, the fabulous source of "gold and silver, ivory, apes and peacocks", where Jonah was headed when he was swallowed by the whale. A case has also been made for placing the lost Atlantis at or near Cádiz.

The Romans knew the peninsula as *Hispania*, which is rooted in a Semitic word meaning "remote, hidden". This western land loomed large in the Mediterranean imagination, and soon it became a target of conquest as well as trade.

Left, Iberian metalwork taught the world to perceive gold as valuable. **Right**, the Lady of Elche blends Iberian and Greek styles.

The future of the Iberian peninsula was to be decided by Carthage and Rome as these two great powers jockeyed for military and economic supremacy in the western Mediterranean. Defeated by the Romans in 241 BC during the First Punic War and subsequently booted out of the island of Sicily, the Carthaginians spent several decades in their North African base rebuilding their armies and preparing for war.

The battle for the peninsula: Carthage made its move into Spain under Hamilcar Barca. With a vastly superior army, Hamilcar took over most of Andalusia, burning Tartessos to the ground in the process. He then proceeded up the Valencian coast, defeating those Iberian settlements foolish enough to oppose him. To bolster the Carthaginian war machine, native Iberians were either drafted into the army or were forced to work as slaves in the gold and silver mines. Hamilcar set about fortifying Carthage's coastal settlements on the peninsula: Barcelona is named after Hamilcar Barca; the second Carthaginian city became Carthago Novo, today's Cartagena.

After Hamilcar's death, his son Hannibal, steeped in his father's hatred of the Romans, led his 60,000-man army out of Carthago Novo and slowly headed northward to the Pyrenees. As he took his troops up the coast, he sought to make alliances with various groups of Celts and Iberians who contributed money and manpower to his army. With his now infamous band of war elephants, Hannibal crossed into France, headed over the treacherous Alps, and swept down towards Rome from the north. In 216 BC he confronted and routed a much larger Roman army at Cannae.

But total victory was to elude Hannibal; for the next 13 years his troops moved up and down Italy, never quite able to defeat the Romans once and for all. The Romans captured his brother-in-law, Hasdrubal, and in a morale-crushing gesture tossed his head into Hannibal's camp. Hannibal hung on in Italy for four more years, but was eventually

Left, statue of a Roman woman. Many Romans made their home in the colonies of *Hispania*.

forced to return to North Africa in 203 BC. A year later, he was soundly defeated in battle near Carthage.

At the same time, Rome had to contend with the Carthaginian base on the Iberian peninsula. In 218 BC, Publius Scipio had landed at Emporia with an expeditionary force. For years he battled the Carthaginians and finally, in 209 BC, he captured Carthago Novo. But there were more furious battles before Scipio's army overran Gadir (Cádiz) in 206 BC, banishing Carthage forever.

The Roman conquest: It took the Romans only seven years to subdue Gaul, but the conquest of Hispania (Spain) dragged on for nearly two centuries. The Spanish wars depleted the Roman treasury and forced the army to adopt conscription, because nobody wanted to fight in Spain. The Phoenicians and the Greeks, who came to the peninsula as traders, had found the natives to be courteous, but the invading Carthaginians and Romans encountered ferocious warriors. The Romans in Spain also had the disadvantage of overextended communications. The countryside over which they marched was hot and bleak, with little water or fodder. The Spaniards, on the other hand, were used to their climate and to deprivation, and they defended their territory desperately.

The most dramatic resistance was that of Numancia, a city of 4,000 inhabitants in central Spain. It took a 60,000-strong army several years to subdue the town and, after months of the final siege, the few citizens who had not perished through disease or cannibalism hurled themselves into the flames of their burning homes rather than submit to the Romans. This battle took on symbolic value, and was invoked centuries later to spur Spaniards to defend their home against invaders. However, Celto-Iberian patriotism did not extend beyond city walls, and tribes often betrayed each other to the Romans. The Iberian lack of unity at first slowed Rome's conquest of the peninsula, since each Roman victory was simply a triumph over an isolated area.

The final stage of the Roman conquest was the Cantabrian War (29–19 BC). Seven Roman legions were forced to participate, and

Augustus himself was called in to lead the final campaign in the Cantabrian Mountains. So defiant were the Cantabrians that they continued to struggle against their conquerors even after their leaders had been nailed on crosses by the Romans. It wasn't until the reign of Augustus (19 BC) that Rome finally established a *Pax Romana*.

Life under the Romans: During the rule of Caesar, Latin became the universal language for the upper classes on the Iberian peninsula. Unified by language, the Spaniards quickly adopted Roman law and customs. As the Carthaginians had discovered much earlier, Hispania was rich in mineral wealth and provided Rome with a seemingly end-

Along with language and customs came religion: Christianity entered Spain in the 1st century AD, during the reign of Nero. It is generally believed that St Paul visited Spain, possibly Aragón, sometime between AD 63–67, and St James, one of Christ's disciples, is said to have preached the Gospel in Spain. Roman resistance to Christianity, however, led to the persecution, torture and the eventual martyrdom of many Spaniards.

Thirteen-year-old Santa Eulalia achieved sainthood when she challenged Roman authority in Mérida's main square by screaming out: "The old gods are worthless, the Emperor himself is nothing…" She was tormented and thrown into an oven; as the

less supply of gold and silver. Rich in livestock and agricultural goods, particularly fruits and vegetables, Hispania became one of the wealthiest, and therefore most exploited, provinces of the empire.

The extension of citizenship proved decisive in the Romanisation of Spain. At first, only colonists of Roman or Italian origin were granted citizenship. Though full citizenship was not granted to all Celto-Iberians until the Edict of Vespasian (AD 74), initial attempts to include the native population in the greater Roman Empire went a long way in establishing at least the appearance of cultural cohesiveness on the peninsula.

account would have it, Eulalia's spirit then flew out of her mouth – in the shape of a white dove – and rose up into the sky, obviously heaven-bound.

Early church history in Spain is full of tales of tortured bodies redeemed by eventual sainthood. A reading of the hymns of Prudentius (AD 348–405) brings to light the tortures – no details spared – that these early Christian martyrs endured.

Yet despite these persecutions, Christian communities began to flourish on the peninsula. Though Spain was predominantly Christian by the time of Constantine's reign (AD 325), it was not until the rule of Theodosius I (AD 379–395) – who was born in Spain – that Christianity became the one accepted religion in the Roman Empire.

The influence of Roman civilisation on the peninsula was enormous, particularly in the fields of construction and architecture. Roman aqueducts, bridges, roads and walls are still in use throughout Spain. Segovia's two-tiered aqueduct is perhaps among the most perfect structures of its kind and still carries water into the town from the nearby hills. Tarragona, on the eastern coast just south of Barcelona, still possesses Roman arches, a three-tiered aqueduct and an amphitheatre, all in mint condition. The Roman theatre in Mérida is still used to stage classic dramas.

became the teacher of Pliny and Tacitus. Though these men were born in Spain, they were all trained in the Latin schools of rhetoric and spent most of their lives in Rome penning works for Italian audiences. Only in the later work of Martial, after he had left Rome – escaping "the togas stinking of purple dye and the conversation of haughty widows" – and retired to his native Aragón, do we find verses that reflect the Spanish landscape.

Vandalism: By the 5th century, the Roman empire was visibly in decline throughout southern Europe. The Visigoths, a warlike Germanic race under the leadership of Alaric, crossed the Alps in 401 and nine

Carmona has a Roman cemetery, and the remains of mausoleums can be found in Fabara, Jumilla, Tarragona and elsewhere.

In literature and philosophy, the Roman occupation gave rise to Spain's Silver Age. Notable Spaniards of the period include the Roman philosopher Seneca, whose Stoical ideals have had a marked effect on the evolution of the Spanish character; the historian and poet Lucan, the poet Martial and Quintilian, the master rhetorician who later

Left, Mérida's Roman theatre is used today to stage classical productions. **Right**, mosaic in Segobriga shows days of the week.

years later sacked Rome. Tribes of Seubians, Vandals and Alans swept across the Pyrenees into Spain and proved to be too numerous for the private armies of Spanish landowners. Notoriously barbaric and ruthless (the word "vandalism" can be traced to the Vandals), these warriors looted and killed as they went, thus effectively ending five centuries of prosperous Roman rule.

The occupation of Hispania by these Germanic tribes was mostly completed by 415. Alliances were forged, power shared, until the Visigoths invaded from Gaul and established their own dynasty on the peninsula. Oddly enough, these barbarian invaders had at one time been Romanised – after having served the Romans as allies and mercenaries – so this new conquest initially brought about few changes. The Visigoths established military rule yet permitted local culture with separate political and administrative organisations, laws and religion. As they numbered perhaps 200,000 among a native population of many millions, this certainly was the expedient course for the Visigoths. In theory the Hispano-Romans had their own separate sovereigns, and their lives proceeded so independently that marriage with Visigoths was not allowed until the reign of Leovigild (568–584).

King Leovigild did more than any other

to convert the Hispano-Romans to Arianism, a form of natural Christianity which refuted the concept of the Trinity and subordinated the Son to the Father. He was liberal enough to allow his son Hermenegild to marry a Christian, but when Hermenegild converted to Christianity and rose up against him, Leovigild sought revenge. He plundered churches, exacted huge sums of money from wealthy Christians, and sent many who opposed him to their deaths.

But the door had been opened. When Leovigild died, his son Recared converted to Christianity and became Spain's first Christian king. With the religious issue resolved, Hispano-Romans developed a new, strong

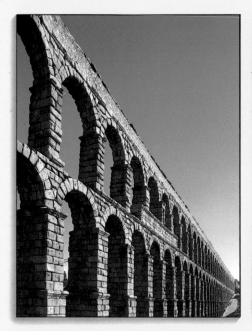

Visigothic king to unite the peninsula. Militarily, he subjugated the Basques in the north, conquered the Seubians who had managed to keep an independent kingdom in Galicia and recovered Baetica (later to become Andalusia) from the Byzantines who had controlled it. He permitted Latin to become the dominant tongue on the peninsula, and for the first time allowed marriages between Visigoths and Hispano-Romans to take place. By stressing cultural, geographical and linguistic unity, Leovigild provided Hispania with a sense of national destiny, totally independent from Rome.

Leovigild failed, however, in his attempt

loyalty to the Visigothic monarchy. Recared's conversion symbolised the victory of Hispano-Roman civilisation over the barbarians, and signalled the beginning of a new alliance between church and state on the peninsula which would continue, with few interruptions, until the present century.

Drawing upon existing Roman precedents, the Visigoths introduced a codified law and a workable tax system. To some extent, they wanted to be the new Romans, speaking Latin and emulating their laws and administration as much as their customs and dress. But they were never willing to undo their belief in an elective monarchy; Visigothic society was an assembly of warriors who cherished the right to elect their king and permitted ambitious nobles to aspire to the throne. There were few smooth transitions to the throne; in the first three centuries of Visigothic rule, there were more than 30 kings, many of whom met bloody deaths.

Decline and fall: Whenever one of the numerous plots threatened the monarchy, the blame was often cast upon the Jews, who had emigrated to Hispania primarily during the reign of Hadrian (AD 117–138). Under Roman rule, Jews had been permitted to move about freely, and they were widely recognised as industrious and intelligent.

Under the Visigoths, they were given the

Jews of Hispania were among the natives who rallied to the Moors when they launched their invasion from North Africa in 711.

When King Witizia assumed the throne in 702, he hoped to side-step the tradition of the elective monarchy and leave the crown to his son Akhila; those nobles who opposed him were soundly beaten and punished. But when Witizia died in 710, Akhila was in the north and Roderic, the Duke of Baetica, was acclaimed king instead by the southern Visigoths. Witizia's family appealed to the Moors in North Africa for help. Fired by his zeal for the new religion of Mohammed, Tarik ibn Ziyad, the governor of Tangier, agreed to join in the battle. His force of

same freedom until the election of King Sisebut in 613. He drafted the first anti-Semitic legislation in Spain: Jews were compelled by royal edict to be baptised or be banished. Thousands suffered the first alternative; those who refused conversion – and remained on the peninsula – were tortured and had their property confiscated. By 693, unconverted Jews were denied access to the marketplaces and were forbidden to trade with Christians. It was no wonder that the

From left to right, Segovia's Roman aqueduct; jewel-studded Visigothic crown; Visigothic carvings on church in Quintanilla de la Vinas.

12,000 men, mostly Berbers, was ferried by boat across the Strait of Gibraltar into Spain. King Roderic was routed in the Battle of Guadalete and perished by drowning.

The year was 711 and the Visigoths were without a king; they retreated to Mérida where they put up a desperate last stand in vain. Tarik should have returned home victorious, but he was fired by two desires; to carry his religion into the land of the unconverted and to seize King Solomon's legendary treasure, purported to be in Toledo. The Moors swept through Spain and by the year 714 they had established control over almost all parts of the peninsula.

The Muslim invasion ended the cultural linguistic and religious unity that the Visigoths had striven to achieve on the peninsula. And yet it would be inaccurate to view the years between 711 and 1492, when the Moors were officially expelled from Spain, as a period in which Moorish values flourished exclusively.

While the Moors took Seville, Mérida, Toledo and Zaragoza, Visigothic nobles regrouped in the mountains of Asturias. In the same region where 700 years earlier hardy mountaineers had held off Roman legions for 10 years, Pelayo's small Christian force faced off against a more powerful invading army.

Though fired up by their zeal for the new religion of Mohammed, the Moors were unable to prise Pelayo's men from their mountain stronghold and the Christians achieved victory at Covadonga in 722. This triumph marked the beginning of the *Reconquista* – the Reconquest of Spain – and came to assume symbolic proportions; the Christians regarded this victory as proof that God had not abandoned his people after all.

Islam sweeps north: But the Moors, intent on conquering all of Europe, were not overly concerned with the defeat at Covadonga. They continued over the Pyrenees into France, until they were stopped at the Battle of Poitiers in 732 by French troops led by Charles Martel, "Charles the Hammer". This stunning defeat forced the Moors to look southward again and to begin the more difficult task of ruling over the land and the people they had recently conquered.

Unlike the Romans who established a link with a strong centralised government outside the peninsula, the Moorish invaders were only nominally the political and spiritual subjects of the Caliphate of Damascus, a distant overlord. As often happens after an invasion, the conquering Moors scrambled among themselves for power and control, dividing up the booty.

These early years of Moorish rule were characterised by numerous rebellions and

Left, *A Spanish King* by Alonso Cano portrays an archetypal medieval monarch.

frequent infighting among the newly formed Muslim kingdoms. Moreover, Spain became the nesting ground for new converts to Islam coming over from North Africa. The Berbers, for example, came from Mauritania and, after a generation of being treated like second-class citizens by the Arab nobles, rose up against them. Years of internecine fighting took place until a new Moorish governor redivided the conquered lands. The Berbers were given much of the territory in the Duero River valley but, after being hit hard by years of famine, many went back home to North Africa.

While the Moors contended with the Berber invasions in the south, Pelayo, followed by his son Favila, set about creating a powerful Christian kingdom in the north. Later, under King Alfonso I (739–757), the Asturians occupied Galicia to the west and Cantabria to the east; under Alfonso II, they moved their capital to Oviedo where the Asturians tried to restore the institutions of the Visigothic monarchy.

Meanwhile, the Basques, usually intent on maintaining their independence, were willing to form alliances with their fellow Christians. All these initial manoeuvrings had one objective: the expulsion of the Moorish invaders and the restoration of Christianity in Spain. When Charlemagne took control of Pamplona and Catalonia late in the 8th century, he set up the Spanish March, a buffer zone meant to keep the Moors out. The Moors had no choice but to build their base in the south of Spain, in the area they called *al-Andalus* or Andalusia.

The emirate: In 756, Abd-al-Rahman I, an Umayyad prince, came to power in Córdoba and established an emirate aligned with, but independent of, the main seat of power in Damascus. He proclaimed himself Emir of *al-Andalus*, and his ascendancy marked the beginning of what would become the most important and advanced civilisation of the Middle Ages.

Córdoba was at the heart of this Golden Age: it became arguably the largest, wealthiest and most cultured city in all of western Europe. At its height in the middle of the 10th century, Córdoba's population had swelled to over 300,000 and there were well over 800 mosques to serve the religious needs of the predominantly Muslim populace. As the Muslims performed daily ablutions as part of their religious obligations, some 700 public baths dotted the city.

The caliphs of Córdoba supported all aspects of learning. During the reign of al-Hakem II (961–976), the city library was established and soon 250,000 volumes were on its shelves. Greek texts, which the Arabs had come across in their triumphant march across the Middle East, were also introduced to Europe for the first time. The works of Aristotle, Euclid, Hippocrates, Plato and Ptolemy were translated and commented

upon by such noted Arabic philosophers as Avicenna and Averroës.

Poets, too, were no less highly regarded. The bloodthirsty al-Mansur was reputed to be surrounded by 30 to 40 poets when he marched off to battle; poets were so numerous and so well-respected that they served a political function similar to television commentators of today. Poetry was written in Castilian, Galician and Hebrew, but the most powerful poetry was written in Arabic: with its fondness for metaphor – a quiet blue river resembled a soldier stretched out in the shade, eyelashes became fish nets or even oars – this Arabic poetry would influence 15th-century Spanish lyrics and, in our own century, the sensuous *casidas* and *gacelas* of García Lorca.

Arabic influence: Over 4,000 words of Arabic origin are still in use in modern Spanish. Agricultural produce introduced by the Moors – *azúcar* (sugar), *berenjena* (eggplant), *naranjas* (oranges) and *sandías* (watermelons) – makes up the daily diets of most Spaniards. Also, words connected with administration, irrigation, mathematics, architecture and medicine can often be traced back to Arabic.

Many phrases and customs still in use in modern-day Spain have their roots in Arabic culture, especially those that express courtesy – *Esta es su casa* (This is your house) and *Buen provecho* (Enjoy your meal) – and the important role of God in everyday life – *si Dios quiere* (if God wills it) and the word *ojalá* which is from the Arabic *wa shá' a-l-lah* (may God will it).

Córdoba also became the scientific capital of Europe during the Middle Ages. The introduction of Arabic numerals into Spain – far less cumbersome than their Roman counterparts – spurred great advances in mathematics; the Moors are thought to have invented algebra as well as spherical trigonometry. Astronomers and astrologers were numerous, and there was a significant following for the occult sciences.

New industries also flourished in Córdoba. The royal factory of carpets was known throughout Spain, and Córdoba's many wonderful silk weavers increased its fame as a place where fine garments could be purchased. Glass and ceramics factories were built, and the old heavy metal tableware was replaced by glass or glazed pottery. Spaniards journeyed to Córdoba to examine the latest designs by its renowned leatherworkers and silversmiths. Moorish physicians were highly prized for their ability to diagnose illnesses and for their surgical skills. The Moors used anaesthetics, and they are known to have performed complicated and delicate surgeries such as the removal of cataracts or the drilling of the skull to reduce pressure on the brain.

But the Moors left their most indelible stamp upon Spain with their architecture. The solid Romanesque churches of earlier centuries were far surpassed by subsequent Moorish constructions which were lighter, airier and more colourful. The cupola, the horseshoe arch and the slenderest of columns, often of jasper, onyx and marble, were all introduced by the Moors and can best be appreciated by visiting Córdoba's *Mezquita* or Mosque. As the Koran forbade the representation of human figures, Muslim artists used geometric patterns which often incorporated the graceful letters of the Arabic alphabet in its designs.

As they were a desert people and because the Koran required daily cleanings, the Arabs were extremely fond of water. In addition to their numerous public baths, the Moors incorporated fountains and ponds into their palaces and villas. This can best be

renaissance of culture on the peninsula. Savagely persecuted by the Visigoths, the Jews were held in high esteem by the Muslim invaders for their role in bringing the invasion about. Generally speaking, they were protected by both kings and nobles for whom they worked in administrative posts. Jews were valued as merchants, ambassadors and emissaries and were often taken into the confidence of Moorish and Christian rulers when their own people could not be trusted. Abd-al-Rahman III's minister of finance was Jewish and, in the 11th century, the vizier of the king of Granada was also a Jew.

Because of their honesty, Jews were used as tax collectors, igniting the hatred and

appreciated in Granada's Alhambra – the Red Palace – and its neighbouring Generalife which served as the summer residence of the caliphs. Built in the 14th and 15th centuries, toward the end of the Moorish occupation, both these structures combine water and greenery to establish a mood of elegance and relaxed splendour.

The Jews in Spain: No story of the Moorish occupation would be complete without including the illustrious, and eventually, tragic, role played by the Jews during this

suspicion of the labouring classes. With the arrival of the Almoravids and the Almohads, fanatical converts to Islam from North Africa, the Jews were either expelled to Christian lands or murdered.

Jews fared well especially under the Caliphate of Córdoba. Maimonides, the great Jewish philosopher and author of the *Guide to the Perplexed*, was born in Córdoba and lived there until he was forced to flee to Egypt during the Almohad invasion. The Talmudic School of Córdoba attracted Jewish thinkers from all over Europe.

Jews were also held in high esteem in the Christian kingdoms, particularly for their

Left, the learned Alfonso the Wise. **Right**, Arabic lettering decorates the Mosque in Córdoba.

administrative skills. They held positions as royal treasurers and physicians, and the Catholic Monarchs came to depend upon their Jewish subjects for financial and medical advice. Alfonso X (1252–84), the "Wise King" of Castile and the founder of the University of Salamanca, created a school of translation in Toledo where Christian, Jewish and Moorish scholars worked together. The Bible, the Talmud, the Cabala and the Koran were all translated into Spanish at the king's behest.

Soon, however, the effect of the Crusades, which fanned fear and hatred throughout Europe, was felt in Spain. When the plague resulted in the deaths of hundreds of Christians, Jews were singled out as the cause. Zealous friars stirred up a wave of anti-Semitism which resulted in the burning of Jewish ghettos and the murder of their inhabitants. In the 14th century, the *Ordenamientos* of Valladolid deprived Jewish communities of their financial and juridical autonomy. But expulsion and the Great Inquisition was yet to come, under the reign of Isabella and Ferdinand.

El Cid: Rodrigo Díaz de Vivar of Burgos, alias *El Cid Campeador*, was expelled from Castile in the middle of the 11th century by Alfonso VI. Taking on legendary proportions, he became the prototypical heroic knight, blending courage and humanity, as he battled Christian and Moorish tyrants alike. After his death in 1099, El Cid became a folk hero celebrated in story and song. His exploits gave rise to the *Cantar del Mío Cid* – The Poem of the Cid – an anonymous epic written in Castilian. Obviously influenced by the French *Chanson de Roland*, the *Cid* stays close to the historical events and gives the reader a clear sense of what life was like for an independent warrior on the frontiers of Spanish society.

Reconquest: The Reconquest, which began when Pelayo defeated the Moors at Covadonga in 722, spanned 750 years. It was not only a battle against an invader, but a war against Islam, despised as a heretical religion that did not recognise Christ as the Messiah.

In the later 9th century, Alfonso II (866–911) took advantage of Moorish infighting and began colonising the Duero River valley, which had been abandoned by the retreating Berbers. To the east, he built many fortresses to repel Muslim attacks. These Asturians, as the first extant Christian chronicles reveal, saw themselves as the heirs of Visigothic power and tradition, responsible for wrenching power away from the Moors.

But when García I moved the Asturian capital from Oviedo to León in 914, the unified Moors – under the rule of the caliphs of Córdoba – wreaked great destruction upon the Christians.

Al-Mansur came to power in Córdoba in 976 and, to distract the Muslims from his own misrule, led what became almost yearly incursions into the five kingdoms of Christian Spain: Asturias, León, Navarre, Aragón and Catalonia. In 985 he burned Barcelona, and its inhabitants were either killed or enslaved; three years later, he plundered Burgos and León. In Santiago de Compostela he destroyed the cathedral – holiest of Christian shrines – and had its famous bells and doors carried by Christian slaves to Córdoba where they were used to make lamps and the ceiling for the *Mezquita*.

When al-Mansur died in battle in 1002, the Christian states counter-attacked. Count Ramón Borrell of Barcelona led troops southward where they joined rebellious Moors. However, progress was slow and it wasn't until 1010 that Córdoba was finally sacked, ending its pre-eminence in *al-Andalus*. Around the same time, Sancho III, "the Great", became the King of Navarre (1000–35); by alliance and warfare, he came to rule over Aragón, Castile, Ribagorza, Sobrarbe and the city of León.

Civil wars and the splitting up of territories into splinter states called *taifas* further undermined Moorish power on the peninsula. The Christian kings took advantage of the fragmentation by playing one Moorish ruler off against another. By weakening the Moors, the Castilians were able to retake Toledo in 1085. This was a significant victory since Toledo, widely acknowledged as the capital of Spain, marked the fall of the first Muslim city and allowed the Christian forces to expand their limits to advance their southern outposts.

Meanwhile, the Aragonese won Zaragoza, and the Catalans retook Lérida and Tarragona. When the daughter of the King of Aragón married Count Ramón Berenguer of Barcelona in 1151, Catalonia and Aragón were united under one ruler.

Holy wars: But the Moors were not going to relinquish Spain easily. To counteract the growing Christian strength, the Muslim kings sought aid from Morocco. The call was answered by the Almoravids – "those vowed to God" – a group of Saharan people who had recently converted to Islam and had conquered much of West Africa.

Under the leadership of Yusuf, the Almoravids brought camels as well as African guards to carry their weapons. In time, they captured Badajoz, Lisbon, Guadalajara and Zaragoza. Though they were repelled at the gates of Barcelona and held at bay in Toledo, the Almoravids remained in control of their territories for 50 years.

Crusade and many Christian kingdoms throughout Europe sent contingents of knights to wage war against the "infidel". A furious battle ensued at *Las Navas de Tolosa* – the Plains of Tolosa – in 1212. Alfonso VIII of Castile united troops from Navarre, Aragón and Portugal against the forces of Miramolin, the Almohad leader. Not only did the Christians achieve victory, but they were now poised for further attacks on the northern border of Andalusia.

The subjection of Muslim Spain was to follow quickly. James I, the "Conqueror King", conquered Valencia and the Balearic Islands. Meanwhile, Ferdinand III, "the Saint", united Castile and León, thus merg-

By the middle of the 12th century, however, the power of the Almoravids was collapsing and the Christians regained most of Andalusia. But then the Almohads, an even more primitive Berber group, left the Atlas Mountain region in Morocco and in 1195 invaded Spain. They defeated and killed the Christian king of Castile at Alarcos and drove thousands of *Mozárabes* (Christians living on Moorish lands) and Jews out of Andalusia.

In response, Pope Innocent III called for a

<u>Above</u>, **Frieze of Ferdinand and Isabella, the Catholic Monarchs, on Salamanca University.**

ing their forces for further attacks on the Moors. Córdoba surrendered to his troops in 1235, followed by Valencia in 1238. Many other Muslim territories futilely resisted the Christian advance. In 1246, Ferdinand III laid siege to Jaén which fell after months of battle. After an even longer siege, which lasted over 16 months and forced the Christians to block the Guadalquivir River with their ships, Seville surrendered in 1248. Many of its houses were burned, vineyards destroyed, fruit orchards cut down and set ablaze; the mosque in Seville was pulverised and only its now famous minaret, the Giralda, was left standing.

With these Christian victories, Moorish domination in Spain was vastly reduced. By the end of the 13th century, only the provinces of Granada and Málaga and parts of Cádiz and Almería had not fallen into Christian hands. A Muslim state under Christian protection was established in Granada, and refugees from the rest of Spain settled there under the rule of the Nasrid Dynasty.

Yet, because of partisan politics and constant feuding, the reunification of Spain was delayed another 150 years. The kings of Spain contested the throne in repeated bloody encounters. Peter or Pedro I, dubbed "The Cruel", ruled from 1350–1369 and left a trail of blood that included the murder of half-brothers, cousins and friends.

Ferdinand and Isabella: Early in the 15th century, the Aragonese took control of Catalonia and Valencia, and the House of Castile assumed charge of Murcia and Almería. Union between these two great powers was achieved in 1474 when Ferdinand of Aragón married Queen Isabella of Castile. But this was a union of crowns, not kingdoms, for each region maintained its own leadership, government and traditions. Moreover, a separate heir would inherit each crown upon the death of its wearer.

From 1483 to 1497 the *Cortes*, or the assembly of nobles in court, did not convene. During these years the Catholic Monarchs, as Ferdinand and Isabella were called, took control over the smallest of kingdoms. Little by little they put an end to the existing feudal order and established an absolute monarchy. They took over the privileges of the old nobility, such as the Royal Council and the courts of appeal, and created a new upper middle class that would become an arm of a new Spain.

The Inquisition: But political unity was not the only objective of Ferdinand and Isabella; they were interested in achieving religious unity for the whole of Spain. In 1478 they obtained a papal bull from Sixtus IV to set up the Sacred Office of the Holy Inquisition to deal with the "evil influences" of the Jews and to ensure the sincerity of the *conversos* (converted Jews) to Christianity.

Constituted as a kind of royal court, the Spanish Inquisition accepted denunciations, applied torture to obtain confessions and not only did it not provide counsel for the accused, but it did not permit them to cross-examine hostile witnesses. Thousands of *conversos* were condemned and subsequently beheaded, hanged or burned while thousands of others fled the country.

Converted Jews could stay, but only if their conversion was total. Many of these *conversos* had risen to new heights not only in the Spanish government, but in the church itself. In 1483, all Jews were ordered to leave Andalusia and Ferdinand commanded that they also be expelled from Zaragoza, but both orders were largely ignored.

In the meantime, the troops of the Catholic Monarchs were laying siege to Granada. Ironically, Ferdinand and Isabella once more sought lands from wealthy Jews to finance the final phase of the *Reconquista*. On 2 January 1492, after 11 years of battle and resistance, the Moorish King Boabdil personally surrendered the keys of Granada to Ferdinand and Isabella who settled in for a brief stay at the Alhambra.

Within two months of capturing Granada, the Catholic Monarchs, on the advice of Tomás de Torquemada, the first Inquisitor-General and son of a *converso* family, ordered the expulsion of all Jews who refused to be baptised. This pleased the lower classes in Spain as they envied the power and wealth of the Jews, but it was both an inhuman and foolish move; at just the moment that Spain needed the Jews, many of whom had attained important positions in commerce, government and the natural sciences, 170,000 were expelled. These Jews, repelled by the notion of conversion, went either to North Africa or to Greece and Turkey where they maintained much of the culture and language of their Spanish ancestors. Indeed, many of these Sephardic Jews have managed to preserve their Castilian speech, known as *Ladino*, to the present day.

For the more than 300,000 *conversos* who remained in Spain, their situation was precarious. They were required to show the solidity of their new faith at all times, and many of them went to extremes to underscore their Christianity or to denounce less orthodox converts. But the Golden Century of Spain would not have been possible without them.

Right, 15th-century painter Pedro Berruguete shows heretics meeting their doom in an *auto-da-fe* or religious execution.

Towards the end of the 15th century Portugal was the world maritime power, aggressively exploring the Atlantic coast of Africa and establishing colonies on the Azores and the Cape Verde Islands.

In 1485 Christopher Columbus, a Genoese navigator who had been in the service of Portuguese captains, approached Ferdinand and Isabella and asked them for the financial support necessary for finding the shortest westward route to India. He offered the Catholic Monarchs new territories, abundant riches and more souls for God.

Columbus was held off for nearly seven years, but once Granada had been conquered, Spain began to concentrate her resources on overseas exploration.

Spain discovers America: On 12 October 1492, about 70 days after setting sail from Spain, Columbus and his crew landed on the island of San Salvador in the Bahamas. He claimed the new lands, which he mistook for India, for the Spanish Crown. The Papal Bull of 1494 ceded much of the New World to Spain, thereby encouraging Ferdinand and Isabella to finance other expeditions. In time, Spain would conquer huge empires in the Americas, notably in Peru and Mexico.

The Spaniards were driven by two distinct, yet equally powerful desires: first, to obtain gold, power and land in the Americas and second, to convert and "educate" the American Indians. As Castilian money had financed the overseas voyages, the Crown insisted that it had the right to control all trade with the colonies and that the *quinto real* – the royal fifth – of all monies should revert to the Crown.

On the more spiritual side, the Spaniards looked upon themselves as missionaries bringing Christianity to distant lands, subjugating barbaric natives who practised human sacrifice; what was before a barren landscape, would become the site of towns, cathedrals, universities.

Along the way, however, several successful Indian empires were destroyed and their

vast mineral wealth usurped in order to finance wars in Europe many thousands of miles away.

When Queen Isabella died in 1504, her daughter Juana, who had married Philip the Archduke of Austria in 1496, became Queen of Castile. After the sudden death of her husband in 1506, she became despondent and was widely judged as mad – thus her nickname *Juana la Loca* – and her father, King Ferdinand, took charge of Castile.

Ferdinand's rule was characterised by a number of struggles in which he attempted to consolidate power under the Spanish Crown. Aragón held Sicily and Sardinia but, when the French intervened in Italy, Ferdinand went to battle; victorious, he annexed the Kingdom of Naples in 1504 and established Spain as a powerful challenger to French designs on the continent. In 1512, he annexed the Kingdom of Navarre, south of the Pyrenees, to Castile. By shrewdly marrying off his children – Catalina to Henry VIII of England, Juana to Philip who was the son of Maximilian, the Emperor of Austria and the Duke of Burgundy and María to King Manuel of Portugal – Ferdinand had succeeded in strengthening Spain's position with several of her European rivals.

The Hapsburgs: When Ferdinand died in 1516, the crown devolved on his grandson Charles, the son of Juana and Philip. The heir to the Hapsburg lands in Austria and southern Germany, Charles was unattractive, inexperienced and spoke no Spanish. When he arrived at Santander in 1517, Spain was extremely apprehensive about being ruled by a foreigner. His arrival and first gestures did not quell fears. The Spanish nobility, especially, resented the King's Flemish advisers and his unwillingness to consult with them prior to making a decision. One such unpopular decision was the appointment of his own nephew to the rich and prestigious Archbishopric of Toledo. To make matters worse, Charles tried to levy new taxes on both the church and nobility, as well as raise the *alcabala* or sales tax.

When his grandfather Emperor Maximilian died in 1519, Charles was elected Holy Roman Emperor as Charles V. But as he was setting sail for Germany, the Castilians, feeling overtaxed and ignored, rebelled.

This was the infamous uprising of the *comuneros* or commoners; led by the town of Toledo, the *comuneros* wanted to dethrone Charles and replace him with *Juana la Loca*, who was still "Queen Proprietress" of Castile. They also declared that no administrative posts should go to people born outside Castile and that the *Cortes* (parliament), not the king, had the right to declare war.

The nobles vacillated, but when they finally aligned themselves with the court, the army crushed the rebels at the Battle of Villalar in 1521. The *comunero* leaders were executed. The power of the monarchy was

became involved in several endless and expensive wars abroad. As Charles V defended southern Italy from Turkish incursions, he became embroiled in hand-to-hand combat with the Ottoman Empire. At the same time, he waged four wars with France; before his reign ended, he had gone to war against almost every European nation.

Spain was forced to use the gold and silver of the Americas as collateral to secure loans from foreign bankers to finance the wars. As prices shot up, the Crown began levying higher taxes and setting up price controls. But as the nobles had invested much of their newly acquired wealth in land, jewellery and decorative objects rather than in industry or

restored and, to show his gratitude for the support of the nobles, Charles V rescinded some of his tax levies.

Charles V's rule coincided with the opening up of the Americas. During his reign, Hernán Cortés conquered the Aztecs and Francisco Pizarro defeated the Incas in Peru; after raiding the treasuries, both conquerors opened huge gold and silver mines in Mexico, Bolivia and Peru. Seville was placed at the centre of the burgeoning metal trade and in a few years the city doubled in size.

Debt and heretics: With peace at home and gold flowing across the Atlantic, Spain – now the most powerful country in Europe –

agriculture, Spain remained economically weak and uncompetitive. Year by year Spain sank deeper into debt while her European rivals developed their industries.

Another of Charles V's struggles was with the Protestant movement. As the ideas of Martin Luther found fertile ground in Germany, Switzerland and England, the Pope appealed to Charles to put an end to a heresy which claimed that "the Pope could not release souls from Purgatory on payment of a fee" and which allowed Christians to communicate directly with God without any intermediaries. Charles responded by giving support to various Catholic military groups, among them St Ignatius Loyola's "Society of Jesus" which fought for the Papacy. In Spain itself there was a Counter Reformation in which certain books were prohibited and the popular humanist ideas of Erasmus were considered heretical.

In 1556, an old and weary Charles V abdicated, retiring to the monastery of Yuste in Extremadura. His brother Ferdinand was given most of the Hapsburg Empire though he left his Spanish possessions, Flanders and parts of Italy to his son, Philip II.

Unlike his extrovert father, Philip was withdrawn, sickly, almost bookish in his imperial pursuits. It was during his reign and under his guidance that the palace, monastery and church of El Escorial was built; this huge granite mansion outside Madrid became one of his favourite retreats.

Philip II: As his kingdom was more limited than that of his father, Philip II generally pursued issues pertinent only to Spain and Catholicism. He was once quoted as saying that he would prefer not to rule rather than to reign over a nation of heretics. When the Calvinists rebelled in Holland, he had their leader beheaded and many of his followers slaughtered, thus cementing his reputation as a religious fanatic and a merciless king. At one point during his reign, he had his own son arrested and accused of treason and heresy; at another, the Primate of Spain was deposed for having voiced his admiration for Erasmus. He was suspicious of all around him, and his cruelty was immortalised in Schiller's *Don Carlos* and Goethe's *Egmont*.

By the 1560s Spain was, despite a surface opulence, in dire financial straits. Her industries were floundering, foreign wars were exhausting her treasury and English pirates began hijacking Spanish ships returning with much-needed gold from the Americas. By 1575 Philip II owed so much money to foreign banks that he was forced to suspend his debt payments.

But Philip's aggressive religious principles dominated his economic considerations. He made the Inquisition hunt out the *moriscos*, Spaniards of Moorish ancestry, many of whom had converted to Christianity during Queen Isabella's rule but were still suspected of adhering to the Muslim faith.

Left, fragment of the Mayan Codex. **Right**, Hernán Cortés, conqueror of Mexico.

Spain's best farmers took refuge in the stony mountains of Andalusia till it was safe to return to their lands.

To encounter the Turks who from time to time had menaced the Spanish coastline, Philip II formed a league with Pope Pius V, Malta and Venice. Under the command of Philip's brother, John of Austria, the alliance defeated – at great financial cost – the Turks in 1571 at the Bay of Lepanto, near Corinth.

Spain sinks: In Philip II's struggle with England, however, economics and religion fused: he prepared the Spanish Armada not only because Queen Elizabeth protected the pirates who attacked Spanish galleons, but also because she persecuted English Catho-

lics and had imprisoned his cousin Mary Stuart. But when the "Invincible Armada" confronted the quicker, more manoeuvrable English fleet led by Sir Francis Drake in 1588, Spain lost thousands of sailors and more than half her ships. Defeat led Philip into a long period of indecision and introspection: had God abandoned the Catholics? What was certain was that Elizabeth's victory established English maritime supremacy for decades to come.

Spain was ruled during the 17th century by the last three kings of the Hapsburg dynasty. When Philip III ascended the throne in 1598, his kingdom included Spain, Portugal, Flanders, much of central and southern Italy, the Americas from California to Cape Horn and the Philippines. But he was indifferent toward his responsibilities, and handed over the affairs of state to the Duke of Lerma who used his position to increase his wealth and to appoint relatives to important administrative slots. In 1609 he advised Philip III to expel the *moriscos* not out of religious considerations, but also to break the power of the Valencian nobles. Half a million *moriscos* were forced out, many of whom were among Spain's best farmers.

With silver production down, agriculture in disarray and corruption everywhere, Spain was drawn into conflict with Holland,

France and England during the Thirty Years' War. Philip IV became king in 1621 and political/military reversals during his reign brought the Empire to the verge of collapse. When in 1640 Philip IV tried to get the Catalans to pay for the maintenance of Castilian troops, they sought help and protection from the King of France; Philip backed down, and he was forced to grant the Catalans nominal independence.

Later that same year the Duke of Braganza proclaimed himself King of Portugal which signalled that kingdom's final independence. Separatist movements were also underway in Andalusia and Naples. The French defeated the Spanish at Rocroi in 1643, and the Peace of Westphalia (1648) marked the end of Spain's role as Europe's supreme military power.

Military defeats were not the only cause of Spain's demise. Spain failed to use gold and silver from the Americas to build strong industries at home: wool sheared in Spain was sold cheaply to Europe's northern countries where it was converted into cloth, then resold on the peninsula at exorbitant prices.

Once the *moriscos* were expelled, the best lands were given over to sheep and cattle grazing; farm goods had to be imported. The church and the nobility were exempted from paying taxes, and so the poorest of merchants and peasants were obliged to support the state. The *escudo*, once accepted as currency throughout Europe, tumbled in value and Spain was unable to secure foreign loans. As a result, the vast armies of the Empire were underfed and underpaid, and morale sank.

Philip IV died in 1665. He left an economy in shambles, deeply in debt, to his only son Charles, a five-year-old who had yet to be weaned. A regency ruled until Charles II took the throne at 15. War with France continued for most of his rule and he was forced to surrender valuable territories in the Peace of Nimega (1678) and Ratisbonne (1684). What France failed to win on the battlefield or at the bargaining table, it figured to gain once Charles II, pallid and sick and without an heir, died.

Charles II left his crown to Philip of Anjou, the grandson of Louis XIV, with the futile hope that he might keep Spain intact from further French incursions.

The Golden Century: Though Spain declined militarily and politically from the enthronement of Charles V to the death of Philip IV, its *Siglo de Oro* saw the country's most brilliant period of literature and art. As the Empire collapsed, the arts prospered.

Literary scholars mark the Golden Age as beginning in 1543 with the posthumous publication of a book of poems co-authored by Juan Boscán and Garcilaso de la Vega. Garcilaso's *Ecologues* tried to convey a bucolic world of perfection in musical, yet unaffected, verse. Fray Luis de León, who spent five years in prison when it was revealed that his great-grandmother was Jewish, wrote mostly prose, but his lyrical output is considered among the most beautiful in Spanish. St John of the Cross (1543–91) led a life of extreme asceticism and his poetry is full of ecstasy and wild lyrical flights.

The prose literature, however, was richer and more varied in the late-15th and 16th centuries. *Tirant lo Blanc*, written in Catalan around 1460, is a masterful work combining military adventures with sexual forays. The autobiographies and mystical works of Saint Teresa de Avila are simply written explorations of her spiritual thoughts and feelings.

La Celestina, published in 1499 by a converted Jew named Fernando de Rojas, is considered the first great literary work of the Spanish Renaissance; it would be a simple

tragicomedy follows the exploits of Don Quixote as he fails to square his idealistic vision with the rough, unjust edges of reality. Don Quixote, Sancho Panza and Dulcinea del Toboso live in the hearts of all Spaniards.

Lope de Vega (1562–1635) was the founder of Spain's National Theatre and the author of about 1,500 plays, some dashed off in a couple of hours. His comedies succeeded in revealing the mood of his age; his language was simple and accessible, thus endearing him to the greater populace.

In contrast was the baroque and highly embellished writing of Luis de Góngora (1561–1625) who is considered the greatest of Spain's sonneteers. Francisco de

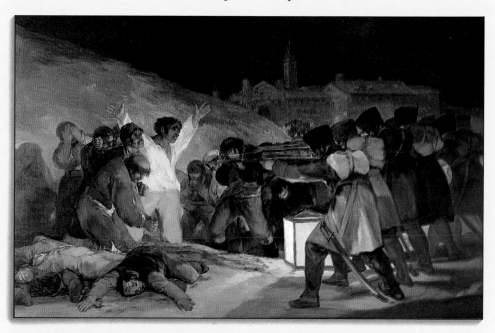

lover's tale if it weren't for Celestina herself, the go-between of illicit lovers. As the seller of all kinds of love potions and charms, Celestina is an incorrigibly modern figure who believes that love – sexual love in particular – is the greatest pursuit of all.

The first, and to many the greatest, novel of all time is Miguel de Cervantes' *Don Quixote*. Published early in the 17th century during the reign of Philip II, this masterful

Left, Federico de Madrazo's portrait of Isabella II. **Above**, *madrileños* who rose up against Napoleon are immortalised in Goya's *Execution of the Rioters*.

Quevedo (1580–1645) was both a poet and a novelist; his writing showed wit and brilliance, though often it was shadowed by an underlying tragic note.

The Golden Age in literature comes to an end with the death of Calderón de la Barca in 1681 whose baroque dramas were admired by Shelley and Schopenhauer.

This 150-year period was also the Golden Age of painting. El Greco (1541–1614), originally from Greece, studied in the studios of Titian before he moved to Toledo where he spent the rest of his days. His brushwork, thick and passionate, was outside the existing art schools in Spain and showed strong Byzantine influences. Diego de Velázquez (1599–1660) was a court painter during the reign of Philip IV but his obeisance to the Crown did not oblige him to relinquish his expressive qualities, using dwarfs and buffoons to convey his sense of a decadent court.

The Bourbons: Lacking in experience, the newly crowned Philip V, the first Bourbon, relied heavily on French advisers. Austria, alarmed by French hegemony in Europe, declared war on France; Catalonia, Valencia and the Balearics saw an opportunity to oppose Philip V and they accepted Charles, the Archduke of Austria and a Hapsburg, as their ruler.

This War of the Spanish Succession lasted 13 years and, for the first time since the Reconquest, a foreign enemy marched across Castile. The Treaty of Utrecht (1713) recognised Philip V as the King of Spain, but not without exacting a heavy toll on the old Spanish empire; Flanders and the whole of Spain's Italian possessions were lost, and Gibraltar was ceded to the British.

The ruling Bourbons embarked on a plan to unify Spain; by diminishing the role of the church, they hoped to strengthen the power of the state. By the middle of the 18th century, Spain's economy had stabilised; its army and navy had been reconstructed, and new industries, primarily in Catalonia, began to develop.

The Frenchification of Spain, both in customs and thought, was launched. The ruling kings adopted French mannerisms and clothes, believed in the Age of Enlightenment and introduced a more liberal church service. Charles III (1759–88) was a devout Catholic but, more than that, a believer in an absolute monarchy: at his behest, church burials were forbidden, and the Inquisitor-General was expelled for drafting a bill without the king's authority. In 1766 he ousted the reactionary Jesuit Order from Spain because of what he perceived as their political intrigues. Unfortunately for the Bourbons, the Spanish masses were deeply conservative and suspicious of any attempt to liberalise life and thought.

Spain truly revived under Charles III. When he first came to Madrid, he was shocked by the squalor of the Spanish capital. During his reign, work on the Royal Palace was completed and the Prado Museum, one of the greatest storehouses of art in the world, was built. He also launched an extensive public works programme which provided funds for the cutting of canals and the building of new roads and highways. A steady rise in prices brought economic development and general prosperity.

When Louis XVI was guillotined in 1793 the Spanish king Charles IV – a nephew of the beheaded French monarch – grew frightened of the growing liberalism on his northern border and declared war on the French. Years of war followed: Spain lost.

Napoleon: Charles IV was a weak-minded and weak-willed ruler. His queen María Luisa and her favourite Godoy – a common soldier who had risen rapidly in rank, eventually becoming Prime Minister – actually ran the state. After Napoleon gained control in France, he turned his eyes toward Spain. On the pretext that he was going to occupy Portugal, Napoleon brought his Imperial Army into Spain and lured the royal family to Bayonne for a meeting. By taking advantage of the intense factionalism among the Spanish royal family, Napoleon was able to broker an agreement: Charles abdicated, his son Ferdinand – who had once been jailed by his parents for opposing them – was banned from Spain and Napoleon gave the crown to his own brother Joseph Bonaparte.

On 2 May 1808, the Spanish peasantry rose up spontaneously in protest; any Frenchman on the Madrid streets became a target. The crack French troops responded swiftly and brutally. Francisco Goya's *The Third of May, 1808* captures in blazing colours the execution of a group of *madrileños* who resisted. Various regional uprisings followed, and France found it increasingly difficult to govern Spain. The War of Independence dragged on until Napoleon was defeated in 1814 by Wellington.

During these years of war, the liberal Spanish Cortes gathered in Cádiz to draft a constitution. In 1812 it was approved, abolishing the Inquisition, censorship and serfdom, and declaring that henceforth the king had to abide by whatever the Cortes decided.

Looking backward: Despite this, Ferdinand VII, however, took over the throne and was pronounced absolute monarch. He refused to pledge allegiance to the constitution and re-established the Inquisition, stifled free speech and allowed the Jesuits to return.

Seeing no hope for accommodation with Ferdinand VII's despotic regime, the Spanish provinces in the Americas rebelled and established their independence.

Ferdinand VII was anything but a forward-looking leader. He turned his back on the three major movements of the 18th century – the Enlightenment, the French Revolution and the Industrial Revolution – and seemed content with keeping Spain apart from the rest of Europe, brooding over her imperial glories and deep religious soul.

When in old age Ferdinand VII married a woman of liberal background, a far right religious group known as the *Apostólicos* rebelled. The conservatives joined them and the Carlists thereby stoking anticlerical fires; when it was rumoured that clerics had poisoned Madrid's water supply, dozens of nuns were slaughtered.

It wasn't until Alfonso XII assumed the throne as a constitutional monarch that this internecine battle came to an end. By signing the Sandhurst Manifesto he attempted to unite all Spaniards: "Whatever happens I shall not fail to be a good Spaniard, nor, like all my forefathers, a good Catholic, nor, as a man of this century, truly liberal."

Liberals and conservatives put down their weapons to engage in the more genteel art of political debate and manoeuvring. Both sides agreed to adhere to the principle of "the

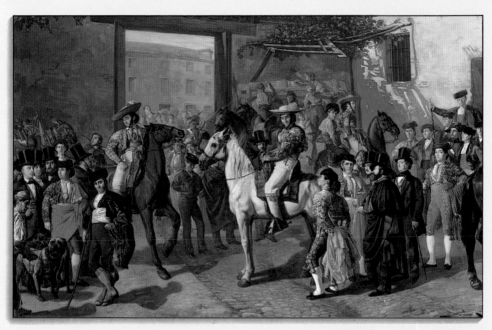

threw their support behind Don Carlos, the king's brother.

The Carlist Wars were actually civil wars between liberals who believed in constitutional government without church domination and conservatives who favoured an alliance between church and state. The liberals were most powerful in the urban areas while the conservative Carlists drew their strength from the countryside, particularly in the northern provinces. The clergy supported

Above, the grandeur of 19th-century Madrid is sentimentally evoked in this painting of the bullring by Manuel Castellano.

peaceful rotation of the parties". The now united troops were sent off to Cuba and the Philippines where the native populations were demanding independence.

Spain's population, as well as its standards of living, increased and there were great advances in the fields of transportation and communications. For the first time in centuries, agriculture was being revitalised on the peninsula. In 1890, under liberal leadership, universal suffrage with a limited electorate became law and, by secularising education, schools began to improve. At the end of the 19th century, Spain found herself hesitantly joining the rest of Europe.

The Civil War in the United States inspired an insurrection in Cuba by those seeking the abolition of slavery on the island and independence from Spain. The rebellion failed, but Cuba was able to obtain a nominal degree of autonomy. In 1895, the Cuban poet and patriot José Martí resumed the struggle for independence and, after his death, the rebellion quickly spread.

Early in 1898 the United States sent the battleship *Maine* to Cuba to protect American interests; whether because of a mine or some mechanical malfunction, the ship exploded in the Havana harbour. Public passion in the United States was aroused; believing that Spain had sunk the ship, President McKinley called for an armistice and the immediate release of all imprisoned rebels. Spain refused.

A series of naval battles followed in which Spain found herself hopelessly outmatched. The US Navy attacked Spanish ships in the Philippines and, on 12 August, Manila surrendered. The Treaty of Paris, signed in December, granted Cuba its independence, ceded Puerto Rico to the United States as indemnity and passed the Philippines to the US for the paltry sum of $20 million.

The end of an empire: This defeat stunned Spain and marked the end of all Spanish pretentions to being an international power. A group of writers and intellectuals, including Miguel de Unamuno, Antonio Machado, and Ortega y Gasset – the famous "Generation of '98" – responded to defeat by declaring that dreams of world supremacy should be abandoned and that Spain should embark on a new, modern course. These intellectuals dug deeply into the nation's history and culture to try and find the true reality of Spain. They issued position papers stressing the need for Spain to revitalise agriculture, reform its tax structure and extend the public education system to all sectors by making school compulsory.

Preceding pages: Picasso's *Guernica* depicts the saturation bombing of a Basque village by German planes in the Spanish Civil War. Left, soldiers in war-torn Madrid. Right, King Alfonso XIII with Eduardo Dato.

It was during this period after the Spanish-American War – referred to as *El Desastre* (The Disaster) – that labour became unionised and radicalised, primarily in the industrial areas of Catalonia. Anarchism, which had had a small following since the 1870s when Bakunin's ideas were introduced, resurfaced more militantly. In 1902 an anarchist union was formed in Barcelona which proposed general strikes.

When the liberal leader Sagasta died in 1903, both liberals and conservatives, whose

leader Cánovas had been assassinated in 1897, found themselves in disarray. The army, comprising mostly Castilian liberals opposed to the absolutist tendencies of the conservatives, was seen by all Spaniards as the traditional upholder of the existing order. But its defeat by the US in 1898 made it vulnerable to criticism, particularly by the Socialist Party and Catalan autonomists.

The people rise up: When the Spanish army found itself under siege in Morocco in 1909, Catalan reservists were called to report for duty by the ruling conservative regime. The Catalans, however, saw no need to risk their lives by clashing with Berber tribesmen. A general strike was called in Catalonia and during this so-called "Tragic Week", 200 churches and over 30 convents were razed by the strikers and, in retaliation, the army shot dozens of strikers and passers-by.

The whole of Spain was temporarily placed under martial law. When a popular Catalan anarchist was unjustly accused and summarily executed for his role in sparking the strikes, mass demonstrations followed. The conservatives were toppled, and the liberal José Canalejas came to power.

Being a liberal in those days simply meant that one believed in parliamentary government, not full democracy. By providing the Catalans with regional control in education and over public works projects, Canalejas sought to block the growing strength of the anarchists. He went further by permitting the Socialists to be part of municipal governments throughout Spain, and he tried to score points with the Far Left by attempting to limit the number of clergy. But when the railway workers went on strike in 1912 he broke the strike militarily, arousing the hatred of many workers. Later that year he was assassinated by an anarchist.

When World War I began, Spain declared its neutrality. It was an expedient move; by continuing to trade with Allied and Axis powers alike, Spain was able to eliminate its national debt and increase its gold reserves. For a few short years Spain became a kind of Switzerland where international and financial issues were resolved.

In 1917 the part-anarchist, part-socialist labour unions called for the first nationwide strike to protest against price increases and Alfonso XIII's appointment of conservatives to the cabinet. The strikes began in Barcelona and Madrid, but soon spread to Bilbao, Seville, and Valencia. The Spanish economy ground to a halt. The army stepped in and crushed the strike, killing hundreds of workers and imprisoning the strike leaders.

When the wartime industrial boom came to a sudden end, thousands of workers were without employment. With the success of the Russian Revolution fresh in their minds, the anarchists resumed their struggle in the streets. Military law was once more imposed in Barcelona.

Popular feeling against the army was quite strong. To make things worse, nearly 15,000 soldiers were killed in Morocco in another attempt to subdue the Muslims. An inquiry into the army's conduct in Morocco brought down the government and García Prieto, an old monarchist who had been liberalised by the turn of events, came to power.

Terrorism against the church and the army intensified – the Cardinal-Archbishop of Zaragoza was assassinated – but the government refused to cede to the army's wishes for a sterner crackdown on protesters. In the September of 1923 the garrison in Barcelona revolted. It was followed by other rebellions throughout the country, and the civilian government collapsed. With the blessing of King Alfonso XIII, Miguel Primo de Rivera, the Captain-General of Barcelona, took control of Spain.

Dictatorship: Like many soldiers and all autocrats, Primo de Rivera had little use for political debate or the trappings of democracy. He immediately suspended the 1876 Constitution and ended parliamentary rule by closing the Cortes; though he claimed that his rule would be temporary, he set about planning for the long-term restoration of the army, the church and the monarchy – Spain's three traditional forces of order. He placed the press under strict military censorship, rescinded Catalonia's nominal autonomy and, by favouring the Socialists within the trade union movement, neutralised the power of the anarchists.

Spain did not adhere to strict doctrinaire fascism, yet relations with Italy were strong. In 1926 an Italo-Spanish treaty of friendship was signed. Following Mussolini's example, Primo de Rivera set up management and worker councils to resolve labour disputes and to draw up collective contracts. A period of economic expansion followed in which new railways and roads were built. Unfortunately, these expansionist policies led to huge budget deficits which became all the more critical because of the world depression of 1929. Moreover, Primo de Rivera began meddling in the army's traditional system of promotion and as a result lost much support. Popular feeling against the dictatorship mounted, anarchism resurfaced and there were frequent battles between workers and the police.

In 1930 Primo de Rivera failed to rally the Captains-General behind him; King Alfonso XIII gave in to pressure and asked for his resignation. General Berenguer assumed power, but his attempts to return to a rotational Constitutional system failed. Berenguer eased censorship, reopened the universities and permitted strikes.

The Second Republic: The elections of April 1931 were crucial. The leftist parties won overwhelming majorities and King Alfonso XIII was forced to leave Spain without formally abdicating. The Second Republic was proclaimed on 14 April, and liberal constitutionalists were installed in power. The monarchy had been overthrown without shedding one drop of blood. For a few brief months it seemed as if much of Spain – industrialists, intellectuals and workers – had united for the first time.

in which the church was subsidised by the state, war was renounced as an instrument of national policy, civil marriages and divorces were to be permitted without church sanction and state-supported education was totally secularised. Overnight, Spain had made a complete about-face.

Manuel Azaña came to power and immediately set about expelling the Jesuits – always considered a fifth column by the Left for their allegiance to the Pope – and confiscating their property.

Other liberal measures were adopted. The Agrarian Reform Act of 1932 expropriated large estates and compensated their previous owners by giving them government bonds;

Yet the constitutionalists were caught in the middle between a Far Right which clung desperately to its privileges and memories of past glories and the growing anarchist unions that were opposed to any form of government. When elections were held for the Cortes, in the June of 1931, the Socialists and anarchists were swept into power. Six months later a new constitution was drafted in which Spain became a "democratic republic of workers of all classes". In one fell swoop Spain ceased to be a Catholic country

War Minister Manuel Azaña poses with optimistic Republican soldiers early in the war.

these lands were either redistributed to the rural peasantry or reorganised on a socialist/collectivist model. Another important piece of legislation granted certain Spanish provinces, including Catalonia and Galicia, semi-autonomy.

In the 1933 elections, the Right – Monarchists, Catholics, and José Primo de Rivera's newly formed Falange Party – achieved a small plurality. A centrist coalition was formed, but it discovered that Spain was now almost irreconcilably split between an organised but divided leftist camp and a rapidly growing Falange Party modelled after the Fascist parties of Italy and Germany. The ruling Centre had to contend with the Basques and Catalans who continued their quest for independence within a federal Spanish Republic, and peasants and Anarchists incensed by the government's decision to halt the expropriation of large estates.

The government was further weakened when striking miners in Oviedo rose up against the army; when the dust had settled a month later, over 1,400 Asturians had been killed and several thousands more injured.

When elections were held in 1936, the Left garnered the majority of the vote; though the Right was almost equal in power, the Centre had crumbled. A new wave of church burnings, coupled with new seizures of land by

moved in from Morocco. They quickly established their control in the rural areas and in the more conservative provinces of Andalusia, Old and New Castile and Galicia. As the army, police and the civil guard sided with the Nationalists, the Republicans were forced to improvise a fighting force by arming the workers.

Franco, the former Captain-General of the Canaries, internationalised the conflict: within days after the rebellion began, Italian warplanes were in Morocco and Italian forces had secured the Balearic Islands. The French and the English responded by setting up a Non-Intervention Committee with Italy and Germany which feebly attempted to

the peasants, followed the elections. Assassinations by the Right and the Left became the daily fare.

The Spanish Civil War: On 18 July 1936, the rightist revolt was launched: the army, supported by the National Socialist parties of Italy and Germany, decided to seize power and put an end to the Second Republic. The Spanish Civil War had begun.

While the Republicans established their base of support in the large urban areas of Madrid and Barcelona and in the provinces of Catalonia, Murcia, and Valencia, the Nationalists – as the rebels proudly called themselves – led by General Francisco Franco

limit the flow of arms into Spain and thereby contain the conflict. The United States, for its part, also decided to respect the arms embargo and in essence abandoned an ally and a legally elected government.

While the Allies pussyfooted, Germany, Italy and Salazar's Portugal poured arms and munitions into the Nationalist forces. By early 1937 Germany and Italy had recognised the Franco regime, Italian troops had taken part in the capture of Málaga and German and Italian ships were patrolling the Mediterranean coast of Spain.

The Republicans, meanwhile, delivered their gold reserves over to Russia to pay for arms and necessary services. In many countries of the world there were calls for volunteers to form International Brigades in defence of the Republic.

Long live death: The Republicans, who saw themselves as opposing Fascism in Europe, were at a terrible disadvantage from the start. In terms of military hardware alone, they were outnumbered by more than ten to one. Furthermore, the Republicans were not united; some of the fiercest struggles of the war took place between the Communists, who wanted to establish disciplined cadres, and the Anarchists, whose militias were loosely organised guerrilla forces where decisions were made communally. The Anar-

licans been more united and had they received more than token support from friendly nations, the end result might have been different.

The Nationalists, on the other hand, were well-disciplined and well-armed troops. They were led by experienced generals and had all the necessary material from abroad. Moreover, with their chant "Long Live Death!" the Nationalists seemed to be on a Holy Crusade to crush the infidels. The death knell for the Republicans sounded early in 1939 when Franco's forces, after weeks of bitter siege, entered Barcelona. The remaining Republicans, numbering over 250,000, withdrew, most crossing into France.

chists had much success, and were able to gain control in Aragón and Valencia where they established skeletal governments, burned churches and killed the much-hated clergy and collectivised the local factories.

But on the battlefield, the Republicans were never quite able to do more than hold off the furious Nationalist charges. The most striking Republican victory was in 1938 when they occupied Teruel. Had the Repub-

Left, Francisco Franco confers with Italian ally Mussolini. **Above**, in a changed political climate, General Franco and his wife welcome President Eisenhower to Madrid.

By 1 April, Franco had entered Madrid and the Civil War was over. In the months that followed, thousands of Republican sympathisers were exterminated in mass executions and millions of others were brought in for questioning and jailed.

The few heroes of the Civil War were clearly those intellectuals who defended the Second Republic. First among them was the great Andalusian poet Federico García Lorca who was shot by the Fascists in 1936 for simply signing a document in support of the Republic. Many writers were either killed or imprisoned by the Fascists, but most – including Rafael Alberti, Jorge

Guillén and Luis Cernuda – were exiled.

Pablo Picasso's horrifying *Guernica*, inspired by the German saturation bombing of a small Basque town, mobilised artists and intellectuals against Franco. The classical composer Manuel de Falla died in exile, heartbroken by the events of the Spanish Civil War, and the great Catalan cellist Pablo Casals refused to perform in Spain so long as Franco lived.

Spain during World War II: Franco attempted to maintain Spain's neutrality during World War II, but his indebtedness to the Axis powers could not be denied. Franco did not want an exhausted and shattered Spain, dependent on western foodstuffs and mineral

The Franco era: When World War II drew to a close, the Allies, angered by Franco's role of professed neutrality and responsive to the clamours of thousands of Republican exiles living within their borders, effectively blocked Spain's entrance into the United Nations and NATO and excluded her from the Marshall Plan. Spain, the only Fascist country left in Europe, found herself isolated by an economic blockade but she survived thanks to huge shipments of meat and grain from Perón's Argentina. In 1947 a referendum was held and the Spaniards, given no other option, voted to establish a Catholic Kingdom with the knowledge that Franco would be head of state for life and would

supplies, involved once more in war, and, when Hitler refused to accede to Franco's demand that Morocco, Tunisia and Algeria be handed over to him, he simply followed a course of non-intervention. He did not, for example, give German troops permission to pass through Spain to attack the British at Gibraltar and, perhaps unbeknownst to Hitler, he allowed thousands of Jews safe passage into North Africa as they fled the Nazis in occupied France.

Yet Spain's sympathies were unmistakable. When Germany attacked Russia in 1941, Franco sent a 17,000-man volunteer division to fight alongside the Germans.

choose a successor of royal blood. Domestically, Franco stifled all dissent and ruled, supported by the church and the army, with an iron hand.

But in 1953 two important agreements were signed which signalled world rapproachment with Spain. As the Truman administration was worried about Soviet designs on Europe and North Africa, Spain's wartime role was cast aside and the United States signed a treaty giving the administration bases on the peninsula in exchange for $226 million in aid.

The second agreement was a concordat signed with the Pope. Roman Catholicism was recognised as the sole religion of Spain, the church was given state financial support and the right to control education, church property was exempted from taxation and all appointments of prelates were to be agreed upon by the Pope and Franco. The Franco regime had been legitimised.

In 1955 Spain was admitted to the United Nations and her isolation ended. The economic situation on the peninsula began to improve due, in large part, to the increase in tourism. As tourist dollars began to reach Spain, Franco earmarked the money for the revitalisation of industry. At the same time, he embarked on a huge public works programme that expanded highways, built

hydroelectric plants and brought cheap water to the dry central plains.

In the social sphere, social security was extended to cover all workers and free medical care was offered to those Spaniards unable to pay for it. Subsidised housing was given to the poor, and vacation retreats were built in the highlands and on the seashores to accommodate the poorest of workers. Education was liberalised, and thousands of Spaniards were given the opportunity to at-

Left, the crypt of the Valley of the Fallen outside Madrid. **Above**, newsvendor displays headlines announcing the death of Franco.

tend university. A powerful upper middle class of executives, managers and technocrats developed. With a million Spaniards working abroad and sending money home, Spain was prospering.

Financial progress brought about a certain amount of liberalisation. Perhaps to gain access into the European Common Market, Spain passed the Religious Liberty Act in 1967, which loosened the grip of the Catholic Church on all worship, and the Press Act of 1968 which made some effort to restrict press censorship. In 1969, Juan Carlos, the grandson of Alfonso XIII, was proclaimed heir to the throne. When General Franco either retired or died, Juan Carlos would become king.

Forty years of Franco: Nearly 40 years of rule under Franco were characterised by order at the expense of freedom. Any protest against the severe restrictions on speech, press and assembly was met sternly. Moreover, the desire of both Basques and Catalans to establish linguistic, cultural and financial autonomy through protest and, at times, violence was rapidly crushed.

Most artists and intellectuals within Spain were forced to take an obscurist path. While many writers wrote religious poems and sonnets in the style of Garcilaso de la Vega, others, including Blas de Otero and Dámaso Alonso, expressed thoughts and emotions in print that most Spaniards were afraid to even whisper to their nearest and dearest.

Franco's regime, until his death in 1975, was empowered by the army, the church and the Falange Party. But as Spain's standard of living rose, a new, more liberal bourgeoisie not haunted by the memories and horrors of the Civil War came of age. These younger Spaniards were receptive to the ideas and customs of the millions of northern Europeans who visited Spain each year.

Franco's death signalled the collapse of the last Fascist regime in Europe. The pomp and ceremony of his funeral service seemed oddly out of place, a remnant of another era. His final resting place was in the Valley of the Fallen, a huge artless mausoleum not far from Madrid, topped by a 450-ft (135-metre) concrete cross, which had been built primarily by Republican prisoners. The cross was to commemorate the half-million dead from the Civil War that Franco himself had helped to launch.

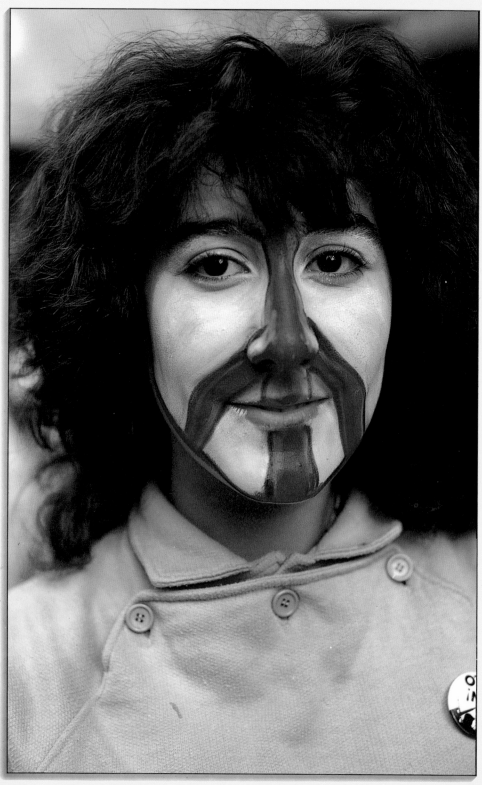

During the 10 years after the death of General Franco, Spain went through political and social transformations which other countries have had the luxury to mull over for decades. The Spanish people more or less decided their political future. They reeled back from violent threats to their new-found democratic system, they took an accelerated course in the sexual revolution and women went from wearing mostly black to wearing some of the most daring clothes walking down the European catwalks.

There were four general elections in that time, in addition to regional and municipal elections, national referenda and regional home-rule referenda. It was a crash course in modernity, which most Spaniards passed with flying colours.

Two days after Franco died, Prince Juan Carlos was crowned King of Spain. The young King, whom former Communist Party Secretary-General Santiago Carrillo mistakenly predicted would be called "Juan Carlos the Brief", had been personally educated and trained by Franco. Few Spaniards had much hope that the dictator's chosen heir was able or willing to lead the country out of the system that had nurtured him.

The last years of Francoism had given rise to all sorts of illegal opposition parties whose leaders realised that Franco's end was near and that their possibilities were about to begin. There was the Communist Party (PCE), the most important of all; there was the Socialist Party (PSOE), which had lain dormant for years and was revived in the early 1970s by future Prime Minister Felipe González and his young comrades from Seville; there were Christian-Democrats, Social-Democrats, Liberals, Maoists and Marxist-Leninists.

There were also parties on the Right which resisted the move away from Fascism; other conservatives, notably the Popular Alliance (AP), led by the former Francoist Cabinet member Manuel Fraga, saw that they would

Left, Madrid girl protests against the Spanish decision to enter NATO. **Right**, marchers in a Corpus Christi procession attest to the still-vital role of the Church in Spanish life.

have to adapt themselves to the new system.

The King's task, then, was somehow to guarantee some sort of political stability at a time when inflation was nearly 30 percent, the prisons still held political prisoners, there were no institutions to speak of which could serve as vehicles for the needed transformations and the armed forces had been recently orphaned.

Three weeks after assuming the throne, Juan Carlos charged the last Francoist president, Carlos Arias Navarro, with forming a

new government. Arias lasted until July 1976, when the King, who never got along well with him, surprised everyone by appointing Adolfo Suárez, the former head of the Falange, the only political party allowed under Franco, as the country's new Prime Minister. The King, Suárez and Santiago Carrillo are the three men generally credited with having successfully brought about Spain's political transition.

Democracy returns: In December 1976 Spaniards participated in the first democratic poll since the Civil War ended in 1939. The "Political Reform Referendum", which was overwhelmingly approved, set things in motion for the first post-Franco general elections in June 1977.

But first there had to be legal political parties. One of the first tests of Suárez's experiment came in April, when the PCE was made legal. The Minister of the Navy resigned in protest and the first sabre-rattling could be heard. It would not be the last time the military threatened to take things into their own hands.

Suárez was Prime Minister but he belonged to no political party which could return him to power. He therefore created the Union of the Democratic Centre (UCD), a hodgepodge of centrist parties which won 27 percent of the vote.

gan straining at the leash, jealous of each other and desirous of more power and freedom of movement.

Finally, in January 1981, Suárez decided to resign as party chief and Prime Minister. But before Leopoldo Calvo-Sotelo could be invested as the country's new head of government, something happened which would shake the country as nothing else had since the death of Franco.

Attempted coup: On 23 February 1981, as the investiture roll-call vote was being taken in Parliament, a group of over 300 Civil Guards and military men burst into Parliament and tried to stage a military *coup d'état*. At the same time, an army general declared

On 12 December 1978, Spanish voters approved the new Constitution, which had previously been passed by Parliament. It is worth pointing out that abstention was 33 percent, considered quite high, and that in the Basque Country the negative votes plus the abstentions were higher than the affirmative votes, indicative of home-rule sentiments in northern Spain.

Once the Constitution had been passed, Parliament was dissolved and new elections were held, in which the results were similar to those of 1977. But by this time UCD was beginning to show signs of stress as the different "families" which composed it be-

a state of emergency in Valencia and tanks began rolling down the city streets. Around six hours after the coup began, the King appeared on television and ordered the insurgents to desist. Twelve hours later they finally surrendered.

The unsuccessful putsch should not have come as a surprise to anyone who was closely following the Spanish military in the post-Franco years. Many coup plots had been hatched, starting in 1977.

Calvo-Sotelo was invested on 25 February, and two days later an estimated one million Spaniards participated in a demonstration in Madrid in support of democracy.

For the first, and possibly the last, time the leaders of all the political parties linked arms and marched together.

The inherently unstable UCD was back in power but its days were numbered. In October 1982 PSOE swept into power with an overall majority, the first time since 1936 that Socialists were in the government and the first time ever that an all-Socialist government ruled Spain. In those same elections UCD virtually disappeared, going from 168 deputies to just 12. In contrast, the conservative Popular Coalition shot up to 106 seats from the nine it had before. Today's bipartisan system was taking shape.

This short, cluttered electoral chronology

illustrates the resolution of the most pressing question following the death of Franco: rupture or reform? Was there to be a clean break with the former regime and the monarchy Franco imposed, or was there to be a gradual adaptation to modern democracy?

Spain joins Europe: The figure of King Juan Carlos was initially rejected by many people in the anti-Franco opposition who saw him as a continuation of the dictatorship. They wanted to return to the Republican system

Left, Prime Minister Calvo-Sotelo meets with Parliament shortly before the attempted coup in 1981. **Above**, King Juan Carlos.

that had been violently abolished with the Civil War. These same sectors demanded that full-scale purges take place in the police, the armed forces and the judiciary once Franco had died.

None of this happened, and the voices crying out for rupture ended up accepting a slower reform as they saw the King was serious when he said he was the "King of all Spaniards" and not just of the victors of the Civil War, as the opposition had feared. The Left and the Right moderated their position, thus guaranteeing the stability of the new democracy.

One of the most important tasks facing the Spanish government since 1975 has been the re-establishment of Spain as a member of the international community of nations after many years of political isolation. After the Civil War, nearly all the world's countries ceased diplomatic relations with Spain. As a result of President Eisenhower's 1953 visit, US military and economic aid was given to the Franco regime, enabling the start of an economic recovery after the very difficult post-war years.

In 1975, Spain still remained isolated. That year, only one chief of state visited the country, and that was Dom Mintoff of Malta. By 1986, however, 29 heads of state had come, an indication of the degree to which Spain had gained equal standing with the rest of the world's industrialised countries.

Immediately after the death of Franco mutual diplomatic relations were reinstated with most of the world's countries. Embassies in the Eastern Bloc nations were set up in 1977, and Israel was finally recognised in January 1986.

By far the most important sign of Spain's desire to become "part of Europe" was its stepped-up campaign to join the European Community (EC), a process which was completed in 1992, and its entry into NATO.

Spain had tried on and off over a 20-year period to join the EC, but its violations of democratic principles impeded its entry. Once the constitutional governments were in power after 1978, however, negotiations were intensified, and Spain finally became a fully fledged member on 1 January 1986.

The story of Spain's accession to NATO is more complicated. The country was originally taken into the Alliance in 1981 by the Calvo-Sotelo government despite the opposition of the Socialists. When the latter party came to power in 1982 it promised to hold a referendum on NATO membership. Over the course of the next four years, though, Prime Minister Felipe González and his government gradually became convinced of the virtues of NATO and began campaigning in favour of remaining a member. In March 1986 the referendum was finally held after a four-year delay and a massive anti-NATO campaign by the country's peace movement. NATO membership was accepted by 52 percent of the electorate.

Economic crisis: While Spain was trying to regain its footing politically, it also had an economic crisis to face. When the interna-

20th century when Spain began a democratic experiment, in 1931 and 1976, have coincided with world economic crises.

By far the most serious economic problem facing Spanish society is unemployment, which by the early 1990s had reached 3 million, or 22 percent, of the labour force. This dramatic figure would signify social chaos in most other countries but the strong family structure in Spain and the fact that an estimated 20 percent of the GNP is produced "under the table", provide a cushion against soaring unemployment. Nevertheless, the strain is tremendous given that only around one-third of the jobless receive any sort of unemployment benefit from the state.

tional recession began to be felt in the early 1970s, other European countries were able to resist the blows because of their advantageous position and their ability to transfer resources from unprofitable sectors to more profitable ones.

But Spain was saddled with an outdated, over-bureaucratic, protectionist and paternalistic economy which had grown up in isolation over 40 years. It lacked any flexibility and when protectionist measures were dropped, businesses suffered. The restructuring of key industries caused the loss of more than 65,000 jobs in the early 1980s. As one writer has noted, the two occasions in the

Regional autonomy: One of the most salient features of Spain's democracy is the home-rule structure. In contrast to Franco's all-powerful centre which ruled with an iron fist, the new federal system has 17 "autonomous regions" with their own government and legislature, and jurisdiction over social services, housing, health, agriculture, culture, city planning and even the police in the case of the Basque Country.

Because Franco and his army were so fervently centralist, the anti-Franco movement believed federalism to be a more progressive stance. The creation of the federal system was a bumpy process, not only because of resistance from the more entrenched right-wing politicians but also because of the differences among the regions.

The Basque Country, Catalonia and Galicia are considered to be "historic nationalities" and have traditionally enjoyed a certain degree of autonomy or even independence since the unification of Spain in the 16th century. In those three regions, local languages are spoken in addition to or instead of Castilian and the fight to get those languages treated on an equal basis with Castilian was one of the main aspects of the "autonomy movement" of the 1970s.

Of all the autonomous regions, the one most known for its separatist leanings is the

nationalism. The widespread practice of torture in Basque police stations; the apparently solid voting base for Herri Batasuna, considered to be the political wing of ETA, which regularly receives around 20 percent of the vote; and the failure of the government to arrive at any effective political solution against terrorism are factors that have made Basque separatism the country's most serious problem along with unemployment.

Although the attempted coup of 23 February 1981 was a failure, it was a powerful reminder that Franco's military was not prepared entirely to let go of the reins. The coup plotters were nearly all given relatively light sentences, which made it unsurprising that

Basque Country. The most obvious manifestation of this sentiment is found in the existence of ETA (an acronym for Basque Homeland and Liberty in the Basque language), an armed separatist organisation which was founded in the early 1960s.

Owing to the particularly harsh repression dealt out by the Franco regime to the Basque provinces, the anti-Franco struggle there became inextricably wound up in Basque

Left, 1981 demonstration for freedom of expression. **Above**, Civil Guard in Madrid. **Above right**, the Basque separatist group ETA makes its presence known.

yet another coup was discovered in the July of that year and then another before the 1982 elections. Even in the 1980s an extraordinary amount of television time was given to military parades, award ceremonies and the like, reflecting the nervousness, masked as respect, felt by the civilian government toward the country's former rulers.

Rapid change: Someone who knew Spain well during the Franco years would have a hard time recognising things today, and a first-time visitor would have a hard time imagining that just a few years ago most aspects of cultural and intellectual life were rigidly controlled by the authorities, that superstition and clichés were a good substitute for knowledge and that personal or sexual freedom were unheard-of concepts which would have been regarded with the utmost suspicion.

The crash course in political affairs has been mirrored, in an even more visible way, by the changes in social questions which affect Spaniards' daily lives. Education, the church, family life, culture and social services – none of these areas came out of the post-Franco transition unscathed.

The stronghold of the Catholic Church and the conservative nature of the regime meant that there was not much room for flexibility in family and personal relations. Divorce, birth control, abortion, homosexuality and adultery were all illegal, although the upper classes often managed to avoid these impediments to their personal happiness.

As the laws were gradually struck down during the centrist and socialist administrations, social behaviour began to resemble that of other European countries. The women's movement was formally launched in December 1975 and its first campaigns were largely concerned with the demand for birth control, a divorce law and an abortion law. Women would have to wait until 1985 for abortion to be legalised, but the law is often criticised for being inadequate; during its first year, just 200 women qualified for a state-sanctioned abortion while an estimated 90,000 women had to go abroad to have abortions. It is believed that many more have illegal abortions within Spain.

As women have fewer children, they have logically begun entering the workforce although to a lesser degree than in other OECD countries. This is partly due to the high unemployment rate in general and partly to sexism. There are no laws to guarantee women equal pay for equal work, and women are often victims of labour discrimination. Nevertheless, the famed Spanish machismo is partly a myth; fathers are often seen taking their children for walks, young couples battle over household tasks just as in other countries and no eyebrows are raised when women enter such professions as law, medicine or journalism.

The church retreats: The education system, despite new reform laws, was largely incapable of responding to the needs of a new society. One indication of this is the enor-

mous popularity of language schools; foreign languages were badly taught, if at all, during the Franco years, but given the country's isolation there was not much need to speak anything other than Castilian Spanish (the country's other languages were prohibited). With Spain's entry into the Common Market, the increased living standard which permits travel and the dramatic inflow of foreign firms, there has been a rush to learn languages, especially English, and regular schools and universities have been ill-equipped to respond.

The church resisted some of the innovations of the education system, fearful of losing its grasp over one of the key areas of society. The church as an institution supported the Franco regime, and was generally regarded as a bastion of conservatism rather than as a force of progress. The exceptions were mainly found in Madrid, where there was a certain "worker-priest" tradition, and in the Basque Country, where the separatists found a great deal of support from priests.

As the church has lost battles over birth control, education, divorce and abortion, as the number of vocations has declined drastically and as the Sunday mass-goers have dwindled, so too has the institution itself lost many of the privileges afforded it by Franco, most importantly its financial subsidies and tax breaks.

Evidence of the church's declining role was clearest during the drafting of the 1978 Constitution. Spain's bishops fought tooth and nail even to get the Constitution to mention the church, and it did so in a less than adulatory way: "The authorities shall take into account the religious beliefs of Spanish society and maintain the appropriate relations of co-operation with the Catholic church and the other denominations."

Media and arts: If the country's youth were to be prepared in schools for the challenges posed by this new society then the adults also needed a daily "school" to open their eyes, prepare themselves for change and learn to think in new ways. That school for most people was the media.

Spain's many national daily papers range from extreme right-wing to left-of-centre, with one that stands out above the rest. *El País* published its first issue on 4 May 1976 and since then has become the obligatory point of reference for most political discourse, so much so that it is sometimes accused of being a mouthpiece for the Socialists. It is lambasted by film directors for its capacity to make or break a movie, and by other journalists who complain that something just hasn't happened if it isn't printed in *El País*. Despite the high number of daily newspapers and weekly news magazines, though, figures show that press readership in Spain is lower than in any other European country except Greece, Portugal and Ireland.

Spaniards thus rely on the radio and state-run television for their news. Until 1981 the radio band was limited to very few stations; it is now open to many more, though not enough, judging from the number of "pirate

stations" on the far end of the FM dial. Private television was part of PSOE's 1982 electoral platform and began to arrive in the late 1980s.

The media may have blossomed but it takes longer to create a generation of writers. It is also true that these two art forms were the ones most exploited for political ends under Franco and the fields most affected by the outward stream of exiles after 1939 and the post-war repression. New young writers are

Above, Socialist Prime Minister Felipe González before his second electoral victory in 1986. González has played a key part in the new Spain.

emerging, but they have yet to make international reputations.

Spanish cinema has fared much better, perhaps because it is a relatively new art form. In fact, during the late 1970s and early 1980s the "new Spanish cinema" began to be commented on and the films won some important international prizes. The Ministry of Culture, which was set up in 1977, provides subsidies for films which demonstrate artistic value and is making an effort to encourage new Spanish directors as well as to recall older directors who were unable to work freely under the Franco regime.

Madrid came of its own as a cultural capital in the early 1980s when it was said that "culture was in fashion". Suddenly one had to choose between a concert, the ballet or an art exhibition. The museums were jammed, particularly after entry for Spaniards was made free in 1983. In 1992 Madrid played the role of European City of Culture.

Spain is different: It is impossible to deny the terrible effects of nearly 40 years under a regime that did all it could to squash the cultural and intellectual aspirations of a people who have produced some remarkable artists, musicians, film directors and writers. These cultural achievements stand as a symbol of resistance during the Franco years, and the speed with which Spain is recovering her role as one of Europe's most interesting and exciting places demonstrates once again that political repression will never succeed in killing dreams and ideas.

In the 1960s, when Spain began promoting itself as a tourist mecca, one of the leading slogans of the publicity campaign was "Spain is Different". Today, the slogan is almost universally looked down upon as symbolising the worst of the era, a clichéd celebration of bullfights, castanets and flamenco dancing that did little justice to the complexity and richness of Spanish culture.

But, in fact, Spain is different. Few countries could have pulled off what she did in the years following the death of Franco. Political, social and cultural reforms have been implemented and accepted. Violent attempts to drag the country backwards have been repulsed. Spain's first chance at democracy was devoured by the Civil War; its second chance has proven a remarkable and inspiring success and now the dictator himself is almost forgotten.

It was the year that human suffering in Bosnia and Somalia reached pitiful new depths; that more than a hundred people died when an Israeli cargo aircraft ploughed into two blocks of flats in Amsterdam; that ethnic riots burned through the streets of downtown Los Angeles; that the foundations of government crumbled in Italy.

But in amongst all the bad news, there were happier times. Like the moment when a solitary archer loosed an arrow of fire to light the massive Olympic flame; and another when it seemed a whole world of balloons filled the sky to mark the start of Expo '92 in Seville.

For 1992 was the year of Spain, the year when three of the country's greatest cities played host to the world. In April, the first universal exposition in over 20 years opened its doors in Seville. In July, the Olympic Games began in Barcelona. And throughout the 12 months, Madrid celebrated its turn as the European Community's Capital of Culture. When 1992 came to an end the country was essentially the same, for the changes which made that special year a success had been quietly taking place for over a decade. But Spain's image among overseas nations was changed forever.

Wave of controversy: It was also, of course, the 500th anniversary of Columbus's exploratory voyage to the New World. Expo '92 was timed to begin and end on the same days as that historic journey had done, and had as its theme "the Age of Discovery". A state-run commission had for several years been planning other special events to mark the anniversary.

Not everyone was laying in the champagne, however. In the eyes of many North and South Americans – descendants of the indigenous civilisations the Spanish conquistadors had destroyed – the anniversary was a cause for dismay rather than joy. "In 1992 there will be a hundred of the richest, whitest and most reactionary families in Lima who will be with Spain, celebrating," Efrain

Orbegozo, the Peruvian Minister of Culture, was reported to have said two years earlier. "And there will be 21 million other Peruvians with Peru, in mourning."

The celebrations of Columbus's voyage and the discoveries which followed were to start on a rather unfortunate watery note. A replica of the *Victoria*, the first ship to circumnavigate the globe, was launched off the coast of southwestern Spain in November 1991. Just 24 minutes later, under the horrified eyes of important persons and local dignitaries who were still toasting its good

fortune back on the shore, the vessel keeled over and the crew had to swim for their lives.

At centre stage: "Madrid, Capital of Culture" got off to a similarly choppy start, amid accusations that its programme of events was elitist, that many would have taken place anyway and that they were being insufficiently promoted. Inadequate publicity caused the hapless Basque Symphonic Orchestra to play to the smallest audience ever recorded in the 2,500-capacity Auditorio Nacional (300 people, many of whom had been specially invited).

The production scheduled to be the curtain-raiser to the Capital of Culture pro-

Preceding pages: South Africa's team in the opening parade of the Barcelona Olympics. Left and right, the world came to Seville for Expo.

gramme – a *zarzuela* or Spanish operetta ominously entitled *Playing with Fire* – had to be postponed, allegedly because the new Teatro de Madrid where it was to be staged had taken longer than envisaged to complete. (Problems included what the Mayor of Madrid called "seats for the blind" since they offered only a limited view of the stage, and an orchestra pit so deep that the conductor could not see singers and musicians at the same time.)

Some scheduled highlights were not just late for Madrid's year of culture: they failed to appear at all. Among them was the rebuilt Teatro Real Opera House, initially due to re-open in October of 1992 but now expected to

ported to have stopped and the project has since quietly faded into oblivion.

Success by stages: Perhaps no programme, though, could quite have matched up to the expectations of the denizens of Madrid, who have very strong opinions about their city and set extremely high standards for it. Despite criticisms and changes of plan, the total of 1,800 events did contain many remarkable attractions.

It also restored to Madrid the Palacio de Linares, superbly refurbished and now a centre for Latin American culture. It led to major rethinks and improvements of the city's museums. It brought the renaissance of the Atocha railway station, made memorably

be out of action at least until 1995. The Museum of the Americas, which had been closed for renovations for eight years, did not, as had been hoped, open its doors in June – or indeed at any time that year.

The most mysterious non-appearance was that of the *Esfera Armilar* planned as an emblem in Madrid of the age of exploration. This monument, representing the solar system and standing more than 300 ft (90 metres) high, was to be built at a cost of 6,000 million pesetas (about £32 million). The scheme had been the subject of controversy from the outset. The first stone was laid in June 1991. Six months later, work was re-

exotic by a steamy tropical garden. And it was the year in which the Thyssen art collection went on public view in the restored Palacio de Villahermosa, making Madrid one of the world's most art-rich cities.

The heat was on: In Seville, preparations paving the way for Expo '92 had also proved traumatic.

Less than nine months before the exposition was due to open, Expo's chief official, Manuel Olivencis, was dismissed from his job and replaced by his deputy, Jacinto Pelón. It often seemed that the race to get things completed on time was not being won, and there were fears that visitors would be deterred by the soaring temperatures of Seville in summer – fears only partly alleviated by an ambitious scheme that would use banks of overhead vegetation to create an air-cooling system. Then in February, just two months before the first of a hoped-for 18 million visitors was due, disaster struck. The Pavilion of Discoveries, the key building of the whole exposition, was destroyed by fire.

The AVE, the new high-speed train being built to link Madrid with Seville in a journey of just two hours 45 minutes, was a further subject for concern. Would it be ready to ferry passengers to Expo? Would it be safe from terrorist attack?

On the night before the opening itself, two for adults. Expo also had its own ambitious arts programme.

The high-speed train outgrew its teething troubles, after an admittedly inauspicious start which included five breakdowns in the first 17 days of operation. Now heavily subsidised, it will carry you swiftly and cheaply to Seville, and has become the fashionable way to get there (advance reservations are vital). Long-term plans are being made for a high-speed train to Barcelona.

Dreams that 1992 would transform Andalusia into a kind of California of southern Spain proved far-fetched, but Expo '92 did bring a new energy and stimulus, and helped put Seville back on its feet. The city acquired

people were shot in a serious incident between rioters (most of them reported to be foreign) and police in Seville.

Then the good news: Ultimately, though, it was a case of "all right on the day". For after this rash of problems, Expo suddenly turned a corner and thereafter things ran smoothly. Millions visited the exposition site on La Cartuja, an island in the Guadalquivir River, and wandered around the dozens of pavilions crammed cheek-by-jowl alongside each other like so many giant toy houses created

Left, a new highway for Andalusia. **Above**, The AVE cut journey times between Madrid and Seville.

a new railway terminus, a much-enlarged airport and several magnificent new bridges on the Guadalquivir river. It is now linked by dual-carriageway, as well as by the high-speed train, to Madrid and by further dual-carriageway to the other major towns of Andalusia. As a result the region as a whole has been transformed from one of the most cut-off to one of the most accessible areas of the country.

The right track: The highlight of the year nonetheless was the Olympic Games. If opinions were divided on Madrid's achievement, and Expo and the 500th anniversary celebrations had had their detractors, no one could question the success of Barcelona. The 1992 Olympics were the first genuinely global games, with more countries than ever before taking part, among them – for the first time since 1960 – South Africa.

It was not an Olympics that could be said to belong to any one competitor. Rather, the Games left a series of stirring mental snapshots of the triumph of the human spirit over adversity. "Magic" Johnson, member of the US basketball "Dream Team", showed how courage could win out in the face of the AIDS virus. Mirsala Buric, a 22-year-old sprinter from Bosnia-Herzegovina, had had to fight a personal battle to compete, training on the streets of Sarajevo when the firing was

at its worst for "it was then that the streets were empty". Algerian Hassiba Boulmerka struck a blow for Moslem women when she won the gold medal in the 1,500 metres.

Barcelona used the Olympic Games to transform itself. An ambitious urban renewal project which had been planned for years became a reality, opening up the city to the sea, getting rid of slums and creating beaches where previously there had been industrial wasteland. It gained a remodelled airport, a new ring road freeing the centre from traffic congestion and new telecommunications and sewage systems. And far from becoming redundant, the Olympic installations on the

hill of Montjuïc have been given a further lease of life as a new "sport university".

Year of living dangerously: One of the greatest – though unspoken – achievements of the year was that of the Spanish authorities in protecting the country and its guests from terrorist attack. The Basque separatist group ETA had threatened Expo and was known to have reconnoitred sites in and around Barcelona. Two other extremist groups were believed to have planted bombs during 1992.

A security force of 20,000 protected Seville during Expo '92, with 3,000 guards on the site and 17,000 police patrolling the city itself. In Barcelona an even greater operation was mounted, including a sea-based force which ran to mini-submarines and even corvettes and minesweepers. Some 16,000 soldiers guarded the new AVE rail-line between Madrid and Seville.

Just before the Olympic Games, ETA offered a two-month truce which the Spanish government neither accepted nor rejected. But the organisation found itself in a considerably weakened position. It was believed to have suffered a massive setback when French police detained its alleged leaders.

After the party: In the last quarter of 1992, Spain – which in the mid-eighties had had the fastest-growing economy in western Europe – went into recession. With the impetus provided by 1992 now on the wane, the economic problems that had dogged neighbouring countries in recent years had finally caught up with Spain.

But Spain's year of years had nonetheless demonstrated what the country was capable of – not just to the world but also to Spaniards themselves. Prior to 1992 the isolation of the Franco years had left a proud people surprisingly lacking in confidence. A desire to match up had been coupled with a fear of failing to do so. Views of the country through foreign eyes were – and are still – seized upon and relayed back home with a self-consciousness redolent of a much smaller nation and one that lacks Spain's illustrious past.

Perhaps no country has undertaken such an ambitious itinerary of events in the same year. It was not all plain sailing, but in 1992 Spain showed the world it could master the great moment.

Left, a new interest in health and fitness. Right, 1992 was good for morale, if not for industry.

Few people can say they have not met a Spaniard, at least in their imagination. To many foreigners, he is short, olive-skinned, raven-haired and fiery-eyed. The men are too proud and strutting for their size. The beautiful women are forever decked out in their frilly flamenco dresses and castanets. They work, in a manner of speaking, but what they appear to do most and best is sing, dance, play the guitar, kill bulls and every now and then kill each other.

As with most stereotypes, there are elements of truth in this popular conception spread by literature, opera and the movies. But it is not the full story, of course.

First of all, while dark looks inherited from the Moorish invaders may be common in the south, Spaniards are not exclusively Mediterranean types. Light-skinned and blue-eyed Celts abound in the northwest and blond descendants of the Germanic Visigoths are to be seen all over the country mingling with the descendants of Romans, who still bear a strong resemblance to statues in Italian museums. Scores of invasions imprinted their features upon the Spanish face and even Britons who came over with the sherry trade left their mark on the *señoritas* and *señoritos* in Jerez.

Secondly, the population is growing, like everywhere else in the world. Army statistics show that young conscripts are an inch taller today than they were 10 years ago, and the upward trend is expected to continue.

A visitor who first meets Spain in one of the big cities like Madrid or Barcelona and rubs shoulders with a few dozen big, blond types may initially wonder where all the guitar-strumming Spaniards have gone. The streets are full of spiky-haired punks, dapper businessmen in suits, people rushing, jumping on buses, streaming out of doorways of impressive modern office-blocks – discussing very serious affairs, to judge by the expressions on their faces – and many other typical characters out of modern-day European life. But after a closer look, you are bound to detect the unique essence of the Spanish nature; an essence that has inspired writers from Dumas to Hemingway and composers from Mozart to Bizet by its sheer colourful force. If a country has ever changed overnight, it has been Spain. But despite the new morning television shows, the new moral codes and the country's adhesion to the European Community, the Spaniard is still his idiosyncratic old self.

History of the Spanish temper: Today's Spaniards, like their predecessors, are individuals who work hard at doing as little as possible and at feeling vastly superior to the neighbour next door. They are still headstrong and quick-tempered, and share a score of other national defects which are greatly overshadowed by one enviable gift – their love of life. In order to understand the predominant traits that blend into what could be called the Spanish temperament, bear in mind four factors: nobility, invasions, regionalism and sun.

From the early Middle Ages, when Christians began regaining territory from the Arab invaders, the ranks of the nobility swelled at such an alarming rate that an estimated 50 percent of Spaniards today have some claim to a title. It is common to hear that even beggars in this country are nobles.

What lies behind this proliferation of nobles was the low-ranking title of *hidalgo*, an abbreviation of three Spanish words that mean "son of something". The term is often linked to the concept of *fueros*, of privileges monarchs granted to peasant-warriors who had reconquered land, enabling them to establish settlements which enjoyed considerable independence from the Crown. But in fact, the title was used as a reward for such diverse exploits as siring seven male children in a row, or promoting industry in the 18th century.

These *hidalgos* were originally barred from doing any work that could interfere with their services at war. But once the periods of the Reconquest and the ensuing conquest of America were over, their social habit had set in such a way that they considered work demeaning. All they became suited for was the army, the church or the administration, and there were not enough jobs to go around. Tens of thousands of people were driven to abject poverty by their social codes. No gentleman would besmirch his name and his title by grovelling for material wealth. Casanova, in his memoirs, describes a visit to a shoe-maker during a trip to Spain. The man apologised, but he could make no shoes. His title of *hidalgo* would not permit him to bend down and measure feet, and meant he could not afford a helper.

This inherited disdain for work, which a foreigner could well mistake for laziness, explains the widespread use of the word *mañana*. It is the reason why the bank manager and the garage attendant are more often out for coffee than at their post. It lies behind the resigned expression on the bellboy's face. And it is certainly at the root of the tiresome inefficiency of government bureaucracy which turns something as simple as getting a passport into a time-consuming ordeal. Any Spaniard who can afford it uses a *gestor* – a person who, for a fee, will stand in the lines, fight with officials, wade through the procedures, pull the right strings for a document that in any other country would take five minutes and a rubber stamp.

The Spanish temperament has also been heavily marked by waves of invasions. At times, Spanish Christians lived side by side with foreign settlers, enjoying an exchange of ideas that left a rich cultural legacy. But more often than not, the onslaught of other cultures helped turn them into proud and arrogant defenders of their own habits and beliefs. The Spaniard became wary of others. He closed ranks with a group he could trust – his region, his village or his family – and only opened his circle of allies according to the size of the current enemy.

Individualism: The result of this ideological isolationism was arrogant individualism. In Spain, the word individualism means egocentricity, not eccentricity. And arrogance, which is pejorative elsewhere, is a term of praise here. Spaniards have a curious habit of taking pride in what could be called their character defects.

Arrogant individualism is noticeable in the national habit of strutting instead of walking, in the way one imposes one's presence by shouting rather than talking and in the marked absence of *"espirit de corps"*. Spaniards envy the ease with which citizens of other countries form associations, act in civilised unison and, by so doing, gather sufficient collective power to get things done. In Spain, where nothing gets done, the reason is often because everyone has his own say in the matter.

When a goal is finally achieved, it is because everyone grew bored with listening to everyone else's reasoning and stepped back, freeing the way for one person to make a final decision.

Fun in Spain goes hand in hand with being in a large noisy crowd. For several reasons, the main one being the sunny weather which keeps everyone outdoors for the best part of the year, gregariousness is the norm. This does not conflict with individualism in the Iberian sense when one realises that the larger the gathering, the larger the potential audience and the opportunity for showing off. Naturally, there is a certain amount of boasting about the number of girlfriends, boyfriends, visible muscles and books read, and there is more and more ostentation of wealth every day. But the pillar of Spanish arrogance is an internal self-sufficiency that needs no external, material supports. It is expressed through wit, grandiloquent phrases, appearance, courtesy, generosity and pride. Often the most arrogant person in a group is the most charming.

On the town: The best place to practice the art of self-adoration is in a bar. The *"ambiente"*, or the amount of noise and people is of utmost importance. Where there is no noise, there is no life, and a Spaniard flees from tranquillity. It is hard to determine what makes more racket in a bar, the patrons shouting at each other – for it would be a euphemism to say that they talk – or the waiters thrashing glasses about. What is certain is that the din is so deafening one can hardly hear the television perched on a shelf in the corner with its volume turned on full.

Anything goes as a subject of lively conversation. The Spaniard is an extremely articulate being with the complete contents of the Royal Academy's Dictionary at his command. A chat can become a literary performance punctuated with quotes and recitations. While the ratio of book readers is low by European and American standards, those who read, choose well. A recent survey showed that in a nationwide list the two best-sellers taken out of prison libraries were volumes of poetry. Among the top 10 was Homer's *Odyssey*.

An insight into the ease with which Spaniards express themselves can be seen on eyewitness news programmes. Bystanders approached and questioned by reporters speak eloquently, with no signs of shyness. This is because of the practice they get giving their opinions most of the day.

In the course of an evening, a group of moderate imbibers will walk into two or three establishments in their neighbourhood and drive to three or four in another part of town. Even in the largest of cities, bars are places where one just happens to bump into friends. *Tapas* or *aperitivos* – bits of skew-

Snobbishness dictates that American cigarette brands are preferable to the perfectly adequate national ones, leading the Spanish Tobacco Company to exploit the image of blond Californian girls on billboards advertising their own products.

With food, however, it is a different matter. Fast-food hamburger joints and pizza parlours are appreciated by the motorcycle-driving teenage crowd, and prove convenient for office workers in a rush. But on the whole, Spaniards prefer Spanish food. The national idea of a feast is cold *serrano* ham, sausage and shellfish, washed down by cool, dry sherry or beer.

At the end of the meal, one self-satisfied-

ered meat, omelette, olives, ham – help keep people sober. A Spaniard's pride will not tolerate a hazy lack of control induced by alcohol. He drinks to enhance his brilliance, but once his words begin to slur, he stops.

Foreigners who visit Spain during fiestas, when whole towns close down for an orgy of indulgence, leave with the erroneous impression that the natives are drunks.

Generosity: A full third of the Spaniard's income is spent on food, drink and tobacco.

Above left, a rural family near Matamoros, Extremadura. **Right**, three generations gather for a traditional big lunch in Madrid.

looking man flamboyantly foots the bill – which could easily add up to half his monthly salary. In Spain, when two people fight to pay a bill, it means they really want to pay it.

The friendly generosity of the Spaniard is one of the characteristics that most astounds first-time visitors to the country. If a local and a stranger embark upon a conversation, it will at the very least end up with an invitation to a coffee or a beer. In the south, bartenders offer so many drinks on the house it is a wonder they can make a profit. Young people rarely seem to buy a cigarette. They approach someone on the street to ask for one, and it is graciously given.

While they find it hard to comprehend a faraway plight such as hunger in Ethiopia, a Spaniard will respond wholeheartedly to anything that appeals directly to his emotions. Most beggars make a living, and some have been hauled into jail for amassing a near-fortune by approaching donors with fake tales.

A Spaniard is also politely helpful and generous with his time. If a stranger asks for an address, he will often be accompanied to his destination. But at the same time, the Spaniard is so loath to disappoint that he is inclined to point down the wrong road rather than admit he does not know the way.

To decorate his arrogant pose, a large

politicians and ideologues. Scores of rulers have attempted, by marriage or iron fist, to unify spiritually and politically this country of nearly 38 million anarchist individualists who speak four languages and seven different dialects. Franco, who after winning the Civil War cried "Spain, one, large and free", did his best to obliterate all manifestations of regional identity. He went as far as to forbid the use in public of any language except Castilian and banned the christening of babies with local names.

Forty years later, the outburst of regionalism has been such that a Spanish-speaking person must arm himself with a dictionary as well as a good deal of patience when he

chunk of the monthly salary goes on clothes. The traditional style of dressing in dark colours or stark white has given way to colourful attire. In rural areas, the habit of dressing in mourning for several years after the death of a relative lingers only among the older generations, who are bound to spend the rest of their lives in black because when one term of grief ends another is likely to begin due to the size of their families. In cities, this custom has largely disappeared.

Regionalism: There are marked differences between people from the north, the south, the east and the centre. It has often been said that the Spanish nation is a myth, a dream of

visits, for example, Catalonia, where the use of Castilian Spanish has been discouraged by the regional government.

Tourism officials have coined a phrase that neatly sums up the varied climates, landscapes and types: "Spain, everything under the sun". Hot and perennially sunny Andalusia personifies the image foreigners tend to identify with Spain. In this vast area, where the Arab influence lingered longest, is the most pronounced joy of life coupled with a piercing tragic fatalism. The Andalusian looks and sees the parched faces of peasants mirroring parched and arid land and knows life is cruel but also exquisitely beautiful. A well-handled bullfight symbolises this particular view of existence. Andalusians are the most arrogant, talkative, humorous and least responsible group in Spain.

By contrast the Galicians, who inhabit the green, rainy land of mist-filled valleys in the northwest, are a conservative, canny people, mostly fishermen, shepherds and farmers with a sprinkling of tobacco smugglers because of the numerous hidden coves, who speak a language close to Portuguese. They have a reputation for dourness, shared with their northern cousins, the Scots. Like them, they descend from the Celts, play the bagpipes and have emigrated in droves after generations of hard work and penury.

Further along the north coast one reaches the land of the hardworking, heavy-drinking Basques, who have traditionally sought independence from the rest of Spain. Many are believed to be descendants of the peninsula's earliest settlers, the Iberians. Their unique language, Basque or Euskera, bears no demonstrable relation to any known language in the world. And their rugged sports, such as wood-chopping and boulder-lifting, have

Spanish males rarely lack self-confidence. From left to right, Andalusian boys pose for a group photograph; guard outside Madrid's Royal Palace; Leonese man takes the sun.

prompted other Spaniards to regard them as little more than boors.

Very different are the sophisticated Catalans, who were for centuries under French rule, soaking up all the refinements of Parisian culture and life. They share one similarity with the Basques, however: a desire to sever ties with the rest of the country.

While the rich Basques and Catalans see anything to the south of their borders as a costly appendage, the Castilians feel they have a divine right to be maintained. After all, the proud and austere Castilian from the unproductive central plains invented the idea of Spain and imposed it on everyone else – a colossal achievement.

Fierce regionalism has been tempered by tides of migrations from the centre and the south to the rich northern and coastal lands, and from rural areas to cities. Today, the most underpopulated parts of Europe lie one hour's drive from Madrid.

Sex and the family: The Spanish family is a large and affectionate clan in which mutual tolerance and staunch support is the norm. Take a stroll through a park any afternoon and it becomes immediately evident that the Spaniard is a happy and adjusted being who will never be an outcast in his own circle. The toughest-looking ruffians are out for a walk with a grandfather leaning on one arm and a baby cousin clinging to a hand.

The honour, rights or jobs of sisters, brothers, aunts, second cousins and even in-laws are defended ferociously in Spain. The worst abuse one can hurl at a man is to insult his mother – and at a woman, to insult her child. The children must surely be the best-dressed and most pampered in the world. But although invariably spoiled, they are good-natured and outgoing. They accompany their doting parents everywhere and stay up with them all hours of the night. From the earliest age, children are made to feel important, which helps explain the egocentricity of the adult later on.

Spanish men are viewed as lustful, dominating macho types. Often, they are. Rarely faithful to one woman, up until recently it was acknowledged and even accepted that married men kept a mistress on the side. The wife, who ran the household and brought up the offspring, was regarded by him as something close to a saint, and certainly treated with all the respect due to a mother figure.

For "dirty things", the husband found less venerable females. Wives generally tolerated these institutionalised escapades, considering that they were part of the man's virility, as long as they remained clandestine. If by any slip, his moral shortcomings were revealed and tainted the family's honour, she would turn into a nagging tyrant. But this was in the days when teenage beauties became dumpy and plain once they had caught their partner and took their wedding vows. Meanwhile the men, involved in their profligate activities, or at least their enthusiastic narrations of imaginary adventures with blond tourists from the north, remained slim and attractive.

Nowadays, men do not keep a second woman – mostly, they could not afford to – but they continue having extramarital affairs. What is becoming more and more common is for women to have them too. But most changes are taking place in the relations between sexes before marriage.

The word *noviazgo*, or engagement, referring to a state which among working-class couples used to last up to 10 years while they got the money together to buy a house, is rarely heard. Don Juanism has become characteristic of both sexes, who before settling into wedlock change partners with almost equal frequency and ease. The frequency of people living together without a wedding ring is indicated by the sharp drop in marriages: 271,347 couples married in 1975; but 10 years later the number of weddings registered had dropped to 180,000.

The changes are largely due to the liberation of women. For numerous reasons, including Franco's ability to ward off progress, the pressure of the church and poverty, female liberation happened later in Spain than in the rest of the developed world. As recently as 1970, wives had to present written authorisation from their husbands to travel within the country or to open a bank account in their own name. Now there are an estimated 400,000 unmarried mothers in the country and 60 percent of women, wedded or single, use contraceptives.

Perhaps most astounding has been the general acceptance of the change in sexual mores except by the most recalcitrant conservatives. But then, the largest section of society has always regarded morality as something to live by routinely, but which

should be broken now and then to add spice to life. Where else could the vice president of the government have a publicly known lover as well as a wife and not cause righteous indignation, even after having an illegitimate child? Or a married Socialist minister date a married jet-setter and arouse only curiosity, approval and generalised glee? Who could disapprove of what an attractive Española does with a Don Juan in the privacy of her boudoir, when the voices of restraint are equated with the dictatorship?

Radical feminist movements that surged following Franco's death have all but fizzled out, indicating that they have become less and less necessary. Few women hold top

jobs, even though university attendance is about half male and half female. But they are making their way in middle-level posts. Now that the birth rate has dropped to 1.3 children per couple and women are less tied to their homes, the situation should improve. What seems certain is that, however much ground women may have covered in their late-coming rush for equality, and however much more they may step into the traditional territory of men, essential femininity and masculinity are a question of aesthetics in Spain, and they will always prevail.

Religion: Strange as it may seem, worldly passion does not clash with religious sentiment. Religious events in Spain are cele- brated with wine and dance and every excess that goes hand in hand with merriment. The nationwide pilgrimage to the Rocío Virgin's shrine in Huelva every spring has been de- scribed as epitomising a pagan celebration and it has broken hearts and marriages year after year. In the early hours of Good Friday in Seville, when Christ was on the way to his crucifixion, a huge float of the Virgin of the Macarena transported on the backs of men begins making its way down the tightly packed moonlit streets. Thousands of voices shatter the night with cries of *"Guapa! Guapa!"* (beauty! beauty!) as the band strikes up a merry tune and the Virgin, de-

the poor. You help me clinch this business deal, find a boyfriend, win that trip abroad and I promise to…")

Virgins and saints are often used as inter- mediaries in the Spaniard's dealings with the Father, and in many churches one finds small candles in front of their images, with a money box nearby. You put in a coin for charity, light one of the candles and then proceed to ask for the holy favour.

To the believer, God is a patient being who understands the weakness of the human flesh and easily forgives. Spaniards sometimes rely so much on his understanding that the relationship becomes one of complicity.

At mass, people act with less formality

spite the diamond tear in her eye, does a sensuous little dance. Lack of respect? No – just familiarity.

In his book, *The Spaniard and the Seven Deadly Sins*, Fernando Díaz Plaja maintains that the Spaniard has something like a pri- vate telephone link with God, a God made in man's image, and not the other way around. It is a God whom he can bribe into private, cosy agreements. ("You help my son pass his exam and I will give ten thousand pesetas to

Left to right, rural women often wear black most of their adult lives; harvesting in Cantabria; lookalike wins Barcelona marathon.

than if they were in the house of a close friend. They arrive late, greet acquaintances out loud, drag chairs and at seaside resorts attend the service in their bathing suits. The ceremony lasts only 20 minutes, but before the priest has given his blessing to the con- gregation there is a stampede for the door.

It is necessary to make a distinction be- tween the Spaniard's comfortable relation- ship with God and his relationship with the institution of the church. To many, the church represents the repression of the dicta- torship. After winning the Civil War, Franco proceeded to sit bishops in Parliament and in the council of the realm and placed the clergy in control of primary and secondary education. People who are now only 25 years old remember endless candle-bearing processions toward religious shrines at dawn and being encouraged by priests at school to place small stones in their shoes for penitence. What became very frustrating for educated adults was how every form of cultural expression had to pass through church censorship. The result was that upon Franco's death, floods of pornography glutted magazine stands and cinemas. Now that curiosity has been satisfied, there has been a drop in the marketability of these products. Many who say they are Roman Catholics swim at nudist beaches that have been opened along

several parts of the Spanish coast. Today, several municipal governments are experimenting with nudist swimming pools for the general public. But it wasn't so long ago that a village priest in Galicia rallied villagers behind him and they fell upon a small group of nude bathers in a hidden cove with sticks and clubs.

Partly because of resentment toward the control the clergy had over their lives (and Spaniards have never been too fond of human intermediaries between themselves and God) and simply because of new winds from abroad, the number of practising Catholics stands at a much-diminished 50 percent of the population. Only 18 percent of these attend mass on a regular basis.

The New Spaniards: At the moment, there is a tendency to classify Spaniards either according to their unique and recent history or according to a modern and homogeneous Europe. They are at the crossroads of two cultures and two continents, Africa and Europe, and of two political and economic systems. The Spaniards themselves, awakening from the lethargy imposed by 40 years of isolationism, are stretching and considering the situation. The man on the street is happy to have joined the European Community. He feels as if he is finally a member of an advanced society, and is proud of the way his country performed when the spotlight was on it for the Barcelona Olympics and the Expo World Fair (even though he was amongst the bar-room cynics during most of the preparations).

But how will he fare in the new competitive society once the new system really gets going? Will he be willing to give up the *ambiente* for the promise of bigger and better cars and video sets?

"A worker gets up bleary-eyed after three hours of sleep, gulps down a black coffee and rushes to work with a heavy head. He abandons the office at 11 for more coffee. Stops for a heavy lunch and a cognac at 2. Takes a siesta. Gulps another coffee before returning to sleep at his desk. Then he leaves at 8, goes out for drinks, a lumbering dinner and back to bed again three hours before the start of the next day. How can we compete with the rest of the world?" asks an exasperated businessman in Madrid.

Economic progress will have to be at the expense of some of the things that make Spain, Spain. More studio apartments will be inhabited by people living far from home for the sake of their jobs. Many will have to be less serious about the things they consider important, and more serious about what they think is trivial. But on the whole, Spaniards will probably be able to strike a delicate balance between the enjoyment of living and the more obscure occupation of "making a living", and enough national idiosyncrasies will remain to make it all worthwhile.

Left, girl from northern Spain shows the fair colouring of Celtic ancestors. **Right**, Zaragoza beauty at the festival of El Pilar.

Alistair Reid, this chapter's author, was born in Scotland and has written about Spain for The New Yorker *magazine for 30 years. He is the author of a collection of essays, "Whereabouts: Notes on Being a Foreigner".*

When I first went to Spain, in the early 1950s, travelling was far from easy: roads were bad, accommodation sparse, comforts minimal. The sun shone steadily, however, and it was not long before sun-starved Northerners – Scandinavians, Celts, Germans – began to

to provide obvious work. The country surrendered itself to alien hordes for a period of about 20 years, something of an indignity to Spaniards, who referred to tourism as *putería*, or prostitution. The mass intrusion had a fruitful side; it put Spaniards in touch with the rest of the world and showed them other ways of being, so that, when the time came to make a new Spain, after Franco, Spaniards impressed everyone with their political sophistication, their native vitality and their determined optimism.

flock to Spain, spearheading what was to become an invasion of mass tourism, that reached its peak in 1974, when more than 30 million tourists, one for every native Spaniard, crossed the Spanish frontier in the course of the year.

Robert Graves, who rooted himself in the Spanish landscape for 50-odd years, gleefully told of an English secretary, newly returned from Spain, who announced to her friends that she had just vacationed in Mallorca. "Where's that?" they asked her. "I have no idea," she replied. "I flew."

Franco, however, badly needed tourism to strengthen his foreign currency reserves and

The tide of tourists forced Spain into a whirlwind of change, grafting the trappings of modernity on to rustic foundations and often bringing the old ways and the new into sharp conflict. Tourists, however, kept to the beaten track, to the concrete meccas created for them on parts of the Mediterranean coast, and much of Spain remained in rural isolation. The remote villages were sought out by sturdy souls, who found a combination of landscape, mode of being and human rhythms that existed nowhere else.

From the 1950s on, I lived for a part of every year in a series of Spanish villages, eventually settling in one to which I would return once a year, like a pilgrim. It is in village life that Spanish qualities most reveal themselves. The elements there are so stark, so boned down, the inhabitants so separate and durable, the rituals so essential and so graceful that living in them feels like a simplification, a purification. In the remoter parts of the country, the quality that Spaniards have of being able to do with less, to wear lack with a kind of pride, often seems like a positive resistance to the trappings of civilisation. My village friends always gave off the air of being self-sufficient in their own skin, of having come to terms with their fate, with the help of the stoic proverb and the cosmic shrug. Conversations took as long as

they had to, work was done in the course of time, and sometimes, sitting down to a long Spanish lunch, I could feel the world outside withdraw, giving way to the small, rich world of the table and the conversation.

From my first visit on, simply being in Spain has always brought me a sudden joy, a physical tingle, from the light, from the landscape, from the language. It springs from intense Spanish particularities: bare village cafés loud with argument and dominoes, or

The unchanging face of Spain: <u>Left</u>, traditional family transport. <u>Above</u>, Andalusian villagers slake their thirst in the traditional way.

else sleepy and empty except for flies; sudden memorable conversations, about life and death, with total strangers; the way Spaniards have of imposing human time, so that meals and meetings decide their own duration. There is a durability about people here, an acceptance of fate that, paradoxically, sharpens their sense of the present, their spontaneity. Their own eccentricities make them tolerant of the oddness of others, which helped them to survive the tourist migrations. The villages have a sparse, uncluttered look, with bare landscapes and stark interiors. The days seem wondrously long, gifts of time, and existence simplifies itself to a vocabulary of elemental acts, like drawing water and making fire.

Over the course of some 25 years, I watched my own village die, in a sense, losing its agricultural self-sufficiency, when bottled gas replaced the charcoal that it had prepared from time immemorial. The population dwindled, as the men left to find work elsewhere, and the school closed when their families eventually followed them. Foreigners, in search of silence, occupied the empty houses, and the village evolved a continuing life, the remaining inhabitants playing the part of custodians, the foreigners their honoured guests.

The tourist occupation of the Franco years was not a destiny that Spain wished on itself, but one which the country has survived well, and has turned to its own advantage. For me, the great satisfaction of recent years has been in seeing the Spaniards themselves assume control of their own destiny not only with great flair and imagination, but also with a genuine national pride. They have also taken a keen pleasure in rediscovering their own country, in maintaining and preserving it, and in making it comfortably available to its own inhabitants, who have taken to exploring it with zest.

They have become enthusiastic about their own country, which makes them the best of hosts. Foreigners, consequently, who had grown used to trudging across Spain at will for so long, have now been moved much more towards the periphery of Spanish life, and behave much more as guests to a host, a change of status that has been eminently desirable for Spain's sake, and has enhanced the pleasures of being in that inexhaustible human landscape.

There is a telling statistic that *madrileños* love to regale visitors with: "Did you know", they say between sips of wine or beer, "that one particular street in Madrid has more bars than all of Norway?" Others say it's Finland; but in either case, the point is clear. In this city of not much over 3 million there are well over 10,500 bars – or about one for every 285 city residents.

Spanish hours: Spain divides its day differently from the rest of the world. In Madrid, as in other Spanish cities and villages, the street life begins at breakfast. After 8am, the typical *madrileño* stops in a *cafetería* for a quick cup of coffee before work. Then around 10.30 he takes a breakfast break – a snack and a beer or coffee to stave off hunger until the traditional two-hour lunch, beginning after 2pm. Later, work over, the city streams into the numerous bars, cafés and *mesones* for drinks and *tapas* until the dinner hour (anywhere from 9.30 to midnight). Then about 2am, no matter what night of the week, the discos begin to fill.

This, at any rate, is the official agenda. But it fails to explain the continuous crowds in Madrid's many cafés and bars at *all* hours of the day, and night. "When do these people work?" is a question asked time and again by visitors to the capital. Of course, it's not at all unusual for business appointments to be made in cafeterias and cafés rather than impersonal offices, but still the phenomenon is a puzzling one: everyone always has time for at least another cup of coffee and the cafés are always full. So when does the work get done?

Heaven-sent: Perhaps the answer lies in the city's patron saint, San Isidro. Legend has it that one day when he was supposed to be working in his master's field, he had a refreshing siesta instead. Two passing angels took pity on him, commandeered his team of oxen and ploughed the field for him. Apparently some of this same blessed good fortune has rubbed off on Madrid itself where it seems that everything keeps going by divine intervention while the city sits and chats.

Preceding pages: poster on Madrid's Gran Via. Left, where the day ends. Right, out for coffee.

These days nobody much takes a siesta, yet somehow the time off allotted for it remains untouchable. At 2pm on the dot, everything comes to a grinding halt with only restaurants, bars, department stores and the offices of a few eccentric foreign companies remaining open. And this in a country which only has seriously hot weather for about eight weeks of the year.

Just to complicate matters a little more, some offices work a *jornada intensiva* from 8am to 3pm, especially in the heat of sum-

mer. For the rest, the early-afternoon break continues to be as sacrosanct as it was.

Thirst things first: It is frequently reported that Spaniards – and especially *madrileños* – sleep less than any of their European neighbours. In a city deprived of its traditional siesta and scraping by on the minimum of sleep at night, coffee plays a crucial role. It is served and described in a plethora of different ways which are guaranteed to bewilder the foreigner.

Café con leche is easy enough for those familiar with *café au lait*, but what about *café cortado* or *café sólo*? The former is a demitasse of espresso with just a dribble of milk and, like *café sólo* (black), is traditionally sipped after dessert, sometimes with cognac either mixed in or on the side. *Café con leche* is almost exclusively a morning beverage, and the hearty, hard-working Spaniard of the old school can still be seen having cognac or anisette with his morning reviver.

A summer variation on the coffee theme is the luscious *blanco y negro*. This is iced black coffee with ice cream, topped with a sprinkling of cinnamon. Then there is *café granizado*, black with lots of crushed ice, and drunk through a straw.

Also popular in the summer is *horchata*, available at most cafés and at special *horchaterias* where it is frequently home-

so must be made fresh daily. Under no circumstances is the bottled version of this marvellously refreshing drink to be considered even a reasonable facsimile of the tasty home-style original.

Bar codes: The various names for Spain's watering-holes can also be confusing. The café is different from the *cafetería*, is different from the *mesón*, is different from the *cervecería*, although they all purvey alcoholic beverages and the distinctions have blurred over the years. As a general rule, however, a bar serves one brand of beer (possibly on tap), wine and mixed drinks; a *cervecería* specialises in beer, usually offering several kinds on tap; and a *mesón* spe-

made. Looking vaguely like milk and having a slightly chalky texture, *horchata* is made from the *chufa* – a tuberous root known in English as "earth almond" – which grows around Valencia. The *chufas* are washed and rinsed, soaked in water for 12 hours, washed again, drained, then mashed with mortar and pestle, put through a blender and soaked again in water for three hours. The juice is subsequently extracted through cheesecloth and sweetened with powdered confectioner's sugar. After this dissolves, the mixture is strained again and then chilled and served with a ladle at the table. In its pure, no-additives form, it doesn't keep very long and

cialises in wine and *tapas* and will often have its own restaurant upstairs or at the back.

On the *tapas* trail: In recent years the craze for *tapas* has spread beyond Spain. *Picar algo, ir de tapas* or *tapear* all refer to sampling these tasty morsels with aperitivos or, if the sampling is ample, making a meal of them. *Tapas*, available most of the day, are, however, traditionally nibbled from noon to 2 pm and again from 7 to 10pm. If any one savoury particularly appeals, ask for a *media ración* (a slightly larger serving of it) or a *ración* (roughly equivalent to a side-order).

The array of *tapas* on offer is likely to include the standard blood-red *chorizos*, mushrooms in oil, potatoes with garlic mayonnaise or spicy *brava* sauce, smoked *jamón serrano* with bread, or Manchego cheese; and perhaps more exotic fare such as octopus salad, fried baby eels in garlic butter sauce, or grilled crayfish (*cigalas*). At some places the *tapas* may be studded with toothpicks and spread out along the bar. In that case just save the toothpicks for the final tally.

When it comes to settling the bill, a magnanimous etiquette prevails. You are rarely expected to pay until you leave. The first round arrives, then the second, and the third, and when everyone's ready to go, it may be hard to get the waiter's attention. And once his eye is caught, he'll likely ask what the

order was…Within a group of Spaniards, it's customary for everyone to pick up a round, usually in successive bars, rather than splitting any one tab. Tipping is appreciated, but not obligatory.

Another thing to keep in mind is that in Spain food and drink will cost more at a table than at the bar. At the most popular spots, however, the remaining space is usually standing room only.

Down and out: After post-dinner coffee and cognac, the fun begins in earnest. Live entertainment at the city's clubs and music bars

Left, café culture by day and, **above**, by night.

usually doesn't start until 11.30pm, and well beyond that Madrid's bars and cafés animate the night. Traffic on the length of the main boulevard, the Castellana, is often as heavy at 3am as at 3pm.

Even when an economic recession has put a slight – a very slight – damper on things, nightlife is still a serious matter… Sufficiently serious, in fact, for national newspapers like *El País* and *El Mundo* to retain nightspot critics. Each week in special Madrid supplements of these newspapers, experts review the latest bars and clubs as gravely as any theatre critic might a production of Shakespeare. The Madrid night scene is constantly changing: consult these supplements for where to go.

In other major cities around the world the night belongs variously to the young, the rich, the lonely, or the aimless. But in Madrid it belongs to everyone. The bars and taverns are the city's living room and on Saturdays entire families, toddlers in tow, will linger well beyond the midnight pumpkin hour. In fact, Spaniards even have a separate word to denote the hours from midnight to morning: they call this period *la madrugada*.

On nights when *la madrugada* passes unnoticed into *la mañana*, there's no point in going to bed. Better head for the Chocolatería San Ginés. An old Madrid institution in the Pasadizo de San Ginés off Calle Arenal, it serves hot chocolate and *churros* (strips of fried dough) from about 5am.

Hot favourites: In the heat of summer, good times move into the open air. From June on, the Castellana boulevard and every other part of town play host to well over a thousand *terrazas*: open-air café/bars serving a burgeoning clientele of theatre people, movie directors, pop singers, transvestites, computer experts, communists and the curious.

As with the old-world cafés, each *terraza* attracts its own brand of clientele, be it yuppie (distinguished by the preponderance of BMWs), young and beautiful (distinguished by the designer creations), or old-fashioned (with a four-piece band serenading them with waltzes). Buskers entertain the idle with their feats of breakdancing, rollerskating, or artful pantomime. And at 3am on a Sunday morning some may still be passing the hat to families with five-year-old children, cliques of high-school students and grandmothers dressed all in black.

First-time visitors to Spain are likely to approach the whole idea of bullfighting with varying mixtures of excitement, fascination, and apprehension. Sitting in the stands and waiting for the initial pageantry to begin, one knows immediately and instinctively that what is about to happen is not a sport. Spanish newspapers categorise the *corrida de toros* as a spectacle; ardent *corrida* advocates fiercely defend its artistic nature, and bullfighting has left its mark on painting, sculpture, music, dance and literature.

religion which was widespread throughout the Roman Empire. The Mithraic priest would slay the bull on a special platform known as the *taurobolium* and the animal's blood was used to anoint the faithful, presumably endowing them with strength, fertility and even immortality.

Spain's brave fighting bull is a fierce, untamed animal, whose bloodlines and pedigrees have been protected over the centuries in order to maintain its purity and the characteristics which make it both fundamental and

Origins: Man has been challenging the bull since time immemorial, not only in pursuit of meat and clothing. The famous paintings in the Altamira Caves, where Neolithic man depicted his slaying of bison and bulls using the very blood of his foes, strongly suggest that the encounter had as much to do with ritual and mystery as with food.

Bulls were the object of worship in ancient Egypt, Mesopotamia and Crete (whence came the famous Minotaur), not to mention the sacred cattle of India. They were the old deities of many pagan religions which often involved curious fertility rites. Perhaps the most notable was Mithraism, the Sun-Bull

particularly apt for the *corrida de toros*.

The fighting bull is not trained to charge; this herbivorous creature is born with the tendency to attack anything that moves or challenges its predominance. It is a fallacy that bulls charge only red for they are colour-blind, but a bull has been known to charge an express train which crossed its path.

It is, in fact, the bull's selected bloodlines, responsible for its innate bravery, nobility and proud bearing, which have preserved it from the slaughterhouse and granted it an almost enviable life. Pampered as a valuable thoroughbred, the *toro bravo* is destined to an existence of four to five years of splendour in the grass before it is faced with the ultimate test, its appearance in the arena.

The aristocratic beginning: Bullfighting goes back for centuries or perhaps millennia, and even Julius Caesar is said to have challenged and speared a bull from horseback.

In fact, court chronicles report that no royal wedding, baptism or peace treaty was held in Spain from the coronation of Alfonso VII to that of Philip V without the corresponding celebration of the bull-fests called *cañas de toros*. Some of the country's most illustrious personages, such as the conquistadors Hernán Cortés and Francisco Pizarro, or the Duke of Medina Sidonia, fought wild bulls from their mounts. El Cid was said to

Bourbon Dynasty, displayed his overt disdain for the spectacle, claiming that he did not want any of the members of his court to risk their lives unnecessarily and in such a "gauche" manner.

This marked a major turning point in the bullfight: its transition from an aristocratic pageant to a popular spectacle.

The first man to turn bullfighting into a profession was the Ronda carpenter Francisco Romero, but it was his grandson, the great Pedro Romero, who is considered the father of modern bullfighting. With the *muleta* (the red cloth draped over a 2-foot-long stick) in his left hand and the sword in his right, Pedro Romero manoeuvred the

have commemorated a victory against the Moors with a display on his horse Babieca before a brave bull in the 11th century.

During Spain's most glorious historic period, bullfighting was an important part of public life. For some 600 years, the aristocracy was responsible for breeding bulls and then fighting them before king and court.

This was the case until the mid-18th century when Philip V of Anjou, the first of the

animal until it was in position for placing the sword. He killed over 5,600 bulls between 1771 and 1799, without suffering so much as a scratch. No matador since has been able to match his feat in terms of physical immunity.

This then was *toreo* in its most rudimentary form; the object of the "show" was to kill the bull. Today, many are the intricate and artistic manoeuvres which have been created with the cape and *muleta*, and the bullfighter is no longer just a mere *matador* (killer); he is a *torero*, one who expresses his sentiments and artistic ability through the art of challenging and dominating a wild beast.

The spectacle itself is filled with colour,

Preceding pages: Madrid's Plaza de Toros; a wounded matador is rushed from the ring. **Left**, walking on to the tune of a *pasodoble*. **Above**, a 5-year-old bull sporting the ribbons of his ranch.

tradition, pageantry, danger, beauty, daring, blood, excitement and sublime art and is certainly worth a closer look. Though there are some, of course, who view it as a cruel slaughter, others see in the bullfight a dramatic dance between man in all his elegant cognisance and the bull in all its natural, earthy fierceness and brutality.

Death in the afternoon: Three is a magic number for understanding the developments of modern-day bullfighting. There are customarily three matadors, who alternate in the fighting of six bulls, which have previously been divided into three pairs of *lotes* in the morning *sorteo*, or drawing of lots.

The bullfight is considered to be one of the

tive *cuadrillas* or teams. Each matador has in his service three *banderilleros*, whose mission it is to assist him in the handling of the bull by using the cape and also in the placing of the *banderillas*, the 2-foot-long, crêpe paper-decorated sticks.

These *banderilleros* were, in their day, aspiring matadors, though few probably managed to progress beyond the novice stage to take the *alternativa*. This is the ceremony in which a veteran matador symbolically cedes the tools of the trade – the *muleta* and sword – to the neophyte, thus endowing him with the right to kill fully grown bulls and therefore to hold the title of *Matador de Toros*.

few events in Spain which is invariably punctual. Train schedules or theatre performances are not necessarily known for this trait, but the opening trumpet or *clarin*, signalling the beginning of the bullfight, waits for no-one.

The *corrida* commences with the pageantry of the *paseíllo* or entrance parade in which the *alguacilillos*, the mounted constables dressed in period attire of the 16th century, lead the march of the bullfighters into the ring to the tune of the *pasodoble*.

The *alguacilillos* are followed into the arena or *ruedo* by the three matadors who precede in turn the three rows of their respec-

The three rows of *banderilleros* are followed by the mounted picadors. Each matador will have two in his employ, one to *pic* each of his bulls.

The *paseíllo* is completed with the no less pompous entrance of the other more mundane bullring employees who will have to put in an appearance in the arena, no matter how insignificant their role: the *monosabios*, who guide the picadors' horses, the *mulilleros*, who handle the mule team used to drag out the dead bull, and the *areneros*, who tidy up the sand.

Once everyone has taken his respective post, the President of the *corrida* will pull out his white handkerchief to signal the entrance of the first bull into the ring. This marks the initiation of the first *tercio* (third) of this live drama in three acts.

The bull will come charging into the arena through the *toril* gate which communicates directly with the *chiqueros*, the individual pens where each bull had been enclosed since the morning's *sorteo*. He will be greeted by a *banderillero*, magenta and gold *capote* (cape) in hand, or by an extremely eager matador.

The *torero* will effect some initial cape passes or lances directed to either horn in order to determine the animal's natural tendencies: whether it favours one horn over the

dor sufficient time and space in which to withdraw from the animal's path.

At this point, the picadors make their entrance, the least understood and appreciated aspect of the *corrida*. The picadors have a multifold purpose. First, they have the thankless task of preparing the animal for the culmination of the matador's work, the *faena*. In order for the bull to be able to follow the cape smoothly it must be slowed down, but not excessively, and its head must be lowered.

The picador is likewise burdened with the responsibility of trying to correct any defects in the bull's charge, such as a tendency to hook to the right or swing up its horns at the

other, has a long smooth charge or swerves about rapidly, sees well, is strong, etc.

As soon as the matador feels confident about the bull's condition he will proceed to perform the most classic and fundamental of the passes, the *verónica*. A tandem of *verónicas* are linked together as the matador leads the bull gradually towards the centre of the ring. The series is concluded with a *media verónica* (half turn) in which the bull is abruptly brought about, giving the mata-

Left, a bull charging from the gate meets a *banderillero*. **Above**, the picador's horse is heavily padded against the bull's horns.

end of each pass, which could prove fatal to the matador who is unprepared for it.

And finally, the picadors have another very important function, that of determining the *toro's* bravery, for the bull is just as significant a figure in the bullfight as the matador and the public calls upon both to perform at their best. A sign of bovine bravery is the animal's repetition of buoyant and determined charges against the padding of the picador's horse. Generally three pics or *puyazos* are administered, depending upon the animal's strength.

The first *tercio* of pics is brightened by the alternating participation of the three matadors in a competitive display. With the cape known as *quites*, each matador is supposed to *quitar* or draw the bull away from the horse and perform, whenever possible, any of the many varied cape adornments: *verónicas, chicuelinas, gaoneras, navarras* and *delantales*, among others.

The President will use his white handkerchief once again to mark the beginning of the second *tercio*, the *banderillas*. Some matadors are skilled in the placing of their own *banderillas*, but 80 percent of the time the public will see the assistants place the sticks in the most expedient manner. This *tercio* gives the bull the opportunity to recuperate somewhat after its cumbersome struggle

reduced to just half the size of the cape.

The right-handed pass or *derechazo*, in which the sword is used to expand the cloth, and the left-handed *natural* are the two fundamental *muleta* passes. More importance is attributed to the *natural*, in which the *muleta* is held in its natural and more diminutive size, with the sword in the right hand. A series of smooth or tempered *naturales* is usually terminated with a *remate* pass, the *pase de pecho*, taking the bull from behind the matador's body and leading it past and off to the right.

Now comes the time to ready the sword for the proverbial moment of truth, the death of the bull. The matador has 15 minutes in

with the heavily padded picador's horse.

The moment of truth: The trumpet now sounds for the third and final act of the drama. Armed with his sword and the red serge *muleta*, the matador will simultaneously salute and request permission from the President to kill the bull. He may choose to then dedicate the animal's death either to a personal friend or a dignitary seated in the audience, or to the general public.

The spectator should bear in mind that the bull is now a good deal more dangerous than when it first made its entrance into the arena, for it has learned the rules of the game and the matador's lure, the *muleta*, has now been

which to create his artistic masterpiece, the *faena*, though he is customarily expected to say everything he has to say in less than 10.

In order to kill in the more common *volapié* fashion, the matador positions the bull, raises the sword to shoulder level and moves in to kill, using the *muleta* to guide the dangerous horns past his right hip. He must move with determination and a steady hand in order to ensure that the sword hits its mark, a 3-inch wide opening between the shoulder blades. If the matador misses his target, he will hit bone and the *pinchazo* will not be appreciated by the public.

If the steel *estoque* is not well placed or

proves to be insufficient for producing the animal's death, the matador will be obliged to make use of the *descabello*. This is a somewhat shorter sword fitted with a cross-bar close to the tip. The matador directs the *descabello* to the rachidian bulb at the base of the bull's skull, producing its instant death, if performed correctly.

As soon as the bull drops to the ground, the *puntillero* will rush out with the *puntilla* or dagger to administer the *coup de grâce* to avoid any prolonged suffering.

At this point the public displays its approval – or otherwise – of the bullfighter's performance. Under satisfactory circumstances the crowd waves handkerchiefs to

Today, the *orejas* (ears) and the *rabo* (tail) are symbolic trophies for a good-to-excellent performance. A matador who performs well but experiences difficulty with the sword might be applauded and invited to take a *vuelta* or lap of the ring.

As the bulls share star billing with the matadors, a brave animal that performs well is applauded as it is drawn out of the arena by the mules. It may even be granted its own turn of the ring and, in exceptional cases, a pardon. A cowardly animal will be the object of irate protests as it is dragged from the ring.

The trumpet will sound again and it is time for the second bull to emerge from its dark pen into the bright sunlight of the arena. The

request the granting of an ear to the matador. This custom dates back to the early 19th century when the *Fiesta Nacional* underwent its transformation from the pastime of the élite to the popular spectacle it is today and the only payment received by the members of that newly created trade – bullfighting – was the carcass of the animal they had just killed. The ear was their token for presenting to the butchers, in exchange for the animal's body or its equivalent worth.

Left, *torero* Joselito placing one of three sets of *banderillas*. **Above**, Lara asks permission to kill before the final *faena*.

first and most senior matador is responsible for dispatching the first and fourth bulls, the second matador, the second and fifth, and the third and least experienced of the trio, the third and sixth. No two bulls are ever alike.

The bullfight season: The Spanish bullfight season officially opens on 19 March (St Joseph's Day) and ends on 12 October (Columbus' Day in America; Hispanic Day in Spain), though fights are frequently held before and after those dates, particularly *Festivales*. These are informal bullfights in which the *toreros* perform merely for their expenses, as the general proceeds of the *corrida* are intended for charity. The bulls' horns are trimmed or shaved for the festivals and bullfighters exchange their silk and sequined *traje de luces* (suit of lights) for the *traje corto* or country costume.

Each town, no matter the size, celebrates its local *fiestas* on behalf of its respective patron saint and the festivities would be incomplete without bullfighting. Madrid honours San Isidro the Farmer on 15 May with the longest bullfight fair of all: 27 consecutive days of *corridas*.

Other important *ferias* are the delightful *fallas* of Valencia in the month of March; the incomparably colourful and gay Seville Fair in April; the Corpus Christi celebrations of Granada in June; the *Sanfermines* of Pam-

Bullfighting today: Bullfighting, also referred to as the *Fiesta Nacional*, is no longer the unchallenged prime national pastime. It is obliged to share the spotlight with increasingly popular soccer matches as well as with all other forms of Spanish Sunday afternoon entertainment.

The bull has evolved from the fierce, erratic bovine faced by Pedro Romero and his contemporaries in Ronda. Years of selective breeding have produced a more tempered, noble stock, but these same years of inbreeding to maintain pure bloodlines have led to a certain weakening of the caste. Additionally, many of the large ranches with their vast expanses of pasture lands have

plona in July, immortalised by Ernest Hemingway; followed by the Valencia Summer Fair; the *Semana Grande* of Bilbao in August; and the busy month of September with the Salamanca and Valladolid Fairs and the Grape Harvests of Jerez and Logroño. The El Pilar Festivities in Zaragoza in mid-October conclude the season.

When buying tickets bear in mind that the bullring is divided into three sections: the more comfortable and expensive shady side, or *Sombra*, the cheaper sunny section, or *Sol*, where, depending upon the season, spectators suffer the summer heat, and the intermediate *Sol y Sombra*.

been sharply reduced. The limited area for exercise and grazing has debilitated the physical stamina of the bulls in many cases.

Ticket prices have also soared. Added to the costs involved in raising a herd of brave fighting bulls for four to five years is the fact that the *festejo* itself is heavily taxed.

One thing which has never changed and surely never will because it represents the very essence of the *fiesta* is the mortal danger to the bullfighters. In one period of 12 months in the 1980s two top matadors died tragically in the arena. The very popular Francisco Rivera, "Paquirri", married to a no-less-famous folksinger, Isabel Pantoja, was killed by the bull "Avispado" of the Sayalero y Bandrés ranch in Pozoblanco (Córdoba) on 26 September 1984. The promising 21-year-old José Cubero, "Yiyo", died instantly in the Colmenar Viejo arena of a horn wound inflicted directly to the heart on 30 August 1985. He was a victim of "Burlero" of the Marcos Núñez ranch.

The fatal gorings of these two star matadors were mourned by the entire Spanish nation, for here the bullfighter is something more than a performer or celebrity. The *torero* in past centuries and in the present one continues to be a unique human being. The very profession itself calls for an individual who possesses courage, grace, elegance,

afternoon, but may very well be in the presence of his Divine Maker at 5.30."

Happily, bullfighters today don't always emerge from very modest homes, searching desperately for fame and fortune in the bullring. More and more would-be *toreros* are coming from middle-class backgrounds and a growing number of sons and nephews of bullfighters are invading the arenas. These budding dynasties, together with the highly positive proliferation of bullfighting schools – *Escuelas de Tauromaquía* – throughout the country, pave an easier way for beginners, who now have fundamental ideas about "body defence" when they enter the ring to face live animals. Once, the only

skill, dignity, physical prowess and agility, artistic sensitivity, a touch of romanticism and perhaps a great deal of madness. The *torero*, without realising it, will develop his own intimate, personalised religion or philosophy which will enable him to risk his life and regularly face death with periodic precision and serenity.

One famous matador expressed it quite well: "The bullfighter is a man who is always aware that he is alive at 5 o'clock in the

Left, bullfighter Espartaco executing a cape pass called *derechazo*. **Above**, he successfully completes a *natural* pass.

way for a hopeful aspirant to learn his profession was through the bumps and bruises received in the village *capeas*.

Bullfighting has served as a source of inspiration for an astonishing range of artists, including Picasso, Dalí, Goya, Hemingway, Lorca, Merimée, Bizet, Michner, Zuloaga, Benlliure, Gautier, Ortega y Gasset and Norman Mailer.

Federico García Lorca called the bulls "the greatest vital and poetic treasure of Spain". In spite of predictions about the demise of bullfighting, the spectacle shows no sign of vanishing. Passionate *aficionados* affirm that it will exist as long as Spain does.

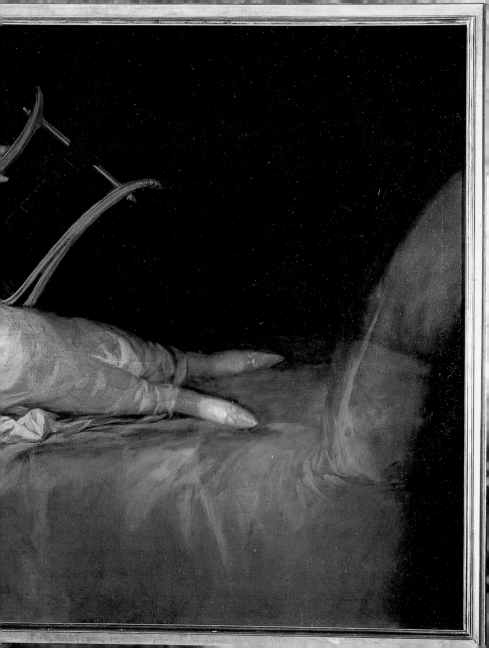

Most of the masterpieces of Spanish art were commissioned by the Church, court and higher aristocracy for Spanish eyes alone. They were meant for lingering contemplation, by a limited number of viewers, of these four subjects: Christ's Passion, the lives of the saints, the nobility of earthly portrait-sitters and, above all, the omnipotence of the Church. It is useful to keep the various propagandist purposes of Spanish painting in mind while dashing through the world's expanding major collections, in almost every one of which Spanish art occupies a place of honour that probably could not have been predicted more than 150 years ago.

The splendid array of painting, sculpture and architectural monuments from every corner and epoch of Spain and Spanish America was discovered in the 19th and 20th centuries. Until the end of the 19th century, tourists who went to Italy to see the great art of the past rarely considered submitting themselves to the hardships of a journey to Spain. The 17th-century Golden Age painters José Ribera, known to collectors as *lo Spagnoletto* (the "Little Spaniard"), and Bartolomé Esteban Murillo, who was imitated in some of the 18th-century English portraits by Reynolds and Gainsborough, were virtually the only Spanish artists whose names were known outside Spain.

It was in France that the ground was prepared for Spain's place in the history of European art. A large collection of stolen paintings by Murillo and other Spanish artists was sent to Paris during the Peninsular War. The best known painting in this stolen collection, one of Murillo's depictions of the Immaculate Conception showing the Virgin standing on a crescent moon surrounded by angels, was bought for the Louvre. The doctrine of the Immaculate Conception was especially popular in Murillo's native city of Seville where, on occasion, paintings like this one were taken from behind the altar and displayed out of doors – a Latin habit also practised in Italy and other Mediterranean

countries. The painting came to the Prado, where it hangs today, in 1940.

King Louis-Philippe of France caused more Spanish paintings to be purchased and brought to Paris, where they were exhibited in his Galerie Espagnole. In the 1840s, Paris possessed by far the greatest accumulation of Spanish paintings yet seen outside Spain. Unfortunately, not all of them were top-quality. Copies, poor imitations, second-rate originals and many misattributions, especially to Ribera, gave a lopsided view of the Spanish School. Still, this period marked the beginning of a true appreciation.

Perhaps more so than today, in the 19th century paintings were relied upon to give an impression of historic events and life in exotic places. Parisians were titillated by chilly cloister scenes and recreations of religious fanaticism such as the Inquisition and excruciating martyrdoms.

Art amnesty: A century later, at the end of the 1940s, the English writer Rose Macaulay visited Spain and romantically concluded that it "grows Roman walls and basilicas and 10th-century churches like wild figs, leaving them about in the most careless and arrogant profusion, uncharted and untended, for travellers to stumble on as they will". Today, in more enlightened and prosperous times, it is not true that Spain's artistic patrimony is, as she put it, "mouldering away". In almost any part of Spain one visits, there are well-catalogued museums and churches.

If few important Spanish art objects are now neglected, many are, however, still uncharted. Many remain in private ownership. In 1986, within a few months of the Spanish government's sensible offer of a tax amnesty forgiving back taxes on undeclared works of art and reducing future taxes, 30,000 paintings turned up, including at least 80 previously unknown works by Francisco Goya. At times Goya was prolific. He painted hundreds of portraits in late 18th-century and early 19th-century Madrid, some extraordinary, some relatively boring. It was a matter of the interest he took in the sitter. A number of Goyas are still owned by the families who commissioned them.

It remains to be seen how many of Spain's

Preceding pages: Goya's *Marquess of Santa Cruz*. **Left**, El Greco's *Gentleman with a Hand on his Chest*.

amnesty treasures, which are said to include works by El Greco and such popular 20th-century Surrealist painters as Joan Miró and the frequently counterfeited Salvador Dalí, will be authenticated by art experts. Family traditions often claim preposterously exalted origins for heirlooms. According to the terms of the art amnesty, owners must allow their freshly rediscovered possessions to be shown for one month in every 12 and cannot sell them outside of Spain. In the past few years large international loan exhibitions in Madrid, London, Lugano, Brussels, Fort Worth/Dallas and elsewhere have gathered the dispersed paintings of Ribera, Murillo, El Greco, Goya, Diego de Velázquez and

toric wall paintings in caves (particularly at Altamira) and early medieval wall paintings hidden under whitewash in Spanish churches began to be rediscovered.

The cave drawings consist of marks which appear to have been primitive notational systems, and elegantly rendered bison, reindeer and other animals. Small stone and bone carvings found with them are now displayed in some Spanish archaeological museums. Prehistoric animal art is commonly believed to be sympathetic magic to ensure good hunting. The vigorous style and spiritual feeling of both cave drawings and early-Christian murals influenced 20th-century artists, notably Miró and Pablo Picasso.

other Spanish artists, so that it has been possible to see a more complete representation of their entire *oeuvre*.

Isolated from the rest of Europe, Spanish painters and their patrons generated one wave after another of powerful, definitely Spanish works of art. An invitation to contemplation, careful observation of life as it is, directness of expression and psychological penetration are qualities that come to mind when one asks what it is that has remained consistently "Spanish" about Spanish art.

Primitive wall paintings: The earliest Spanish masterpieces were the most recent to come to light. Only 100 years ago, prehis-

Spanish art of all periods is noteworthy for its cosmopolitanism and high sophistication. In the Middle Ages, pilgrims' trails and trade routes fed the stylistic influences of French and Italian, Netherlandish and German, Near Eastern and North African art into Spain's ecclesiastical network. All of the artists patronised by the Church were affected by these influences. Thus, the bold decorative figures and rich colours, sharply outlined, of medieval wall paintings are also found in illuminated manuscripts in the libraries of León Cathedral, El Escorial and other cathedrals and museums. Early medieval manuscripts, in turn, were another influence on the work of Miró, Picasso and other 20th-century artists.

One of the most surprising ensembles of rediscovered early medieval mural paintings is in the little pre-Romanesque church known as "Santullano" (or San Julian de los Prados) in Oviedo, built in the early 9th century. Mosaics from Roman villas have been excavated near Oviedo; Roman wall paintings similar to those preserved at Pompeii, in Italy, inspired the *trompe-l'oeil* decoration of this Asturian church.

In León, around two hours south of Oviedo by car, the architecturally advanced, mid-11th-century Panteón de los Reyes, a royal crypt adjoining the Colegiata de San

which the angel appears to the shepherds, is often cited as an example of Spanish realism. Completely ordinary details such as a shepherd feeding his dog are found in the sacred art of other European schools too; but in the frequency and directness with which they are usually presented in Spanish art, many people read a special Spanish sense of the dignity of everyday life. In view of the classical origin of the Oviedo wall paintings, it is interesting to note that the suggestion has been made that this scene is an adaptation of a manuscript illumination illustrating a passage from the Roman poet Virgil.

Another 11th-century church containing 12th-century frescoes is the Ermita de San

Isidro, possesses unusually well-preserved wall paintings dating from 1175, including a vaulted and frescoed ceiling supported by columns with beautifully carved Romanesque capitals which were once also painted, although the colours have faded.

León is on one of the pilgrimage trails to Santiago de Compostela, so it is quite possible that French artists painted the relatively naturalistic Christ in Majesty and scenes from the New Testament. One of them, in

Left, 12th-century church mural from Maderuelo, Segovia. **Above**, fresco from Galicia showing the Moors and Christians at war.

Baudelio de Berlanga in the village of Castilla de Berlanga, in Soria near Burgos. Both its architecture and its wall paintings are outstanding examples of the *mozarabic* style; palm-like, the church's central pier branches out to form vaults. It was completely surrounded by Biblical scenes, exotic animals – a bear, a dromedary and an elephant – and symbolic hunting scenes, energetically executed by at least two artists.

Although the church at San Baudelio became a national monument in 1917, in the early 1920s certain villagers created a scandal by selling most of the wall paintings, detached and mounted on canvas, to an art dealer. Their removal caused further damage to the already much-abused frescoes, some of which had long been covered with whitewash. Eventually, 22 sections found their way to the United States and were exhibited together in Providence, Miami, Indianapolis and Toledo before their dispersal to various museums.

The sections in the Prado, consisting of the elephant, the bear, a bearded warrior with shield and a hunting scene with dogs, are on permanent loan from the Metropolitan Museum in New York. In the Prado, the 12th-century frescoes from the apse of Ermita de Santa Cruz in Maderuelo, Segovia, are believed to show evidence of the same hand as

is said to have been propelled to Spain from Jerusalem. To look at Spanish art with an analytical eye is to be reminded that Islam and Christianity were both Eastern religions. The Catalan Romanesque style, in particular, shows the effects of the Byzantine influence. Its ritualistic figures are almost expressionless, even when they undergo horrifying martyrdoms as on the 12th-century painted wood altar frontal from Ermita de Santa Julita de Duero, Lérida, now also in Barcelona. Besides exemplifying the exposure to Byzantine prototypes, the Tahull frescoes include examples of Spanish anecdotal detail in the scene in which Lazarus, leaning on his crutch, is licked by an ecstatic dog.

one of the unknown artists who worked at San Baudelio.

Catalan Romanesque: Art historians see another similarity in style between the frescoes from Maderuelo and those of about 1123 from the little Pyrenean church of Sant Climint in Tahull, in Lérida, part of a large group of Catalan "primitives" in the Museo de Arte de Cataluña in Barcelona.

The Moors who entered Spain from North Africa reinforced the Spanish artists' flair for flat, linear, brightly coloured stylisation. However, the oriental gift for patterning also wafted across the Mediterranean, via Italy, from Byzantium, just as the body of St James

Regional Schools: As the *Reconquista* progressed, regional Spanish Schools developed. The product of their workshops was naive and at times positively homely, but they were not completely cut off from the innovations of the artists who worked in busy Flemish and Italian commercial centres. During the 14th and 15th centuries, at the end of the Middle Ages and the beginning of the Renaissance, despite the cultural and ideological differences between kingdoms in one part of Europe and another, the technical breakthroughs of the increasingly realistic northern European and northern Italian Schools profoundly affected the artistic styles of the whole continent. In the early 14th century, the Florentine painter Giotto de Bondone broke away from the Italo-Byzantine style. Gifted with much originality and dramatic power, he settled solid, stolid, block-like figures in spacious landscapes. It is unclear how many Spanish artists visited the Netherlands or Italy.

An artist's biography was normally of little interest before the humanist Renaissance, and Giotto was one of the first anywhere to have been acclaimed as a genius in his lifetime. However, in the fresco cycle by the Catalan Ferrer Bassa, presumed to have studied in Italy in the 14th century, are the squared, three-dimensional figures and striking narrative scenes which indicated that Bassa was one of the *Giotteschi*, or imitators of Giotto. One of his Marys tenderly pulls at Christ's shroud – the Spanish anecdotal flourish.

Towards the end of the 14th century, a style which was still basically Gothic spread from the Burgundian and French courts. Integrating the Flemish artists' careful drawing of meticulous detail and the Italo-Byzantine love of pattern and colour, the international Gothic style was characterised by courtly elegance and a new sensitive interest in individual psychology. A superb example of what could be achieved with this 15th-century stylistic mix is the influential Flemish painter Roger van der Weyden's *Deposition* in the Prado, an altarpiece of around 1435 which came into the huge Spanish royal collection in the 16th century. Lluis Borrassa's altarpiece of Sta Clara, *circa* 1412, in Barcelona is a Catalan version of the international Gothic style.

The altarpiece, a polychrome (that is, painted) sculpture or a painting on a wood panel, was the most important commission for the artist of the *Reconquista*. In this lively period, Spanish fresco painting died out, the altar frontal disappeared and the retable, or *retablo*, stretched out, became a wallful of panels and climbed up to fill and tower over the typical Spanish church's east end.

There is Spanish directness and persuasive sincerity, and International Gothic decorativeness, in the panels from the altar-

piece of the Legend of St Michael in the Prado, the work of an anonymous Aragonese artist of the first half of the 15th century known as the Master of Arguis.

Hispano-Flemish: Lluis Dalmau, a Catalan, was sent to Bruges to study in the 15th century; upon returning to paint in Barcelona, he passed on his training to the younger Jaime Huguet. In Dalmau's impressive altarpiece, the *Virgen des Concellers*, in Barcelona, he placed a Spanish Virgin and Child on a Gothic throne in a Flemish landscape. A panel by Huguet in the same museum is filled with charming Spanish anecdotal details: *ex-votos* hanging over the corpse of the miracle-working St Vincent, and a tiny devil

escaping from the mouth of one of the cured.

The Hispano-Flemish style peaked at the centralising, art-collecting court of Ferdinand and Isabella. Flemish or Flemish-trained artists painted his portrait (now at Windsor Castle) and hers (now in the Royal Palace, Madrid). Fernando Gallego (*Piedad* in the Prado), the outstanding Castilian practitioner of this style, combined the decorativeness of international Gothic with the monumentality that had been developing since Giotto.

It might have been thought that the classically inspired Italian Renaissance would not "take" in dour, backward, priest-ridden

Spain. Admittedly, the Church and the Inquisition militated against the portrayal of idealised nudes and mythological subjects. Nudes have, in any case, rarely been portrayed in Spanish art – one reason Goya's *Maja* is so shocking. High Renaissance perspective like that in Andrea Mantegna's Italian masterpiece, *The Death of the Virgin*, in the Prado, brought to Spain by Philip IV, was attempted by only a few Spanish artists. The figures in Spanish paintings continue to occupy shallow Flemish or Byzantine pictorial space. Empirical perspective, used even in the highly accomplished 17th and 18th centuries, gives Spanish painting a modern look even today.

Between the skills Spanish artists brought back from Italy and the collecting fever of the Hapsburgs, beginning with Charles V, Spanish painting lost much of its provincial character without losing its Spanish flavour. Among the pleasing details in the *Saint Francis* in the Prado, painted by one of the dozens of lesser Golden Age Masters, Francisco Ribalta, is a lovable Spanish lamb climbing on to the saint's plank bed.

Realism: The late 16th-century Mannerist style, a spiritualistic reaction against the High Renaissance, was created by Italian and Spanish artists together. The greatest Mannerist, Domenikos Theotocopoulos, better known as El Greco, came to Spain in hopes of painting for the pious Philip II at the Escorial, but his weird, hovering, realer-than-real Byzantine figures wiped with eerie bluish light did not appeal to Philip, who had expected something entirely different from a pupil of the Venetian Renaissance genius Titian, his father's friend and favourite.

El Greco specialised in the two kinds of paintings that could command an audience in Spain: portraits and religious subjects. His portraits reveal the more realistic side of his painting: in *The Gentleman with a Hand on his Chest* the dark background emphasises the features of the man's face and his aristocratic tapered fingers. In religious painting, he displayed an independence from traditional expressions of piety as well as a streak of mysticism. The Inquisition was ambivalent about religious ecstasy, but the number of contemporaneous copies of his work attest to his popularity during his lifetime.

The Golden Age of Spanish painting extended from the reign of Ferdinand and Isabella to the deaths of Philip IV, the last great Hapsburg patron, and his friend and court painter Velázquez, who painted almost nothing but secular subjects. Velázquez devoted himself to capturing not only Spanish dignity but also Spanish nobility.

Ribera, a Spaniard who worked in Spanish Naples, and the three Sevillans, Velázquez, Murillo and Francisco Zurbarán, inserted beautifully painted *bodegones* (Spanish still-lifes) into larger narrative paintings suffused with unsentimental tenderness. Velázquez was to some extent inspired by Rubens, and his *Surrender of Breda* in the Prado, painted for Philip IV's Buen Retiro, recreates a gesture of genuine magnanimity at the conclusion of the siege a few miles north of Rubens' studio in Antwerp. *Las Meninas*, also in the Prado and recently cleaned, records one of the royal family's visits to Velázquez' studio in the Alcázar. The bold technique, the extraordinary sense of depth created by the figures in the mirror and, above all, the offhand, snapshot quality of the royal portrait, have made this picture one of the masterpieces of universal art.

Posthumously, after centuries of learning from Netherlandish and Italian artists, Spanish painters became highly influential themselves in the 19th century. The French Impressionists were stunned by the way the two great Spanish court painters, Velázquez and Goya, had represented with unblinking realism and expressive paint-handling whatever lay in front of them. Goya, one of the most original artists produced by any country, is sometimes considered the first "Modern" artist since, for him, realism included the portrayal of nightmares. Hemingway claimed that he "painted his spittle into every face" in his portrait of the degenerate *Family of Charles IV* in the Prado.

Like a number of other Spanish artists, Picasso was both painter and sculptor. According to Gertrude Stein, he "had in him not only Spanish painting but Spanish Cubism which is the daily life of Spain". Goya and Picasso, appearing miraculously, long after the Golden Age, communed daily with the artists of the past; and, like Goya, Picasso thought of himself as a Spanish realist.

Right, Miró's *The Wine Bottle*, like several other 20th-century works of art, is indebted to past Spanish Masters.

Seven men gather around the evening's camp on an Andalusian hillside as night falls. The flames of a fire now illuminate what was once in sunlight. The enveloping darkness is punctuated by the animated banter of the companions, who share a meal and pass full *botas* of wine. As the talking continues, it turns to harsher things. They recount to each other the difficulty of supporting life in a harsh land, the betrayal of a lover, remorse over a tragic death. When speech can no longer bear the weight of the emotion that descends around the campfire, one of the men begins to sing a *soleares*, a lament of abandonment and desolation.

Sometimes I would like
to go mad and not feel,
for being mad takes away grief,
grief that has no solution.
Death came to my bedside
but did not wish to take me,
as my destiny was not complete;
on its departure I began to weep.
I am living in the world devoid
of hope;
it is not necessary to bury me
as I am buried alive.

The song moves another man to pick up his guitar and he begins to strum chords that the singer recognises, by its progressions of harmonies and its rhythmic inflection, to be a *seguiriyas*. The guitarist completes his introduction and the singer begins. The song becomes a dialogue between sung verses and instrumental commentary, both men free to express their deepest emotions because they both know intimately the patterns which must be followed in this particular song. They are creating their *flamenco*.

Flamenco is the artistic legacy of the rich confluence of cultures which occurred on the Iberian peninsula. The seven-centuries-long occupation of southern Spain by the Moors has left the strong mark of the Arabic musical art. Other oriental features of flamenco come from Spain's adherence to Byzantine Christian ritual through the 11th century, and from the liturgical chant of the small but

important Jewish community of medieval Spain. Finally, the form crystallised around the many gypsy refugees who had entered Spain in the mid-15th century, bringing with them performance practices of Hindi origin.

Though its development has centred principally on the region of Andalusia, flamenco has embraced many of the folk traditions of the northern provinces and has become, along with bullfighting, the popular signature of Spain.

The flamenco attitude: The exact origin of the use of the word flamenco for this distinctive style of music has been obscured by time. In Spanish *flamenco* literally means Flemish, and some say that the Castilians, appalled by the wild and boisterous behaviour of the court retainers from Flanders who accompanied the arrival of Charles V in 1517, began using the word to describe unrefined behaviour in general. Another possibility is that it is a Spanish derivation from the Arabic words *felag mengu*, meaning "fugitive peasant", as this music early on came to be associated with gypsies who lived on the periphery of Spanish society. Other theories have it that its use came from the rigid and highly stylised postures of gypsies performing this music (resembling a flamingo) or from the German *flammen* (to blaze), referring to the intensity of the performer's expression.

Whatever the true origin, it seems fairly certain that *flamenco* was used to characterise a type of behaviour before it began to designate a specific style of music-making and dancing. And even today, one can be a *flamenco* without being a musician or a dancer. It is an attitude toward life of which the music is but one manifestation. To "proper" society, *flamenco* came to mean a type of person who was emotionally uninhibited, more concerned with grasping the pleasure of the moment than with industriousness, and who often resided on the edge of the law.

To the *flamenco*, it is a term of honour which marks a person who treasures freedom of movement over acquisition of property, and individual spontaneity and depth of expression over routine.

Left, even at its most flamboyant, the essence of flamenco is sorrow and loss.

The first recorded use of the word *fla-menco* in its modern musical sense dates from the mid-18th century. It was during this period that theatres presented short scenes focusing on rustic life and featuring popular song and dance as interludes between the acts of operas. Gypsy performers figured prominently in these scenes and indeed the colourful aspects of the itinerant gypsy life were such a rich source of material for these interludes that the words *flamenco* and gypsy became interchangeable. The gypsy people, though not the sole creators of fla-menco, were its guardians and chief per-formers from this period until the 1930s.

Musical roots: Song (*cante*) is central to the

written documentation simply doesn't exist.

The quality of voice that is sought after in the singing of flamenco is one that is more expressive than conventionally beautiful. Especially in the more serious songs, it is desirable to have a singer whose voice has a roughness, a texture of gravel which mirrors the torment in the text.

Deep song: Flamenco encompasses the full range of human emotion from ecstasy to despair, bitter hatred to subtle irony, but the songs which are considered to be the highest manifestation of the art are those which deal with the darker and more tortured aspects of life. The family of songs which constitutes this group is called the *cante jondo* or deep

art of flamenco and it vividly exhibits the intricate weave of oriental influences in this Spanish art. Two melodic features of fla-menco which come from the East are the repetition of a single note, reminiscent of ritual incantations, and the singing of figures which turn around a central note as an inflec-tion of an important word in the text. One also finds frequent use of sliding between notes and the use of pitches which are not found in western scales, singing notes which would fall "between" the keys of a piano.

There is the added difficulty that, like all folk music, the tradition is transmitted orally from master to student and therefore proper

song and is the type of flamenco song most closely identified with the gypsies. The two central song forms of the *cante jondo* are the *soleares* and the *seguiriyas*.

The *soleares* are sometimes called the "mother of the *cante*", as their melodic and rhythmic structure has been so important in the development of flamenco in the 19th and 20th centuries. Its name is the gypsy pronun-ciation of the Spanish *soledades*, meaning solitude or loneliness, and the texts are ex-pressions of alienation and isolation. The *soleares* were created in the Triana district, the gypsy quarter of Seville during the 19th century, and are based on even more ancient flamenco songs, the *polos* and the *cañas*.

Love and loss: Of all the songs which give vent to the most profound emotional expression in flamenco, the one that is considered to be the ultimate test of the singer's art is the *seguiriya*. The verses of the *seguiriya* are a passionate cry of the soul which rages against persecution and imprisonment, the fleetingness of love and man's relationship with his ever-present companion – death. Like the *soleares*, the *seguiriyas* are also related to an older song, the *playeras*.

The *seguiriyas* and the *soleares* are both examples of songs that are sung with a precise rhythmic inflection. This rhythmic pattern is called the *compás*. It is important that

the accompanist knows the *compás* properly for each type of song in order to support the stresses in the verse. In the 18th and 19th centuries the guitar became the most popular method of accompaniment but, prior to and even after this time, the *compás* was also created with hand-claps, foot-tapping, strokes from a staff or rod, even the rapping of knuckles on a piece of resonant wood or a tavern table.

Not all songs of the *cante jondo*, however,

Left, *cante*, **or song, is the heart of flamenco. Above**, **Doré etching of gypsy camps at Sacromonte, near Granada.**

have this fixed rhythm or *compás*. The *saeta* is a *cante* which is sung in free rhythm. Its name means literally "arrow of song" and is sung as a lament on the agony of Christ's crucifixion.

During the week of Easter, images of Christ and the Virgin Mary are carried through the streets of cities and villages throughout Spain, accompanied by bands performing a sombre religious march. From time to time, a devotee will be moved to sing and the statue bearers will lay down their burden as the procession listens to the notes of a *saeta* arching towards heaven. In Seville, it is said that if the *saeta* is not done well the procession will resume its march before the singer finishes.

The *saeta* is one of the few songs of the *cante jondo* that is not associated with the gypsies, and bears a resemblance to the liturgical chant of the Sephardic Jews in Spain.

A meaningful presentation of the *cante jondo* demands an absolute identification of the performer with the emotional atmosphere of the song. It requires an abandonment of self-consciousness and the capacity to reside at the edge of despair and to look at it boldly.

Duende and juerga: This inspired state of artistic expression is crucial to the correct performance of flamenco music. *Duende* means literally spirit or demon and is used to describe those moments when the relationship between artist and act is no longer controlled by volition but is guided by revelation. Calculation is the enemy of the *duende*. The *duende* is not within the artist but exists in the struggle between thought and expression.

True flamenco performance is therefore a community venture. The *juerga* is a type of informal and unplanned celebration which can last for hours or days, depending on the stamina and desires of the participants. It is the classic flamenco gathering in that everyone is both performer and audience by turns. The shouts of encouragement and hand-clapping from those who are not singer, dancers, or instrumentalists are an essential component of the *juerga*.

These all-night carousals have antecedents in Moorish celebrations in Andalusia. In fact, the most typically Spanish exclamation of *Olé!* at a particularly *jondo* performance gesture derives from the similar cries of

Allah! that accompanied Arab musicians and dancers. Its most profound aspect, the *juerga*, is not an opportunity for diversion but a situation created to enhance the possibility of a visitation by the *duende*.

Though the *cante jondo* is sometimes taken as representing all the flamenco songs, it really represents just one group of songs in the *cante flamenco*. The modern classification of the *cante* divides it into three groups: the *cante grande*, the *cante intermedio* and the *cante chico*.

The *cante grande* includes all of the song forms of the *cante jondo* – the family of songs which is most closely identified with the gypsies. The *cante intermedio* are less

emotionally bleak than the *grande* family though some can still be very moving. They are associated with Andalusian performers. The *cante chico* are generally characterised by a quick and rhythmically propulsive *compás*. The verses of the *cante chico* are humorous and jaunty as a rule.

For the beginner, a daunting fact about flamenco is that there are more than 70 songs. However, in some cases as many as seven or eight songs are only regional variants of one central song form. The *fandango*, or more properly *fandango grande*, is a good example of this.

The *fandango grande* is a song of the *cante*

intermedio which seems to derive from an Arabic stylisation of the *jota*, a dance indigenous to the northern province of Aragón. As *fandango* became more popular throughout Andalusia in the 18th century, each local community that adopted and altered the form gave birth to a new *cante*. In the city of Ronda, the *fandango* became the *rondeña*, in Málaga the well-known *malagueña* and in Granada the *granadinas*. Miners in the area of the Levante sing a variant known as the *taranta*.

The *bulerías* (from the Spanish word meaning to joke or ridicule) is a member of the *cante chico* and, with its lively *compás*, represents the most exciting song in flamenco. Its infectious rhythm makes it also one of the most popular dances.

Dance: Flamenco dance (*baile*) expresses through movement all the emotions found in *cantes*. The gestures in traditional flamenco are not symbolic or storytelling by nature but seek to reveal an architecture of feeling.

In two important ways, the *baile flamenco* differs from the dance as it developed in the rest of Europe. The choreographies of other European dances try to create an illusion of freedom from gravitational forces and the independence of limb movement in relation to the torso. Flamenco dance, with its majestic foot placements, seeks to secure the dancer's connection to the earth; and the most expressive movements of the arms and legs always return to the centre of the body.

In flamenco dance of the 19th century, there were differences in focus between men and women dancers. The male tended to emphasise complex footwork and rapid rhythmic patterns created with heel and toe taps called *zapateado*, while the female worked to achieve grace of line and fluidity of motion in arm and hand movements. This is not to say that there was no overlapping of technique. In the 20th century, these distinctions no longer really exist, as women have now incorporated the *zapateado*.

The *compás* of the dance is punctuated not only with footwork but through the use of *pitos* (finger-snaps) and *palmas* (clapping). Castanets are sometimes found in popular flamenco dance but are not used in the purest forms of flamenco as they restrict the ability of the hands to gesture.

The actual movements to be used in any given dance are not prescribed, allowing a freedom of form to the dancer that is not possessed by the singer or guitarist.

Popular support: Spain has always, to a greater extent than any other European nation, supported the public performance of its folk music; first in the use of rustic *tableaux* as operatic interludes, then in the creation of a national opera, called a *zarzuela*, based on traditional idioms.

With the reorganisation of Europe away from the aristocracy and towards the will of the people, a new interest in historical identity was forged. This lent prestige to the exploration and performance of folk music throughout the continent. Ironically, these same forces which propelled flamenco music into international popularity also created conditions which ultimately threatened its authenticity.

Frontera and other cities throughout Andalusia to create a more intimate setting for flamenco *aficionados*, one closer to the original atmosphere of the village *juerga*.

The *cafés cantantes* gave rise to a basic ensemble of performers called the *cuadro flamenco*. This *cuadro flamenco* consisted of a group of singers, dancers and guitarists seated in a semicircle on an elevated platform. During the course of an evening's entertainment, the different members of the *cuadro* would be featured in turn as soloists, with the remaining performers serving as accompanists.

Flamenco guitar: It was within the *cuadro* that the guitar began to develop its voice as

All of these currents in the mid-19th century created a demand for the public performance of flamenco music that had not previously existed. Troupes of gypsy performers became a popular entertainment at public festivals and in local taverns. In the 1840s *cafés cantantes* (similar to cabarets) began to open in Seville, Cádiz, Jerez de la

a soloist in flamenco music. Before the *cafés cantantes* era, the guitar had always been confined no greater function than pure accompaniment. Though this still remained its principal task, introductory passages and interludes between sung verses began to be increasingly complex.

The foundation of flamenco guitar technique and the hallmark of its distinctive sound is the *rasgueado* – a vast array of finger movements in the right hand used to strum out different rhythmic patterns. *Rasgueado* technique includes a wide selection of possible finger patterns, from one finger strumming to the thumb and all four

Left, the experience of *duende* begins young. **Above**, the duration of a *juerga* depends upon the mood and stamina of the participants.

fingers organised into a continuous flurry of motion, creating great waves of sound. The *rasgueado* alternates with the playing of melodic filigrees called *falsetas*. Flamenco guitar technique also benefited from the renaissance of the classical guitar in Spain in the 1870s and 1880s. Techniques of arpeggio playing, *tremelo* (the repeated sounding of a single note) and new harmonic possibilities were all incorporated.

Even with the inclusion of certain aspects of the classical guitar repertoire and its visual resemblance to that instrument, the flamenco guitar retains a very distinct identity with a sound imitating features of the flamenco *cante* and *baile*. The strings on the flamenco guitar are set very close to the neck and create a resonant jangle when struck, mirroring the roughness of the singer's voice. From the dance, the guitarist has taken the sound of the intricate footwork, or *zapateado*, and transferred it to his own instrument. He mimics by tapping the body of the guitar with his fingertips and knuckles, a technique called *golpe*. There is also a subtle resonance between the guitarist's *rasgueado* and the precise choreography of the flamenco dancer's hand postures.

From the heart: Early on, the period of the *cafés cantantes* supported a period of creativity and a growth in technical virtuosity that has never been equalled in the long history of this art. Previously, flamenco music and dance had been created by herder and blacksmith, miner and mother, villager and wanderer. Music for these early *flamencos* was not something done for hire at a prescribed hour but part of the fabric of everyday life. It was a gift given freely and, therefore, priceless. The frequent performances required by the *cafés cantantes* created a new class of professional flamenco performer.

This new professionalism changed flamenco forever, for good and for bad. By providing musicians and dancers with a livelihood, it allowed them the time to explore and refine their technical equipment. Other effects were less salutary. Competition among performers for the limited number of openings in the cafés became a temptation to introduce gestures of calculated flamboyance to appeal to a public often ignorant of the true nature of flamenco. In addition, café owners faced with the task of providing nightly entertainment were forced to reward performers who were often more reliable than revelatory.

El "Shows": The demands of public performance introduced an element of routine and repetition that attacked two ideas at the very heart of flamenco – that of spontaneity of creation and the integrity of the performer's impulse. The *duende* was under siege.

By the turn of the century, a period of decadence had set in during which the dance became a caricature of its former vitality and the song forms were grotesquely distorted. This picture-postcard flamenco unfortunately exists in certain performances today.

A modern revival of classical flamenco was attempted in the 1920s when a group of influential Spanish artists, among them the composer Manuel de Falla and the poet Federico García Lorca, organised a competition in Granada to reassert the importance of the traditional song and dance techniques. But it has been the art's fate that even to the present day, two flamencos exist: one based on *duende* and the other on the dollar.

There is an added difficulty today as to what can properly be called *flamenco*. While the contemporary history of other folk traditions of the West is one of research and conservation, the history of flamenco is a story of assimilation and it is a music that prizes the movement of creation. Can this growth have an end?

To traditionalists, flamenco is the flamenco style that was codified during the golden age of the *cafés cantantes* and was continued principally in the singing of rural artists untouched by the commercial interests of the 20th century. But to many of the serious young creators of flamenco today, that gold does not merely exist to be displayed, but to be used with respect – to be hammered and shaped into designs that acknowledge new influences.

In this sense, flamenco is not a petrified style but an aesthetic capable of unlimited expansion, an expansion created with a knowledge of the past that is conscious of the present. One thing is certain: as long as there is love and despair, honour and deceit, beauty of gesture in the face of death, there will be flamenco.

Right, regularly scheduled flamenco shows have somewhat changed the nature of this spontaneous musical form.

Bullfights and beaches, *fiestas* and flamenco. These are the highlights of Spain for millions of international tourists crowding the *costas* every year. Too few realise that Spain is also host to a wide range of fascinating wild animals and birds.

So extensive is the list of rare and exotic creatures that, for some naturalists, Spain is Europe's last Eden. Enthusiasm and concern starts at the top. King Juan Carlos has declared: "Nature conservation is one of the great public endeavours of our age."

Imperial Eagle: Yet with varying attitudes and policies across Spain's autonomous regions, from dedicated and protectionist to indifferent or even antagonistic, conservationist ideas may have come too late. Itself a regal symbol, the Spanish Imperial Eagle, for example, has been reduced by habitat destruction and heedless development to isolated pockets of existence.

But with patience and a bit of luck, you can see, high above the coastal heathland in southwest Spain, pairs of these magnificent eagles in flight, displaying their remarkable mating behaviour.

It starts with a series of elegant circlings, wings and pinions fully extended. After soaring together for a few minutes, one bird takes the initiative and dives at its mate. Both male and female then take part in an uninhibited display of aerial swoops and chases. One bird eventually rolls on its back in mid-air and presents its unsheathed talons to the other. Finally, the birds plunge earthward, interlocked, before levelling out and flying apart a few hundred feet above the ground.

The large ramshackle nest this couple will build on top of a cork-oak tree is made up of branches, twigs, dried grass and ferns. Two or three eggs produce plump balls of white fluff. After about a month, the young are large enough to be left for spells as both parents go out hunting. At two months, the young eagles, now with cinnamon-brown feathers, are already learning to soar and to dive at prey. Within a year, with adults ready to mate again, juveniles are on their own.

Southwest Spain encompasses the exten-

Left, Imperial Eagle feeds a snake to its young.

sive protected area (nearly 100,000 hectares or 250,000 acres under different classification) of Coto Doñana National Park, a habitat of six world-protected species including the imperial eagle, and the winter retreat of thousands of migratory aquatic birds. It seemed for years as if Doñana would disappear as its fragile environment suffered assault from developers and commercial pressure groups. Now the tide appears to have turned and its future seems assured. For the general visitor, though, limited to short guided trips around the National Park, it's not always easy to see what the battle was about.

Lynx: It could be even harder to see, in this southwestern region of Spain, one of the shyest of exclusively Iberian creatures. But if a cat with the look of a leopard cub streaks across the road in front of you, you'll have had a rare glimpse of the handsome Spanish Lynx. Weighing around 30lb (12 kilos), it has markings even more pronounced than its first cousin, the European lynx.

The lynx is king of Spain's wildcats, a family that includes the slender genet with its characteristic long banded tail. Fur pattern apart, the lynx can be immediately distinguished by large and tapering ears, topped with tufts of black hair. These act as antennae, sensitive to air currents during up-wind stalking and to the slightest rustle in the undergrowth. Monitoring sounds inaudible to a human ear, they also compensate for a weak sense of smell. Strong, padded paws, a surprisingly short tail, exploratory white whiskers and a mottled-ochre coat – perfect camouflage in sun-dappled vegetation – complete the picture.

So lithe as to appear boneless, the lynx is a nocturnal hunter in sandy scrubland bushes, tangled heather and juniper clumps. It is an agile tree-climber; it's also an expert swimmer. With eyes that can be green or amber, it possesses ultrasensitive sight – enabling it to spot and select its supper at a considerable distance on a moonless night.

Living in coverts that can be flooded by rain or chilled by snow, the lynx stays active as a matter of survival. A female lynx with kittens will leave her lair to hunt across exposed areas. Desperation is the lynx's driving force, skill and cunning its protection.

Storks: Relax under an oak in rural Spain and you might hear the unexpected sound above you of a saw cutting wood. Look

carefully for the carpenter. It could just be a Black Stork or *Cigüeña negra*, back in Spain from its winter sojourn in Africa. A big bird with jet-dark plumage, it returns to the same large, untidy nest as the previous year.

Unlike the large, more common White Stork visible in nests on bell towers and tall chimneys throughout Spain, the black species prefer lonely elm or oak woods, river cliffs or rocky platforms in the *sierras*. A true stork for all its ebony features, the *Cigüeña negra* is something of a solitary bird, flying alone or in small groups during migration.

Seemingly adverse to using their heavy wings, the storks do a good deal of gliding, and need thermal upcurrents to maintain

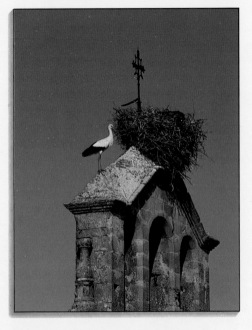

altitude. Since there are practically no thermals over large expanses of water, the birds tend to seek the shortest possible crossing, like the Straits of Gibraltar, for their north and southbound journeys.

The Black Stork shares a curious habit with its white counterpart. On emerging from the egg, the nestling lays its head on its back and makes rapid snapping movements with its bill to signal it is hungry. Though silent at first (the infant stork's bill is soft), in this way begins the bird's lifelong characteristic clacking. And if, in an adult, the habit looks like a bad-humoured warning of attack, it can also signal excitement and love.

Male and female Black Storks look alike, but the male's courtship – preening of wings, leaping into the air, seizing nest-sticks – signals his sex and intentions to other storks. The demonstration attracts a mate, and the pair, heads thrown back, engage in a riot of mutual bill-clapping. When eggs appear, male and female share responsibility for the hatching and, once chicks emerge – three to five of them, with snowy white feathers – the storks are exceptionally faithful parents. So much so that if the female dies or is killed, the male will remain alone at the nest to guard the eggs and rear the chicks. If all goes well, both parents raise the nestlings, their early tuition including warnings against such traditional

west Spain you could do with wings or a stargazer's telescope. Even scientists who aim to study them can end up encountering only one or two of the shaggy giants (at about 7 ft or 2.1 metres tall, they are among the largest land animals). But a shrunken colony of bears *is* there, forced from the foothills to take refuge in forests near the peaks after centuries of persecution by hunting parties.

At one time in history these Brown Bears numbered in hundreds. Today some 80 or fewer survive in the mountain range. In winter, the bears disappear entirely, holed up in caves and crevices for their long hibernation.

During hibernation, a prolonged light sleep on a bed of leaves, the respiration of both

enemies as the predatory Eagle Owl.

Boar and Bear: If you're planning a walk through thick forest, watch out for Wild Boar. The same animal that featured prominently in medieval banquets is still the curse of farmers, whose crops it raids, and target of not always legal hunters. The boar are understandably shy but are also fiercely protective of their engagingly-striped piglets and have been known to attack.

To see anything of the Brown Bear families of the Cantabrian mountains of north-

Left, White Stork and nest. **Above**, well concealed Spanish Lynx in the Coto Doñana.

male and female bears sinks to some five breaths every couple of minutes. Heartbeats become accordingly slow, though body temperatures drop only about 10 percent. Females which have given birth lie in the den, making a warm circle for their hairless cubs.

Since 1973 the Spanish bears have been legally protected. Hunting or killing carries fines of millions of pesetas, possibly imprisonment. But still occasionally you will hear accounts of farmers boasting of a trophy, though certainly the kill will be claimed as self-defence or the protection of lambs.

Flamingos: In contrast to the secretive bears, Greater Flamingos are eminently visible –

particularly in the large Fuente de Piedra lagoon north of urban Málaga, or on the mud-flats of the Guadalquivir River estuary in Doñana and the shallow coastal lakes, floodwaters and salt marshes of the south – a sub-tropical climate where there is normally a good food supply of algae, molluscs and crustaceans. The rose-pink and white flamingos, wading or in serried flight, are an ornithological treasure. Their stilt-like legs and long necks allow them to "graze" the shallow water for nutritious algae, feeding with their heads upside-down.

Totally gregarious, Greater Flamingos "talk" to their companions with much trumpeting and, when flying in formation, goose-

Great Bustard: Turning from one leggy bird to another, you may see on the plains of Spain the fascinating and bizarre Great Bustard. About 30lb in weight (12 kilos), it has a moustache of white bristles, an ostrich-type head and legs and barks like a dog when excited. It has also been called a goose with eagle's wings.

Spain is the last European stronghold of the Great Bustard, almost grotesque on the ground yet spectacular in flight. One of the world's largest flying birds, it is legally protected. The courtship of Great Bustards, in spring often performed by dozens of birds in open spaces, is quite a spectacle. Uttering gruff barks, the males (or *barbons*) attract

like gabbles. They breed in company, building circular, mud-heap nests a few inches above brackish water where almost no other bird nests. By April, each has produced a single egg. This is hatched after about a month among an assembly of mud-pie nests.

The greyish-brown chicks, puny and vulnerable, struggle to keep up in the water with their elders as they feed. But in the warm places they favour lies danger to the flamingo populations. A searing summer will shrink or dry up water habitats. Lakes become salt-pans and the birds can only breed there irregularly. Even trigger-happy hunters can be a threat.

the assembled females with displays of their gorgeously-striped plumage and fan-tail, and showy and prolonged dancing rituals. After the ball is over, the female seeks long grass or a field of cereals for her nest. The principal enemy to her hatchlings is the raven.

Other birds: The friendly little Hoopoe is found searching the grass for insects all over Spain. If you walk extensively in Spain, you are likely to see its unmistakable fanned crest of black and pale gold, pinkish-brown plumage and barred black-and-white wings. The Hoopoe's singularity and seemingly playful ways give it a considerable charm.

Spain is rich in wild birds, particularly

woodpeckers. A rare prize would be a glimpse of the swamp-dwelling Purple Gallinule. The lovely, egg-thieving Azure-winged Magpie of the Coto Doñana is also a notable character, which inhabits only two regions of the world, thousands of miles apart. One is eastern Asia, including China, the other – Spain.

Another striking bird, the Spanish Imperial Heron, is the most exalted of its species, a dramatic figure with a black crest and long, graceful, boldly striped neck. It nests and breeds in colonies, hidden in beds of dense reeds. The question arises why this bird, *Ardea purpurea,* with its dark plumage, is "imperial" in Spain when elsewhere it is simply a Purple Heron. The answer perhaps

lies in subtleties of sheen or colouring, but the Spanish name seems appropriate – one that is very different, moreover, from the truly purple, red-legged, red-billed Gallinule. Virtually all the two have in common is that they are secretive dwellers of the wetlands.

Two other vastly different creatures inhabit the high Pyrenees: the Bearded Vulture with its 9-ft (nearly 3-metre) wingspan and the odd, mole-sized Desman. The Desman's distinction is that it is one of the rarest animals on earth. Related to the mole, it is a sightless nocturnal rodent with a long, flat-

Left, **Iberian Ibex. Above**, the friendly Hoopoe.

tened, red-tipped snout, clawed front feet, large webbed hind feet and a rat-like tail.

Visually unappealing, rarely photographed – and unknown to science before the 19th-century – there's nothing like it in the animal kingdom. Peasants joke that "God's hand shook when He created the Desman". An aquatic mammal, it feeds on caddis, the larva of mayfly and stone flies, probing icy river beds with its sensitive proboscis. Water pollution has driven it ever higher into the mountains; for all its unwholesome appearance, the Desman can only survive in the purest water.

Vulture and toad: The Bearded Vulture (or Lammergeyer) is in decline due in part to shooting by hunters and its unfortunate habit of eating poisoned meat put down by shepherds for wolves. Its main diet is the remains of wild or domestic animals. As the garbage collectors of the mountains, the birds are a vital component in the scheme of nature.

Splendid gliders, Bearded Vultures will stay aloft for many hours of the day, scanning the landscape in search of food. Carrion creatures though they are, the birds' flight silhouette is not unlike the falcon's. Lacking the long, bare neck that gives other vultures a repulsive image, the birds in flight are impressive and beautiful.

The Bearded Vulture supplements its food by a neat trick. Its wings extended – primaries outstretched like slim fingers – it will soar over rocky ground strewn with bones left by predators. Swooping, it picks up a bone, then lets it drop from a height so that the bone cracks, exposing a tasty morsel of marrow. Thus their Spanish name of *quebrantahuesos*, or bone-breakers.

Travel slowly and you will see wild creatures virtually everywhere – including, below ground near ponds, the strange little Spanish Midwife Toad, its eggs on its back. However you are unlikely to see any of the few remaining Iberian Wolves, mainly in the west, but you could be luckier with the striking Iberian Ibex in the Gredos mountains near Madrid and, in Galicia, the heathlands' wild horse, the Garrano.

Of the protected areas, Coto Doñana is well-known, but among others are Cazorla in the southwest, Monfragüe in Extremadura in the west, Albufera and the Delta del Ebro in the east and Ordesa in the northeast below the Pyrenees.

Spain

80 km / 50 miles

Pta. de la
Estaca de Bares

La Coruña

Avilés

Gijón

Cueva de
Altamira

Santander

Oviedo

Santiago de
Compostela

Lugo

Picos de Europa
▲ 2648

Bilbao

Ga
(V

CORDILLERA CANTABRIA

Ebro

Orense

Miño

León

Burgos

Logro

Vigo

Astorga

Bragança

Benavente

SIER

Braga

Vila Real

Zamora

Valladolid

Duero

Sc

Porto

Douro

Tormes

Salamanca

Segovia

▲ 2430
Peñalara

Guadala

S
A
D
E
G
U
A
D
A
R
R
A
M
A

Mondego

Ciudad
Rodrigo

Valle de
los Caídes

Madrid

Alcalá de
Henares

Figueira da Foz

Coimbra

Covilhã

Talavera
de la Reina

Tajo

Aranjuez

P O R T U G A L

Tajo

Caceres

S P A I N

Toledo

Caldas
da Rainha

Tejo

Valencia
de Alcántara

Mérida

Puebla d. A.

Ciudad
Real

L A   M A N C H A

Sintra

Lisbon

Badajoz

Valdepeñas

Setúbal

Guadiana

Gândola

Fregenal
d. l. Sierra

Espiel

Úbeda

Sines

Beja

S I E R R A   M O R E N A

Guadiana

Córdoba

Écija

B E T I C A

Sagres

Lagos

Faro

Seville

Huelva

Genil

Granada

SIERRA NEVADA

▲ Mulhacén
3478

Guadalquivir

S I E R R A S

Antequera

Pico Veleta

Jerez
de la Frontera

Málaga

Alm

Cádiz

COSTA DEL SOL

Atlantic

Ocean

La Linea
de I.C.

Algeciras

Gibraltar

Strait of Gibraltar

Tanger

Ceuta

MOROCCO

Tétouan

F R A N C E

Moissac

■ Aven
Armand

Avignon

Toulouse

Nîmes

Aix-en-
Provence

Montpellier

Arles

Canal du Midi

CAMARGUE

Biarritz

Bayonne

Béziers

Marseille

Narbonne

Pau

Tarbes

Carcassonne

Golf de Lion

Donostia
(San Sebastian)

Pamplona

Garonne

Gavarnie
■

Pico de Aneto

P Y R E N E E S

ANDORRA

Puymorens
1915

Perpignan

3404
▲

Andorra
la V.

Huesca

Figueres

Ebro

Vic

Girona

C
O
S
T
A

B
R
A
V
A

LA VIRGEN

Zaragoza

Lleida

Terrassa

atayud

Monestir
de Poblet ■

Barcelona

RRA DE CUENCA

Ebro

Reus

C
O
S
T
A

DAURADA

Tarragona

Monreal
d. C.

COSTA

AZAHAR

DEL

B A L E A R I C   I S L A N D S

Ciutadella

MENORCA

uenca

Castellón
de la Plana

Alcúdia

Maó

MALLORCA

Manacor

■ Cuevas
de Arta

Sagunto

Palma
d. M.

■ Cuevas
del Drach

Valencia

*Golfo de
Valencia*

Santanyí

Júcar

S. Antoni A.

IBIZA

Albacete

Eivissa
(Ibiza)

Alcoy

FORMENTERA

Ifach

C
O
S
T
A

B
L
A
N
C
A

Alicante

M e d i t e r r a n e a n   S e a

Caravaca
d. l. Cr.

C
O
S
T
A

Murcia

orca

Cartagena

Algiers

Tizi-Ouzou

Ténès

Blida

Bouira

D
A
H
R
A

Mostaganem

Ech Cheliff

ALGERIA

Aïn-M' Lila

«Las Señoritas de Avignon».

The territory covered by Spain's 50 provinces is vast and breathtakingly mountainous. It is a land of illusions: in the clear, bright air the windmills on the horizon seem close enough to touch, and nearly every journey is longer than it appears on a map.

This following section of the book has divided Spain into her four main climatic zones, beginning with the central plateau, or *meseta*. At its heart is Madrid, Cultural Capital of Europe in 1992 and home to the Prado Museum and the opulent Royal Palace. Toledo and El Escorial, both near the capital, offer insights into Iberia's mixed cultural past and the stern Catholicism that fuelled her empire. Extremadura, the *meseta* region running southwest to Portugal, is an arid, hilly country which has traditionally bred conquistadors and brave fighting bulls. Less known in this area are the intact medieval towns, windswept and stork-filled in their isolation.

The second zone is Andalusia, the Spanish South. This is the sunny Spain of legend and travel brochures, with its Moorish architecture and passion for flamenco. In addition to the three gem-like cities of Seville, Córdoba, and Granada, Andalusia is sprinkled with lovely white villages. Another Andalusian treasure is the Coto Doñana, a wildlife refuge for migrating birds and camels who sauntered off the film set of *Lawrence of Arabia*.

In the Levant, the zone along the Mediterranean coast, the weather is mild and humid and the soil, deposited by mountain runoffs, is the most fertile in Spain. For more than a thousand years, the city of Valencia has been prospering from agriculture made possible by Moorish irrigation genius. North of Valencia are the spectacular coastlines called the Costa Dorada and the Costa Brava. Between them lies Barcelona, the capital of Catalonia which itself offers trout fishing, hiking and skiing in the Pyrenees.

Finally, the Spanish North is the most geographically and culturally varied part of the country. Navarre and Aragón offer rugged alpine vistas, Romanesque churches and the splendid festivities of San Fermín and El Pilar. The Basque Country, with its lush hills and gentle coast, is Spain's gastronomic paradise and home to a blue-eyed people with a prehistoric past. Cantabria's wide beaches draw well-heeled holidaymakers from Madrid, while Galicia remains somewhat hidden behind her mist-shrouded mountains.

Preceding pages: Castilian plain; Ubeda Cathedral in Andalusia; Saffron festival in La Mancha. **Left**, mural pays homage to Picasso in Caltojar.

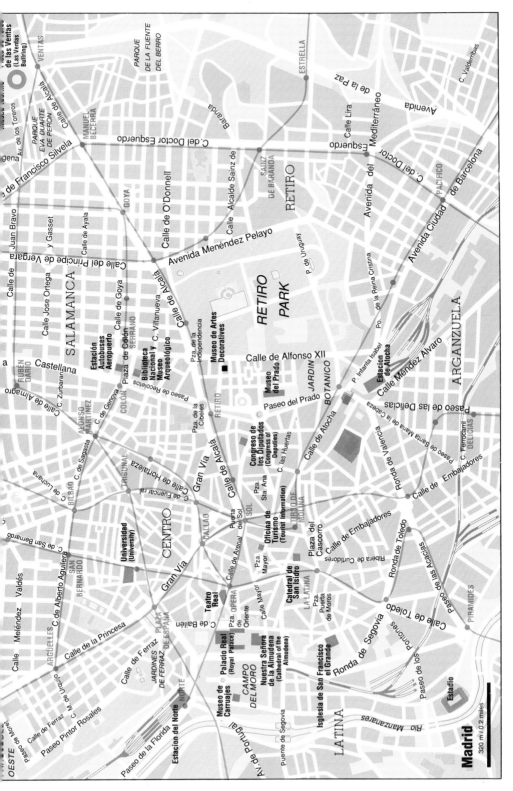

Madrid

320 m / 0.2 miles

145

MADRID

From Madrid to heaven, with a hole in the sky to look back at her.
      – Madrileño proverb

Think of Paris or Rome, and familiar images spring to mind. But Madrid is more elusive, and a city which takes getting to know. With so many other destinations in Spain to lure the holidaymaker, it may well be Europe's most undervalued capital.

The charm of its older quarters, the colour of its street life, the vibrance of its long, long, night, the exquisite duck-egg blue of its skies: these are a few of the joys of Madrid. In the last few years, democracy has brought a new dynamism to the capital which was created on the caprice of a king in 1561, and the landmark year of 1992 has added further attractions.

Sixteenth-century Madrid was a placid farming community within sight of the **Guadarrama Mountains**. The high terrain with its clear, dry air and the dense surrounding forests had once attracted the Moors, who built a fort called *Magerit* on a rise over the **Manzanares River**. It was captured by the Christians in 1083, but the two religions coexisted in relative tranquillity, remote from the politics and fervour of other Castilian cities.

When Philip II proclaimed Madrid the capital, reluctant courtiers speculated that it was simply because the town was convenient to his royal palace at El Escorial. Nevertheless, noble houses, convents and monasteries were hastily assembled in order to be near the new circles of influence. As the city grew, uncontrolled cutting of forests for construction led to erosion, drought and an increase in temperature; Madrid's climate was changed for ever.

After the Hapsburg line came to an end, the incoming Bourbons were horrified by the unpresentable state of the 18th-century capital. The streets were filthy and crime-ridden; the housing squalid; the slapdash brick churches gave no outward sign of the artistic treasures within. The Bourbons set about putting that right. Philip V built the present royal palace, the Palacio de Oriente; Ferdinand VI created the Academy of Fine Arts; Charles III was responsible for the Puerta de Alcalá and the superb neoclassical building which houses the Prado collection.

Civic improvements weren't always received gratefully by *madrileños*. Charles III believed that the long capes and broad-brimmed hats worn by Spaniards were conducive to Madrid's many cloak-and-dagger incidents, but his decree that citizens wear European short capes and tricorner hats caused a mutiny that ended in bloodshed. Joseph Bonaparte initiated a programme of trees and open spaces in Madrid, but he had been brought to power by a revolutionary invasion, and his beautification efforts earned him the nickname of "*Rey Plazuelas*" – the Courtyard King.

By the turn of this century, imposing bank buildings along the **Calle Alcalá** marked the capital's growing financial power. Sweeping boulevards and monumental fountains had given Madrid a truly majestic appearance, yet she couldn't quite shake off her cow-town reputation, particularly among fellow Spaniards. Basque novelist Pío Baroja called Madrid "an overgrown village of La Mancha".

Officially, this city of well over 3 million inhabitants is still called by its Hapsburg title of "the Village and Court", and there are those who claim that, in spite of Madrid's avant-garde arts scene and sophisticated nightlife, it's still a mass of villages. *Madrileños* are known for being open and unaffected, and it's possible that those very traits have eased the city's rapid political and cultural transformation.

Orientation: Situated at 2,000 ft (600 metres) above sea level, Madrid is the highest capital in Europe. Pollution from the city's 2 million vehicles and the continuing use of heating oil have made the air rather less champagne-like than it was said to have been in the 19th century, when European princesses often came to Madrid to give birth, but on

Preceding pages: view of Madrid from atop the Hotel Plaza. **Left**, beloved Don Quixote and Sancho Panza in the Plaza de España.

a clear day the Guadarrama Mountains seem within walking distance, and the glittering sun will prove hazardous to photographers and the fair-skinned.

Even if it's overcast, midday (2 to 3 pm) is a good hour to retreat indoors for lunch and a nap. Around 5.30 pm the streets begin to come alive again: the lovely long *tarde*, which lasts until 9 or 10, is the time for strolling, café-sitting, observing and being observed. The city's dense population appears even more so because of the Spanish belief that crowds are for joining.

The heart of it all is the **Puerta del Sol**, an oval plaza surrounded on all sides by cream-coloured 18th-century buildings. It's Spain's Kilometre 0 and the centre of most metro and bus lines; the bronze bear statue in the middle is the city's most obvious spot for a rendezvous, judging from the number of people always standing around it with their arms folded. At midnight on New Year's Eve *madrileños* gather here to eat the traditional 12 grapes, washed down with plenty of fermented grape juice, in time to the striking of the clock.

In the past, less festive public gatherings in the Puerta del Sol included a bloody battle with Napoleon's Egyptian forces, depicted in Goya's *Charge of the Marmelukes*, and an 1830 uprising against Madrid's friars, who were rumoured to have poisoned the city water supply. The Second Republic was declared here in 1931, and in the 1980s the Puerta del Sol was the centre of demonstrations in favour of freedom of expression and against NATO.

Feeding into the Puerta del Sol from the north is **Calle Preciados**, where Madrid's two largest department stores, **El Corte Inglés** and **Galerias Preciados**, face each other across a pedestrian walkway. Both stay open all day.

Following the **Calle Alcalá** to the northeast, you'll pass the **Royal Fine Arts Academy of San Fernando**. It houses paintings by artists of the Spanish School, including Goya's *Burial of the Sardine*, a portrayal of a mock-tragic funeral for a fish which takes place in Madrid on Ash Wednesday.

The 18th-century Puerta de Alcalá.

Alcalá intersects the **Paseo del Prado** at the spacious **Plaza de la Cibeles**, graced by a fountain dedicated to the goddess Cybeline. The white building opposite resembling a wedding cake is the **Correos** (post office), sometimes called the **Palacio de Comunicaciones**. Facing it on the northeast corner of the plaza is the aristocratic **Palacio de Linares**. Neglected for years, this was restored for 1992 and now houses the **Casa de América**, a centre for Latin American culture. In the mornings guided tours, some in English, reveal its fantastic 1870s interiors, the walls groaning with gold leaf, silk and marble. There are murals in the grand manner, lowering mirrors and burgeoning chandeliers.

Further along Alcalá is the Puerta de Alcalá, built as a triumphal archway for Charles III in 1778.

Frame and fortune: The **Paseo del Prado**, the southern stretch of the Castellana boulevard, has become home to a "Golden Triangle" of art collections. But of the three, the **Museo del Prado** remains in a class of its own. If it were Madrid's sole attraction, it would still be worth the trip.

The idea of opening museums to the public is only as old as the Enlightenment and, ironically, it was Joseph Bonaparte who put forth a plan to make Spanish works of art available to the Spanish public. Bonaparte was ousted during the Peninsular War, but Ferdinand VII completed the project. In 1819 the collection was opened in a building originally designed to hold a natural science museum. As notions of what public morals could bear became more enlightened, pictures such as Titian's *Venus* and Rubens' *Three Graces* were unveiled. Today it owns more than 7,500 paintings, less than a sixth of which are on permanent display there.

The best strategy for a single visit to the Prado is probably to head for the upper floor first to see the 17th- and 18th-century Spanish masters and the Italians; and then pick and choose according to taste on the ground floor, which includes Goya's "black" paint-

ings, Flemish, Dutch and German masterpieces and earlier Spanish works. Don't miss the roomful of paintings by Hieronymus Bosch.

A ticket to the Prado is also good for its annexe, **El Casón del Buen Retiro**, which houses the collection's 19th-century works. For years it was also the home of *Guernica*, Picasso's disturbing allegory of the bombing of the Basque town of that name during the Spanish Civil War. But in 1992, amid fierce controversy, the painting was moved down the road to Madrid's new showcase for modern art, the **Centro de Arte Reina Sofía**.

In fact controversy has dogged the Reina Sofía all the way since its initial opening in 1986. Satirically referred to as "El Sofidú" in allusion to the Pompidou Centre in Paris, it has undergone seemingly endless renovations and is reported to have cost the Spanish tax-payer over £100 million.

Just off the Paseo del Prado at its southern tip in Calle Santa Isabel, the gallery is housed in the 18th-century former General Hospital of Madrid, its formidable exterior jazzed up by futuristic transparent lifts – source of yet more controversy. But perhaps controversy is appropriate to a setting for innovators like Picasso, Dalí, Miró and Juan Gris. The Reina Sofía has a lively programme of exhibitions, and more worldly visitors will enjoy its gift shop.

The Thyssen trove: This collection of art came to Spain, amid hot competition from other countries, for an initial period of nine and a half years, but now it will be staying for good, its treasures on permanent view in the **Palacio de Villahermosa**, almost across the road from the Prado.

The lion's share of the art collection of Baron Hans Heinrich Thyssen-Bornemisza, reckoned the greatest in private hands after that of Queen Elizabeth, was bought by the Spanish state for 44,100 million pesetas (£232 million). The 700-odd pictures are superbly lit and displayed in such a way as not to overwhelm, though the salmon-pink wash on the walls does not elicit universal approval. The collection,

spanning the centuries from 1290 to the 1980s, is particularly notable for its 17th-century Dutch Old Masters; 19th-century North American paintings; 20th-century Russian Constructivists and German Expressionists.

A palatial past: Both El Casón del Buen Retiro and the adjacent **Army Museum** are remnants of a palace built by Philip IV in the 17th century, which explains the ceilings by Velázquez and his disciples in the latter building.

The **Naval Museum**, five minutes' walk away at Paseo del Prado 5, is dedicated to the once-invincible Armada. Among its attractions are model ships, weapons, charts, nautical instruments and the first map ever to show the New World, dating from 1500.

For a sensual retreat from battle, head for the **Museum of Decorative Art** around the corner in Calle Montalbán. Here are six floors of Persian carpets, tapestries, gold-stamped Cordovan wallpaper, baroque beds with velvet hangings, inlaid tables, silk and feather fans and exquisite dolls' houses constructed for royal children. On the top floor is an old-fashioned kitchen decorated with Valencian tiles.

Sunday in the park: Originally, **El Parque del Buen Retiro** was conceived as a park where the Spanish nobility could retire from the unpleasantness of the 17th-century Madrid streets. Inside the wrought-iron gates, garden parties and tableaux reached lascivious heights during the reign of Philip IV, a king who was "lewd in his pleasures, a blind adorer of art and beauty... a child in whose indiscreet hands the precious and complicated machinery of government became a pastime", according to the Spanish historian Mesoneros. The floating ships of musicians, and celebrants dressed in Greek costume running through the trees vanished with Philip's death, and the park was virtually abandoned. It was badly damaged during the Peninsular War, and Ferdinand VII began its restoration and opened its gates to the public.

Fountains, statues and the delicate **Crystal Palace** still give the Retiro the air of a royal garden. Joggers and roller skaters are now a part of the landscape, but for most *madrileños*, a day in the park is a dress-up affair, from dapper old gentlemen in black suits to little girls gleefully scuffing white shoes through the dirt.

The nearby **Royal Botanical Garden** was created in 1774 by Charles III. There's a small admission charge, but even if you can't tell a Japanese maple from a dahlia, it's shady and aromatic.

Outside the southern wall of the garden is the **Cuesta de Moyano**, a year-round outdoor book fair. Sunday morning is the peak browsing time for bestsellers and the odd rare edition. Meanwhile, up the road in the **Plaza de la Lealtad**, well-heeled diners will be enjoying the fashionable Sunday brunch at the **Ritz Hotel**.

On other mornings of the week, literary pilgrims can follow the **Calle Cervantes** from the Paseo del Prado to the **House of Lope de Vega** at number 11. Here the great playwright created his most important works. The furnishings and personal effects are not his, but they show how a 17th-century Spanish household might have looked. (Closed afternoons and Sundays).

Returning to the Puerta del Sol along the **Carrera San Jerónimo**, you'll pass the parliament building, the **Palacio de las Cortes**. The bronze lions in front are made of melted-down cannons captured in the war with the Moroccans in 1860. It was here on 23 February 1981 that a Civil Guard named Antonio Tejero held the entire Spanish lower house at gunpoint overnight, as part of an abortive coup attempt.

Further up the street is the **Museo del Jamón**, a delicatessen with artful displays of the many kinds of Spanish ham and sausage. Be sure to try *serrano*, a tender, cured ham similar to the more widely known prosciutto.

Old Madrid: South of the Puerta del Sol is one of Madrid's oldest and most colourful neighbourhoods: a tangle of narrow cobbled streets lined by adobe apartment houses with wrought-iron balconies and chilly, musty foyers. If you want to sample some of Madrid's

Parque del
Buen Retiro.

CREAM OF THE CAFÉS

Most of us think of a café as a place to have a cup of coffee and a sinful pastry. But not so the Spaniards. To them it is variously a place to watch the world go by, an academic arena, a setting for cultural input or a therapeutic refuge from the world beyond its velvet curtains.

To experience the Spanish café at its traditional best, visit the Café Gijón on the Paseo de Recoletos. Now more than a century old, this is the *grande dame* of the café as cultural institution. The group at the next table to you may be immersed in a *tertulia* – a lengthy discussion usually on some artistic or political issue. The exigencies of modern life are putting an end to the tradition of *tertulias*, though the cafés which are their natural habitat have made a comeback in the last few years.

Probably no other café in modern Madrid goes back as far as the Gijón. The somewhat stark interior of the Lion, on Calle Alcalá close to the Plaza de la Cibeles, is one of the few authentic survivors from the late 1920s.

But the delightful Art Nouveau-style decor of El Espejo, also on Recoletos, is deceptive. Its tiled pictures and huge mirrors date from 1978, while the pavilion extension, a seemingly turn-of-the-century confection of glass and tiles, appeared only in 1990. Another comparatively new entry in the old style is the Café de Oriente, opposite the royal palace. Draped with velvet, padded with plush and trimmed with lace, the café specialises in exotic coffees and homemade patisseries, though its menu is very versatile.

The 19th century was the heyday of the Madrid café. The fear and repression inflicted by Franco on his fellow Spaniards stifled much of the political and philosophical rhetoric that were the mainstay of the capital's cafés before the Spanish Civil War; but the cafés at least provided a welcome refuge from the winter cold. As indoor plumbing and central heating became more common in the late 1960s and early 1970s, the old-world café came to the verge of extinction. But it has made a comeback since the rebirth of democracy. While the chrome and plastic of the new generation of cafés are a world away from the polished panelling and lace edging of the more traditional variety, the social impetus that sparked them is as old as the capital itself.

In Spain, patronizing one café over another is not just a matter of convenience and taste: it is a question of personal conviction and one's station in life. There are right-wing cafés and left-wing cafés; cafés for the literati, for yuppies, for the film crowd, for the *outré* and progressive. At the Circulo de Bellas Artes, near the Puerta del Sol at Alcalá 42, you'll see the pale-faced girls and Balzacian types you'd expect at the Fine Arts Circle. The café's fabulous interior – columns, chandeliers, painted ceilings and a magnificent sprawling nude as you walk in the door – dates from 1926.

Late in the evening at the Café Central (Plaza del Angel, 10) you can listen to great jazz played live in an Art Deco setting, while in the next street, the Salon del Prado (Calle Prado, 4) offers live classical music on its small stage lateish on Thursday nights.

The capital's cafés are of a variety to suit every taste. They offer the chance to talk, drink, read, listen to jazz or sonatas, admire paintings, or simply watch – and who knows just whom you might meet? ■

Outside the Café Gijón.

legendary bars and *tapa* bars, head for the **Plaza Santa Ana** and the adjoining **Plaza del Angel**. Among names to look for are **La Trucha** (in the pedestrian passageway of Manuel Fernández y González, 3), great for inexpensive *tapas*; **Viva Madrid** (same passageway, number 7), with an unforgettable interior; **Cervecería Alemana** (Plaza Santa Ana, 6), a bit of history preserved; and **Los Gabrieles** (Calle Echegaray, 17) whose fantastic walls give new life to the phrase "a night on the tiles".

Be street wise: In this area, the prudent will give calles **Cruz** and **Espoz y Mina** a miss, since both have seen better days. Madrid, like other big cities, has its share of street crime, much of it drugs-linked. Most of the drug markets are on the outskirts of town but one is right at its heart, in the streets around the Puerta del Sol and the Gran Vía. Notoriously bad for muggings is the area directly to the north of the Gran Vía, especially around Calle Ballesta.

If you plan extensive wanderings on foot through the downtown area (Centro), leave your jewellery, vital documents and large amounts of cash in the hotel strongbox. It makes sense to take precautions.

Madrid's **Plaza Mayor** or main square is a 17th-century beauty superbly restored, even if it is no longer the centre of town as it was in ages past, when *autos-da-fé*, bullfights and coronations took place there. The wide cobbled square is closed to traffic and is a pleasant spot to have coffee and make plans, since the main tourist office is located here.

Just west of the Plaza Mayor is the **San Miguel Market**, enclosed in a lacy turn-of-the-century ironwork building. Redolent with *chorizo* and voluptuous heaps of fruit, a Madrid market will also give you an idea of why this city is sometimes called the best seaport in Spain. Fish and shellfish are flown into Castile daily.

Further along **Calle Mayor** is the **Plaza de la Villa**, a pretty pedestrian square which is a showcase of Madrid architecture from the 15th to the 17th

Sunday stamp market in the Plaza Mayor.

centuries. The main attraction is the baroque **Casa de la Villa**, or town hall. As in most country towns, the municipal building also served as the jail, which explains the double entrance.

Also worth noting here are the **Torre de los Lujanes**, one of the few examples of 15th-century secular architecture in the capital, and the **Casa de Cisneros**, a Plateresque 16th-century structure with a tapestry museum. Facing the town hall is the former **Hemeroteca Municipal** (periodicals library).

On a Sunday morning, head south to the **Church of San Isidro**, whose gloomy interior houses the remains of Madrid's peasant patron saint. Just beyond the church, people say, Madrid becomes Magerit again – the **Rastro**, an enormous open-air bazaar, fills the streets for several blocks in all directions. Clothes, furniture, animals and electronic wares can all be haggled for, as well as specialised items such as rings of skeleton keys, old liquor stills and Fascist memorabilia. (Beware pickpockets here).

The Rastro takes place in a section of the city locally described as *castizo*; a word which means "pure" but has a similar connotation to the London "cockney". Here Madrid's throaty urban accent is thickest; it's the pulse point of the August festival of the Virgin of the Paloma, when women in kerchiefs and flounced skirts dance through the streets with their waistcoated partners to alternate blasts of traditional *chotis* and rock music. Just to the south in the **Puerta de Toledo**, the old fish market has been cleverly transformed into a tasteful, triple-decked complex with small, upmarket, fashion, crafts, antique and food shops.

Fit for an angel: Sacred architecture is not one of Madrid's strong suits, but most of the notable churches are located in the vicinity of the Plaza Mayor.

The capital's long wait for its cathedral came to an end on 15 June 1993 when Pope John Paul II consecrated the **Cathedral of Santa María la Real de la Almudena,** alongside the Royal Palace. The church houses the image of the

Combing the Rastro for bargains.

Virgin of the Almudena, patroness of Madrid. Work on the building had started in 1883: indeed, King Alfonso XII hoped it would be the burial place of his beloved first wife and cousin, María de las Mercedes. A devotee of the Virgin of the Almudena, she had died aged 18 in 1878, and could not be interred in the Royal Pantheon at El Escorial as she had not produced heirs. "When you pass beneath the vaults of this church", said the King, laying the first stone, "pray for the memory of that angel in heaven to whom is owed the initiative of this idea." A century later Madrid has its completed cathedral, but María de las Mercedes is buried at El Escorial.

Also close to the Royal Palace is the neoclassical **Basilica de San Francisco el Grande**, which was built on the site of a 13th-century monastery purportedly founded by St Francis during a pilgrimage to Spain. The rotunda was first designed by a monk named Francisco Cabezas, but the plans were discovered to be structurally unsound and the building was eventually completed by the Italian architect Sabatini in 1784.

The interior is mostly decorated in florid 19th-century style; one mural shows an apparition of St James in the act of killing Moors. There is also an early fresco by Goya, which contains a bright-eyed self-portrait.

Just a couple of streets to the northeast is the **Capilla del Obispo**, an exquisite Gothic chapel which originally formed part of the palace of the Vargas family. (It has been closed for restoration, so check first with the Tourist Office if you wish to visit it.) Also very close is the **Capilla de San Isidro**, considered one of the best examples of baroque architecture in Madrid.

The **Monasterio de la Encarnación** was built near the royal palace and was once connected to it by a passageway. Apparently the convent was meant to be a refuge for the women of the royal family, "in case of some novelty", as its founder Queen Margaret of Austria hinted darkly in a letter. The cloister houses royal portraits, including one of an illegitimate daughter of Philip IV

Left, Madrid's new Cathedral of Sta María. Right, celebrating the La Paloma festival in old Madrid.

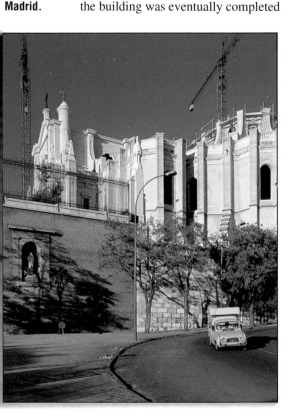

being received into heaven. The church is a splendid example of 18th-century Madrid architecture by Ventura Rodríguez. In the reliquary is a vial of a saint's blood which is said to liquefy every year on 27 July.

Just beside the Monasterio de la Encarnación is an ideal restaurant for those in search of an authentic taste of Madrid. **La Bola**, at Calle Bola 5, serves some of the capital's finest *Cocido Madrileño* – a Spanish *pot-au-feu* traditionally presented in two or even three courses. Set in what was once a wine shop, this is one of the capital's oldest restaurants. Its attractive interior is liveliest at lunchtime.

The nearby **Monasterio de las Descalzas Reales** (Royal Barefoot Franciscans) was founded by a sister of Philip II and contains a number of art treasures donated by blue-blooded nuns' families. Many of the works of sacred art have to do with children, who represented the triumph of life over death for Golden Age painters.

The Royal Palace: For its spectacular

location and opulent interior, the **Palacio de Oriente** is the second most dazzling tourist attraction in Madrid. On Christmas Eve, 1734, the Hapsburg Alcázar burned to the ground, enabling Philip V to build a palace more suited to the requirements of a Bourbon monarch. Of the lavish result, designed by Italian masters Sacchetti and Sabatini, Napoleon claimed that his brother Joseph had better lodgings than his own at the Tuileries in Paris.

Alfonso XIII was the last inhabitant of the palace, although Franco's body lay in state here in 1975. The present royal family prefers less elaborate quarters outside town and the palace is now used only for official functions. The stately **Campo del Moro** gardens were opened to the public by King Juan Carlos in 1977.

Interesting annexes to the palace include the **Royal Armoury**, containing the swords of Cortés and Ferdinand the Catholic, the **Carriage Museum** and the **Royal Pharmacy**, with glass cases full of the exotic medications of centuries past. Guides also urge visitors to see the **Royal Tapestry Factory** across town, where craftspeople still patiently turn out Goya designs by means of thousands of hand-tied knots.

Familiar refrain: The **Teatro Real**, opposite the palace, opened as an opera house in 1850 – due to a string of delays, it had taken 38 years to build. Legend has it that the cast of one production included live elephants, but in recent years it has been used only for concerts. Now renovations are under way to make it an opera house again. Tardiness seems to have become a tradition, however: the opening production scheduled for 1992 has been postponed until 1995…

Zarzuela or Spanish operetta is usually performed in the **Teatro Lírico Nacional La Zarzuela** on Calle Jovellanos. Nostalgic and full of colourful local details, *zarzuela* is an unusual Spanish art form in that it takes a sentimental, not tragic, view of the past.

The centre of the western end of Madrid is the **Plaza de España**, where larger-than-life bronze statues of Don Quixote and Sancho Panza ride toward

Outside the Palacio de Oriente.

the sunset. The square lies at the end of the Gran Vía.

The Lily Palace: Just north of the Plaza de España is the **Palacio de Liria**, the magnificent 18th-century home of the Duchess of Alba. Designed by Ventura Rodríguez, who worked on the royal palaces of Madrid and Aranjuez, the house contains an outstanding collection of furniture, miniatures and European paintings. The gallery may be visited by prior appointment.

The Duchess of Alba comes from a venerable line of art patrons, including the 13th Duchess Cayetana, the beautiful and lively friend of Goya. She was long rumoured to have posed for Goya's *Naked Maja*, but art historians generally agree that the gleaming, idealised female body must have been painted from the artist's imagination. (Nineteenth-century Spain was not alone in finding the picture shocking. In 1930, letters bearing the 10-peseta stamp of Goya's nude were barred from circulating in the United States, and as recently as 1991 a reproduction was removed from Penn State University's music room as it was held to constitute sexual harassment.)

Exquisite painting by Goya is one of two good reasons for making a pilgrimage down to the **Paseo de la Florida** to visit the **Ermita de San Antonio**. After completing this frescoed ceiling showing St Anthony raising a murdered man from the dead, Goya was appointed first painter to the court, despite the fact that his portrayal of scrofulous street people was a startling departure in church art. The little chapel is now his mausoleum. The popularity of the shrine – St Anthony is the patron of disappointed lovers and lost objects – has necessitated the construction of a replica chapel next door.

Also important is the rambling stone restaurant beside the hermitage: **Casa Mingo** offers an Asturian feast of roast chicken, cheese and strong, tart, cider.

Other sights in this part of town include the **Temple of Debod**, given to Spain by Egypt in gratitude for helping with the construction of the Aswan

Goya frescoes in the Ermita de San Antonio.

Dam. It was built by the Pharaoh Zakheramon in the 4th century BC. Nearby, you can board a funicular and sail over the **Parque del Oeste** and the Manzanares River to the **Casa de Campo**, an enormous scrubby park with an amusement park and a zoo. Among the pines below your cable car you can see traces of Civil War trenches from the city's three-year siege.

Rebel roots: Madrid's centre for the counterculture element is the area known as **Malasaña**, between Calles **San Bernardo** and **Fuencarral** south of **Calle Carranza**. By day this area is redolent of old Madrid, with local people going about their lives. Storefronts attract customers with brightly-coloured 19th-century mosaics. A former pharmacy on the corner of Calles **San Andrés** and **San Vicente Ferrer** has memorable tiles advertising turn-of-the-century miracle cures.

But when night falls the neighbourhood changes character. Bars resound with rock 'n' roll, semi-clandestine drug deals are agreed on street corners and the streets are generally less safe.

The centre of the neighbourhood, the **Plaza Dos de Mayo**, was the scene of a fierce battle with Napoleon's forces; citizens rushed to the streets with whatever weapons they could lay their hands on. The civilians lost but casualties on both sides were heavy; the archway in the middle of the plaza commemorates the fallen.

Some years ago, when plans were made to tear down the old houses and put up new apartment blocks, the neighbours once again mobilised in defence of the *barrio*. This time Malasaña was saved without bloodshed and it enjoyed a brief period as a fashionable bohemian district.

The **Municipal Museum**, on nearby Calle Fuencarral, is installed in a former poorhouse with an ornate late-baroque facade. During the 19th-century rage for neoclassical design, the building was held up as the embodiment of bad taste. The exuberant mouldings and statuary are restored and now historic rather than merely out-of-date. The **Parque del Oeste.**

museum contains exhibits on the history of Madrid from the Palaeolithic period to the present day. Among its attractions are Goya's *Allegory of the City of Madrid*, an exquisite 1830 model of the capital and photographs dating from 1850.

Noble pasts: The **Romantic Museum** at **Calle San Mateo 13** is housed in a mansion formerly belonging to the Condes de la Puebla del Maestre, and made into a museum by the Marqués de Vega Inclán. Most of the furniture and pictures here have to do with the reigns of Ferdinand VII and Isabella II; objects which one associates with the peculiarities of the 19th century include a pair of duelling pistols instrumental in the death of satirist José de Larra, scatological moving pictures and a water closet with a velvet seat, which once belonged to Ferdinand VII.

While in this area, enthusiasts of the work of the architect Antoni Gaudí should see the **Palacio de Longoria** at **Calle Fernando VI, 6** (at the corner with Calle Pelayo). Designed by the Catalan architect José Grases Riera, of the Gaudí School, it dates from 1902 and is one of the best of the few examples in Madrid of Catalan Modernism. These days the building is the headquarters of the Society of Authors, which has restored it to its original splendour.

A couple of streets to the south-east, **Calle Almirante** has become a showcase for Spain's more innovative fashion designers. **Casa Gades**, at **Conde de Xiquena 4**, is an attractive and inexpensive Italian-style restaurant named after the flamenco dancer Antonio Gades, who was one of its founders. The nearby **Teatro María Guerrero**, on **Calle Tamayo y Baus**, is a pretty, state-run theatre staging classic works.

On a pedestal: The **Jardines del Descubrimiento** alongside the **Plaza de Colón** – which translates as "Square of Columbus" – are graced by a statue of the discoverer on a neo-gothic column and huge beige sculptures which resemble large decayed teeth. At the western end, an attractive, noisy waterfall guards the entrance to the **Centro Cultural de**

Bar in Malasaña.

la Villa, an arts complex with a theatre, concert hall and exhibition space.

Alongside this plaza is a monolithic Hellenic structure enclosing the **National Library** facing west and the **National Archaeological Museum** facing east. The library, inaugurated in 1892 to mark the 400th anniversary of Columbus' voyage, contains manuscripts dating from the 10th century.

The Archaeological Museum has rich displays from prehistoric Spain, Iberian treasures such as the mysterious, impassive Lady of Elche, Roman statues and mosaics and a Visigothic crown studded with jewels. In the garden are reproductions of the Altamira cave paintings in a reconstructed cave.

The *barrio* of **Salamanca** was constructed in the late 19th century for the Spanish aristocracy who wanted to move away from the noise and congestion of the city centre. The project was bankrolled by the Marqués de Salamanca, a soldier, politician and entrepreneur who made and lost three fortunes and whose picaresque business dealings once forced him to flee to France in disguise. Today the neighbourhood is the soul of respectability. While there are few outstanding individual examples of architecture, notice the seigneurial touches to the buildings: the ornate glassed-in balconies, the doorways cut wide enough to allow the entrance of carriages. Many of the mansions are now foreign embassies, but the area is still a comfortable enclave of the well-to-do, evidenced by the exquisite delicatessens, antique shops and fur-clad ladies sipping afternoon chocolate.

The main shopping street is **Calle Serrano**, where French and Italian boutiques are gradually making room for Spanish names such as **Loewe** and **Adolfo Domínguez**. Prices for shoes and leather goods are no longer low, but quality, on this street in particular, is unsurpassed. In a nearby street the disco/café complex within the trendy **Téatriz**, a converted theatre, is worth a glimpse for the architecture alone.

Further north, just before Serrano crosses Calle María de Molina, is one of

Salamanca street corner.

Madrid's loveliest museums, the **Lázaro Galdiano**. The turn-of-the-century Italianate palace surrounded by a lush garden was the private residence of a publisher who bequeathed his art collection to the Spanish government in 1948. On the first floor are display cases of deep blue medieval enamels, silver and gold chalices and reliquaries, coffers, a 12th-century ivory Virgin and a small head of San Salvador. On floors above are clocks, armour, crystal and ceramics, as well as painting from Spanish and Flemish primitives to Constable and Turner.

Elegant boulevard: The **Paseo de la Castellana** bisects the city between the **Atocha** train station to the south and the **Chamartín** station to the north. This wide, tree-lined road is said to be Madrid's solution to the poor impression made by the scrawny Manzanares river.

Most of the 19th-century palaces along the Paseo have been converted into banks, or torn down to make room for new architecture of glass and chrome, but it's still a delightful promenade. Traffic islands shielded by potted palms and privet make oddly intimate outdoor cafés, since the swoop of cars is loud enough to keep conversations private. In summer these open-air *terrazas* become popular night-spots.

Driving north up the Castellana, you leave the past behind. **Nuevos Ministerios**, a dismal grey complex of post-war government buildings, gives way to unremarkable apartment blocks.

But long before you reach the Plaza de Castilla at the top, you'll see two extraordinary modern buildings which lean towards each other at an angle of 15 degrees. To *madrileños*, these are *las torres de Kio* – the Kio towers, named after the Kuwait Investment Office (KIO) which financed their construction. But their official title is **La Puerta de Europa**: the Gateway to Europe.

Why two towers set deep in the *meseta* of central Spain should constitute a gateway to Europe remains a mystery... as mysterious, in fact, as a king's decision to set his capital here all those centuries ago.

Below, One of the Kio towers. **Right**, Paseo de la Castellana.

TOROS en TOLEDO
Empresa GONZALEZ VERA · Representante: FELICISIMO TEJEDOR

Martín Font

Martín Font

JUEVES, 1 DE JUNIO DE 1972 ● FESTIVIDAD DEL CORPUS CHRISTI
se verificará, si el tiempo no lo impide, con permiso de la Autoridad y bajo su presidencia, la

TRADICIONAL CORRIDA DE TOROS

BRAVOS TOROS, cuyos defensas están íntegras,
con divisa en ambas rejas, con divisa negra y
amarilla, de la ganadería de los herederos de
PISATEJOS (Portugal), serán picados, banderilleados y muertos a estoque por los siguientes

Don Alberto Cunhal Patricio
ESPADAS

EGO · **PACO** · Francisco Rivera

UERTA · CAMINO · PAQUIRRI

Acompañados de sus respectivas cuadrillas de picadores y banderilleros

La corrida empezará a las SEIS en punto de la tarde

 CAJA DE AHORRO PROVINCIAL DE TOLEDO
60 SUCURSALES EN LA PROVINCIA
Su ahorro en "La Caja" beneficia a los toledanos

EL DIA 23 DE MARZO 1975 ● Domingo de Ramos
se verificará, si el tiempo no lo impide, con permiso de la autoridad y bajo su presidencia, la

¡TRADICIONAL CORRIDA DE TOROS

6 Soberbios Toros de Don JOSE y Don FRANCISCO ORTEGA SANCHEZ, par

CURRO ROMERO
RAFAEL de PAULA
PACO ALCALDE

Acompañados de sus correspondientes cuadrillas de picadores y banderilleros

La corrida empezará a las CINCO en punto de la tarde

DESPACHO DE LOCALIDADES: A partir del Jueves día 20 en TOLEDO, en el BAR «LAS PANDERETAS», y en MADRID, en el BAR «LAS PANDERETAS», Jardines.
Teléfono 231 00 12 · ABUNDANTE SERVICIO DE AUTOCARES CON BILLETES DE IDA Y VUELTA · ESPECTACULO NUMERO 12

FUTBOL - Campo Municipal - Toledo
EL DOMINGO, 23 DE MARZO - A las DOCE de la mañana **REAL MADRID - C. D. TOLEDO**

TOLEDO AND EL ESCORIAL

Two different day trips from Madrid lead to two of the most important and contradictory historical spots in Spain: the city of Toledo and the monastery of El Escorial. Whereas the former harks back to the Middle Ages, El Escorial is a monument to the immense 16th-century Spanish empire.

Toledo has always played a prominent role in Spanish history. She was the capital of Spain and home to Romans, Visigoths, Moors, Jews and Christians. Today Toledo is a small regional capital (pop. 62,000), but such is her beauty and history that the entire old city is a national monument, and also listed as part of the UN's World Heritage.

The city lies around 45 miles (72 km) south of Madrid. The unusual neo-*mudéjar* train station is a good starting point for a visit. Just outside the station, the city's majestic patrician profile rises above the **Tagus River** gorge. Cross the river on the **Alcántara Bridge**, the oldest bridge leading into town. It was built by the Romans, then refurbished successively by the Moors and the Christians. On the hill opposite the city is the **San Servando Castle**, built by the Romans to protect the bridge.

The main entrance to the city is through the **Bisagra Gate**, the most impressive of the nine toll-collecting gates along the old city walls. In the **Cambrón Gate**, at the west end of the city, you can still read the medieval plaque advising gatekeepers that Toledo residents need not pay.

Privileged position: Toledo's strategic and geographic advantages have long been appreciated. The Romans reached here in AD 192, though little is left of their occupation: a **Roman circus** off the **Avenida de la Reconquista**, a few mosaics and reconstructed buildings.

By the 6th century AD the Visigoths had set up court in Toledo. The Visigothic Councils, the name given to the meetings between the Visigothic king and his advisers, were held on the site where the **Cristo de la Vega Her-**mitage now stands, near the Roman ruins. This little hermitage, with a fine *mudéjar* apse, was also the site of a celebrated miracle. According to the legend, a young man swore eternal love to a young lady while standing before the crucifix in the church. But the young man left his love jilted, and she called in a judge to decide the case. When asked to produce a witness, she took the judge to the church and asked Christ to verify her story. Sure enough, the crucifix slowly moved, which is why one of Christ's arms is off the cross (a replica).

To get a sense of the Visigothic presence in Toledo, visit the church of **San Román**, where the **Visigothic Culture and Councils Museum** has been installed. San Román was originally a Visigothic church, but it has been retouched with *mudéjar* work, Romanesque murals and a Renaissance dome. In the museum are copies of the Visigothic kings' crowns.

Melting pot: In AD 711 the city was conquered by the Moors. Until 1085, when King Alfonso VI reconquered To-

ledo, an unusually fluid relationship between Moors and Christians existed here. Because the city had not resisted the invasion, it was rewarded with a certain degree of independence, although tribute was paid to the Moorish court in Córdoba. Until the end of the 14th century, this harmony also included the Jews, whose population in Toledo was 12,000 in the 12th century.

This tolerance lasted long enough to leave its mark on the city's architecture and art. The *mozarabic* style of architecture was developed by Christians living under Moorish domination, while the *mudéjar* style was the work of Moors who remained in the areas reconquered by Christians. Less apparent are the remains of Jewish influence in the city. Of the 10 synagogues, only two managed to survive the 14th-century pogroms.

The departure of the Jews in 1492 and Philip II's decision in 1561 to move the capital to Madrid meant that Toledo's splendour was doomed to decline. By the middle of the 17th century, her population was half what it had been 100 years before.

Churches, synagogues and mosques: Visible from quite a distance on the *meseta*, the **Cathedral** itself is testament to Toledo's long history as Spain's spiritual capital long after the court moved to Madrid (even today it keeps Castile's archbishopric). The Goths worshipped on this site before the Moorish invasion, and the Moors converted their church to a mosque. The present structure was begun in 1226 and finished 300 years later, during which time *mudéjar,* baroque and neoclassical elements were added to the predominantly Gothic building. The large polychrome retable depicting the life of Christ; the famously excessive baroque Transparente altarpiece, built to allow in natural light; the sacristy, with its collection of paintings by El Greco, Titian, Goya and Van Dyck; the sumptuous walnut choir stalls and the *mudéjar* ceiling in the chapterhouse are all worth a lingering look.

The other major Catholic structure in **Toledo.**

Toledo is **San Juan de los Reyes**, located in what is left of the *judería,* the old Jewish quarter. The Gothic church was built by the Catholic Monarchs, Ferdinand and Isabella.

The **Cristo de la Luz Hermitage** is possibly one of the oldest buildings in the city; Alfonso VI held mass here when he conquered Toledo in 1085. There is a pleasant garden behind the church which leads to the top of the **Puerta del Sol**, the old Moorish gate. The church is also known as Cristo de la Luz Mosque, due to the fact that it was used as such for 400 years.

The major synagogue which survived the 14th-century pogroms is known today as **Santa María de la Blance**, located on **Calle Reyes Católicos**. The most striking feature of the synagogue are the capitals, which reflect a Byzantine or Persian influence. The iris, symbol of honesty, and the Star of David play prominent roles in the synagogue's interior ornamentation. Except for the three chapels at the head of the building, added in the 16th century, this syna-

gogue is basically the same as it was before it was converted into a church in the latter half of the 15th century. The other synagogue is **El Tránsito**, a simpler 14th-century structure which today houses the **Sephardic Museum**.

El Greco: Many kings and queens of Spain held court in Toledo, and many philosophers and artists contributed to the city's splendour, but one stands out above all: Domenico Teotocopulos, better known as El Greco (The Greek), arrived in Toledo in 1579 after Philip II had dismissed him from El Escorial. He lived here until his death in 1614.

El Greco's paintings are spread throughout the city. One of his masterpieces, *The Burial of the Count of Orgaz,* is in the church of **Santo Tomé** on **Calle Santo Tomé**. The complexity, the blend of the temporal and the spiritual and the presence of many portraits, including El Greco's own, make this painting a highlight for art lovers who visit Toledo. The **Santo Cruz Museum**, just off the central **Zocodover Plaza**, holds some 20 El Greco paint-

Toledo Cathedral's sumptuous altarpiece.

ings as well as several rooms of liturgical objects, manuscripts, tapestries and the banners flown by Don Juan of Austria when he won the Battle of Lepanto in 1571. The building itself is beautiful, particularly its Plateresque entrance and staircase and the splendid *mudéjar* wooden ceilings.

Outside the city walls the **Tavera Hospital**, built in the 16th century, holds El Greco's *The Holy Family*, *The Baptism of Christ*, and several important portraits of saints. One of the few Renaissance interiors which has kept intact much of an original art collection, it also has fine paintings by Caravaggio, Titian and Tintoretto.

El Greco lived in the Jewish section of the city just behind the El Tránsito synagogue. His house is no longer standing but a nearby 16th-century dwelling has been restored and is known today as the **El Greco House and Museum**, which contains several of his paintings including the famous *View of Toledo* – painted from the north of the city – and possessions.

Symbolic fortress: The **Alcázar** (the word means "castle" in Arabic) dates back to the era of El Cid, and its occupants, architects and purposes have been numerous. From the patio you can get a good sense of the strategic importance of the place. The Alcázar is the result of the work of Spain's finest 16th-century architects, though now heavily restored. It was burned and sacked by both English and French invaders and was the site of a famous siege during the Civil War. Today it is a symbol of Franco's triumph over the "Communist hordes" of the Second Republic, as the commemorative plaques say.

Marzipan and steel: Although Toledo is not famed for its cooking, you can't go wrong ordering braised partridge and crayfish soup, both local dishes. Rich, sweet marzipan, a Toledo speciality found in shops and cafés – for example, around the Plaza de Zocodover – is an especially reviving snack.

The best known crafts in the town are the very striking *damascene* (black enamel inlaid with gold, silver and cop-

Damascene, Toledo's unique copper and black enamel work.

per wire), steel knives, swords and the fine ceramic work from nearby **Talavera de la Reina**.

El Escorial: The "eighth wonder of the world", a "monotonous symphony of stone", and an "architectural nightmare" are just three of the ways that **San Lorenzo de El Escorial**, Philip II's most enduring legacy to Spain and the world, has been described since it was completed in 1584. This combination monastery-palace-mausoleum is located about an hour away from Madrid in the foothills of the **Guadarrama Mountains**. There are frequent trains from Madrid's Chamartín station, via Atocha, or you can drive along the N6 and turn left on the C-600.

The origin of El Escorial is most likely 10 August 1557, the day Philip II's armies defeated the French at the Battle of St Quentin, in Flanders. In honour of Saint Lawrence (San Lorenzo), whose feast day it was, Philip decided to build a tribute to the saint.

The King sent two architects, two doctors and two stone masons out to seek a site for the new monastery that was to be neither too hot nor too cold nor too far from the new capital. After a year's search they came up with what is now San Lorenzo de El Escorial.

The stony monarch: Aside from his predilection for St Lawrence, Philip II was an introverted, melancholy, deeply religious and ailing man who wanted a place to retreat to from his duties as king of the world's mightiest empire. He wanted to be surrounded by monks, not courtiers; besides a royal residence, El Escorial would primarily be a monastery for the Order of St Hieronymous. Philip did not permit anyone to write his biography while he was alive, but in fact he left it himself, written in stone. The battles he won and lost, the glories and defeats of the empire, the succession of deaths and tragedies and his obsession for learning, art, prayer and order are all reflected in El Escorial. The location of the enormous church in the centre of the complex shows his belief that all political action should be governed by religious considerations.

El Escorial.

Construction began in 1563 and took 21 years to complete. The chief architect was originally Juan Bautista de Toledo, a disciple of Michelangelo, but after he died the task was picked up in 1569 by Juan de Herrera, who is credited with having provided the inspiration for the final design.

El Escorial is built of grey granite and measures 683 by 531 ft (208 by 162 metres). It has 15 cloisters, 16 patios, 13 oratorios, 300 cells, 86 stairways, nine towers, nine organs, 2,673 windows, 1,200 doors and a collection of more than 1,600 paintings. Some people believe that the shape of the building is like an upside-down grill, a reminder of the martyrdom of St Lawrence, who was grilled alive.

The northern and western sides of the monastery are bordered by huge patios called *la lonja,* while the southern and eastern sides are the site of gardens with excellent views of the monastery's fields and orchards and the Madrid countryside beyond. In fact, there is a statue of Philip II there doing just that, looking out beyond the **Jardín de los Frailes**, where the monks rested from their labours. Below the garden on the right is the **Gallery of Convalescents**.

Architecture and painting: Visits are unaccompanied, although guides are available. The route currently starts in two small new museums (**Nuevos Museos**), the first of which explains the building's architectural history through drawings, plans, tools and scale models. Exhibits include intriguing bits of machinery dreamed up by Herrera to cope with technical problems.

Flights of stairs then lead up to nine rooms of magnificent 15th to 17th century paintings. As in the Prado, the range and quality – from Bosch to Veronese, Tintoretto and Van Dyck, as well as the Spanish School – illustrate why the Spanish Hapsburgs were the greatest patrons of art of their time. The Flemish School, collected by Philip's grandmother Isabel, and Titian, court painter to his father Charles V, are especially well represented.

Hapsburg frugality: The first room of

Elegant Bourbon apartments in the otherwise austere El Escorial.

the Hapsburg living quarters belonged to Philip II's favourite daughter, Isabel Clara Eugenia, who took care of him when he was dying. The austerity is broken only by the important collection of paintings and the Talavera ceramic skirting on all the walls in this section of the palace. But even the word "palace" is not the right one: Philip II himself said that he wanted to "build a palace for God and a shack for the King".

The simplicity continues in the Sedan Room, where you will find the unadorned wooden chair in which Philip was carried from Madrid once his gout was bad. In the adjacent Portrait Room, so-called for its portraits of the Spanish Hapsburg dynasty, you can also see the little chair on which Philip rested his painful leg.

A hallway leads on to the Walking Gallery, whose old leaded windows give the best views out over the gardens. The doors, made of 17 different types of wood – surprisingly splendid – were a present from Maximilian of Austria in 1567. This leads through to the Ambas-sadors' Salon, or waiting room, and, finally, the King's bedroom, adjacent to the main altar of the church, so that Philip II could hear Mass from his bed. When his gout permitted, he would walk through a small door that leads directly from his room to the church.

Stairs and corridors lead round to the four Chapter Rooms, where the monks once held their meetings. Now the walls are hung with paintings, among them Velázquez's masterpiece, *Joseph's Tunic*, in the first room and Bosch's *Garden of Pleasures* in the last.

Royal remains: One of Philip II's motivations for building El Escorial was to construct a mausoleum for his father, Emperor Charles V, whose remains were brought here in 1586. But it was not until the reign of Philip III, in 1617, that this splendid bronze, marble and jasper pantheon began to be built directly below the main altar of the church. The remains of all the kings of Spain since Charles V lie here, with the exception of Philip V, who could not bear the gloom of the place and asked to

Left, portraits of Philip II and **Right**, the King's favourite daughter, Isabel Clara Eugenia, from the Portrait Room.

be buried at Segovia, and Ferdinand VI, whose tomb is in Madrid. The queens who produced male heirs are also buried here, while across the way in the 19th-century **Princes' Pantheon** lie the remains of princes, princesses and queens whose children did not succeed to the throne.

Dashing bastard: Of the three empty tombs, one is reserved for Don Juan Borbón, the first non-monarch to be honoured by burial here. His son and present King Juan Carlos – and, more generally, the Spanish people – felt his defence of democracy under Franco and ceding of the throne to his son to ensure a peaceful transition deserved this final sigh of respect.

Church and library: While some illustrious visitors have praised the church's perfect grandeur – the French writer Alexandre Dumas referred to the Kings' Courtyard as "the entrance to eternity" – others have complained about its oppressive size. French writer and intellectual Theophile Gautier wrote: "in the El Escorial church one

feels so overwhelmed, so crushed, so subordinate to a melancholy and inflexible power that prayer appears to be entirely useless".

The frescoes on the ceilings and along the 43 altars were painted by Spanish and Italian masters. The main retablo was designed by architect Juan de Herrera himself; between the jasper and marble columns are paintings of the lives of Christ, the Virgin and the Saints. On either side of the retablo are the royal stalls and the sculpted figures of Charles V, Philip II and their families at prayer.

Second only to the Vatican library, the library at El Escorial holds the writings of St Augustine, Alfonso the Wise and Santa Teresa. It has the largest collection of Arabic manuscripts in the world, illuminated hymnals and works of natural history and cartography from the Middle Ages. It is the only library in the world to store its books facing backwards, a measure taken to preserve the ancient parchment.

The ceiling, painted by Tibaldi and his daughter, represents the seven liberal arts: grammar, rhetoric, dialectics, arithmetic, geometry, astronomy and music. The two key sciences, theology and philosophy, are represented on either end. Pope Gregory XIII ordered the excommunication of anyone who stole a manuscript from here. Today, most of the books on show are facsimiles.

Coming up for air: During the reign of the Bourbons, part of the living quarters were converted and two small palaces were built near the monastery to be used as hunting lodges and guest houses. **The Prince's Pavilion** (Lower Pavilion), around a half-hour's walk down toward the train station, is a showpiece of Pompeian ceilings, Italian painting, bronze, marble and porcelain. **The Upper Pavilion**, located 2 miles (3 km) along the road leading to Ávila, is closed at present. Continuing along the Ávila road a bit, and then taking a fork to the left, leads to **La Silla de Felipe II** (Philip II's seat), a group of large boulders up on a hill from where the King supposedly gazed out over his monstrous monastery as it was being built.

The Princes' Pantheon.

CASTLES IN SPAIN

A drive or train ride across the plains of Castile might turn out to be initially disappointing to the romantic traveller. The dry fields are endless; the sun seems to have flattened out all colours and shadows. Then, gradually, it becomes apparent that the land isn't flat – it rises and falls like choppy water. A thin row of poplars comes into view; a village the same colour as the earth appears to be growing out of a bluff, and above it is a sight which causes the motorist to gasp with pleasure: a castle, with rounded turrets and crenellated battlements – as perfect and pretty as a toy.

Castile (Castilla) is the land of castles; most of the 10,000 in Spain are located in this region. During the seven centuries of the Reconquest, the various small kingdoms of the *meseta* were uneasy allies, and castles were built as bulwarks against other Christians as much as against the Moors.

Many have a history far older than the Middle Ages. Their strategic locations are the sites of Celto-Iberian forts known as *castros*; hence the Latin word *castellum*; castle. The *castros* were made first of wood and later of stone.

The castles of the Reconquest were often built of materials taken from earlier buildings, which is why there are so few pre-medieval ruins in Spain. At the time of their construction, there was nothing fanciful about castles – they were meant to be as utilitarian and menacing as aircraft carriers. The entrance was approachable only by a drawbridge, and usually placed between two towers, making its defence easier. Windows were slits in the stone protected by iron bars. The soldiers' quarters, stables and storerooms were further enclosed by a second layer of walls and iron gates; the *torre de homenaje*, which quartered the lord of the castle, had the best view and was reached by a series of winding staircases. Other essential elements were the chapels and prisons. Decoration was limited to a coat of arms over the entrance.

The castles built by the Moors, however, had irregular floor plans and elongated rooms; there was decorative iron fretwork at the entrances and the inner walls were usually adorned with moulded stucco. The 10th-century castle of Gormaz, in Soria, is a fine example of Moorish architecture.

Mudéjar style, in which buildings were constructed by Moorish workmen under Christian direction, is characterised by the use of cheap materials, such as brick and adobe, to rich aesthetic effect. Two well-preserved examples are Coca, near Segovia, and Medina del Campo, near Valladolid.

After the Reconquest in 1492, Ferdinand and Isabella feared for Spain's tenuous unity and obliged the feudal lords to leave their strongholds and live at court. Castles began to be abandoned at about that time, and the expression "building castles in Spain" came into use to describe a pointless undertaking.

Some castles, such as the Alcázar in Segovia, retained a military use until fairly recently. Others have become museums, farming co-operatives, trade schools, or well-appointed hotels in the national chain of *paradores*. Many are just empty, and can be visited by hunting down the person in the village with the key. The key-keeper will probably say there is no admission charge, and by that it's understood that a tip would be most appreciated. ■

Mudéjar style at Coca, near Segovia.

177

CASTILE-LEON

For centuries Old Castile has been the geographical and spiritual heart of Spain. Most of the great notions of Spanish history germinated here: the unification of the ancient Iberian kingdoms, the *Reconquista* and the exploration and conquest of the New World. Philip II chose the dead centre of Castile as the vantage point from which to rule his empire.

The empire in turn grew and then gradually disintegrated as a result of the mismanagement and short-sightedness of Castilian governments. This process caused Ortega y Gasset to lament, in 1921, that "Castile made Spain and Castile has been her undoing".

General Franco increased the force of the Castilian centrifuge by decreeing that *castellano* was to be the nation's only legal language. It isn't surprising, then, that Spaniards in other parts of Spain regard Castile somewhat warily, as they might regard an idealistic but potentially oppressive older sibling.

Deadpan and dignified, Castilians themselves often express mixed emotions about their landscape. "Nine months of winter and three of hell", is their wry assessment of the climate. The poet Antonio Machado described the rocky terrain, "crossed by the shadow of Cain", with a blend of affection and weary despair.

A visitor could well conclude that Castilians protest too much. The winters are mild; autumns are long and richly coloured. The sierras are stark but beautiful, the wide plains are windswept and intense.

Ancha es Castilla: "Wide is Castile", says the plain-spoken Castilian proverb. After the democratic government granted autonomous status to Spain's various regions, Old Castile got in on the act and in 1983 became the Autonomous Community of Castile-León, a territory covering one-fifth of the nation, or 36,350 sq. miles (94,147 sq. km), and including the provinces of **Ávila.**

Ávila, Burgos, León, Palencia, Salamanca, Segovia, Soria, Valladolid and Zamora, each with a capital of the same name. The fragrant native scrubland of ilex, thyme and *jara* of past centuries has in large part been replaced by wheat fields with vineyards and olive groves; most of the provincial capitals are developing smog-producing industry.

While many Castilian villages are ancient, they cannot be described as quaint. Built as outposts against the Moors, they still have a frontier feeling.

Some, too, are virtually ghost towns. In the past decades the rural population has been steadily declining, as young people leave to look for work in cities. Often, what remains are three or four streets of adobe houses, a crumbling church with a dazzling gold retable inside, old women sewing in the late afternoon sun and old men driving ageing tractors home

Ávila: Sealed within its perfectly preserved medieval walls, **Ávila** has been compared by poets to both a coffin and a crown. It lies 69 miles (111 km) north-west of Madrid, making it a good place to begin a tour of Castile, as well as a plausible day trip from the capital. At 3,700 ft (1,131 metres), it is the highest city on the peninsula, and the pure air has made it a haven for swallows. Along the walls, storks' nests soften the stern effect of turrets and battlements.

Hercules was the city's legendary founder, although it is probably older than the Greek invasion of Spain: stone carvings of pigs and bulls found in the area point to a Celto-Iberian origin. Ávila was Christianised in the first century by Bishop San Segundo, but passed back and forth between Moors and Christians until Alfonso VI claimed it definitively in 1090. He promptly transferred his best knights from the northern kingdoms to the city, and they began constructing fortifications.

The walls, which average 40 ft (12 metres) in height and 10 ft (3 metres) in width, have 88 round towers and nine fortified entrances. The perimeter is 8,438 ft (2,572 metres). In the gardens next to the **Parador Nacional Rai-**

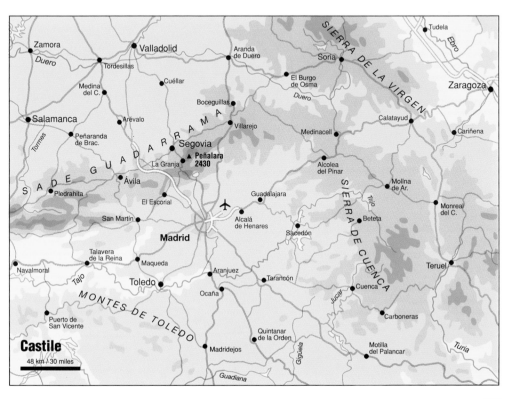

Castile

48 km / 30 miles

mundo de Borgoña, you can climb the walls and look out across the surrounding plains.

Knights and nuns: Granted home rule by Alfonso the Wise, Ávila spent the next few centuries in proud hermetic isolation, resisting the unifying efforts of Charles V. A more recent show of local independence occurred in the late 1970s, when the city fathers rejected Ávila's nomination as a National Historical Artistic Monument, a designation usually greatly coveted by Spanish towns. Some five years later, however, the commercial advantages of the title obliged them to relent and suffer the indignity of being a tourist attraction.

Unofficially, the city has been a magnet for pilgrims since the late 16th century, as the birthplace of Santa Teresa, an outspoken nun who founded a reformed religious order and wrote about the presence of God in her life in distinctly physical terms.

Teresa de Cepeda y Ahumada was born in 1515 to a noble family with Jewish roots, who, possibly to keep their daughter out of the way of the Inquisition, sent her to a convent school. About the day she later left her father's house to enter the Carmelite Order, at her own choice but with misgivings, Teresa wrote: "I did not think the day of my death would be more upsetting", but as a nun she thrived. She began to have face-to-face conversations with Christ, beginning with an encounter with the child Jesus on the convent stairs.

Her objections to the opulent lifestyle of the Carmelites, who often brought servants and family silver into the convent with them, spurred her to begin her own order, the Unshoed Carmelites, and she spent years riding around Spain founding convents. Her insistence on austerity made her unpopular with the nuns of her own city, and her unorthodox writings did bring the eye of the Inquisition upon her, but she was canonised 40 years after her death in 1582. "Ávila of the Knights" is the city's nickname, yet within the stone walls Teresa's personality dominates. Her shrines are numerous. Nuns of various orders walk the streets; egg yolk confections called *yemas de Santa Teresa* are sold in every souvenir shop.

Ávila's **cathedral** is set into the city walls, and has a matching military air. The original design was Romanesque, with Gothic and Renaissance elements added later. Inside is the mottled red and white stonework characteristic of churches throughout the city. Of particular artistic merit are the choir stalls, by the Dutch artist Cornelius, and the retable, painted with scenes from the life of Jesus Christ. Of interest to literary pilgrims is the chapel of San Segundo, where playwright Lope de Vega was chaplain.

Follow **Calle Santo Tomás** southeast out of town to the **Monastery of Santo Tomás**, founded by Ferdinand and Isabella in 1482. Its adornment includes carvings of pomegranates, or *granadas,* illustrating the royal determination to capture the city of the same name. The church has a retable considered to be the masterpiece of Pedro Berruguete, depicting scenes from the life of St Thomas Aquinas. Here also is the tomb of Prince Juan, the only son of the Catholic Monarchs. His sudden death at the age of 20 was a tragedy from which his parents never recovered, and it thrust Spain into the unsteady grip of his sister, the mad queen, *Juana la Loca.*

Memorabilia: Enter the town again through the **Plaza de Santa Teresa**. The white statue of Santa Teresa in the Plaza was built in honour of the Pope's visit in 1982, at which time she was named Doctor of the Church, the first woman to hold the title.

Monuments to the saint include the **Convent of Santa Teresa**, built over the site of her childhood home. Her finger is among the objects on display in a museum in San José Monastery (also known as the Convento de las Madres), the first convent she founded. The more appealing relics in this museum include her saddle, her toy drum and a letter written in her fine handwriting.

A guided tour of the **Convent of La Encarnación**, where Teresa spent nearly 30 years, takes visitors to her cell, and the **locutorio** where she carried on animated conversations with her confessor and fellow mystic, San Juan de la Cruz. In her memoirs Teresa describes a scene in which she and "my brother Juan" became so ecstatic during a theological exchange that they levitated, each on opposite sides of the wooden screen. Today the cloistered nuns at Encarnación follow Teresa's dictates, and only leave the convent in cases of personal illness, or to vote.

The southern part of Ávila province is traversed by the **Sierra de Gredos**, a weekend retreat beloved by *madrileños* for its fresh air, pine woods and ski slopes. The Gredos is full of picturesque stone villages, such as **Arenas de San Pedro**, with its 15th-century castle and Gothic bridge. Two other lovely alpine hamlets are **Guisando** and **El Arenal**. Driving north of Ávila, an interesting historical detour is **Madrigal de las Altas Torres**, featuring the ruins of the palace where Queen Isabella the Catholic was born.

Salamanca: The golden university town of **Salamanca** "is the pinnacle; the greatest triumph and honour Spain has ever had", wrote a historian in the court of Ferdinand and Isabella. While Salamanca's finest days are probably over, this lovely honey-coloured sandstone city is not weighed down by its glorious past. A lively student atmosphere dispels the native Castilian sobriety. Great scientists no longer flock here to listen to earth-shattering theories, but today's visiting scholars in the university's *cursos para extranjeros* (courses for foreigners) seldom leave without a new respect for history, a love of poetry, a smattering of Arabic and a changed perspective.

Salamanca was an important Iberian city 2,000 years before the university was founded in 1218. It was Hannibal's westernmost conquest, and a Moorish town until it was captured by the Christians in 1085. The victors filled the city with churches: **San Julián**, **San Martín**, **San Benito**, **San Juan**, **Santiago**, **San Cristobal** and the **Old Cathedral** all date from a century of feverish Romanesque construction.

Salamanca Cathedral.

Historians suspect that Alfonso IX of León established the university in response to the foundation of one in Plasencia by his cousin and rival, Alfonso VIII of Castile. Salamanca quickly absorbed the latter school, and less than 30 years later the Pope proclaimed it one of the four best universities in the world. Columbus presented his starting project before the Department of Theology, at the same time that the first woman professor, Beatriz de Galindo, was teaching Latin here. Cervantes is thought to have taken classes in Salamanca, as did conquistador Hernán Cortés.

The Inquisition put an end to the university's reputation as a haven for new ideas and for thinkers, and during Philip II's reign Spanish students were forbidden to study abroad. By the end of the 19th century the colleges were decimated by war and neglect, although the 20th century brought another brief moment of triumph when the philosopher and novelist Miguel de Unamuno became University Rector. Unamuno's

Tragic Sense of Life is a lucid, poetic exploration of the Spanish soul.

Unamuno died driven mad by the atrocities of the Civil War, and the Franco period saw Salamanca, like other Spanish universities, fall into a long sleep. Now, however, it is regaining its reputation for Spanish literature.

The University: Salamanca has three universities, but the entrance to the original **Universidad** can be found in the **Patio de las Escuelas**. The Plateresque facade contains likenesses of the Catholic Monarchs surrounded by a jungle of literary, pagan and religious symbols. According to one critic, the facade looks "as though the artists were merely instructed 'Adorn'."

Downstairs are several historic lecture halls, including the one where Hebrew scholar Fray Luis de León, after four years in the prisons of the Inquisition, began his first lecture with: "As we were saying yesterday…" Upstairs is the **Old Library**, with 50,000 rare volumes plus valuable ancient manuscripts.

Across the Patio are Plateresque doors leading to the **Escuelas Menores**. One of the old classrooms here has a ceiling painted with the signs of the zodiac, a reminder that Salamanca once had a Department of Astrology.

The **Plaza de Anaya** is a graceful quadrangle surrounded on three sides by university buildings from several epochs and dominated by the **New Cathedral**. This imposing Gothic church was begun in 1513, when Salamanca's fame was such that the smaller Old Cathedral would no longer do. It contains a magnificent gate and choir stalls by Alberto Churriguera. The Old Cathedral, which leans against the new one like a chick under the wing of a hen, is now a museum. It's the more attractive church of the two, with its Byzantine dome and Romanesque frescoes.

In the adjacent **cloister** is the **Santa Barbara Chapel**, where students were quizzed while they rested their feet on the tomb of a bishop for luck. Exam results were made public, and a crowd of townspeople waited outside to pelt with rubbish those who failed. Those who passed were carried triumphantly **Salamanca's Plaza Mayor.**

around, and allowed to paint the word "Victor" on the walls of the university in bull's blood. Franco, who never attended a class here, also painted his "Victor" on the wall in 1939.

While there are those who will argue that Seville and Santiago are prettier cities, no one disagrees that Salamanca's **Plaza Mayor** is the most magnificent in Spain, for both architecture and ambience. The square, designed in 1729 by Churriguera, is bordered by an arcaded walkway lined with fashionable boutiques and voluptuous pastry shops. A *paseo* in the Plaza is a tradition beloved by students and locals alike, although boys and girls no longer stroll around in opposite directions, as they did even 20 years ago.

East of the Plaza Mayor, in the **Plaza del Mercado**, is a string of student bars serving strong red wine and a type of delicious greasy sausage called *farinato*. More substantial student fare is offered at **Mesón Cervantes**, in the Plaza Mayor; and an elegant Castilian meal of excellent suckling pig and garlic soup can be savoured at **El Candil**.

Wildlife: Through the ups and downs of the university's history, student life has always been spirited. "To Salamanca go the prostitutes, on the Eve of St Luke", was a medieval couplet honouring the commencement of classes in October. "Monday of the Waters", when working girls were allowed back into the city after Holy Week, is still commemorated by rowing parties on the **Tormes River**.

Students belonging to musical groups called *tunas* walk the streets on weekend nights, strumming guitars and dressed in doublets and hose. However, entertainment is not stuck in the Middle Ages; Salamanca is full of discotheques open until dawn.

Close to the Plaza Mayor is the oddlooking **Casa de las Conchas**, a noble mansion decorated all over with carved scallop shells. Following the **Calle San Pablo** from the Plaza Mayor leads you past the **Casa de la Salina**, where the unpopular Bishop Fonseca took revenge upon his many enemies by cari-

Drawing water in a Castilian village.

caturing them in gargoyles around the house. Further down the same street are two gorgeous examples of the Plateresque style at its zenith: the 16th-century **Convent of Las Dueñas**, and the **Monastery of San Esteban**, which looks as though it were made of sugar.

Continue downhill as far as the river and cross over on the **Roman Bridge**, for a splendid look at the city rising above the bank.

Zamora: The "Very Noble and Very Loyal City of **Zamora**" – so named by Henry IV – lies 37 miles (60 km) north of Salamanca. This plain-looking town on the banks of the **Duero River** has a 12th-century **cathedral** which makes it well worth a stop. The Byzantine dome of the cathedral is a striking addition to the Romanesque-Gothic structure. Inside, it's easy to see why Spaniards call the dome a half-orange. The cathedral contains a painting of *Christ in Glory* by Fernando Gallego, and 15th-century choir stalls whose carvings are spiced up by lewd satires of monastic life.

Outside the cathedral are the remains of Zamora's walls. The city was the site of centuries of bitter struggles between Moors and Christians; such that a complaint about how long something takes in Spain will sometimes bring the reproof: "Zamora wasn't captured in a day." Sancho II was treacherously murdered here, and the spot is commemorated by **Traitor's Gate** in the ruined **castle**. Two Zamora buildings are connected with the Spanish national hero El Cid: the 11th-century **Casa del Cid** and the church of **Santiago de Caballeros**, where he was knighted.

León: Cool, regal **León** is in many respects a gateway city, with ancient ties both to Castile and to the green regions of Asturias and Galicia to the north. Its location at the base of the Cantabrian Mountains, 195 miles (314 km) from the coast, makes it one of the less-travelled peninsula cities, yet both Spanish and foreign travellers return from a chance visit exclaiming over its dignified medieval beauty. The city's proudest century was unquestionably the 10th, when Ordoño II moved his

León Cathedral.

court here. León became a model of reasonable, civilised medieval government, and the assault and burning of the city by the Moor Almansor in 996 is an event still spoken of with regret. The city was recaptured in the 11th century, and was for a time capital of Spain as well as the seat of the Reconquest.

Stained glass: A visit to León should begin with the **cathedral**, which ideally ought to be returned to at various times throughout the day in order to see the effect of changing light on nearly 20,000 sq. ft (1,800 sq. metres) of magnificent stained glass windows.

Construction was begun in 1205, in the Romanesque style, but the soaring upper portions are Gothic at its best. In the morning and afternoon the splendid rose windows should be seen from the inside, while at night the illumination turns the exterior into a glittering jewel box. The church contains several thousand-year-old sepulchres, including the delicate and ornate tomb of Ordoño II. The 14th-century **cloister** and the **cathedral museum**, containing many Romanesque treasures, may be visited with a guide.

The **Colegiata de San Isidoro** is a shrine dedicated to San Isidoro of Seville, whose remains were brought here to escape desecration by the Moors. Adjacent to the Romanesque and Gothic church is the **Panteón de los Reyes** (Kings' Pantheon), which holds the tombs of early royalty of León and Castile. The frescoes in the pantheon are generally described as "The Sistine Chapel of Romanesque art". But these delightful paintings belong to a less accomplished, homelier age.

The vanguard: One of the most exotic sights in León is the **Casa de los Botines**, designed by Barcelona architect Gaudí. The construction of this hallucinatory, fairy-castle house (now a savings bank) caused a local uproar in the León of 1894. It appeared here because of a friendship between the Botines family and Count Güell, the architect's strongest patron.

The **old city** around León's Plaza Mayor is an attractive quarter of winding cobbled streets and wrought-iron balconies. It has become the domain of the hip younger crowd, and nearly every block has a bar or pub offering jazz, quirky decor and tolerance for marijuana smoked openly.

Palatial prison: The **Hostal San Marcos**, on the banks of the **Bernesga River**, is worth a visit even if you aren't a guest at the five-star **Parador** inside. It was built in 1168 as a hospital for pilgrims on the road to Santiago. The ornate Plateresque facade, by Juan de Badajoz, was added in 1513. The hostel subsequently became a political prison (the poet Quevedo was the most illustrious of the guests) and then a barracks. The cloister and sacristy now house the **Provincial Archaeological Museum**. Of particular note are the 11th-century ivory Christ and a 10th-century *mozarabic* cross.

León's *fiestas* occur from 24 to 29 June, between the days of San Juan and San Pedro. Reflecting the Leonese character, they lack the gypsy wildness or drunken abandon of Seville or Pamplona. The streets are hung with tiny lights, there is dancing and the highlight is usually a concert of haunting medieval ballads, performed in the cloister of the cathedral.

Burgos: Situated in the middle of the high plains of Old Castile, **Burgos** has been a Spanish crossroads for a thousand years. Motorists tend to use it as a place to stop for lunch; a good choice particularly in winter, when substantial *burgalese* fare – roast lamb, suckling pig, *morcilla* (blood sausage) and bean stew – is just the thing to take the chill off. (When George Orwell wrote that Spanish cold was colder than any other kind, he was on the *meseta* slightly east of Burgos.) Winter or summer, the city merits more than a meal and a digestive sprint around the cathedral.

El Cid: Founded in 884 as a fortification against the Moors, Burgos is a relatively young city. Most of the landmarks have to do with its beloved native son Rodrigo Díaz de Vivar, better known as El Cid. The Cid (from *Sidi*, Arabic for leader) began his own campaign against the Moors after being sent into exile by Alfonso VI. He terrorised the Moors, and eventually captured the city of Valencia. While historians tend to agree that his biographical poem, *Cantar de Mío Cid*, is largely fiction, the personal bravery and individualism he represents are as prevalent in modern Spain as are the dreamy descendants of Don Quixote.

The **cathedral**, begun in 1221, is considered to be the Cid's mausoleum. Described as "the work of angels" by Philip II, the gunmetal Gothic building dominates the city. As roads fanned out from Burgos, churchwardens began to lock the main door so the church would not be used as a thoroughfare, a custom which continues to this day.

Perhaps no other cathedral has so many curios, as well as artistic treasures. Visitors are usually as anxious to see the marionette clock **Papamoscas** and the life-size Christ made of animal skin and human hair as they are to admire the **Golden Staircase** by Diego de Siloe, the opulent Isabeline **Condestable Chapel** and the **Santa Ana Chapel**, with its magnificent retable showing the Virgin's family tree.

The **cloister** contains a similar mixture of art and folklore. Here you may see a parchment bearing El Cid's promise of gifts to his future wife Jimena, and the coffer which he filled with sand to trick Jewish moneylenders (the legend hurries to add that he repaid them with interest). The Cid and his wife are buried in the middle of the cathedral transept, under a marble slab inscribed with a verse of the poem.

As an antidote to the still, dark air of the church, cross the **Plaza Santa María** to the esplanade along the **Arlazón River**. The turreted **Santa María Arch** was part of the 11th-century city walls and was decorated in the 16th century as a tribute to a visit from Charles V. The sculptures show the King surrounded by the Cid and other local heroes. Enter the city again at the **Plaza Primo de Rivera**, passing the statue of the Cid with his cape billowing around him like a vampire's.

Four stops: The **Chapterhouse of Miraflores**, less than 2 miles (3 km) east of Burgos, was built by Queen Isabella as a memorial to her parents. The sculptures of Juan II and his queen are considered to be the most elaborate tombs in Europe. Here also is a tomb with a kneeling statue to Don Alfonso, whose early death made Isabella's succession possible. This gloomy place, inhabited by cloistered nuns, was described by the poet Lorca as "a sombre house, imbued with the coldness of the region".

Near Miraflores is the **Monastery of San Pedro de Cardeña**, from where the Cid went into exile. He asked to be buried here along with his wife and his horse Babieca, but the human remains were spirited away to the cathedral during the Peninsular War. Apparently the French then spitefully damaged the empty tombs. In the 1940s the Duke of Alba financed excavations around the monastery and the bones of a horse were discovered, thus enriching legend with hard evidence.

The **Monastery of Las Huelgas** is a 12th-century nunnery where only women from the highest rank of society were admitted. The abbess was second in rank to the Queen of Spain, and it was said that if the Pope were allowed to marry only the abbess of Las Huelgas would be worthy of the honour. In addition to tombs of many early monarchs of Castile, there is a **Museo de Ricas Telas** (Museum of Rich Cloth), containing brocades and jewellery discovered in some of the tombs.

Northwest of Las Huelgas is the Plateresque **Hospital del Rey**, built by Alfonso VIII for poor pilgrims on the road to Santiago. Even then, Burgos was noted for its hearty lunches. One traveller who stopped at the Hospital several centuries ago wrote: "They provide food and drink until one is sated."

Villages of Burgos: The province of Burgos is full of villages which strongly evoke the days of chivalry. A detour from the N-I highway south can be made to accommodate visits to two particularly haunted spots. Some 2 miles (4 km) east of **Quintanilla de las Viñas** is the ruin of a 7th-century Visigothic chapel, which is one of the earliest Christian edifices in Spain. Only a square apse and transepts remain of the original church, which may be visited in the company of a guide from the village. The squat building, standing all alone on a desolate plain, is decorated with emblems of the sun and moon, pointing to a still-powerful pagan sensibility.

Passing the ruins of the **Monastery of San Pedro de Arlanza** leads you to the village of **Covarrubias**, with its 10th-century tower where Doña Urraca, one of Spain's most tragic princesses, was imprisoned. The **Colegiata** contains the tombs of the Doña's parents.

Catching up with the N-I at **Lerma** allows a stop at this Baroque town rising like a mirage over the Arlanza River. The conjunction of churches, convents and towers looks medieval but isn't; it was built by the Duke of Lerma in 1605. The city's fortress-like appearance is peculiar considering the time when it was built, and is testimony to 17th-century Spain's longing for the glory and drama of the Middle Ages, a nostalgia which Cervantes poked fun at in his novel. It is said that 17th-century Spain

laughed at *Don Quixote,* the 18th-century smiled and the 19th and 20th centuries wept.

City of the poets: Of all the cities of Castile, **Segovia** may be the one whose charms are most evident at first sight. Situated only 57 miles (92 km) from Madrid on a good highway, Segovia fills up with *madrileños* every weekend, who come to admire the Roman aqueduct and the fairytale Alcázar, and feast on the cuisine for which the province is justly famous. The city has been compared to a ship sailing between the **Clamores** and **Ledesma Rivers**, or the aqueduct to a harp made of stone.

Segovia became important under the Romans, who built the aqueduct around 50 AD. The city was long favoured by Castilian royalty, and Isabella the Catholic was proclaimed Queen here in 1474. In 1480 it became the headquarters of the dreaded Inquisitor Torquemada; a flourishing textile industry further increased its power and influence.

Economic recession, war and a 1599 plague nearly brought Segovia to ruins,

but it rose again under the Bourbons, who built their summer palace at La Granja nearby. It became a city known for its writers and artists, the most famous of whom was the early 20th-century poet Antonio Machado. The elegant **Parador Nacional**, on a hill overlooking the city, is now a favourite retreat of film directors, actors and other luminaries of the Madrid arts scene.

Among Castilians, Segovians have a wide reputation for gaiety and humour, exemplified by the February festival of Santa Agüeda, when women dress up in traditional costumes and take over the administration of the provincial villages. Segovians with a contemporary turn of mind, however, say it's time this ritual stopped being treated as a joke.

Roman marvel: All roads to Segovia lead to the **aqueduct**. One of the largest Roman constructions still standing in Spain, its 128 pillars rise as high as 96 ft (29 metres) over the **Plaza del Azoguejo**. The huge granite blocks stay in place without mortar, which may have fed the medieval legend that the Devil built the aqueduct (which still carries water) in one night. Recently the granite was found to be crumbling and traffic has been banned from passing underneath.

From the Plaza del Azoguejo, follow the **Calle de Cervantes** uphill to the **old city**, past the **Casa del los Picos**, a noble house decorated in the 15th century with diamond-shaped blocks of stone. A few steps beyond is the **Plaza de San Martín**, with the beautiful Romanesque church of **San Martín** and a circle of Renaissance mansions. In the middle of the plaza is a statue of Segovian hero Juan Bravo, who led the citizens in their disastrous resistance against the army of Charles V.

The church of **Corpus Christi**, consecrated in 1410, was once the largest synagogue in Segovia. As the seat of the Inquisition, the city saw particularly harsh persecution of the Jews. The old Jewish Quarter, or *judería*, along **Calle San Frutos**, still has houses with tiny windows which allowed the inhabitants ventilation, but not a view of the street. Around the **Plaza Mayor** are the

Segovia's Alcázar.

church of **San Miguel**, where Isabella was proclaimed monarch, and the late-Gothic **cathedral**, designed by Juan Gil de Hontañón and his son Rodrigo.

The Isabeline **cloister** was transplanted here from the old cathedral, which was burned during the insurrection against Charles V. It contains the tombs of the architects and that of María del Salto, a Jewish woman wrongly accused of adultery. She was flung from a cliff and saved by the Virgin, whom she prayed to as she fell. In the **Santa Catalina Chapel** is the tomb of Prince Pedro, who slipped from his nurse's arms from a balcony to his death at the Alcázar. The horrified nurse then jumped in the same manner, and ended her own life as well.

Fairy castle: The **Alcázar** stands at the western end of the city, the prow of the Segovian ship. Destroyed by fire in the 19th century, its 1882 restoration combines reconstruction of some *mudéjar* elements with contemporary taste in castles, and the end result looks like a child's elaborate dream of a castle. Two of the most interesting rooms are the **Sala de Reyes**, containing wooden carvings of the early Castilian, Leonese and Asturian kings, and **Sala del Cordón**, decorated with a frieze of the Franciscan cord.

According to legend, Alfonso the Wise once ventured the heretical opinion that the earth moved around the sun. A bolt of lightning followed this remark and, terrified, he wore the penitential cord for the rest of his life. The arduous climb up the **Torre de Juan II** is rewarded by sweeping views of the Segovian countryside and the Guadarrama mountains beyond.

There are 18 Romanesque churches in Segovia, but the most beautiful is **San Esteban**, behind the Plaza Mayor, with its golden arcaded tower. Nearby, in the **Calle de los Desamparados**, is the house where the poet Antonio Machado lived. The house can't be visited, but the **Bar Poetas** on the corner is a sort of shrine to him.

Little Versailles: The French-style palace of **San Ildefonso**, or **La Granja** (the farm), lies 7 miles (11 km) southeast of Segovia. It symbolises the vast differences between the Bourbon monarchs who built it and their dour Hapsburg predecessors. As if it were a portent, the old Hapsburg retreat in these mountains burned to the ground after a visit from Charles II, the imbecilic end of the Hapsburg line. Philip V of Bourbon bought the farm and commissioned a palace suitable for the retirement of an enlightened 18th-century despot.

A team of French and Italian architects built something along the lines of a modest Versailles, the royal residence outside Paris. The palace has interesting collections of marbles, paintings, furniture, lamps, clocks, porcelains, carpets and Flemish tapestries, with the inevitable Spanish touch of a chapel full of saints' bones and teeth. The most splendid part of San Ildefonso are the gardens and fountains, which surpass their French model. The fountains play only on certain days, but the gardens are especially pretty in autumn, when the yellow linden and elm trees are reflected in the pools.

Segovia's Roman aqueduct.

EXTREMADURA

Bordered to the west by Portugal and to the north and south by granite mountain ranges, the arid plains of Extremadura are sweet with the scent of wild thyme and eucalyptus. Cattle- and sheep-raising are traditional occupations here; forests of cork oaks provide rooting grounds for future Extremaduran hams.

"Land of the conquistadors, land of the gods", is the modest refrain a traveller to this region may hear. You might also come across the apocryphal remark attributed to a French soldier, who declared that Extremaduran cooking made Spain worth invading. *Extremeños* are hospitable, expansive, horse-loving and, historically, inclined to large-scale undertakings.

Archaeological evidence, including cave paintings, point to an extensive prehistoric settlement of the area. Mild winters and generally fertile soil made it the site of several Roman colonies, most notably Mérida, which became a kind of luxury retirement community for distinguished soldiers. Subsequent invasions of Visigoths and Moors disturbed the *Pax Romana*, however, and during the Reconquest the region became a no-man's land between Moorish and Christian armies. In the 13th century the victorious Christian soldiers were granted huge tracts of land to resettle, and rural life in a vast, lonely territory is said to have bred the intrepid character of the conquistador.

Conquistador gold: About a third of the Spaniards who set out to explore and conquer America came from Extremadura; those who survived and triumphed returned to build magnificent palaces in their home towns. Some of these houses are still inhabited by their descendants, while others have become hotels or public buildings, or been abandoned to storks. Money and glory passed quickly through this land, leaving it as remote as ever. Walk through the honey-coloured medieval section of an Extremaduran town on a hot afternoon. A town clock built with conquis-

tador gold strikes the hour; a cloud of garlicky smoke puffs out of a Plateresque courtyard; there is little to disturb the illusion that this is not the 20th century. In spite of its baroque splendours, Extremadura isn't a regular tourist destination, and locals are likely to be pleased, although not particularly surprised, by a stranger's admiration.

Shrine and spa: Perched amid wooded sierras, 133 miles (214 km) from Madrid, the town of **Guadalupe** is a striking point of entry to the region. Since the late-13th century, when a shepherd chanced upon a buried image of the Virgin Mary purportedly carved by St Luke, Guadalupe has been an important place of pilgrimage.

Alfonso XI dedicated a battle to this Virgin in 1340; when she brought him victory he ordered the construction of a splendid monastery in which to house her. Christopher Columbus brought the first Indians to be baptised to Guadalupe, where the rite was performed at the town fountain. Cervantes journeyed here to give thanks for his release from prison. Over the next few centuries wealthy pilgrims enriched the monastery's order of Hieronymite monks and donated funds for additions to the original building, which served as a combination palace, church, fortress and royal hotel.

By the 15th century the shrine was known as the "Vatican of Spain" and possessed hospitals, a Fine Arts school, 30,000 head of cattle and what was possibly the world's best library. Its medical school, strongly influenced by the Arabic medical tradition, was one of the most advanced in Europe. The monks were unusually successful surgeons, due probably to the fact that Pope Nicholas V issued a special dispensation which allowed them to practise on cadavers. Guadalupe was also a renowned centre for the treatment of syphilis, and had a hospital specialising in the "sweat cure". The old Hospital San Juan Bautista, with its graceful 16th-century patio, is now the **Parador Zurbarán**, just across the street from the monastery.

In 1531 the Guadalupe Virgin appeared to Mexican peasant Juan Diego, and thus began her own conquest of America. Schools, churches, convents and more than a hundred cities in the New World bear her name.

Such became the wealth and power of the monastery that a popular refrain went: "Better than count or duke, to be a monk in Guadalupe." The place was sacked by the French in 1809 and in 1835, when the Spanish government ordered the sale of church property, the Hieronymites fled.

The Virgin's treasures: Presently the monastery is inhabited by Franciscan monks, who provide both lodging for visitors and a tour of Guadalupe's treasures. A visit begins in the 14th-century *mudéjar* **cloister**, with its brick horseshoe archways and lovely fountain surrounded by a miniature temple. The old **refectory** houses a dazzling collection of priests' robes, embroidered with gold threads and encrusted with pearls. There is also a black velvet funeral robe, adorned with white silk skulls. Of further interest is the collection of illuminated choir books, and a room containing the Virgin's own rich wardrobe, necklaces and crowns, given to her by kings, presidents and popes.

The artistic highlight of the tour is the **sacristy**, which contains eight paintings by the 17th-century Extremaduran master, Zurbarán. Up a red marble staircase is the **camarín**, where the Virgin resides. She is a small cedar figure, who looks lost in her gorgeous robes. Her hands and face are dark brown after her 700 years underground, and, according to the Franciscan guide, because the Moors tried to set her on fire. Around her in the room are marble statues of the eight strong women of the Bible.

The town of Guadalupe grew up around the shrine, and still lives mainly by religious tourism. The cobbled streets wind among traditional Extremaduran slate houses, their wooden balconies full of potted geraniums. In addition to devotional souvenirs and pottery, you can also take home a bottle of *gloria*, a local drink made of *aguardiente*, grape juice and herbs.

Roman mosaic celebrates the grape harvest.

Lonely statue: Crossing the **Guadalupe Range** south takes you through the mountain villages of **Logrosán** and **Zorita**, the former boasting the remains of a pre-Roman town on a nearby hillside. Catch up with the main highway, the N-V, at **Miajadas**. From there you can take an 17-mile (28-km) detour to **Medellín**, birthplace of the conqueror of Mexico, Hernán Cortés. Climb up to the ruined **castle** and survey the **Guadiana River** shimmering below. Medellín is a pleasant, quiet village, indistinguishable from dozens of others in Extremadura, except for the outsize bronze statue of Cortés in the town square – a rare representation, since there are no statues of him in Mexico.

Formerly Emeritus Augustus, Mérida lies 79 miles (127 km) south of Guadalupe, on a sluggish bend of the Guadiana. Founded in 25 BC, the city became a prosperous capital of the Roman colony of Lusitania, and Roman ruins are Mérida's pride today. Naturally it is a mecca for archaeologists, who daily uncover treasures on digs in the city's outskirts. "If only we could tear the town down and dig underneath it", the director of the new archaeological museum says.

It's just as well he can't, because Mérida, capital of the Extremadura autonomous region, is a lovely city, whose buildings and hedges of myrtle and hibiscus give a flavour of the Spanish south. One of the streets running into the Plaza España has been renamed **Calle John Lennon**.

In July, Mérida hosts a classical theatre festival, which attracts some of the best Spanish and international companies and directors. Performances are held in the old Roman theatre and **amphitheatre**, which seat 6,000 and 14,000 spectators, respectively. People are matter-of-fact about their 2,000-year-old monument: why not use it? The acoustics are excellent.

Nearby are the hippodrome, formerly used for chariot races, and the **Casa Romana**, which was actually a small palace. The caretaker will give a guided tour of the house, which is helpful since only the floors of most rooms are still intact. Of particular interest are the mosaic floors depicting the four seasons, and the remains of a sauna.

Modern museum: Across the street from the theatres is the **Archaeological Museum**, finished in 1989, a superb modern building which holds the largest collection of Roman artifacts outside Italy. The main hall of the museum, with its high brick archways, has the feeling of a cathedral nave, and is an impressive backdrop for the colossal statues. Two storeys of galleries built around the main hall are dedicated to theme exhibits, and full use is made of natural lighting.

A somewhat startling monument is **Trajan's Arch**, just off the Plaza de España. The triumphal arch, measuring 50 ft (15 metres) by 30 ft (9 metres), dwarfs the narrow street and nearby houses which have grown up around it.

Two other important remnants of Roman times are the **bridge** over the Guadiana, with its 60 granite arches (now open only for pedestrian traffic), and the **Milagros Aqueduct**, which

Mérida's Archaeological Museum.

brought water to Mérida until quite recently. The aqueduct leads from the **La Prosepina Reservoir**, which is now used for windsurfing.

13-year-old saint: After noticing cafés, video parlours and streets dedicated to Santa Eulalia, you may be curious to see the **hornito**, or "little oven", where the teenaged Christian martyr was baked by the Romans. The monument, outside Santa Eulalia Church on the Avenida de Extremadura, is not really an oven but a tiny chapel built of fragments from a temple to Mars. Before her execution, Santa Eulalia was compelled to ride naked through the streets of the town, but a fog suddenly appeared to shroud her. The heavy mist rising from the Guadiana in the early morning is still called "the fog of Santa Eulalia".

Badajoz: The capital of the southern Extremaduran province is 37 miles (60 km) west of Mérida, and 3½ miles (6 km) from the Portuguese border. Following the universal habits of border-dwellers, the Portuguese come to Badajoz to shop, while the Spaniards cross over to Elvas, just inside Portugal.

Originally a Roman town named Pax Augustus, it rose to prominence as Batalajoz, capital of a Moorish principality, and once dominated half of Portugal, including Lisbon. It was captured from the Moors in 1229, but its strategic location made it the site of many bloody sieges over the centuries.

In August 1936 it was captured by Nationalist forces, and, in one of the darkest moments of the Civil War, many Republican defenders (possibly several thousand but the exact figure is unknown) were herded into the bullring and shot. The poverty which made the city a Republican stronghold has been partially alleviated by the Badajoz Plan, a government programme of land expropriation and irrigation, begun in the 1960s.

Moorish imprint: Badajoz is now the largest city in Extremadura, and her somewhat stolid appearance is given spark by the monuments left by the Moors. The part of the city bearing the strongest Arab imprint is on a hill called **Cáceres.**

194

Orinace, 200 ft (60 metres) over the Guadiana River. Here, the Moorish kings built their castle, the **Alcazaba**. Many of the original ramparts and towers remain standing, the most interesting of which is the octagonal **Espantaperros**, so called because the vibrations of its ancient bell were at a pitch that terrified dogs. The Alcazaba has pretty gardens and palm trees left over from Arab times, and the keyhole doorways are particularly evocative of the city's greatest moment.

Nearby is an **Archaeological Museum**. Two other sights in Badajoz worth a look are the **Puerta Palmas**, the old city gate, designed by Herrera, and the Gothic **Cathedral** which has impressive Renaissance choir stalls and paintings by Morales and Zurbarán.

Buy a *bocadillo* (sandwich) of the good local ham or sausage and retreat from the Extremaduran sun into the **Parque de la Legión**, resplendent with palms, bougainvillaea and tinkling fountains.

Cáceres, the capital of the northern Extremaduran province, is a city lifted out of the pages of an illuminated book of chivalry. Film directors have used its cobbled streets to make period films, such as Ridley Scott's *Life of Columbus*. Over the years Cáceres has been miraculously spared the sieges and bombardments which destroyed parts of other Extremaduran cities, so that its entire medieval quarter has been declared a national monument.

The old city is separated from the new by well-preserved walls and towers, and is best approached on foot from the **Plaza Mayor**. Leaving the plaza, with its parking lots and cafés, and climbing the steps leading through the **Arco de la Estrella** is a dramatic ascent into an old city which appears to be inhabited by storks and swallows.

Noble hotheads: During the Middle Ages the atmosphere was rather more hectic. When Alfonso IX took the city from the Moors in 1229, it became the seat of a brotherhood of knights called the *Fratres de Cáceres,* who eventually became Spain's most noble order, the Order of Santiago. At one time there were 300 knights in the city, their palaces just a few steps from one another. Each *solar*, or noble house, had its own defensive tower, and the continual factions and rivalries meant that there was always a small war in progress somewhere around town.

In the interests of peace Ferdinand and Isabella ordered the destruction of most of the towers, save those belonging to their favourites. Of the few which are left, the most striking is perhaps the **Torre de las Cigüeñas**, or Stork Tower, in the **Plaza San Mateo**.

Provincial museum: Directly opposite is the **Casa de las Veletas**, a baroque palace built on the site of the Moorish castle. The Moors held Cáceres for almost 400 years, and were responsible for building a large portion of the city walls. In the basement of the Casa de las Veletas is an enormous arcaded *aljibe*, or cistern, which looks like a flooded mosque. Upstairs is a museum containing artifacts from prehistoric Cáceres, Roman coins and local handicrafts and costumes. There are also reproductions

Statue of the conquistador Pizarro in Trujillo's Plaza Mayor.

of the cave paintings in the nearby caves of **Maltravieso** and contemporary Spanish art is on display next door.

To the left of the museum is the church of **San Mateo**, with a beautiful bell tower, and the **Convent of San Pablo**, inhabited by cloistered nuns. The nuns run a sweet shop in the vestibule of the convent, and use a dumbwaiter to conduct business, thus avoiding showing their faces to the world.

Palaces: Cáceres was the birthplace of several conquistadors, who returned to build their own palaces alongside those of the ancient aristocrats. Therefore, while the facades of the houses range in architectural style from Gothic to Plateresque, there is a similar ponderousness to all the granite buildings.

Palaces of particular note include the **Casa de los Solís**, with its coat of arms in the shape of a sun, and the **Casa del Mono** (monkey), now a Fine Arts museum. Near the 16th-century church of **Santa María la Mayor** are the **Bishop's Palace**, the **Palace of Ovando**, with its lush green patio, and the **Casa Toledo-Montezuma**, which was once inhabited by the descendants of the conquistador Juan Cano and Montezuma's daughter.

Behind Santa María is the **Casa de los Golfines de Abajo**, a house belonging to a family of French knights invited here in the 12th century to help fight the Moors. They ended up terrorising Moors and Christians alike, so that, according to a contemporary chronicler, "even the king cannot subject them, though he has tried". Inscribed in one of the palace stones is the ominous legend: "Here the Golfines await Judgment Day." It's believed that the Spanish word *golfo*, meaning "scoundrel", is derived from this family's surname.

On 29 September 1936, Franco was proclaimed Chief of State in the house of the Golfines. His followers swore, under his mandate, "to make ourselves worthy of our noble forefathers".

The best way to see medieval Cáceres is simply to wander, preferably at dusk, so you can watch the street lights come on. Many of the noble houses are still

Nuns at San Carlos Palace tell the story of Trujillo's miracles.

inhabited, and their patios may be peeked into (tip the porter).

Crowning a dusty hill surrounded by pastureland, **Trujillo** is just 29 miles (47 km) from Cáceres. Hardly more than a village in size, its number of extraordinarily beautiful monuments make it well worth a two-day visit.

Trujillo's long and dramatic history is said to have begun with its founding by Julius Caesar, but the city's proudest moment was clearly the conquest of Peru by native son Francisco Pizarro. His bronze equestrian statue dominates the **Plaza Mayor**, and palaces built with Inca treasure are sprinkled throughout the city. Like Cáceres, Trujillo had an overabundance of knights and noble houses long before the New World was discovered.

The conquerors: The conquistadors were not, as they are sometimes depicted, village louts but often the second or illegitimate sons of aristocrats, with grand surnames and military training, but limited expectations in Spain. Francisco Pizarro was the bastard son of a nobleman who, together with his two half-brothers, set out to capture the fabled wealth of Peru. Even in that delirious time the expedition was known as "*de los locos*", mad. During one desperate moment in the jungle Pizarro drew a line in the sand with the point of his sword and dared his comrades to cross it and head home. All but 13 did.

The inroads made by those 13 convinced Charles V to give Pizarro the ships and armies he wanted, with which he was able to conquer and kill the Inca. The **Marqués de la Conquista's Palace**, built by Francisco's brother, Hernando, stands across the plaza from the statue. On the ornate facade are busts of Francisco Pizarro and his wife Inés Yupanqui, daughter of the Inca. Above them is the coat of arms ceded to them by Charles V.

Behind the equestrian statue is the 15th-century church of **San Martín**, whose bell and clock towers provide ample nesting ground for several storks. Inside the church the most valuable work of art is a Baroque crucifixion,

Tuesday is market day in Plasencia.

known as the *Cristo de la Agonía*.

Across the street from the church is the **Palace of the Duke of San Carlos**, a 16th-century palace with a striking Baroque facade. The house is now inhabited by nuns, who are happy to give a tour of the patio and staircase, as well as tell the story of miracles which occurred in Trujillo.

Also in the Plaza Mayor is the **Palace of Chaves Cardeñas**, an ornate mixture of late Gothic and Baroque. A son of this family founded Santa Cruz, Bolivia. A few steps outside the plaza is the **Palace of Pizarro de Orellana**, also run by nuns, boasting an exquisite Plateresque patio. Francisco de Orellana was a Pizarro cousin, and the first European to navigate the Amazon. He claimed the river for Spain, and eventually perished along its banks.

Miracles: Each step uphill in Trujillo is a step further back into the past. Follow the **Cuesta de Santiago** past the **Torre del Alfiler** (Needle Tower) up to the Moorish **castle**. Pause for breath at **Santa María la Mayor**, a 15th-century church containing the tomb of Diego Paredes, the "Samson of Spain". As a young child he was said to have carried the stone baptismal font from the church to his mother's bedside, and Cervantes wrote that as an adult soldier, Diego "defeated the entire French army and held them at the end of a bridge". His tomb, however, is the normal small size of a medieval man.

The castle is largely intact, and from the walls there is a panoramic view of the town and the surrounding countryside. Upstairs is a chapel dedicated to the Virgin who enabled the Christian armies to take the castle from the Moors by illuminating a dark fog which had enveloped them. A coin-operated machine allows the modern visitor to illuminate the granite statue of the Virgin; her bright light can be seen from the Plaza Mayor below.

An attractive town on the banks of the Jerte River, **Plasencia** is 27 miles (43 km) north of Trujillo. Settled by the Berbers, it was conquered by Alfonso VIII, who granted it a coat of arms with the title *Placeat Deo et hominibus*

(Pleasing to God and Man). Up until 1492 the city continued to have large Jewish and Arab populations, reflected by the narrow, winding streets in which these minorities lived, as well as by street names, such as **Calle de las Morenas** (Street of the Dark Women). Try to arrive in Plasencia on a Tuesday, when the market takes place in the **Plaza Mayor**, as it has for 800 years.

Plasencia has an impressive **cathedral**, which is actually parts of two cathedrals joined together. The first is 13th-century Romanesque, with some touches of Gothic, while the second is 15th-century Gothic with a Plateresque facade. The first one was never completely torn down and the second never finished; from the outside they form an imposing monolith roughly the shape of Gibraltar. The older church houses a museum of religious art.

The choir stalls are some of the most beautiful in Spain; the carving represents both sacred and, on the backs of the seats, profane subjects. The sculptor, Rodrigo Alemán, declared that even God couldn't have made such a masterpiece. Apparently it was this blasphemy, rather than his lascivious artwork, that got him locked into a nearby castle tower. According to legend, he ended his days by falling from the tower, flapping home-made wings.

There are several palaces in Plasencia, the grandest of which is the **Palace of the Marqueses de Mirabel**, in the **Plaza de San Vicente.** The house is occupied by the present marquis, but the porter will give an impromptu tour of the Italian-style patio and several of the downstairs rooms if the marquis is out. He will also talk about the family's fall from favour in the 15th century, when they backed the wrong side in the struggle for the throne between Isabella the Catholic and her niece, Juana.

Jewish ghost town: An interesting detour from the road back to Madrid is **Hervás**, a mountain village surrounded by pine and chestnut groves, which contains one of the best-preserved Jewish quarters in Spain.

It is thought that Hervás became a predominantly Jewish settlement in the early Middle Ages, as the Jews fled Christian and Muslim persecution of the larger cities. Perhaps because of the remoteness of the area, Hervás escaped the massive pogroms and fires of 1391. When the Jews were expelled from Spain in 1492, their neighbourhood was left intact, and their possessions ceded to the local Duke of Béjar. Stripped of its wealth, the town fell into oblivion, although its breezy mountain location is turning it into a popular spot for building *chalets*, or vacation homes.

The intricate, maze-like streets make this village an intimate one. Neighbours bring their chairs and sandwiches outside and sit together in the sunshine. There is little sign of the town's former inhabitants, although a plaque near the entrance to the quarter, in Spanish and Hebrew, is dedicated to Spanish-Jewish friendship, and a modern hotel near the train station is called Sinagoga.

Summit: From Hervás, a narrow but spectacular road, not to be attempted in bad weather, crosses a portion of the **Sierra de Gredos** which soars to 7,000

ft (2,100 metres). The summit is treeless and breathtaking, and still fits George Borrow's 1836 description in *The Bible in Spain*: "I proceeded down the pass, occasionally ruminating on the matter which had brought me to Spain, and occasionally admiring one of the finest prospects in the world. Before me outstretched lay immense plains, bounded in the distance by huge mountains, whilst at the foot of the hill which I was now descending, rolled the Tagus, in a deep narrow stream, between lofty banks; the whole was gilded by the rays of the setting sun."

An appropriate last stop in Extremadura is the **Monastery of Yuste**, inhabited by Charles V from his retirement in 1557 until his death in 1558. The head of the globe-spanning empire declared he wanted a simple place in the Guadalupe Mountains where he could tend to his hobby of clock mending and think about the other world. The bare, black-draped rooms where he reputedly rehearsed his own funeral are indeed austere, except for the view.

Hervás, the Jewish quarter.

SEVILLE

Seville. Córdoba. Granada. A resounding triumvirate of southern (Andalusian) Spanish cities whose very names roll from the tongue with a hint of arrogance. Flashy, flamboyant, proud.

Warm of weather, attractive of scenery and easily accessible by sea, Andalusia was vulnerable to the successive settlements of the Phoenicians, Greeks, Romans, Visigoths and Moors. But it was the Arab and Berber presence that bequeathed Andalusia the richly sensuous medieval culture of silver filigree and ornate mosques that bewitches travellers today.

Under the Moorish dominion, this region was the centre of the most highly developed civilisation of the Middle Ages. But its reputation for riches and flair for hospitality hark back to an even earlier incarnation as the Roman province of Baetica, when Andalusia purveyed all make and manner of luxuries to the connoisseurs and *cognoscenti* of imperial Rome.

Such 19th-century visitors as Washington Irving, George Borrow and Richard Ford were inspired to record its charms in their various travel chronicles and thus helped to convert the salient features of Andalusia into the universal Spanish stereotype.

Sherry wines, well-disciplined horses, brave bulls and flamboyant flamenco were the stuff of Andalusia. And who from a colder and soggier climate could resist the promise of 3,000 hours of sunshine annually and a mere 12 inches (30 cm) of rain?

Generally, Andalusia's winters are mild and its summers scorching. And throughout, the climatic catchword is "dry", as evidenced by the number of bridges spanning parched riverbeds, some of which are under cultivation.

Fellow Andaluces: Until the Reconquest of Granada by the Catholic Monarchs Ferdinand and Isabella in 1492, Andalusia had rarely been united under one ruler. Internecine strife among the *emirs* and *taifas* of Córdoba, Jaén, Gra-nada and Seville undermined Moorish domination well before the increasing pressure of Spain's northern Christian kingdoms ultimately vanquished it.

Today Andalusia is Spain's most populous region, tallying 33,695 sq. miles (87,270 sq. km), 6½ million inhabitants and comprising Spain's eight southernmost provinces. Comparable in size to Portugal, it stretches from that country in the west to Murcia in the east. Its northern reaches are marked by the Sierra Morena and its southern boundaries by the Atlantic Ocean and Mediterranean Sea.

The people of the provinces of Almería, Granada, Jaén, Córdoba, Málaga, Cádiz, Seville and Huelva, each with a provincial capital of the same name, are at once fellow *Andaluces* and individual *Almerienses, Granadinos, Cordobeses* and *Sevillanos*. Says one Seville taxi driver: "Seville is different from the rest. Here there is more sympathy, and we are more polite in everything. We all call ourselves *Andaluces* because we share the same flag. Of course, Cádiz is somewhat similar to Seville, but the *Granadinos* are coarse fellows, as if they weren't even *Andaluces*."

These provincial rivalries have their roots in a not-so-playful past of seesawing fortunes among the former Moorish kingdoms of Granada, Seville and Córdoba.

For a long time foreigners and fellow countrymen from Spain's industrialised north have characterised the *Andaluces* as lethargic and overly fond of their afternoon siesta. But at the same time all consider them to be refreshingly spontaneous andwitty, balancing an exaggerated sense of tragedy with a robust sense of humour.

"Here are two classes of people to whom life seems one long holiday, the very rich, and the very poor", writes Washington Irving in *Tales of the Alhambra*, "one, because they need do nothing, the other, because they have nothing to do; but there are none who understand the art of doing nothing and living upon nothing better than the poor classes of Spain. Climate does one half and temperament the rest… Talk of poverty! With (a Spaniard) it has no disgrace. It sits upon him with a grandiose style, like his ragged cloak. He is an *hidalgo* even when in rags."

Witness today the supreme cleanliness of even the sorriest of Andalusian streets and the smallest of its white houses – it is, quite simply, a matter of personal dignity.

Recently a southern farmer had this to say about his native *tierra*: "This is a land boiling over, yes, but here the fiestas and other things are born and die; what is important is the ephemeral, the fleeting, paper lanterns and flashes, but one doesn't build, one doesn't put cement to anything. What delights is the arrival of the heat to signal the siesta."

Historic leap: It is true that ever since the Christians eclipsed the Moors in Andalusia, the Spanish south has been largely poor. Not the overt, searing poverty of the Third World, but rather an undercurrent of rural poverty not readily detected by the casual tourist.

Fortunately, Andalusia's reputation as "a rich land inhabited by poor men"

is declining. While unemployment remains obstinately high (well over 20 per cent), official statistics tell only part of the story as there is a thriving underground economy and rural workers, long neglected, now enjoy an unheard-of range of social services.

The 1980s brought unprecedented prosperity to Andalusia. Spain's entry into the European Community in 1986 spurred development, which was further boosted by the colossal investment in infrastructure to prepare for Expo '92, the world fair in Seville celebrating Columbus's voyage to the New World. Having Seville native Felipe González as prime minister was helpful too.

Although the dream of making Andalusia the "California of Europe" still seemed distant as the worldwide recession of the 1990s slowed activity, the region has entered a new era of progress. Four-lane highways now connect it with Madrid and the rest of Europe and a high-speed train, the AVE, has halved travelling time from Madrid to Seville.

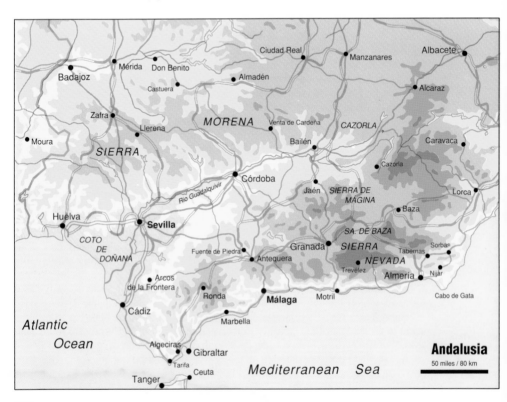

Abundant sunshine and fertile farmland are two enduring resources. The sunshine has converted the coast, particularly the Costa del Sol, into a favourite vacation and residential area for pale-faced Northern Europeans, but efforts are underway to open up less-known areas inland to attract hikers and wildlife *aficionados*. Modern methods are being applied to farming and thousands of acres of what once was desert in Almería Province have been transformed into plastic-covered greenhouses, where export crops, from melons to carnations, flourish all year.

Flirtatious Seville: Seville, Spain's fourth largest city, host of Expo '92 and Andalusia's capital, is the most coquettish of the three grand cities of the south. Says an old Spanish refrain: *Quien no ha visto Sevilla, no ha visto maravilla.* (He who has not seen Seville, has not known marvel.)

George Borrow, author of *The Bible in Spain*, considered it "the most interesting town in all Spain", standing beneath "the most glorious heaven…"

Even through a rare veil of fine December rain Seville is pretty. In the bright Andalusian sunshine, she is dazzling. A fitting setting for Byron's Don Juan, Bizet's Carmen, and Rossini's barber to play out their fictional lives.

Some of the real lives that got their start here are those of the poets Gustavo Adolfo Bécquer (1836–70) and Antonio Machado (1875–1939), and the painters Diego de Velázquez (1599–1660) and Bartolomé Esteban Murillo (1618–82).

Romance has apparently always coursed through the city's veins. The Muslim historian Al-Saqundi, captivated by its endless charm, once proclaimed: "If one asked for the milk of birds in Seville, it would be found."

Saint Teresa was so taken with its beauty and boldness that she confessed she felt that anyone who could somehow avoid committing sin in Seville would be doing very well indeed.

Unfortunately, today's visitors are too often sinned against themselves as wallets disappear from pockets and

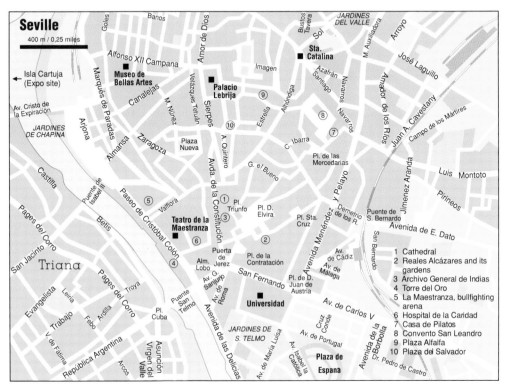

Seville

400 m / 0,25 miles

← Isla Cartuja (Expo site)

1 Cathedral
2 Reales Alcázares and its gardens
3 Archivo General de Indias
4 Torre del Oro
5 La Maestranza, bullfighting arena
6 Hospital de la Caridad
7 Casa de Pilatos
8 Convento San Leandro
9 Plaza Alfalfa
10 Plaza del Salvador

purses from sightseeing shoulders or restaurant tables.

Roman rule: "Hercules built me; Caesar surrounded me with walls and towers; the King Saint took me." This terse recapitulation of Seville's multi-tiered history was carved long ago on the Jerez Gate. In later years, Seville's port would bustle with New World activity as Spain built a lustrous but short-lived overseas empire.

In the era of discoverers, when the Netherlands, England and Spain were fighting for supremacy at sea and in the New World colonies, Seville was one of the richest cities in the world. But it had already known previous fame and fortune. Founded by the Iberians, it was usurped by Julius Caesar for Rome in 45 BC. Made an assize town and named *Hispalis*, it was given the title of *Colonia Julia Romula* and quickly became one of the leading towns of the flourishing Roman province of Baetica, roughly corresponding to present-day Andalusia.

There followed several lacklustre

centuries under the Vandals and Visigoths, the latter having Seville report to their capital at Toledo.

Glory days: Then in 712 came the Moors, who renamed it *Ishbiliya*. Later, as part of the Caliphate of Córdoba, Seville rivalled that capital in material prosperity and as a seat of learning. When the Caliphate broke up in the 11th century, Seville pursued an independent course. Beginning in 1023, it saw the successive rule of the Abbadites, Almoravids (1091) and Almohads (1147). Under this last dynasty a new period of prosperity reigned that left behind many of Seville's fine buildings, including the Giralda.

In 1248, Seville was reconquered for Christianity by Ferdinand III, the King Saint, who died and was buried here.

The wave of New World discoveries that raised Seville to the crest of its fortunes in the 16th century also dashed it in its wake when the empire ebbed a century later. In 1519, Magellan set sail from here to circumnavigate the globe. But Seville's moment of glory was all too fleeting, and decline set in again in the early 17th century, subsequently hastened by maritime competition from Cádiz, the snowballing loss of the Spanish colonies that had brought so much trade, the troubled state of 19th-century Spain and a brief French occupation lasting from 1808 to 1812.

Its historic momentum lost, Seville strolled into the 20th century trailing a tarnished heritage that nevertheless stirred great feelings of pride among *Sevillanos*. Seized early in the Civil War by the Nationalists, Seville served as a base for attacks on the rest of Andalusia. Emerging from the war physically starving and spiritually spent, the city gradually regained its legendary *alegría* under the entrenched Franco dictatorship. But for a long time its gypsy bravado resounded with a tragic note.

From 1940 to today, Seville's population has almost doubled to the current 650,000. With the granting of regional autonomy, Seville – as capital – received a boost in importance. But it was Expo '92 that proved to be "the sort of

Seville's Giralda.

cold shower we needed", in the view of one *sevillano*. The flux of professionals from other regions and countries shook up the status quo in a community where class barriers and conservative attitudes seemed immovable. They brought new money and fresh ideas to a city frozen in its ritualistic ways.

Expo also transformed Seville physically, with splendid results. Scores of old buildings were restored, half a dozen new bridges now span the Guadalquivír, fine walkways run along the riverside and Seville finally has an opera house. A new railway station accommodates the AVE high-speed train, the airport has been enlarged and a bypass sweeps around the city, sparing through traffic the nightmare of negotiating the narrow streets.

Most striking of all is the change wrought in the **Isla de la Cartuja**, once a boggy wasteland with only one building, the Monasterio de Santa Maria de las Cuevas where Columbus was first interred. Cartuja was the site of Expo '92. Part of the island is now a high-

Expo '92 brought the future to Seville.

technology research area, while the rest is open to the public as the Parque de los Descubrimentos. This features many of Expo's most interesting pavilions including that of Navigation and of Discovery, a cable-car, a monorail train, a large auditorium and varied entertainment, with everything from laser shows to flamenco and rock.

On a huge scale: Virtually everything in Andalusia is of a human scale – except the **Cathedral** of Seville. Some 380 ft (116 metres) long and 250 ft (76 metres) wide, it is the third largest Christian church in the world (after St Peter's in Rome and St Paul's in London) and the largest Gothic one. Built between 1402 and 1506 on the site of a former mosque, it contains five spacious aisles, a large main chapel with a wrought-iron screen and vaulting that towers 184 flamboyant feet (56 metres) above the transept. Allegedly it was the chapter's aim in 1401 "to construct a church such and as good that it never should have its equal. Let Posterity, when it admires it complete, say that

those who dared to devise such a work must have been mad."

Hidden in its sombre shadows are many relics and treasures, including paintings by Murillo, Zurbarán and Goya; a cross said to be made from the first gold brought from America by Columbus; and a funerary monument claimed to hold the explorer's remains. In fact, he almost certainly reposes in Santo Domingo, capital of the Dominican Republic. His leaden tomb was taken from Seville to Santo Domingo Cathedral in 1544, in 1795 what were believed to be his remains were transferred to Havana and a century later from there to Seville. But somewhere there was a mix-up and it is believed that the bones in Seville may be those of his son Diego.

On Corpus Christi, the Immaculate Conception and the last three days of Carnival, a peculiar custom takes place in front of the Flemish high altar in the cathedral's sacristy. Ten choristers in traditional 17th-century pages' costume dance a slow minuet known as the Dance of the *Seises* (there used to be six). Its origins, suspected to be secular, are largely unknown.

Moorish treasures: Adjacent to the Cathedral is the chequerboard **Patio de los Naranjos**. Now neglected, it was the court of the city's main mosque, a shaded oasis of orange trees and sparkling fountains used for the ritual ablutions of Islam.

Exiting through the **Puerta de Oriente**, you are at the base of Seville's trademark **Giralda**, a slender, rectangular tower rising 305 ft (93 metres) alongside the Cathedral. Erected between 1184 and 1196, it is the remaining minaret of the mosque which was destroyed a century later.

Across the **Plaza del Triunfo** from the Cathedral stands a Moorish fantasy in filigree: the **Alcázar**. Built between 1350 and 1369, it is a *mudéjar* elaboration of an original Moorish citadel and palace. For nearly seven centuries, it was the palace of Spanish kings. Most notorious among them was Pedro the Cruel, who had his half-brother

Tomb of Columbus in Seville Cathedral.

Fadrique assassinated in 1358 and murdered his guest, Abu Said of Granada, for his jewels. The skulls painted over Pedro's bedroom door supposedly suggest the fate of five unjust judges who crossed him during his reign.

Though less grandiose and expansive than Granada's Alhambra, Seville's Alcázar has a special cosiness and charm derived from its sense of intimacy and its careful attention to polychrome detail. Its fanciful floors, ceilings and walls are intricate works of art, reaching heights of richness in Charles V's room and the **Salón de Embajadores**. The **Patio de las Doncellas** is noted for its friezes, *azulejos* (tiles) and stucco work. Well-manicured gardens, redolent of orange groves, palm trees and roses, contribute to an overall sense of an elegant summer sanctuary.

Jewish quarter: Stretching beyond the walls of the Alcázar is the **Barrio de Santa Cruz**, the former Jewish quarter turned fashionable neighbourhood. The walls are so white, the flowers so bright and the iron everywhere so exquisitely wrought that you quite expect a *señorita* in full flounce to come around the corner any minute, castanets clicking. When tourists are in season, guitar-packing gypsies also regularly flock to the local taverns. In the off season they often play until dawn for local *aficionados* at clubs, bars and private gatherings, for flamenco is a child of the night.

Amidst the chic shops and rustic restaurants of this *barrio*, you can see many traditional Andalusian homes. Open-work, wrought-iron gates mark the entrance porch and iron gratings the windows where cape-draped gallants once wooed the *señoritas* caged within. A square inner courtyard, cool and inviting with its abundant greenery, dado of Moorish tiles and central fountain is covered with an awning in the summer and used as the living-room; in winter the family retreats upstairs. In 1828, writer Washington Irving stayed in the **Calle Mezquita**.

Near the Cathedral, the shelves of the **Archives of the Indies** sag with the weight of history. Since 1785, it has

The Barrio de Santa Cruz.

been accumulating the heavy tomes that contain some 36,000 files of documents chronicling the adventure of discovery, the trails of colonisation, the trivia of colonial administration and the minutiae of trade that recall a 16th-century Seville that was the headquarters for New World trade and, as a result, one of the richest cities in the Old World.

Park and plaza: To enter into the spirit of a bygone Seville, tour **María Luisa Park** and the **Plaza de España** in one of the horse-drawn carriages perpetually lined up in front of the Cathedral.

The park is dotted with buildings left over from the Spanish-American exhibition of 1929. One of these now houses the **Archaeological Museum**.

The Plaza de España is marked by a long semicircular series of arches bearing ceramic crests of all the provinces of Spain. Several ceramic-and-brick bridges span the small, concentric stream that flows through this expansive plaza. Its impressive buildings now house both military and government headquarters. Between the Plaza and

the Alcázar is the old tobacco factory where Bizet's Carmen was one of 10,000 employees. The building is now part of Seville University.

The river: Seville straddles the banks of the **Guadalquivír River**, which makes a port of the city 70 miles (113 km) from the sea. Known by the Romans as "Baetis" and the Moors as the "Wadi el Kebir" ("great river"), part of its 400-mile (644-km) course also flows through Córdoba; but to hear the *Sevillanos* talk about it, you'd think the Guadalquivír was their very own.

Frequent droughts render this river less than impressive to those who have barged down the Thames or taken a steamboat on the Mississippi, but to citizens of Seville, it is every bit as revered as the Amazon.

Once upon a time in Seville you could be born on the "wrong side of the river". Over there, across the river from the Cathedral, the bullring and the up-and-coming Barrio de Santa Cruz was the nefarious **Barrio de Triana**, haven of violence and vice. Reputed to be both

Plaza de España.

unsavoury and unsafe, it was the lair of the little-loved gypsies. Today, though, it is largely a residential suburb fast becoming every bit as respectable as its neighbours across the water.

Back on the "right" side of the river, you'll see along the **Paseo de Cristobal Colón** the enigmatic **Torre del Oro**; enigmatic because the origin of its name and its very purpose are a matter of dispute. Some say it got its name from the golden colour of its *azulejos*; others maintain that it was a warehouse for New World gold. In times of danger it held one end of a chain that stretched across the river to a companion tower, now vanished, on the other side. The 20th-century purpose of this 13th-century, 12-sided, battlemented tower is to house a small maritime museum.

Pilate's house: This 16th-century palace, just north of the Barrio de Santa Cruz, was indeed named after the famous Biblical magistrate whose house in Jerusalem inspired some of its features. Also incorporated in this mansion of the first Marquess of Tarifa are

mudéjar and Renaissance elements rendered in remarkable *azulejos* and moulded stucco.

A day in the life: Late morning, Seville begins to stir. Along the **Calle de las Sierpes**, a pedestrian thoroughfare winding from **La Campana** to the **Plaza de San Francisco**, friends meet to do business, exchange confidences and just generally pass the time. At No 52 once stood a prison that quartered the not-yet-prominent Cervantes, author of *Don Quixote*. Also in the neighbourhood is the **Museum of Fine Arts**, housed in a former friary and displaying numerous Murillos, several Zurbaráns, a smattering of Velázquez and a single El Greco.

From the more sophisticated pubs of the **Plaza de Cuba** to the kiosks on the corner of **Altozano**, an assortment of establishments chalk up on their blackboards such memorable *tapas* as bull's tail, stewed giblets, baby squid, kidneys in sherry, and clams in their own juice. Less adventurous eaters are always safe ordering cheese.

Pilate's
house.

After dinner hour (9pm to 11pm), the bars of both Santa Cruz and Triana come explosively alive. Triana's **Calle Salado** is the centre for do-it-yourself flamenco.

Those driving in this city should be warned of Seville's web of one-way streets. You may well circle your destination several times before deciphering how actually to attain it, and cars parked on the curbs of already too-narrow streets will cause you to inch along.

Feria de Abril: Every April (usually two weeks after Easter) Seville dresses to the nines and lets down her hair in a confluence of Andalusian stereotypes: wine, bulls, horses and flamenco.

The day begins around noon with a mounted parade of handsome horses outshone only by their more handsome riders: men in leather chaps with scarlet cummerbunds, short jackets, and broad-brimmed hats and women riding pillion wearing full-skirted flamenco dresses with vivid polka dots. Alternating with the horsemen are horse-drawn carriages, harness bells gleaming.

All around, pavilions, public and private, bubble with friends and visitors sharing *tapas* and *manzanilla* and gossiping. Amidst all the rejoicing, dancers perform the classic *sevillanas*, the most popular modern flamenco.

The pavilions, arranged in rows and decorated with flowers, flags and paper lanterns, fill the **Prado de San Sebastián**, former site of the Inquisition's *autos-da-fe*, the burning of heretics. Between them, the roadway is carpeted with golden sand.

After lunch and a brief siesta, the late-afternoon bullfights begin, in an atmosphere of great excitement. Beneath the floodlights and fireworks of night, the flirtatious merriment continues until dawn. For this is the time when Seville's southern belles search for and show off their dashing *novios*.

The *Feria de Abril* began in 1848 as a rural livestock fair. To be sure, cattle-dealing still goes on, with gypsies playing their traditional role, but today the essence of the Feria is simply Seville celebrating life itself.

Señoritas get into the spirit of the *Feria*.

214

HOLY WEEK

The week preceding Easter is *Semana Santa,* a time of national ritual in Spain. In every corner of the country processions snake their way, day and night, from the local parishes to the main cathedrals and back again.

In the larger cities there may be more than 30 different processions in any 24-hour period. Depending on the size of the municipality and its economic means, each day is marked by regalia of varying colour, elaborate floats showing scenes from the Passion and centuries-old music. Since the 16th century, this has been the Spanish way of commemorating Holy Week.

These celebrations attain a feverish pitch of pageantry and colour in the south. From Palm Sunday to Easter Sunday the communities focus on the trials of Christ and the tears of the Virgin. It has often been alleged that the *andaluces* are more demonstrative in their faith because of a need to live down the Muslim-Moorish legacy.

In Seville, a fervent "thunder" fills the Cathedral on Wednesday with the rending of the veil of the temple and resounds again on Saturday just before all join in singing "Gloria in Excelsis" and ringing every bell.

In Córdoba, on the afternoon of Good Friday, mass is celebrated in the church within the mosque with a full symphony orchestra and a massive chorus.

In Granada, mantilla'd ladies all in black dripping with jewellery and rosaries march through the city among the floats.

For everywhere *pasos,* or floats, are a fixed feature of *Semana Santa.* They bear life-size and extremely lifelike polychrome and gilded figures depicting every Passion scene from the Last Supper and the Garden of Olives to the Descent from the Cross. The figures wear wigs and real costumes that may cost up to $150,000.

As the proud parishioners watch their particular Virgin pass by they may weep, applaud, sing, or even throw her some saucy compliments. Some admirers are so moved by a particular *paso* that they spontaneously sing the traditional, melancholy *saeta.*

The trappings of the processions are solemn. Penitent processioners wear long robes gathered with belts of esparto grass

Holy Week crucifix.

and tall, pointed hoods covering their faces except for two slits for the eyes. Called *capuchones,* these are the hoods of the Spanish Inquisition and the equally insidious Ku Klux Klan. Some carry up to five crosses, making one wonder what they've been up to.

But the strong Andalusian sense of fun cannot be long suppressed. The processional ranks are constantly broken as people cross through the parade to greet friends and share a beer or a *boccadillo* (sandwich).

In the side streets off the parade route tables and chairs are set up to provide rest and sustenance. *Torrijas,* a fried, milk-soaked confection, and *flamenquines*, deep-fried slices of veal wrapped around snow-cured ham and cheese, are traditional snacks.

Folklore or religion? The celebrations of *Semana Santa* seem to be both. Almost everywhere in Spain, the end of *Semana Santa* signals the beginning of the bullfighting season. In Arcos de la Frontera a local version of the "running of the bulls" takes place on Easter Sunday, and in Málaga you can go straight from the last Easter mass to the season's first *corrida.* ∎

CORDOBA

Handsome, honourable and forthright, Córdoba is harsher than Seville and without the benefit of a marked gypsy grace note to soften its keen masculine edge. In its no-nonsense streets there is no sense of the benign chaos that chokes rush-hour Seville, nor is there in the town centre a subtle layering of eras as in Granada.

There are just the old and the new, clearly demarcated by an intermittent, well-tended Moorish wall. To one side are the twisted antique alleys, to the other wide, straight streets with a 20th-century purpose.

Just look at a map of Córdoba and you'll see the old quarter meandering down to the banks of the wide, shallow Guadalquivír in a Rorschach maze of tiny alleyways doubling back on themselves or sometimes leading nowhere. These will test the mettle of even the most seasoned navigator.

Visitors are advised to leave their cars outside the old quarter and go on foot with good reason. Most of the roads are barely wide enough to accommodate the most fuel-efficient of vehicles, and you might well find yourself suddenly backing a hasty retreat down a one-way street under the reproachful gaze of an impatient horse, tourists in tow, eager to return its carriage to the shaded queue outside the *Mezquita* walls.

Patrician colony: Looking at Córdoba today, it is hard to imagine the truly heady heights this city achieved in earlier epochs. The history of Córdoba, like that of Granada and Seville, is a dizzying account of soaring success and dismal failure.

Like Seville, Córdoba was an important Iberian town. In 152 BC its fate passed to Roman hands when the consul Marcus Marcellus made it a colony favoured with the title *Colonia Patricia.* As the Roman "Corduba", it became the capital of *Hispania Ulterior;* and under Augustus, it came into its own as the prosperous capital of Baetica Province

The archways of the *Mezquita* in Córdoba.

and Spain's largest city at the time.

At this stage in its life it sired Seneca the Elder (55 BC–AD 39) and his son, Lucius Seneca (4 BC–AD 65), noted philosopher and preceptor to Nero. His statue now stands by the **Puerta de Almodóvar**, the principal entrance to the old town.

From the 5th to the 8th centuries Córdoba was ruled by the Visigoths, who gave it its first taste of Christianity. The Moors entered some two centuries later. With the help of the city's disaffected Jewish residents, harassed by the Visigoths, the invaders quickly established their supremacy and ultimately raised Córdoba to the pinnacle of prestige and prosperity.

The Caliphate: At the beginning of the 8th century, emirs from the Damascus Caliphate had already established themselves in the city; but with the arrival of Abd-al-Rahman I in 756, a discernible dynasty was founded capable of consolidating the power to rule over all of Muslim Spain, which the Moors called *al-Andalus.*

Under Abd-al-Rahman III (912–61) and his successor Hakam II (961–76), the blessings of the Caliphate of Córdoba rained down on the city like manna from heaven. Its overstuffed coffers, luxurious appointments and richly brocaded cultural achievements defied even the gifted hyperbole that was second nature to the Moors and is a lingering trait among their present-day Andalusian offspring.

Córdoba was then possibly Europe's most civilised city. In the 10th century it founded a university of great renown. Literature and science were encouraged, schools of philosophy and medicine were strongly promoted and libraries were established.

The city's inhabitants, numbering between half a million and a million, were served by 3,000 mosques, 300 public baths and 28 suburbs. At its supreme moment of glory Córdoba was surpassed in size and opulence only by the city of Baghdad.

But bad news was just around the corner. At the beginning of the 11th century internal dissent and revolt laid a

foundation for its downfall. In 1031, the powerful Caliphate split up into petty kingdoms called *taifas,* and some 40 years later Córdoba itself was subsumed by the kingdom of Seville until its recapture for Christianity by Ferdinand III in 1236.

Córdoba's decline was then given even greater impetus as many inhabitants fled and the Christians turned an indifferent eye upon the industry, trade and agriculture that had fed the city's enviable affluence.

For centuries to come Córdoba wallowed in the doldrums, a dull provincial capital with a dormant past. But over the last 50 years its spirit has been steadily reviving, and the city is once again picking up speed. Since 1950 its population has grown by over 50 percent to more than 250,000. To see the city at its liveliest, visit during the Patios Festival, held in the second week of May, or the *Feria,* 25–28 May.

Córdoba's mosque: Whether you see it as a travesty or a triumph, the **Mezquita** is a product and a symbol of the grafting

The *mihrab* of the mosque.

of Christianity on to Muslim Spain.

As the great mosque of the Umayyad caliphs, it enjoyed such profound artistic and religious stature that it saved the city's inhabitants the arduous pilgrimage to Mecca, whose mosque was the only one of greater size and importance. Begun in 785, the mosque was two centuries in the building, expanding with the city's population before reaching its full size of 570 by 450 ft (174 by 137 metres).

Inside, a forest of about 850 columns produces a repetitive motif of criss-crossing alleys not unlike the effect of a hall of mirrors. Uneven in height (average 13 ft, or 4 metres), and varying in material and style, these pillars support an architectural innovation of the time: two tiers of candy-striped arches that lend added height and spaciousness.

Most notable and memorable among the Moorish flourishes is the *mihrab,* or prayer recess, along the wall facing Mecca. The workmanship is a masterpiece of Moorish mosaic art. Interlaced arches sprout from the marble columns surrounding the vestibule; and, more exquisitely decorated still, is the octagonal *mihrab* itself topped by a shell-shape dome.

Newly Christian Córdoba soon claimed the mosque as its own Church of the Virgin of the Assumption, building chapels against the interior walls and closing up the open northern facade to allow access only through the **Puerta de las Palmas**. But construction of the cruciform church in the centre of the mosque did not begin until 1523.

Massive as the church is, you are not immediately aware of its looming presence upon entering the mosque. Only after considerable slaloming beneath the arches do you suddenly stumble upon a 180-ft (55-metre) long Renaissance structure with a choir, a **Capilla Mayor**, a 50-ft (15-metre) wide transept and a lavishly adorned ceiling.

Its hodgepodge of styles (Gothic, Renaissance, Italian and baroque) required nearly a century of construction; and when Charles V, who had given his unthinking permission for the building, **Córdoba is one of Spain's hottest cities.**

218

first saw the architectural and artistic disfigurement it caused, he reproached those responsible for the transformation. "You have built here what you or anyone might have built anywhere else", he said, "but you have destroyed what was unique in the world." It is still unique, but in a rather freakish way.

Outside the mosque but within its surrounding battlemented walls is the requisite **Patio de los Naranjos** entered through the **Puerta del Perdón** at the base of the distinctive 305-ft (93-metre) Christian belfry that replaced the Moorish minaret. A stairway inside the belfry leads to the top for an overview of the mosque, the surrounding city, the Guadalquivír and the plains beyond.

From the nearby **Calleja de la Flores** (Alley of the Flowers), you can see the belfry framed in postcard splendour between the flower-studded walls of this narrow street. In true Córdoban fashion the flower pots are attached to the walls with wrought-iron rings.

Religious persecution: The site and size of Córdoba's **Jewish Quarter** indi-cates that here, as elsewhere, the Jews were long considered a breed apart. And like elsewhere, they were a learned, accomplished and wealthy breed that seemed never to be allowed to prosper between periods of persecution.

Disgruntled with their lot under the Visigoths, the Jews of Córdoba aided and abetted the Moorish victory; they subsequently enjoyed a welcome period of peace and prosperity under the tolerant Muslim yoke.

Córdoba itself was at one time home to the distinguished Moorish physicist, astrologer, mathematician, doctor and philosopher Averroës (who lived here from 1126 to 1198) and to Moses Maimonides (1135–1204), noted Jewish physician and philosopher. In the **Calle Maimonides** today stands his monument, along with the striped remains of a small, 14th-century synagogue built in the *mudéjar* style. To visit it, apply to the caretaker.

Trivial pursuit: Heirlooms deposited in the environs of Córdoba by the various tiers of its history are beautifully dis-

Lunch in Córdoba's El Churrasco restaurant.

played in the **Archaeological Museum** in the **Plaza de Jerónimo Paéz**. Housed in a Renaissance palace of the same name, the extensive collection contains prehistoric, Roman, Visigothic, Moorish and Gothic remains. Striking among them are a bronze stag from nearby Medina Azahara, Iberian sculptures vaguely reminiscent of Chinese temple dogs and an original Roman foundation upon which the building rests. The museum also contains the world's largest collections of lead sarcophagi and Arabic capitals.

Horse and buggy: Many tourists may feel that it's trite to see the sights in a horse-drawn carriage, but such a trip in Córdoba is highly recommended. Not only will it save you the bother of navigating the old town's tiny, tortuous streets on your own, but your driver/guide will undoubtedly point out many esoteric sights you might otherwise have missed.

Among the less esoteric ones is the Manolete monument in the **Plaza del Conde de Priego**. Born Manuel Rodríguez in 1917, Manolete was a local boy who found fame and fortune in the bullrings of Spain. Unfortunately, he encountered an untimely death by goring in 1947. The equally famous *torero* El Cordobés was actually born Manuel Benítez in 1936 in the town of Palma del Río 36 miles (58 km) west of Córdoba.

El Cristo de los Faroles is a well-known crucifix standing starkly in a hidden plaza surrounded by wrought-iron lanterns. A return visit at night is highly recommended.

The 17th-century **Plaza Mayor**, also known as the **Plaza de la Corredera** because of its earlier use for bullfights, is nothing to write home about. The four-square, three-tiered structures marking its perimeter have a sagging, grade-B-western-movie quality.

In contrast, the **Plaza del Potro** has remained vigorous since the days when Cervantes allegedly stayed at the *posada* in this square and wrote a part of *Don Quixote*. The square's fountain-statue of a colt is mentioned in the book.

Arts and crafts: In an old hospital in the same square is the **Fine Arts Museum,** which has Goya and Carreño paintings.

All along, you'll notice shops offering Córdoba's prime crafts in trade: silver filigree and stamped leather. Since the time of the Moors these crafts have flourished here, but in the 16th and 17th centuries the latter in particular flourished through a prevailing fashion dictating that all walls and seats should be covered with leatherwork, properly embossed, tooled, tinted and gilded.

Just west of the mosque, in the vicinity of the much-restored Roman bridge spanning the Guadalquivír, is the old **Alcázar of the Umayyads**, now largely supplanted by the bishopric. Remaining are some attractive Moorish patios, some Roman mosaics and the Arabic gardens, lively with pools and shaded with cypresses.

Medina Azahara: About 5 miles (8 km) northwest of Córdoba at **Córdoba la Vieja** stand the emerging remains of an extensive palace complex begun around 936 by Abd-al-Rahman III to satisfy the caprices of his favourite wife

A Córdoba courtyard sports the head of a once-brave bull.

Zahara (meaning "flower"). Allegedly the funding for this ambitious project came from an immense fortune bequeathed to the caliph upon the death of one of his concubines.

The new city stretched up the **Sierra de Córdoba** foothills of the Sierra Morena mountains, adapting itself gracefully to the terraced terrain. Its area of approximately 275 acres (110 hectares) is divided into three levels. The highest, which has seen the greatest amount of excavation to date, contains the Alcázar; the middle, the gardens and orchards; and the lowest, the mosque and city proper.

The account of its construction, as rendered by the Arab historian El-Makkari, gives some impression of its scale. Ten thousand men, 2,600 mules and 400 camels worked for 25 years, he reports, to erect the palace, gardens, fish ponds, mosque, baths and schools.

Some of the city's 4,300 columns came from Carthage, some were made of marble, others of jasper. The royal entourage included 12,000 men in the garrison, 4,000 servants in the palace and 2,000 horses in the stables. There were hanging gardens, aviaries, zoos, streams, courts and kiosks, gold fountains and a quicksilver pool.

But the life of the city was as fleeting as its very being was fantastic. In 1010, just 74 years after its conception, the Berbers attacked and burned it. From that moment on, its marble and jasper and lavish appointments were systematically plundered to become part of other Islamic structures on the Iberian peninsula and in North Africa.

The excavation has been carefully done and is now proceeding apace. At the entrance is a small display of fragments and relics, but the more important pieces have found a home in Córdoba's Archaeological Museum.

According to numerous Arab chroniclers, Medina Azahara, the most beautiful of all sights in all *al-Andalus*, was a formidable rival to the monuments of Baghdad and Constantinople and, as such, a fitting fixture for the then capital of the western Muslim world.

Medina Azahara.

GRANADA

Dale Limosna, Mujer,
Que no hay en la vida nada
Como la pena de ser
Ciego en Granada.

Give him alms, lady, alms,
For there is no pain in life so cruel
As to be blind in Granada.

Inscribed on the ramparts of the legendary Alhambra, these words point to the beauty of the setting that distinguishes **Granada** from Seville and Córdoba.

Nature was generous here, endowing the city with much greenery and placing it at the foot of three mountain spurs, from which it gracefully stretches up toward luminous blue skies against the blue-green backdrop of the Sierra Nevada to the southeast. Bounding the city to the west is a broad, fertile *vega* (plain). To the north, the dainty Darro, a mountain stream, flows through the city between two of its three picturesque hills, those of the **Alhambra** and the **Albaicín**. The third hill, **Sacromonte**, is due north of the Alhambra.

After the relative flatness of Seville and Córdoba, Granada's hills are a welcome change of scenic pace. The world is three-dimensional once again not only topographically but climatically, for almost all year you can see snow on the Sierra Nevada, a popular winter retreat for skiers.

While Seville sprawls open-ended under the abundant Andalusian sunshine and Córdoba goes about its business with a minimum of fuss, Granada savours in its municipal valleys the romantic promise of the three hills that are the pillars of its tourism trade and the core of its own unique character.

Early history: Granada, the last stronghold and longest-running kingdom of the Moors in Spain, began life as the obscure Iberian settlement of Elibyrge in the 50th century BC. From there it went on to become the equally obscure Illiberis of the Romans and Visigoths.

It is to the Moors, then, that it owes a debt of gratitude for its current national and international stature. Its name derives from the Moorish "Karnattah" and not from the Spanish word for pomegranate (*granada*), which it has nevertheless adopted as the city arms.

While Seville and Córdoba both tasted wealth and glory under the Romans, Granada first knew grandeur as a provincial capital during the time of the Caliphs of Córdoba. As Córdoba's prominence waned with the fall there of the Umayyads in 1031, Granada's political stock began to rise. For some 60 years the city was the capital of an independent kingdom, but successive inroads by the Almoravids eventually resulted in its integration into the kingdom of Seville.

When Jaén fell to the Christians in 1246 under the relentless assaults of Ferdinand III, Ibn al-Ahmar moved his capital to Granada and, as Mohammed I, founded the Nasrid Dynasty that ruled for 250 years.

Golden Age: During this "golden age" under the Moors, the Jewish presence in

Left, entering the Alhambra in Granada. **Right**, the Alhambra's Court of the Lions.

Granada was important and strong. In fact, for a time Granada was known as the "City of the Jews". Here, as elsewhere in Muslim Spain, the Jews were doctors and philosophers and even diplomats and generals.

Politically, however, Mohammed I found it expedient to remain on friendly terms with Christian Castile, and even went so far as to help Ferdinand III capture Seville, which little helped the *granadinos* ingratiate themselves hereinafter with the *sevillanos*.

For the first time in its life, Granada was indisputably on top. In the wake of successive Christian victories in Córdoba, Seville and elsewhere throughout *al-Andalus*, Muslim refugees flocked to Granada, contributing to the trade and commerce of this up-and-coming kingdom.

As surrounding Muslim kingdoms failed, Granada reaped an unprecedented prosperity. The fertile *vega* to the west enjoyed elaborate irrigation. Science, arts and the humanities flourished. Out of this impressive synergy of material, intellectual, and spiritual well-being was born the greatest triumph of Moorish art, the Alhambra.

During this period Granada's population swelled to 200,000, over four times that of the London of its day and just shy of its current headcount.

Love affair: Then under Muley Hassan (1462–85) it all started to unravel over a family affair. Hassan fell in love with a Christian and entertained thoughts of repudiating his queen Ayesha, mother of his son Boabdil, for the beautiful Zoraya. Conjugal jealousy and concern for the regal inheritance of her son caused Ayesha to flee the city, which was already torn by feuds between the Abencerrajes, in support of her, and the Zegris, in support of Zoraya.

Mother and son soon returned, however, to dethrone Hassan and his brother, weakening the kingdom. Preying upon this weakness, Ferdinand V of Aragón captured Boabdil, the Boy King (*El Rey Chico*), offering him liberty at the price of remaining passive while the Catholic Monarchs gobbled up more **Arabic lettering over a Granada café.**

and more of the Moorish territory.

When in late 1491 Ferdinand and Isabella beat down the door of Granada, the city's spirit had already been broken and Boabdil put up but a token resistance. By 2 January 1492, the capture of the sole remaining stronghold of Muslim Spain was complete.

As the cross and banner of Castile cast their first Christian shadows across the 9th-century Alcazaba, Boabdil and his followers retired to the Alpujarras mountains. As Boabdil turned for a final look at the flickering glory of Granada, his mother allegedly reproved him, saying: "You weep like a woman for what you could not hold as a man." To this day that very spot is known as the *Suspiro del Moro*, the Moor's Sigh.

Unfortunately, the resounding Godspeed that reverberated throughout Christendom with the fall of Granada never came to fruition. Religious intolerance culminating with the expulsion of the *moriscos* in 1609 drained the city of its most enterprising citizens and the glory they had wrought. By 1800, its

The Alhambra represented exotic Spain for 19th-century travellers.

population had dropped to just 40,000.

But like the rest of Andalusia, Granada is again enjoying a new prosperity resulting from improved irrigation and intense agricultural activity. Also important are the visitors who enthuse over the artistic legacy that is the swansong of the Moors. Here, after 781 years of rule, Spain's Moors went out with an architectural bang.

The Alhambra: "Al Qal'a al-Hambra", "the Red Fort", sits, the only surviving monument of Moorish Granada's great artistic outpouring, on a scarped ridge crowning a wooded hill.

No amount of description can prepare you for its great playfulness or do justice to its exquisite delicacy and proportions. Proclaimed one of the unofficial wonders of the world, it is the epitome of Moorish imagination and artistry, the consummate expression of a sophisticated culture. For many, it serves as a kind of bridge between the Oriental and Western minds, a personal point of contact with the magical world found in the tales of the *Arabian Nights*.

Its pleasing splendour resides not in the architectural structures themselves, but in the masterful ornamentation that makes them seem almost an apparition, in the intricate delicacy of its carved wooden ceilings, the lace-like reliefs of its plaster walls, the repeated motifs of interlaced arabesques and the finely perforated tracery of the arched arcades on slender columns of white marble.

Knowing a good thing when they saw it, the Catholic Monarchs had the Alhambra repaired and strengthened after their 1492 conquest and used it whenever they were in town. Subsequently, Charles V, who had given the uninformed nod to the construction of the church inside Córdoba's mosque, deemed it insufficiently magnificent for him and pulled part of it down to make way for the palace he taxed the Moors to build. Beautiful in its own right as an example of the Italian Renaissance style, his palace is nevertheless incongruous in its Aladdin's lamp setting.

The **Alcazaba** at the western extremity of Alhambra Hill was a 9th-century Moorish citadel. Today, its vista takes in the palace, the Generalife, the Albaicín and Sacromonte sections of Granada, and the Sierra Nevada.

The royal residence of the Moors within the Alhambra is highlighted by the **Court of the Myrtles**, and the **Court of the Lions**. The former is an open court 360 ft by 255 ft (110 metres by 78 metres) bisected by a narrow fishpond tucked between hedges of myrtle. At either end, within the arcaded alcoves, you can see fine stalactite vaulting.

Off the northern end of this court is the lofty **Sala de los Embajadores**, the audience chamber of the Moorish kings. A dado of *azulejos* underscores the intertwining polychrome patterns and inscriptions stamped upon the stucco. Pairs of horseshoe windows admit enchanting views of Granada. And topping it all off is a domed ceiling of cedarwood.

Leading off the southern end is the Court of the Lions (measuring 90 ft by 50 ft, or 28 metres by 15 metres), built

Granada from the gardens of the Generalife.

around a massive antique fountain resting on the backs of 12 diminutive grey marble lions.

Off its northern end is the **Sala de las Dos Hermanas**, containing the most elaborate of the Alhambra's honeycomb cupolas. This one is said to comprise over 5,000 cells.

Washington Irving: Some 19th-century writers were fortunate enough to spend some time in the Alhambra. During his three-month stay in 1829, Washington Irving began his *Tales of the Alhambra,* a collection of romantic sketches of the Moors and Spaniards that continues to sell well in Granada's souvenir shops. Richard Ford, author of the *Hand-Book for Travellers in Spain,* paid the palace a visit in the summers of 1831 and 1833; and George Borrow, author of *The Bible in Spain*, visited in 1836.

East of the royal apartments are the terraced **Partal Gardens** and charming **Torre de las Damas**.

But this account barely scratches the surface of the vast resources of delight embedded in the Alhambra's many rooms and alcoves; its capacity to impress and astound is seemingly limitless, taxing to the utmost even those with the keenest eye for detail.

Gardens of seduction: Adjoining the Alhambra and overlooking both it and the city are the grounds of the former summer palace of the sultans, the **Generalife**, dating from 1250. Blessed with gardens that far outclass the sparse beauty of its restored buildings, this palace is cool and green and full of restful pools and murmuring fountains.

Known in Arabic as *Jennat al-Arif*, meaning "garden of the architect" (who, by the way, remains unknown), it is filled with statuesque cypresses, diminutive shrubs, orange trees, hedges and flowers. Rumour has it that Boabdil's sultana kept trysts with her lover Hamet in the enclosed **Patio de los Cipreses**. Who can blame them? This garden is a veritable invitation to indiscretion.

The **Patio de la Acequia**, within the gardens, has pretty pavilions at either end linked on one side by a gallery and

Geraniums in the Albaicín.

on the other by the palace apartments.

At some point be sure to pass along the **Camino de las Cascadas**, where runnels of water cascade down a series of conduits. Every summer from 15 June to 15 July, the International Music and Dance Festival is staged in the grounds of the Generalife.

Royal tombs: Proud of their conclusive victory over the Moors, the Catholic Monarchs wished to be buried in the city where Muslim Spain met its final demise. So a decorative royal chapel was built between 1506 and 1521, and Ferdinand and Isabella now share this mausoleum with Philip the Handsome and Juana "The Mad". Many of their royal accessories are on display, and hanging in the sacristy are many works from Queen Isabella's personal art collection, containing Flemish, Spanish and Italian paintings of the 15th century.

The pretentious **Cathedral** adjoins the Royal Chapel. Begun in 1523 in the Gothic style and continued in 1528 in the early-Renaissance style, it has been described as "one of the world's archi-

tectural tragedies, one of the saddest of wasted opportunities". Not completely finished until 1714, it is overall a rather awkward and tasteless structure.

Take five: Sightseeing in Granada always seems to be more intense, more all-consuming than in either of the other grand cities of the south. Perhaps it's the desire to drink in every last detail of the Alhambra, or to spend an afternoon just smelling the flowers of the Generalife, or to see yet again the small house of **Manuel de Falla**, just below the Alhambra, which is now a museum.

Whatever it is, there just doesn't seem to be enough time left over to give the many cafés and bars of Granada their proper due.

Especially good value in the heart of the city is the Spanish custom of dropping into a bar or three for *tapas*. Wine bars specialising in Andalusian vintages serve a drink popular with *granadinos* called *falleza*, a mixture of sweet Málaga wine and soda water.

In the heart of the city are also any number of cafés outfitted with marble columns and counters that evoke images of handlebar moustaches and pomaded hair, but in reality they are frequented by little old ladies in floral-printed dresses aggressively fanning themselves in summer alongside black-leather-clad punks sipping their *café con leche* (coffee with milk). In the evening, crowds congregate at the **Plaza Bibarrambla** behind the cathedral, which was once the site of medieval jousts and bullfights.

Albaicín: This quarter, the oldest part of Granada, covers a slope facing the Alhambra on the north side of the Darro. It was home to the first fortress of the Moors and the haven to which they fled when the Christians reconquered the city. Today it offers the typical tangle of Andalusian alleys and simple whitewashed homes that might not be so simple at all on the inside. Often the area's long walls signal some luxuriant gardens discreetly enclosed for privacy.

The **Mirador de San Nicolás** offers a postcard view of the Alhambra that is particularly striking at sunset. Farther up, beyond the ruins of the Moorish

Born of Granada's gypsies, flamenco is the true song and dance of the south.

walls, is the **Mirador of San Cristóbal**. En route, you will come across a number of Moorish houses. In the **Calle del Agua**, note No. 37.

Sacromonte: The hillside opposite the Generalife has long been a gypsy enclave. Its character is changing and most gypsy families have moved away. But every evening gypsies stage flamenco shows in their caves. It is strictly tourist fare, but among the performers there could be one destined for international fame as more than one flamenco great has started his career here.

At first glance flamenco seems anything but subtle: shrill singing, foot stomping, the clacking of castanets. But the emotional thread that binds song and dance is as ephemeral as gossamer.

Shaped by influences as far removed in time and spirit as the migration of the Indo-Pakistani gypsies and the colonisation of Cuba, flamenco is a musical idiom for an affair of the heart. The song is akin to the sound of a howling wind reaching forth in gusts and fluttering tones. The guitar is melancholy and bold. The dance is proud, haughty and aggressive. Between mortal pain and vital joy, flamenco feels. To Spain's gypsies, it is a way of life.

For reasons largely known, gypsies began emigrating *en masse* from northwestern India between the 8th and 9th centuries, their numbers increasing when Tamerlane expelled them in the 14th century. Many found their way to Spain where their rhythms and music mixed with those of the Arabs and Jews to forge flamenco.

When newly united Spain began persecuting its Jews and Moors, it went after the gypsies as well. Out of the shared isolation and fear of these refugees, flamenco grew.

Federico García Lorca: Born in 1898, 11 miles (17 km) from Granada and raised in the city, García Lorca, one of this century's greatest Spanish poets and dramatists, saw the gypsy as symbolising the most profound elements in the Andalusia psyche. His *Gypsy Ballads*, published in 1928, brought him national fame.

But his political views – and his homosexuality – made him many enemies in his home town. Ill-advisedly, he returned to Granada at the start of the Civil War. He was arrested by the Nationalists, who had seized power, and executed. A memorial park now marks the spot where he was shot, near Viznar, just outside the city.

Only after the return of democracy was it possible to speak freely of Lorca's murder and for his work to receive the attention it deserved. His plays, often based on folk themes, such as *Blood Wedding* and *Yerma*, are widely produced and some have been adapted for films. His birthplace at **Fuente Vaqueros** is now a museum, and the Huerta de San Vincente, an old farmhouse on Granada's outskirts where he wrote several famous works, is also to be opened to the public.

Lorca often left Granada, but always yearned to return. He once said of these leave-takings: "It will always be like this. Before and now. We must leave, but Granada remains. Eternal in time, but fleeting in these poor hands…"

Federico García Lorca.

SOUTH TO GIBRALTAR

Within the irregular triangle defined by Seville, Córdoba, Granada and the Mediterranean Sea lies much to be seen that is little known to the general tourist population. This is the Andalusian heartland, the province of the *pueblo* where the spice of life is simplicity, peace and home hospitality.

Whether you spend your holiday vagabonding from village to village or simply make inland excursions from the coast, you will marvel at the spontaneous beauty and variety of Spain's landscape. Like set changes in the theatre, Andalusia's villages and vistas seem to spring suddenly out of thin, dry air. Now you *don't* see it, now you *do.*

The only redundant element in this ever-shifting scene is the ubiquitous olive tree. The first hundred groves are interesting; the first thousand, a curiosity. But when it seems that you've seen tens of thousands, the novelty begins to wear thin. Fortunately, at one turning in the road they grace plains; at the next, gentle slopes; then suddenly they cling to a steep mountainside. Somehow their ubiquity never succumbs to monotony.

The white towns: The white towns are the innumerable small villages of the Andalusian hinterland whose sparkling whitewashed houses cap the mountaintops or slide down their slopes like wilting whipped cream topped with burnt-orange cherries. The Ministry of Tourism thoughtfully publishes a map of these towns, indicating the major routes that crisscross the provinces of Cádiz, Málaga and Granada, as well as some of the dead-end spurs leading to the more remote towns.

All along these winding secondary roads, the fields and trees, wild flowers and donkeys come to the road's very edge to greet you.

The warmth and hospitality of the rural Spaniard can be overwhelming. The visitor may wander into an olive grove at midday and be invited to share the workers' hearty lunch of coarse

Andalusian olive groves.

peasant bread, cheese, sausages and fortifying red wine.

Then, should you lack for formal accommodation in your white-town wanderings, you'll surely find a family willing to rent you a comfortable spare room for the night by making inquiries at one of the local bars.

Common to all these towns nowadays is a very special brand of serenity. But it wasn't always so. You'll notice that many of the white towns share the tag *de la frontera* ("of the border"), because often throughout Andalusia's ping-pong history they found themselves on the contentious frontier between Christianity and Islam.

Arcos and Jerez: Between Seville and Cádiz, two notable towns are **Arcos de la Frontera** and **Jerez de la Frontera.**

Arcos, a sizeable town of some 25,000 inhabitants, sits on a sharp ridge above a loop of the **Guadalete River**. Steep streets lead up to the panoramic *parador* looking out across the mottled browns and greens of Andalusia's farmland and the blue of a large lake.

The rolling landscape between Jerez and the Atlantic, known as The Sherry Triangle, is ideally suited to raising the grapes that the wineries of Jerez convert into extraordinary sherries and brandies. The brand names are quite familiar: González Byass, Pedro Domecq, Sandeman. Tours and tastings are informative and readily intoxicating.

At the beginning of September, Jerez's 167,000 inhabitants are joined by many visitors in celebrating the Wine Harvest Festival where local wines are amply sampled and soberly judged.

But more important still is the city's annual *Feria del Caballo* (Horse Show) at the start of May, following on the heels of Seville's *Feria de Abril*. Proud of its pure-bred line of Carthusian horses, Jerez shows them off in racing, dressage and carriage competitions. All year round these handsome Arabian animals can also be seen strutting their stuff at the **Andalusian School of Equestrian Arts** where they are put through much the same paces as the horses of the Spanish Riding School in

White town of Caseres.

Vienna. Performances are usually limited to holidays and other special occasions, but visitors can watch practice sessions between 11am and 1pm.

Jerez also offers a well-endowed **Clock Museum**, the bare-bones remains of an 11th-century *alcázar* and Moorish baths.

Bandido **country:** Heading inland from the coast towards **Ronda**, the countryside gradually grows wilder. Last century, travelling here meant taking your life in your hands. The hills were full of highwaymen. During and after the Civil War, the more remote of these villages harboured Republican refugees. Of course, the bravura of the *bandido* is now but a thing of legend, and the restoration of democracy has liberated any lingering exiles.

To reach **Castellar de la Frontera**, a side road climbs up a rocky hillside, passing through private yards and public chicken crossings along the way. The archetypal castle stands crumbling, deserted, devoid of all purpose, like a splendid wedding gown yellowing forgotten in an attic. The next castle, too, sits on its own hilltop, crumbling. At its feet the town of **Jimena de la Frontera** spills like white paint down the hillside where mules graze below on the steep, grassy slopes.

Between Jimena and Ronda, a distance of about 35 miles (56 km), stop somewhere by the roadside and indulge your senses. The scent of herbs perfumes a silence smooth as silk.

Cliff dwellers: Whether you approach **Ronda** from the north or south, you are given no clues that you are about to enter a bustling town of 30,000 perched on a rocky bluff with sheer walls falling away a dramatic 600 ft (180 metres) on three sides. A deep ravine some 300 ft (90 metres) wide divides the old and new sections.

Near the **Puente Nuevo** that links the old and new towns a path leads down to a fine view of this bridge that spans the vertiginous gorge. Built in the 18th century, it is beautifully unobtrusive in design, allowing the magnificent scenery to shine through. Thanks to its auspi-

Decanting sherry in a Jerez *bodega*.

Ronda.

cious position, Ronda was to a large extent impregnable and remained the capital of an isolated Moorish kingdom until 1485.

The 18th-century bullring in the new town is one of the oldest in Spain and contains an interesting **Bullfight Museum** displaying suits of lights, documents, photos, posters and Goya prints pertaining to this uniquely Spanish art.

It was here in Ronda that bullfighting on foot first began. Earlier, as the sport of nobles, it had been practised strictly on horse-back. According to Collins and Lapierre in their book, *Or I'll Dress You in Mourning*, it was in Ronda that "During one of these spectacles, at the beginning of the 18th century, a noble and his horse were upended by a bull's charge. As the bull poised to drive those horns into the nobleman's body, one of the village poor leaped into the ring. Using his flat-brimmed Andalusian hat as a lure, he drew the bull away from the helpless rider… [and thus began] the ritual of the modern bullfight, a conflict between a bull, a dismounted man, and the lure of a fluttering piece of cloth."

Cut-throat den: Throughout the Serranía de Ronda, the mountain range surrounding the city, are more storybook white towns. **Grazalema**, 20 miles (30 km) west of Ronda, boasts that it gets more rain than anywhere else in Spain. Long a haunt of smugglers and brigands, it was described by Ford as a "cut-throat den".

Not far away, through wild, pine-clad sierras, at the foot of a mountain, lies the bigger **Ubrique** (14,000 inhabitants), noted for its leatherwork. Also in the neighbourhood is the village of El Bosque, with its trout hatcheries.

Most of these villages have spectacular settings, but that of **Zahara** ("de la Sierra" to distinguish it from Zahara de los Atunes on the Costa de la Luz) is truly breath-taking. A brilliant beacon of white, it stands on a steep crag northwest of Ronda. Neat, bright and whiter than white, it offers another ancient castle and superb views.

In contrast, much of the village of **Setenil** huddles in a chasm, its houses

built right under menacing lips of rock.

North of Málaga, **Antequera** is an attractive town with 28,000 inhabitants and innumerable churches and convents. Seek out the ruined Moorish Castle, near the 16th-century church Santa María la Mayor, for a fine view. To the east you will see a curiously shaped rock, the Peña de los Enamorados, which looks like a human face in profile. It gets its name from a legend of two thwarted lovers who hurled themselves off the top.

Antequera's most unusual attractions are three dolmens, or ancient burial chambers, which were constructed with huge slabs of rock around 2000 BC. The Cuevas de Menga and Viera are close together on the edge of town, while the Cueva de Romeral is down the road near a defunct sugar factory, where a guardian is on duty.

Costa del Sol: Most of the Sunshine Coast is in Málaga province, running from east of Gibraltar to the province of Granada. Development has been heavy – often excessive – all along the coast. However, there are still some nooks and crannies where you can avoid the crowds, as in the western section between Gibraltar and San Pedro where resorts are relatively scattered. From then on the pace quickens and the crowds thicken, with lush golf courses interspersed with luxury villas.

The area between the flashy marina **Puerta Banus** and **Marbella** is known as the Golden Mile and is the playground of showbiz celebrities, sheikhs, millionaires, royalty and bullfighters. Expensive restaurants, a casino, signs in Arabic and a mosque testify to the presence of Middle East oil money.

The coast goes down-market approaching **Fuengirola**. From there to Málaga tourist traffic is intense. Highrise hotels and aprtment blocks crowd the water's edge, summer beaches are packed with bodies and discos and bars compete raucously, reaching a climax at **Torremolinos**, which was a poor fishing village until the early 1960s when it was "discovered" and the cement-mixers moved in.

Donkey taxis: Up in the mountains just behind the coast the white town of **Mijas**, once a quaint mountain village, now uses its donkeys for photo opportunities rather than for farming and seems to have more shops than residences.

Málaga (pop. 550,000) boasts it is the capital of the Costa del Sol. However, it is not a tourist resort but a bustling, colourful port which was founded by the Phoenicians and whose people pride themselves on enjoying life. You can visit the house where Picasso was born, on the Plaza de la Merced, try some character-packed *tapa* bars and, for fine views, climb up to the Gibralfaro, a Moorish castle with a parador next door.

If west of Málaga there is too much going on, to the east there is relative peace and quiet – and a lot of Moorish towers, intensive cultivation and a spectacular cliff-side switchback coastal road, which can be slow going.

Underground art: Nerja is one of the larger resorts on this part of the coast and offers some vast caves nearby. On display inside are some of the Palaeo-

Costa del Sol.

lithic remains discovered here along with photos of the excavations. Also, over 500 cave paintings have been uncovered here, but will be accessible only to researchers until study of them has been completed.

A 1½-mile (2-km) path leads through the colourfully lit caverns, representing about one-fifth of the area projected to be opened to the public. As yet, the full extent of this underground wonderland remains unknown. But what there is, is wonder enough. It is like an underground cathedral in an abstract Gaudí style with stalactite pipe organs and stalagmite spires. And here and there one seems to glimpse the hand of Dalí. Every July these bizarre natural sculptures are the backdrop for an international festival of concerts and ballet performances.

Salobreña, raised on a rock above a sea of sugar cane, is yet another white-walled coastal village, but its special situation between the mountains and the sea makes it well worth a look. It is capped by yet another Moorish castle, which has been handsomely restored.

Port city: Modern construction totally lacking in charm lines the narrow isthmus leading to the 3,000-year-old heart of **Cádiz**, the oldest inhabited city of the western world. It is hard to believe that the population of Cádiz is almost the same as that of Jerez, for the density and intense activity of this town suggest a populace far surpassing that of the tranquil and sprawling Jerez.

But this is a city that has repeatedly lost its *raison d'être* and is getting decidedly seedy round the edges, especially in the old quarter.

Its safe inner harbour first attracted the Phoenicians, who established "Gadir" as early as 1100 BC. Known to the Greeks as "Gadeira", its prime stocks in trade in the 7th century BC were tin and amber. In 501 BC came the Carthaginians, followed later by the Romans under whom the city of "Gades" grew rich. When Rome fell, so did Gades, which for the succeeding Visigoths and Moors was little more than an insignificant port of entry.

Windsurfers at Tarifa, near Cádiz.

With the discovery of America, Cádiz rose again to become the wealthiest port in western Europe and, as a result, the target of attack for the Barbary corsairs and the envious English naval fleet. Sir Francis Drake burned ships at anchor here in 1587, delaying the sending of the Armada and boasting afterwards that he "had singed the King of Spain's beard".

With shipbuilding in decline, Cádiz has been forced to attract other industries, including car-manufacturing. Fishing is important and fish farms have been established around the bay. Not surprisingly, the city is famed for its fresh seafood and a visit to one of the better restaurants is recommended.

The **cathedral**, a grandiose structure capped by a dome of golden tiles, was described by Townsend as "a disgrace to taste" and by Richard Ford as "a stranded wreck on a quicksand". Restoration work has been going on for some time. An impressive collection of church treasures can be viewed and in the crypt lies the tomb of composer Manuel de Falla, a Cádiz native, whose music is highly evocative of the magic of Andalusia.

In the **Oratorio de la Santa Cueva** are some Goya works, but you need patience to gain entry. **San Felipe Neri** church is a place of pilgrimage for democracy-loving Spaniards, since it was here that parliament gathered in 1812 to proclaim a liberal constitution.

Despite its vacillating fortunes and the ramshackle appearance of some quarters, the *gaditanos* love their town and have a reputation for being among the liveliest of Andalusians. Many leading flamenco artists hail from the Bay of Cádiz and the city runs wild every year during the crazy days of Carnival.

The coast of light: From Cádiz to Tarifa stretches the southernmost section of the Atlantic Costa de la Luz, which starts at **Huelva**. **Vejer de la Frontera**, one of the prettiest of the white towns, lies just off the coastal highway on the sheer cliff of a mountain. Here are a partially restored castle and some long-forgotten windmills facing the sea.

The Rock of Gibraltar.

Tarifa, at the southernmost tip of the coast, is a point of departure for ferries connecting Spain with the continent of Africa and a mecca for windsurfers.

The Rock: Continuing along the coast past the undistinguished town of **Algeciras**, the major kicking-off point for Africa, you eventually come to disputed **Gibraltar**. Since the border with Spain was reopened after the 1969 Spanish blockade, only a passport and valid car insurance are required to allow you to cross on to the limestone rock over the airport runway that bisects the narrow isthmus. If anyone stops you as you approach the border and offers, for a small commission, to facilitate your getting an insurance card, drive on. This is a time-consuming scam. All rental cars are insured, and anyone driving into Spain is required to have proof of valid car insurance before actually crossing the border.

Since 1704 Gibraltar, one of the ancient Pillars of Hercules, has been a bone of contention between Britain and Spain. But before that it had been passed back and forth a number of times between the Spaniards and the Moors, who first took it in 711 under the Berber leadership of Tariq ibn Zeyad and gave it its name "Gebel Tarik", the mountain of Tariq. The Moor's Castle, now in ruins, was his legacy. In 1462, the Spanish regained it one last time before the British seized it in 1704.

Despite periodic importuning by the Spanish, and despite a high Spanish-origin ethnic population, the British won't budge. They stand firm in carrying out the wishes of the populace as reflected in a 1967 referendum, whose vote was 12,138 to 44 in favour of keeping it British.

Peaking at 1,396 ft (425 metres), Gibraltar measures less than 3 sq. miles (7 sq. km) and is home to some 30,000. The strategic strait it controls links the Atlantic and Mediterranean and is 36 miles (58 km) long and 8 miles (13 km) wide at its narrowest point.

Wildlife: Oddly enough, this seemingly barren rock enjoys some fame for its wildlife. The origin of its distinctive Barbary apes is not known, but they are not found on the Spanish mainland. Legend has it that the British will remain as long as the apes survive. When extinction threatened them in 1944, Churchill ordered reinforcements.

More impressive still is the extraordinary variety of birds that stop here during their annual migrations to and from Europe. Among them are honey buzzards, griffons, black storks and short-toed eagles.

A curious military feat are the Upper Galleries tunnelled into the rock at the time of the Great Siege by France and Spain between 1779 and 1783. By the end of this war the tunnel measured 370 ft (113 metres).

Curious, too, is the evident cultural mixture on the Rock. Arab women in full-length dress and modified *chador* cross paths with British officers, Spanish-speaking merchants and dark-skinned descendants of the Moors. Equally mixed are the linguistics. In a local bar the TV plays in Spanish, the radio in English and the bartender speaks with a hybrid accent.

One of Gibraltar's Barbary apes.

CANARY ISLANDS

Marooned out in the Atlantic is an isolated archipelago, often forgotten in any survey of Spain. Some of the islands in this archipelago are razor-sharp, steep and volcanic, their tops in cloud; a couple of them are slivers of sand, like slices cut at a stroke from nearby mainland Africa and rolled flat by blistering sunshine. This archipelago boasts one of the highest mountains in Europe, always capped by snow; it has beaches of black sand and seas of volcanic lava that are still hot, and it has moss-cloaked and mist-shrouded forests which have survived from the tertiary era.

These are the Canary Islands, and are perhaps better known to Europeans escaping the mid-winter blues than to Spaniards. They are Europe's equivalent of Hawaii, and no fewer than seven million tourists come here every year, outnumbering the locals by five to one. They are attracted by a remarkably consistent climate and all-year-round sunshine: the average temperature of 17 degrees centigrade in winter increases to 24 degrees in summer, with a cooling offshore breeze.

From having been an isolated cul-de-sac of Spain, the Canaries have been transformed by tourism into a diverse, multi-cultural society. The seas are covered in sails and condominiums cling to the slopes. The well-equipped resorts are little cities in themselves, with a babel of different languages filling the streets and the bars: there are whole districts that are almost entirely British, Dutch, French, German, Scandinavian and of course Spanish; you can buy genuine fish and chips made by a man from Macclesfield, or genuine sauerkraut made by a man from Stuttgart.

And yet, despite this annual invasion, there are still plenty of surprises on the islands. Even the origin of the name is unexpected: it is not the sweet-singing birds that are celebrated, but dogs – *canes* in Latin – which the islands' conquerors discovered roaming wild in great numbers. Some historians suggest that these 'isles of the dogs' were virtually unpopulated when the Spanish first arrived in the 1600s; a more likely story is that the unfortunate Guanches, the original islanders, were all but wiped out in the conquest. Their language has gone – unless you count *silbo*, the whistling language still practised on La Gomera, which supposedly developed after the conquistadors cut off the survivors' tongues.

Since then, all sorts of other things have happened on these shores which haven't entirely come to the world's attention: Columbus interrupted his momentous voyage of discovery here to lie for a couple of months in the arms of the Countess of Gomera; Nelson lost his arm here trying to capture Spanish bullion; and General Franco launched the Spanish Civil War from here.

There are seven islands in the Canaries: Gran Canaria, Fuerteventura and Lanzarote in the Eastern Province, and Tenerife, La Palma, La Gomera and El Hierro in the Western Province. Only a couple of centuries ago the Spaniards

Preceding pages: Puerto de la Cruz, Tenerife. **Left**, beach on Tenerife. **Right**, local transport.

believed there were eight; they even mapped the eighth, which they called San Borondon, and visited it regularly. The myth continues, but the elusive San Borondon has not yet been picked up on any satellite picture.

The Eastern Canaries: Although Tenerife and Gran Canaria share equal status within the autonomous region of the Canary Islands, the latter is currently the seat of local government, as well as the main commercial and communications centre. **Gran Canaria** is the third largest of the islands (592 sq. miles, 1,532 sq. km) and has a population of 600,000. Its capital city **Las Palmas de Gran Canaria** (pop. 355,000) covers its northern tip.

Las Palmas has a long sea-frontage like Havana's, the largest port in Europe in terms of sheltered water, and was once a major stepping stone on the long haul to South America; it's also both aristocratic and seedy in the way that Havana once was, with broken ships on the Corniche and whispers on the street. In addition, Las Palmas has one of the best downtown beaches of any city in the world; you can emerge dripping from the surf on Playa de las Canteras one moment, and be inside a Las Palmas department store the next – still dripping. Also notable in Las Palmas is La Vegueta, the old quarter to the south, built in Spanish colonial style. The cathedral, Columbus' house and museum are located here.

The south of the island is the main tourist destination, with more hours of guaranteed sunshine and resorts like Playa del Ingles (350 restaurants and 50 discos) and Maspalomas with its famous sand dunes. Until 20 years ago the south was a remote, arid spot; now the whole of the southern shoreline is virtually one continuous urbanisation. Beyond the more upmarket resort of Mogan, the coast returns to its semi-wild state, with locals still pursuing their livelihoods of fishing or agriculture. In the northwest the two attractive towns of Agaete and Galdar are particularly active in local cultural life, with festivals and Guanche remains.

The Vegueta district of Las Palmas.

Gran Canaria has a wild, steep and scenic interior, rising to 6,496 ft (1,980 metres) at the Pico de las Nieves. There is an excellent view of the central summits from Cruz de Tejeda, where the parador is situated. In these inland areas there are still cave villages, particularly Artenara and Atalaya, and the island's most famous ravine – the Barranco de Guayadeque – has cave restaurants.

Volcano island: The fourth largest of the seven islands **Lanzarote** (307 sq. miles, 795 sq. km) has a population of 50,000, vastly outnumbered by tourists. It is a destination that visitors either love or hate. At the wrong time of year, when the light is sluggish and the ground unproductive, the island looks like what it is – the scab on a volcanic wound, still bubbling hot, red and raw underneath. At other times there are moments of rare beauty in this landscape, whose sparse, minimal features can come together in a memorable way. They say that the islanders paint their windows and doors green to compensate for the lack of green in their landscape.

Lanzarote's Timanfaya National Park is a massive volcanic wasteland of mangled rock and twisted lava created by eruptions in 1730 and 1736. In Timanfaya the *malpais* or badlands are so severe that moss barely manages to grow. Park rangers give dramatic demonstrations of the continuing power of the earth, and the park's El Diablo restaurant cooks with volcanic heat.

Elsewhere on the island the prickly pear cactus is widespread, either growing wild or hosting colonies of cochineal beetle (in a kind of white dust on the side of the plant) which is used as a food dye. This was once a major industry, but synthetic colourings have all but supplanted cochineal, which is now a luxury product used by those who prefer their food colourings to be natural.

Most tourist developments on Lanzarote are tastefully done, and the majority are no more than two storeys high. Local architect Cesar Manrique is responsible for memorable features such as cave conversions (Jameos del Agua and Cuevas de los Verdes), museums

Lanzarote islanders paint their doors green.

and viewpoint restaurants (Castillo de San Gabriel and Mirador del Rio). **Arrecife**, the island's main town, has been condemned by Manrique as an urban disaster.

Dry land: The second largest of the Canary Islands at 668 sq. miles (1,731 sq. km), **Fuerteventura** also has one of the smallest populations (25,000). Like neighbouring Lanzarote and not-so-distant Africa only 60 miles (96 km) away, Fuerteventura doesn't have the height to be able to prod the passing clouds into letting go some of their water. The island is consequently very barren and sandy, and its fragile economy is based upon goats, tourists and the military (there's a Spanish foreign legion base here). The main town of **Puerto del Rosario**, which surrounds the port, is straggling and unattractive. Inland, the ancient city of Betancuria is little more than a hamlet. But Fuerteventura does also have the Canaries' best beaches.

Most of the resort areas are either on the northern tip at Corralejo, where there are two large hotels, or on the southern Jandia peninsula. The latter was at one time separated from the rest of the island by a wall, La Pared, erected by the original Guanche kings. This southern part of the island was isolated again during and after World War II, when it was given to a German by General Franco. An airstrip was built here and all islanders were excluded; rumours about what went on behind the wall are still circulating.

The Western Canaries: The western islands – Tenerife, La Palma, La Gomera and El Hierro – are taller and more beautiful than the eastern group; the latter three, little known to tourists, could together compete for the title of European Bali, with craggy *campesinos*, lush valleys, weird fiestas, brilliant sunshine and deep and ancient forests.

The largest of the islands (794 sq. miles or 2,057 sq. km), **Tenerife** has a population of 600,000 and boasts the highest mountain in the whole of Spain (El Teide). In fact, the majority of the island's bulk is the volcanic Teide, which rises to 12,188 ft (3,715 metres), with **Lighthouse on Tenerife.**

forests, villages, lush valleys and finally beaches on its lower skirts.

Tenerife's main town, **Santa Cruz de Tenerife**, is a more pleasant but rather smaller place than Las Palmas, and its shopping centres do not have the same wealth of goods. Santa Cruz is also in the shadow of the Anaga mountains, which form the northern part of the island, and conceal remarkable and rugged scenery and tiny hidden villages in their folds.

As with Gran Canaria, the main tourist resorts on Tenerife (Los Cristianos and Playa de las Americas, for example) are in the south of the island, where the sunshine is guaranteed and where the main airport is now located. The original airport, above Santa Cruz, is still in use, but it was the site of the world's worst air disaster when two Jumbo jets collided on the runway. Most international flights now arrive in the south.

There is a tradition that says that tourism to the Canaries was started by London taxi drivers, who needed somewhere sunny to go in the winter when business back home was not so busy.

In fact the history of tourism here is far longer; it really began in 1850, with the first steamship service between the islands and Cádiz. In the 1880s Mrs Olivia Stone, a formidable Victorian traveller, toured the islands on donkeyback. In a letter to *The Times* of London she wrote that "the Canaries require only to be known to be much resorted to by the English". When her book *Tenerife and its six satellites* was published, she noted with satisfaction that "visitors have poured into the islands" as a result.

Those days, of course, only gentry could afford to travel. They came in particular to Puerto de la Cruz and La Orotava in the fertile Orotava Valley on the northwestern coast, seeking the supposed health benefits of the mid-Atlantic climate. The lush valley is still known for its banana plantations, although the Canary banana is now judged too small for European supermarkets and the elegant colonial-style mansions and narrow cobbled streets are focused on tourism rather than agriculture.

La Orotava during the flower festival.

Both towns still have some of the gentility bestowed on them by the early travellers. However, because the sea of this northern coast is rough and wild, Puerto lacks one major feature that the modern tourist expects – a sandy beach. This problem has been circumvented by the elegant Lido Martianez, a series of swimming pools sculpted out of the rock at sea level by Lanzarote architect César Manrique. Canarian ingenuity doesn't stop there, either; around the top of the island from Puerto a new beach has been created at Las Teresitas with the aid of 3.5 million cubic feet of sand from the Sahara.

Tenerife's National Park is Las Canadas, the ancient crater around Teide, which has been dormant since 1798. Las Canadas is easily reached by good roads, and contains some unusual rock formations as well as a government-run *parador* and a visitors' centre. El Teide's peak is reached by a combination of a cable-car ride and 20-minute scrabble.

Best of the rest: On a clear day the other three western islands are easily visible from the top of Teide. **La Palma** is the greenest and fifth largest of the islands (281 sq. miles, 728 sq. km), and has retained much of its population of 72,000 thanks to its suitability for agriculture. The island is very steep, rising to 7,959 ft (2,426 metres) at the Roque de los Muchachos, and falling away sharply to the sea most of the way around the rocky coast, thus denying mass tourism much of a foothold.

Much of the northern part of the island is occupied by the Caldera de Taburiente, one of the largest volcanic craters in the world at 5½ miles (9km) in diameter. The Caldera is another National Park, and on its rim is the Observatorio de Astrofisica, an observatory shared by several European countries, with the largest telescope in Europe. Here the air is so clear that you can easily see the rest of the moon when the lit bit is only fingernail thick. La Palma was the scene of the most recent volcanic activity in the Canaries, when an eruption in the side of the old volcano of Antonio in 1971 formed a new cone.

En route for La Gomera.

Distinguished by being Columbus' chosen stepping-off point for the New World in 1492, things have changed little in **La Gomera** since then; this, the sixth largest island (146 sq. miles or 378 sq. km), has a population of 20,000, vastly depleted in recent years thanks to the attraction of working in tourism in Tenerife. Gomera's main town of **San Sebastian** is linked to the south of Tenerife 20 miles (32km) away by a regular shuttle ferry service, and many of the visitors to the island come on day trips.

Gomera's limited tourist areas are the Valle Gran Rey, a deep and luxuriant valley on the southeastern corner of the island, which attracts young and longer-staying backpackers, and Santiago, the site of the island's main resort development around the Hotel Tecina. Beach areas are limited: the island rises steeply to its highest point (Mt Garajonay 4,879 ft/1,487 metres) and the centre of the Garajonay National Park, which is notable for its ancient tertiary-era forest made up of moss-cloaked laurel and cedar trees.

The *parador* (government-run hotel) in San Sebastian is one of the finest in Spain; it is also likely to be the only place visitors could be sure to hear *silbo*, the whistling language once used by the Gomerans to communicate across a landscape of ravines and terraces. Now it is used by the *parador*'s gardeners.

The smallest of the islands at 107 sq. miles (277 sq. km), **El Hierro** is also the most backward and least populated (6,000 inhabitants). Cattle and livestock farming are the mainstay of the community, and wine is still made on the island. The principal town, **Valverde** (literally "green valley") is the only island capital situated inland, indicative of the fact that Hierro has always laid greater stress on its agriculture than on seaborne trade.

Hierro also has its own massive volanic crater, although one side has since collapsed into the sea; the result is El Golfo, a calm, wide gulf, and the island's most peaceful spot. Actually, on El Hierro, finding peace and quiet is not a problem.

These, then, are the Canary Islands.

Balconies in La Palma.

VALENCIA

Valencia's site is enviable. Just 1½ miles (3 km) from the Mediterranean and straddling the **Turia River**, it lies in the middle of one of Europe's most densely developed agricultural regions. The fields surrounding the city can yield three to four crops a year. Pomegranate, orange and lemon trees line the roads. Rice grows alongside sweet corn. Mulberry trees are used for silkworm production. Shimmering canals weave their way through the land, giving it life.

This is the *huerta*, a cultivated and irrigated plain that feeds the nation and that was considered by the Moors to be heaven on earth. Even the Spanish hero El Cid was taken by it. On his entry into Valencia he proclaimed: "From the day when I saw this city I found it to my liking, and I desired it, and I asked God to make me master of it."

The city he so desperately wanted had already seen the glories of four empires. Originally a Greek settlement, it was taken over by the Romans in 138 BC and turned into a retirement town for old soldiers. In 75 BC it became the capital of the colony *Valentia Edentanorum*. Chosen for its mild year-round temperatures, the Romans took advantage of the sunshine and the runoff from the surrounding mountains to turn the rich soil into some of the most efficiently irrigated farmland in their domain.

Paradise: The Visigoths and Moors knew a good thing when they saw it, and continued to improve the complex system of canals and channels. To the desert-dwelling Moors it was a paradise, and one that could effectively feed their people. They controlled the land for 500 years and built a city impressive enough to draw the Cid's attention. He conquered Valencia in 1094 but after his death it fell back under the jurisdiction of the Moors.

In 1238 the city was finally wrestled from Arab domination and incorporated into the kingdom of Aragón by James I, *El Conquistador*. The 15th century saw Valencia blossom into its Golden Age as it overtook Barcelona as the financial capital of this Mediterranean empire. Aside from its agricultural riches and its burgeoning port, the city held claim to a growing ceramic and silk industry and set up the nation's first printing press in 1474.

The city continued to prosper until 1609, when it was dealt a disastrous blow by Philip III – the expulsion of the *moriscos* from Spain. No area was as hard hit as Valencia, which lost one-third of its people, most of them farm labourers. The city never really fully recovered. While it still reigns as the nation's bread, fruit and vegetable basket, it has never regained its place as the most important Spanish port on the Mediterranean.

Its political fortunes have also gone the way of the port. It was here in 1814 that Ferdinand VII declared the Constitution defunct and restored the old monarchy. During the Civil War the city was hard hit for being the last Republican hold-out. The effects of bombardment are still visible; broken buildings leave

Preceding pages: Ibizan roof-tops; tiled kitchen in Valencia. **Left**, the Valencian *huerta*, based on Moorish irrigation. **Right**, papier-mâché giants celebrate the *fallas*.

gaping holes in otherwise normal neighbourhoods.

But the scars are easily overlooked. Signs of *huerta* wealth brighten up this rather drab city of over 800,000 people. Streets are given life by an overabundance of fruit and vegetable stands. Corns on the cob roasting on open fires turn busy corners into quick picnic spots. The main square is saved from being just another traffic jam by meticulously groomed flower stalls.

Like most main squares, the **Plaza del Ayuntamiento** lies in the centre of the city and is the location of the city hall, post office, telephone office and bus stops. Until recently this triangular plaza was called the "Plaza of the Valencian Nation". While their separatist feelings are not as strong as the Catalans' or the Basques', Valencians do not forget that the city gained its importance long before it was joined to Castile. They are proud of their own traditions and language. The language, *valenciano*, is actually a dialect of Catalan and today is being used with more and more frequency. Manifestations of this regional pride can make it easy for the visitor to get lost – most of the street signs in Spanish have been covered over with the "correct" street name handwritten in *valenciano*.

The history of this nation is told in a small museum housed on the second floor of the **Ayuntamiento** (City Hall). Unfortunately, there is nothing here regarding the Cid, since most of the exhibits date from the time of James I, who is considered by Valencians as the true saviour of the city from the Moors.

Of special interest is the first map of the city drawn at a time when Valencia, with a population of 80,000, was bigger than Barcelona, Madrid and Genova. The map, drawn in 1704, took five years to complete as the cartographer, Padre Tosca, measured the city street by street with a tape. It's still one of the most accurate city maps in existence.

Glorious food: To the north of the Plaza del País Valenciano is the **Plaza del Mercado**, site of the central market. The brick and tile market is a veritable

254

cathedral to food. The domed building with stained-glass windows and ornate doorways is over 9,600 sq. yards (8,027 sq. metres) which makes it one of the largest markets in Europe.

Across the street is the **Lonja de la Seda**, the old silk exchange, built in the 15th century for the ever-increasing mercantile industry. The prosperity that necessitated the building of a larger exchange is reflected in the elegant **Transactions Hall**. High-ceilinged and supported by eight twisted columns, the hall's delicately traced windows allow the sun to cast shadows across the red and black tiled floor. Upstairs is the old Maritime Council, or port authority.

The western windows of the upstairs hall afford a view of the church of **Santos Juanes**, a typical example of the state of most Valencian churches. Its beaten-up appearance is the consequence of two distinct events. The first occurred in the 17th and 18th centuries, when contemporary architectural taste caused elaborate Churrigueresque stucco to be applied to plain Gothic interiors. Later, many churches were fire-damaged in the Civil War. Unfortunately, what is left is a hodgepodge of half-ruined buildings.

Following **Calle de San Vicente**, a wide street that slices through the crooked lane of the old town, you'll come across three such churches before reaching the **Plaza de Zaragoza** and the jumble of architectural styles known as the cathedral.

The **cathedral**, built on the site of a Roman temple to Diana and later a Muslim mosque, was begun in 1262 in traditional Gothic style. In the 1700s its interior was covered over with a neoclassical facade, which has been removed. The west side, facing the Plaza de Zaragoza, is Italian baroque while the south door is Romanesque. The focal point of the structure is the still unfinished 15th-century octagonal bell tower known as the **Miguelete**, or *Micalet* in *valenciano*. From the top is a fine view of the glazed tile roofs of the town and of the *huerta* stretching beyond it to the nearby mountains. The

Valencian fishmonger.

cathedral museum contains a small purple agate cup purported to be the Holy Grail.

Water power: Around the corner from the Miguelete is the cathedral's **Door of the Apostles**, a 14th-century portal adorned with crumbling statuary. In this antique doorway, every Thursday at noon, the *Tribunal de las Aguas*, or Water Tribunal, meets.

Eight men, each representing one of the original irrigation canals built by the Romans over 2,000 years ago, govern the 2,300 acres (930 hectares) of the *huerta*. Any questions concerning the intricate system of canals, channels and drains must be brought before them. The tribunal, which has met without interruption for over 1,000 years, still conducts its business in *valenciano*.

The crowd which always gathers to watch the Tribunal spills into the **Plaza de la Virgen**, one of Valencia's most tranquil and attractive squares.

Taking up the east side of the plaza and connected to the cathedral by a small bridge is the chapel of **Nuestra Señora de los Desamparados** (Our Lady of the Abandoned), the patron saint of the city since the 17th century. The original image of the Virgin was carved in 1416 for the chapel of Spain's first mental institution. A replica is located beneath the cupola.

Across from the chapel is the **Generalidad Palace**, a 15th-century Gothic palace used as the assembly hall of the ancient *Cortes* and today housing the *Diputación*, or city council. The *Cortes,* a group of elected citizens whose job was to keep the nobility in check, were disbanded in 1707 by Philip V, who feared their power. One of their duties was to collect a "general" tax (so called because everyone had to pay it) and hence the name of the building. Its most notable features are the inner courtyard and an orange-tree garden that fronts the Plaza de la Virgen.

Calle de Caballeros, running north from the palace, is the old main street. Its commercial importance has waned but its former glory can be seen in the Gothic residences that are interspersed

Irrigation disputes are settled by the Water Tribunal.

256

with shoe-repair shops, fruit and vegetable stands, bars and cafés. Most of the houses have retained their beautiful patios, the sure sign of 15th-century Valencian success.

Night watchmen: The maze of streets that branch off from Caballeros form the oldest part of the city. As late as 1762, Valencia was still a network of 428 narrow streets held within fortified city walls. In 1777 the dangers of these dark alleyways gave rise to the establishment of the first corps of *serenos*, or night watchmen, who later became a standard feature of most Spanish towns.

Follow **Calle de Serranos** to the **Torres de Serranos**, a town gate built in the 1390s and one of two left standing. (The other is the **Torres de Quart** at the end of Caballeros.) The tower is a massive fortification that once formed part of the city walls, torn down in 1865. The walls, broken by 10 gateways, followed the boundaries set by the present-day streets of **Avenida de Guillem de Castro** and **Calle de Colón** on one side, and the curve of the Turia River (now a dry river bed converted into a garden) on the other.

Painting and pottery: Across the river are the **Royal Gardens** with an outdoor theatre, a small zoo and the **Fine Arts Museum**, one of the most important provincial galleries in Spain. Housed in a four-storey baroque convent, the museum's most interesting paintings are the works of Valencian Impressionists. Year-round sunshine, the colours of the *huerta* and the simple life of the farmers were suited to the impressionist brush of artists like Joaquín Sorolla.

The craft which Valencia developed into a fine art, ceramics, is represented in the **Marqués de Dos Aguas Palace** which houses the National Ceramic Museum, with over 5,000 exhibits. The industry dates back to the 13th century, when ceramic work came into use as a means of home decoration. Tapestries, which were used in colder climates to help retain heat, were never needed in Valencia and the use of *azulejos* (coloured tiles) became popular. The oldest pieces in the museum come from two villages in the *huerta*, Paterna and Manises. Their porcelain was once much sought-after by European royal families. Today only Manises keeps up its potteries.

The palace itself appears to be made of ceramic. Its grey and rust marble facade is in perfect Churrigueresque style: on either side of the alabaster entryway is a carved muscled Greek pouring water from an urn, illustrating the Marques' name.

Around the corner is the 16th-century **University**, whose library retains a copy of *Les Trobes*, the first book printed in Spain, and the **Colegio del Patriarca**, with a two-storeyed Renaissance patio and the tomb of Juan de Ribera, prosecutor of the *moriscos*.

The *fallas*: Look on almost any building in Valencia for the small plaque guaranteeing that the structure is insured against fire. Fire insurance is essential in the city with the most explosive fiestas in Spain: the *fallas*.

The custom dates back to the Middle Ages when Valencia's carpenters burned their accumulated wood shavings in huge bonfires on the eve of 19 March, the feast of St Joseph, patron of woodworkers. Over the years, the traditional woodchips were replaced with papier mâché and cardboard figures lampooning politicians, local customs and current events. For a week, 700 of these temporary works of art are on display throughout the city. The moment of truth, the *cremá*, arrives on 19 March, and the streets, plazas and balconies fill up with citizens, tourists and, most importantly, firemen. One by one the colourful images are put to the match, so that at midnight the entire city, illuminated with an orange glow, appears to be burning down.

Aside from the *fallas,* food is also taken seriously in the *huerta*. The most typical of Spanish dishes, *paella,* has its origins in the rice paddies south of the city. Replete with saffron-seasoned rice, *paella* contains a variety of meats, seafood and vegetables, depending on the cook's taste. Valencian drinks include fresh orange juice and *horchata*, a refreshing summer cooler which tastes faintly of almonds.

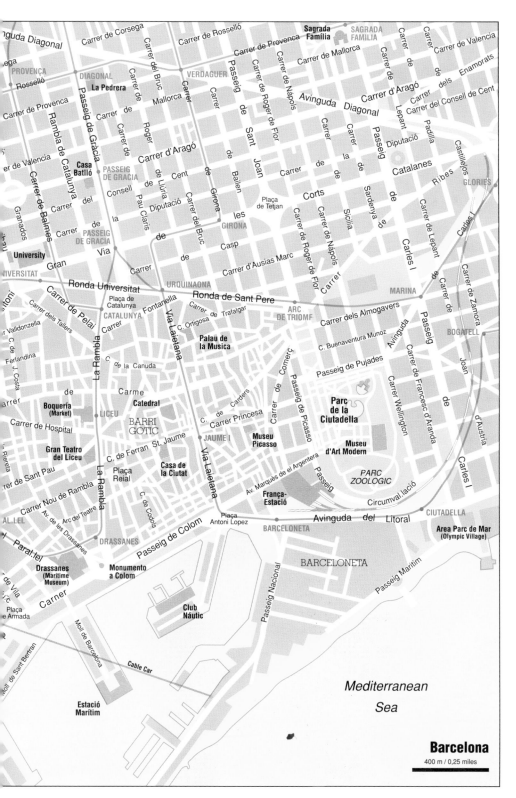

Barcelona

400 m / 0,25 miles

BARCELONA

The largest city on the Mediterranean, key port and capital of Catalonia, Barcelona is one of the most vibrant destinations in Europe. A bilingual city – Spanish and Catalan, and French too – with one foot in France and the other in traditional Spain, it seems as close to Paris, Rome and Munich as it is to Madrid, and it has long been the Spanish link to Western Europe.

The city symbolised by the radical architect Antoni Gaudí has produced other world-figures in the arts – Pablo Picasso, Joan Miró, Pablo Casals, Josep Carreras and Montserrat Caballé – and it likes to think of itself in the forefront of European fashion and design. This was the image it managed to convey in the 1992 Olympic Games, for which it was given an enormous facelift. Its fine medieval buildings were renovated, new ones put up, a ring road created and the whole city was re-orientated towards one of its most neglected assets, the sea.

Catalonia and Spain: Understanding Barcelona requires some insight into the Catalan-Spanish duality. Although about half of the city's 3½ million inhabitants have emigrated from other parts of Spain, Barcelona is historically and culturally a Catalan city, the capital of Catalonia and the seat of the Generalitat, which is the Catalan autonomous government.

Catalonia was an independent nation with a parliament – the Council of 100 – well before the formation of the Spanish State. Catalonia became a commercial power in the Mediterranean during the 14th and 15th centuries, developing a merchant class, banking and a social structure significantly different from the feudal model which continued in most of Spain. Later, while the rest of Spain colonised, mining New World wealth, Catalonia industrialised, becoming the world's fourth manufacturing power by 1850.

Catalan, a Romance language derived from the speech of the occupying Romans, is closely related to the Provençal and Langue d'Oc French spoken in southern France. The strength of Catalan culture has fluctuated with the region's political fortunes.

After uniting with the kingdom of Aragón in the 12th century, Catalonia found itself part of a new nation – Spain – when Ferdinand of Aragón married Isabella of Castile in 1469. Centuries-old privileges and institutions were suppressed by Castilian centralism over the next 300 years, most notably in 1714 when the newly installed Spanish King Philip V, grandson of Louis XIV of France, militarily seized Barcelona and abolished all local autonomous privileges. During the 19th century Catalonia's industrial success fostered new independence movements and a *renaixença* (renaissance) of Catalan nationalism. But its last experiment in autonomy was crushed by Franco's victory which ended the Spanish Civil War in 1939.

Since Franco's death in 1975, Catalonia has undergone a spectacular cul-

Left, Columbus statue by Barcelona Harbour. Right, buskers in the Gothic Quarter.

tural resurgence. Catalan, a forbidden language for 36 years, is once again taught in schools, published in books and newspapers and accepted as the co-official language. There is, as well, Catalan radio, television and cinema. The Barcelona Olympics was a high point of this new cultural golden age, with Catalan accepted as an official language.

Orientation: Bordered by the sea on one side and by the **Collserola** hills to the west, Barcelona is intersected by great avenues – the **Diagonal** and the **Passeig de Gràcia** – and punctuated by open spaces of parkland which provide welcome relief from the city's human and architectural density. The hills of Montjuïc (by the port) and Tibidabo (behind and inland) tower over the city's chaotic sprawl.

In the 19th century Barcelona broke out of the old Gothic city into the **Eixample**, the orderly grid of wide avenues planned by Idelfons Cerdà, which occupies the middle ground between the old city and its backdrop of hills.

This grid system was extended down to the sea front on the northeast side of town when the old industrial area of **Poble Nou** was pulled down to build the 2,000 apartments of the Olympic Village and the new leisure port.

Gothic Quarter: Barcelona's old city, known as the **Barri Gòtic** or Gothic Quarter, is a stunning display of solid stone, sprinkled with small shops, cafés, taverns and gourmet restaurants. Although most of the major architecture was completed between the 13th and the 15th centuries, there are traces of Roman civilisation.

Barcelona's acropolis – the highest elevation in the Barri Gòtic – was originally the Iberian village of Laia. The Romans conquered the town in 133 BC, erected the Temple of Augustus and fortified their *Mons Taber* with walls in the 4th century.

The itinerary which best clarifies the city's archaeology and history begins facing the **cathedral** at **Plaça Nova**, crosses to the left in front of the cathedral steps and continues round to the

Left, in the Gothic Quarter. **Right**, the *sardana*, the traditional Catalan dance.

right down **Carrer Tapineria** to the **Plaça de Ramon Berenguer el Gran**, which was the eastern limit of the Roman walls. After another section of Carrer Tapineria, cross through **Plaça de l'Angel** and along the **Carrer Murallas Romanes** where original sections of the Roman walls can be seen. After cutting in behind the wall to **Plaça Sant Just** and doubling back up to **Carrer Llibreteria**, the **Carrer Veguer** leads up to the **Plaça del Rei** where **Santa Agata Chapel** and the **Royal Palace** are located.

Santa Agata is an extraordinarily pure example of Catalan Gothic construction and was the chapel of the Palau Reial or Royal Palace, the residence of the Counts of Barcelona, who became kings of Aragón in 1137. The **Museum of the City of Barcelona** is the key entry point to this complex. It is built over Roman foundations which can still be seen in its basement. The **Saló del Tinell**, the early Gothic Great Hall of the Royal Palace, and the adjacent **Palau del Lloctinent** complete the

buildings around the old, regal square.

The Cathedral: Begun in 1298 in a transitional style, Barcelona's **cathedral** was completed over the next two centuries, with the exception of the main facade which was not finished until towards the end of the 19th century. The two octagonal bell towers are, perhaps, the cathedral's most monumental features, while the interior cloister with its magnolias, palms, orange trees and geese is one of the city's most beautiful spots.

The **Canonja**, **Degà** and **Ardiaca** houses which ring the square outside the cathedral, as well as the **Santa Llucia Chapel** at the corner of **Carrer del Bisbé** are also important architectural gems and should not be missed before moving up the Carrer del Bisbé toward the **Plaça Sant Jaume**. There are often guitarists or flautists along the way – usually music students – playing medieval compositions echoed and amplified by the acoustics of stone.

Seat of government: Down Carrer del Bisbé and to the right emerging into

Artist's impression of the Casa de la Ciutat.

Plaça Sant Jaume is the **Generalitat**, the seat of the autonomous Catalan government since the 14th century. Any lingering doubts about Catalonia's view of herself as a nation are quickly laid to rest with a tour of the stunningly ornate Generalitat building.

Constructed principally from the 15th to the 17th centuries, the main points of interest are the **Gothic patio** with its exterior staircase, the **Sant Jordi chapel**, the **Patí dels Tarongers** (Patio of the Orange Trees) and the **Saló Daurat** (Gilded Room), with its lovely murals of Catalonia's mountain ranges, valleys, plains and beaches.

The Plaça Sant Jaume itself is a striking work of art. At Christmas a 100-ft (30-metre) pine tree is brought in from the Pyrenees and decorated in the centre of the square.

The neoclassical facade directly across the Plaça Sant Jaume from the Generalitat is the **Casa de la Ciutat** or Town Hall. Inside the building the main elements include the black marble staircase leading to the main floor, the **Saló de Cent** (Hall of the Hundred), which was the meeting place for one of Europe's first Republican parliaments.

Sailors' church: The **Barri de Santa María** is the area around the superb **Santa María del Mar** church, a supreme example of Mediterranean Gothic architecture. Begun in 1329, Santa María del Mar was the centre of Barcelona's new seafaring and merchant community and the crowning glory of Catalonia's hegemony in the Mediterranean. "Santa María!" was one of the war cries of the Catalan sailors and soldiers as they stormed into Sicily, Sardinia and Greece.

The church is one of the simplest and most elegant structures in the city. It's three naves are vast and of similar height, reducing interior support to the bare minimum. The church's massively-tall stone columns, rose window, two bell towers and virtually all of the side chapels and stained-glass windows are exemplary. The acoustics are also worthy of note – they produce a six-second delay which is capable of converting a dulcet medieval melody into a polyphony of powerful echoes and overtones.

The **El Born** area on the eastern side of the church was the site of jousts, tournaments, processions and celebrations from the 13th to the 17th century. The house at No. 17 **Plaça del Born** is the only surviving structure of the *palau barcelonin* model of the 14th century. The others were rebuilt in the 17th and 18th centuries. The Born became the central marketplace for maritime Barcelona, its iron hangar of a market building constructed in 1874 by Josep Fontserè. More recently, the area has become popular with artists.

An immediate left turn leaving the east end of Santa María del Mar leads to **Carrer Montcada**, one of Barcelona's most aristocratic streets in the 14th century and one of the most beautiful today. Nearly all of the 14th-century palaces on this street are in perfect shape. The most important are the **Cervelló** palace at No. 25, the **Dalmases** palace at No. 20, the house at No. 23 with its typical three-part windows and the **Palau d'Aguilar**, which houses the **Picasso Museum**. The building is, in fact, almost as interesting as its contents.

The Picasso Museum provides an insight into the early evolution of the artist's talent. From caricatures of his teachers in school texts to studies of anatomy as an art student and including his first great paintings in the styles of the Masters – Goya, Velázquez, El Greco – Picasso's extraordinary vitality comes through.

Continuing on to **Carrer Corders**, you will find the 12th-century **Marcus Chapel** which, even though presently connected to a baroque house constructed in 1787, retains its character as a Romanesque hermitage. Around the corner at No. 12 Carrer Corders is the **Hostal de la Bona Sort** (Good Luck Inn) which has a well-preserved 14th-century patio.

Carrer Corders leads up to the **Plaça de la Llana**, another typical medieval space. From there, continue along the narrow alleys which run parallel to Via Laietana, walk through the refreshing **Santa Catalina market** and on up

Carrer Mare de Deu to the stupendous **Palau de la Música**. Erected in 1908 by the Modernist architect Domènech i Montaner, this riot of form and colour in concert-hall shape will pull you right back to the 20th century.

Beaches: The best finale to a morning of wandering through the Gothic Quarter is to head for the beach in colourful **Barceloneta** which has the feeling of a southern European fishing town, with brightly-painted balconies and houses, laundry hanging over the side-walk, narrow streets and delicious aromas of fresh seafood from its specialist restaurants. From the church of **Sant Miquel de Port**, which stands in a lovely square just off **Passeig Nacional**, it's a 15 or 20-minute meander out to the beach and the start of the new 2-mile (4-km) waterfront, encompassing seven beaches, which is a lasting legacy of the Olympic Games. On the port side of Barceloneta towards its tip is the end-pylon for the cable car which crosses to the hill of Montjuïc and provides a spectacular panorama of the city.

Ciutadella Park: Philip V built the Citadel, **La Ciutadella**, in reply to Barcelona's long and bitter resistance in the siege of 1714. Believing that the city needed a major show of force to ensure peaceful relations with the new regime, the Spanish King set about building one of Europe's largest fortresses. Some 1,162 houses were torn down in the waterfront district known as the **Barri de Ribera** to make way for the fortress which was always a focal point of subsequent anti-centralist resentment. Never of any use to anyone, it was finally razed in 1888. Only the **Governor's Palace**, the **chapel** and the **armoury** remain.

The Ciutadella Park is now the site of the **Barcelona Zoo** (its star is an albino gorilla), the **Aquarium**, the **Museums of Zoology** and **Geology**, a botanical garden, a children's library and – most importantly – the **Museu d'Art Modern**. This excellent collection, which will move to the Place Nacional on Montjuïc when refurbishments are complete, includes works by the

The port.

Catalan painters Casas, Miró, Nonell and Sert.

La Rambla and the port: Barcelona's famous **Rambla**, its lively, mile-long pedestrian thoroughfare, has something for everyone. Originally a stream bed, the Rambla runs from **Plaça Catalunya** down to the Christopher Columbus monument at the port.

Across the street from the top of the Rambla, where the city's Metro surfaces, is the **Café Zurich**, a handy place to have coffee in the sun, read the paper and meet friends. The section of Rambla at **Font de les Canaletes**, around a cast-iron drinking fountain, is a traditional gathering point where crowds of soccer enthusiasts passionately debate the fortunes of Barcelona's *fútbol* club.

The next section of the Rambla, the **Rambla dels Estudis**, has the renovated **Betlem Church** on the right and, on the left, the **Palau Moja**, an 18th-century palace now used by the Generalitat as a bookshop.

The **Rambla de las Flors** or **Rambla de Sant Josep** is the next section of the main promenade, lined with flower stalls and overlooked by the **Palau de la Virreina** and the spectacular **Boquería** market. Ramon Casas, Catalonia's first Impressionist painter, is said to have discovered his best model and, subsequently, his wife among the beautiful flower-sellers of the Rambla.

The 18th-century Virreina Palace, named after the widow of the Viceroy of Peru, is a brilliant Louis XIV-style structure, richly endowed with sculptured ornamentation. It now houses the city's information centre. The Boquería is Barcelona's largest open market, covered by a high-roofed, steel-girdered hangar. The arrangements of fruits and vegetables under bright lighting, the fresh salt and iodine fragrance of the seafood and the busy din of the marketplace, with its tiny, marble-countered bars, make the Boqueria market one of the most important stops for any visitor.

The **Rambla del Centre** or **Rambla dels Caputxins** begins at the small

Left, balconies off the Rambla. **Below,** on the Rambla.

square – which has a pavement mosaic by Joan Miró – in front of Barcelona's famous opera house, the **Liceu** (1862). The **Café de l'Opera** across the way from the Liceu is a well-frequented meeting spot. A short side-trip down Carrer Cardenal Casañas to **Plaça del Pi** is advisable. The Plaça and the surrounding lanes of small antique shops make an interesting diversion; artists sell paintings in the square on Sundays. Just off the Rambla on Carrer Nou No. 3, is the **Palau Güell**, designed in 1890 by Antoni Gaudí and now housing a **Theatre Museum**. The **Hotel Oriente** is one of the few surviving formerly religious buildings that once lined this side of the Rambla. It was originally the Franciscan Sant Bonaventura college.

The **Rambla de Santa Mònica** is the next and final part of the Rambla, extending from the entrance to **Plaça Reial** down to the port. The Plaça Reial, with its palm trees and uniformly porticoed 19th-century facades, is one of Barcelona's most appealing spots. The beer halls and cafés surrounding the square, tucked in under the columns, are cosy places for beer, *patatas bravas* (potatoes with hot sauce) and *calamares* (squid), but the Plaça Reial, now closed to motor traffic, has become a marketplace for every other kind of traffic – especially drugs and stolen goods. After dark the Rambla de Santa Mònica, from Plaça Reial down to the port, is given over to delinquency and prostitution – although it was much cleaned up for the Olympic Games.

The bottom of the Rambla is flagged by one of the city's most famous landmarks, the **Columbus Monument**, designed by Gaietà Buïgas for the Universal Exhibition of 1888. A lift takes visitors up to the top of the 200-ft (60-meter) column. This was the former landing point for the city and today small pleasure boats, *goldrinas* (swallows), offer trips round the port.

To the south is the **Drassanes Maritime Museum**, in the vast Gothic shipyards that once turned out 30 war galleys at a time. To the north is the refurbished **Moll de Fusta** with a jokey lobster on top of the Gambrinus restaurant overlooking the yacht clubs. There are always interesting sailing ships in this part of the port.

Gaudí's Barcelona: Few architects have marked a city as Gaudí has Barcelona. Born in nearby Reus in 1852, Antoni Gaudí i Cornet created revolutionary forms which coincided with the Art Nouveau or *modernisme* artistic movements. Gaudí's works and those of his contemporaries and disciples can be found all over Barcelona – undulating, polychromatic, sculptural shapes determined to avoid straight lines and right angles.

The young Gaudí's work can be found in Pere Fontserè's **Cascada** in the Ciutadella Park where, prior to 1878, as an architecture student and Fontserè's assistant, he designed the rocks of the cascade itself. The Plaça Reial lamp posts, their branch-like arms extending at different heights, are also early Gaudí products. His 1889 **Casa Vicens**, in the **Gràcia** neighbourhood (at 24–26 Carrer de les Carolines), was his first major project and the debut of totally

The Boquería market.

polychromatic architecture. Gaudí's most important works in Barcelona are Güell Park, Casa Batlló, Casa Milá (sometimes also known as La Pedrera), and, of course, his great temple of the Sagrada Família.

Güell Park was commissioned by the Barcelona financier Eusebi Güell as an urban project: a combination of gardens and living spaces in the upper part of the city, above Gràcia. Between 1900 and 1914 Gaudí designed a covered market, a large central square, a series of paths across the side of the mountain and the plots for the construction of houses, of which only two were finally built. The wall surrounding the park, decorated with a ceramic mosaic, is the first notable feature of Güell Park, followed by the two houses near the entrance with their bizarre shapes and multicoloured roofing.

The market is known as the **Sala de les Cent Columnes** (Hall of the Hundred Columns). There are actually 86 Doric columns supporting an undulating ceiling decorated with mosaics. The dream-like, leaning arcade upstairs to the left leads around to the park's entrance. The central square, surrounded by ingeniously decorated benches, uses a wide range of found objects, tiles and rubble, all spontaneously mixed and built into the ceramic finish. A serpentine pathway winds up the mountainside above Gaudí's dream-like walls, across fantastic bridges, eventually leaving the park at **La Farigola**.

The **Casa Milá** (**La Pedrera**) and **Batlló** are apartment houses on the **Passeig de Gràcia** in the Eixample. The Casa Batlló (at No. 43) forms part of the famous "mançana de la discordia" (city block of discord), so-named for the contrasting architectural styles of the three neighbouring buildings designed by the city's greatest 19th-century architects. Apart from Gaudí's Casa Batlló, there is Puig i Cadafalch's 1900 **Casa Ametller** at No. 41 and Monènech i Montaner's 1905 **Casa Lléo Morea** at No. 35.

Casa Milá, at No. 92, is a more natural fantasy by Gaudí – repetitions of sandcastle waves, shadows, elaborate wrought-iron balustrades. Even the mouldings, the door knobs and the window casings of the apartments are designed or inspired by Gaudí.

El Temple Expiatori de la Sagrada Família (The Expiatory Temple of the Holy Family) was begun in 1882 as a neo-Gothic structure under the direction of Francesc P. Villar. In 1891 Antoni Gaudí took over, completed the crypt and designed an enormous project which would reach a height of over 500 ft (150 metres).

Gaudí worked on the Sagrada Família until his death in 1926. Conceived as a symbolic construction, the cathedral features three gigantic facades: the Nativity Facade to the east, the western side representing Christ's Passion and Death and the southern facade – the largest – portraying His Glory. The four spires of each facade symbolise the 12 apostles; the tower over the apse represents the Virgin Mary; the central spire (as yet unbuilt), dedicated to Christ the Saviour, is surrounded by four lesser towers representing the Evangelists: Matthew, Mark, Luke and John. The decorative sculpture and ornamentation covering the different elements of the structure are of extraordinary quality and density. Work is still in progress here, but much of the site can be visited.

Notable in Gaudí's buildings is the extent to which the architect attempted to integrate the shapes and textures of nature. The influence of the peaks and heights of Montserrat, Catalonia's religious retreat near Barcelona, is certainly evident in the Sagrada.

A deeply religious man and a mystic, Gaudí, when struck by a trolley car at the age of 74, was so unassuming in physical appearance that he was unidentified for some time and died in paupers' accommodation at Domènech i Montaner's modernist Hospital de Sant Pau i de la Santa Creu, not far from the Sagrada Família itself. His body is buried in the crypt of the unfinished temple which was virtually his life's work, and which continues to grow around his tomb even today.

Just beyond the Sagrada Família is **Plaça de les Glòries Catalanes** where

Gaudí's unfinished temple of the Sagrada Família.

the city's big flea market, **Els Encants**, takes place every Monday, Wednesday and Friday. A new **national theatre** is being built nearby, designed by the trendy Barcelona architect Ricardo Bofill, who is also responsible for the new airport design.

Pedralbes: From Glòries the Diagonal whistles up to the top of the town to the smart residential area of Pedralbes. The **Palace of Pedralbes**, which lies on the north side of the thoroughfare, was built by the city council for Alfonso XIII in 1925 and part of it houses a fine **Ceramic Museum**. A dragon wrought-iron gate by Gaudí on the road up to the right of the palace is a clue that this was all once part of the Güell farm estate. Continue past it to reach the beautifully preserved **monastery of Pedralbes**, where masterpieces from the Baron Thyssen-Bornemisza collection are on show. The bell tower, cloister and Sant Miquel Chapel are perfect examples of Catalan Gothic.

Above Pedralbes is **Sarriá**, a small town swallowed up by the city, which has managed to maintain its special flavour, some of its peace and quiet and a sense of community. Occasionally a hunter returns from the Collserola hills or a *boletaire* carrying a basket of wild mushrooms appears at the station heading downtown. Near the station is the **Plaçeta de Sant Vicens**, Sarriá's patron saint. This picturesque spot still has the air of a village square.

On the south side of the Diagonal, below Pedralbes Palace, is Barcelona's **football club**, where visitors can see the trophies and stand in the directors' box. Designed in 1957 by Francesc Mitjans, **El Camp Nou** has a capacity of 150,000 and is considered one of the most beautiful soccer stadiums in the world. Fútbol Club Barcelona, for 40 years the *only* means of expressing Catalan nationalism, is a monolithic organisation with top professional and amateur teams competing for every amateur national championship available.

Between here and the hill of Montjuïc lies the area of **Sants**. Like Gràcia, the district above the Diagonal at the top of

Admiring the port from Montjuïc.

the Passeig de Gràcia, it has a grass-roots, working-class and, above all, distinctly Barcelona tradition. Mercé Rodoreda's moving novel, *La Plaça del Diament* (translated as *The Time of the Doves* by David Rosenthal), gives an excellent account of life in Gràcia during the 1930s and 1940s. **La Torre de Rellotge** (the clock tower) at Plaça de Rius i Taulet is one of the centres of life in Gràcia, which has the most vibrant of the city's local fiestas every August.

The whole area around Sants was one of several that benefited from the Olympics. The station was redesigned with the **Parc Industrial d'Espanya** in front of it, where boats may be hired on the small lake. Beyond it on the Carrer D'Aragó is **Parc Joan Miró** dominated by the artist's colourful 70-ft (22-metre) statue *Woman and Bird*.

Olympic site: Barcelona's sea-front hill, **Montjuïc**, overlooks the port and was the principal site of the 1992 Olympic Games. Its attractions include the **military fortress** which guards the entrance to the harbour, an **amusement park**, track and field facilities, baseball and rugby fields, an amphitheatre and four museums: the **Museum of Catalan Art**, the **Archaeological Museum**, the **Miró Foundation** and the **Spanish Village (Poble Espanyol)**.

The following tour of Montjuïc can be followed by a cable car trip over the port to Barceloneta. Start at **Plaça Espanya** and walk up between the exhibition pavilions past the **Magic Fountains** towards the imposing **Palau Nacional**, which has been undergoing major renovation. It houses one of the finest collections of Romanesque art in the **Museu d'Art de Catalunya**. Most of the murals come from the Catalan Pyrenees and date from the 10th–12th century. The museum's Gothic collection is also superb.

To the right of the Magic Fountains is Mies van der Rohe's restored **Pavilion**, built originally for the International Exhibition of 1929 which was the reason why the Palau Nacional and most of Montjuïc's grand edifices came to be here. Most eclectic and most popular of

Montjuïc's
Magic
Fountains.

these projects is the **Poble Espanyol**, where a collection of buildings were erected to show the different styles of all the regions of Spain. Today it is flourishing as a tourist centre, where craftsmen work and sell their wares, and as a popular place for a day or evening out: one of the city's most famous nightclubs, Torres de Avila, is at the entrance gates, its interior the work of the city's two best-known designers, Alfredo Arribas and Javier Mariscal (the latter was responsible for creating the Olympic mascot, Cobi).

Behind the Palau Nacional are the principal Olympic sites: the brown sandstone **stadium**, enlarged from Pere Domènech i Roure's 1927 original, and beside it on the **Plaça Europa**, a wide and elegant terrace overlooking the delta of the Llobregat and the sea, are the modern lines of Irata Isozaki's **Palau Jordi**.

On the opposite, city side of the hill, on the way up to the amusement park and the hill-top **castle** and **military museum**, is the **Miró Foundation**, one of Europe's finest modern galleries built in 1988 by the artist's friend Josep Luís Sert.

Hill top spectacular: Barcelona's other hill, **Tibidabo**, the highest point of the Collserola hills behind the city, derives its name from the Devil's temptation of Christ as reported by Saint Matthew: *Haec omnia tibi dabo si cadens adoraberis me*, I will give you this if you adore me. Catalans say that the view from the 1,700-ft (518-metre) peak, towering over the city of Barcelona on one side and looking out over the interior of Catalonia to the north and west, was the most diabolical temptation imaginable.

Part of the charm of a visit to Tibidabo is the process of getting there via train, tram and funicular. Barcelona's Tibidabo train line ends at the top of **Carrer de Balmes**. From this point the blue tramway still runs up to the funicular where there is an excellent restaurant, **La Venta**, with outside tables for warm weather.

The **Sagrat Cor** church with its famous boys' choir, the **Hotel Florida** and the **amusement park** are all points of interest at the top of Tibidabo, but the panorama is the main reason for being up there. The tremendous views of the city and the Mediterranean on one side, the fields of Catalonia and the jagged peaks of Montserrat on the other and, to the north (only visible on a clear day) the snowcaps of the Pyrenees are, indeed, a tempting display of the city's and Catalonia's riches.

The most essential single excursion from the city – excluding beaches – is to the **Benedictine Monastery** and **Sanctuary of the Mare de Deu de Montserrat**, 45 minutes from Barcelona by car, train, or bus. It is a Catalan religious shrine of great power and mystery. For many years, Montserrat performed the only marriage ceremonies and celebrated the only masses in the Catalan language. *La Moreneta*, Catalonia's beloved Black Virgin, presides over the church itself, nestled among the natural stone spires which rise up from the valley floor like the flutes of a gigantic organ.

Left, Miró sculpture in Parc Joan Miró. **Right**, Montserrat.

CATALONIA

Catalonia appears to have everything: rocky coasts, sandy beaches, lush plains, steppe, foothills and high sierra, all within a couple of hours of a major European metropolis. There are historic cities and towns, tiny fishing villages, mountain hamlets, some 1,000 Romanesque chapels, Roman bridges, centuries-old stone farmhouses, vineyards, wheat fields, orchards, trout streams and wild boar – all in this one province. The presence of so much variety and density within such a small area, which has kept its own identity and language, is a continual surprise, even to longtime admirers of this corner of the earth.

Catalonia's 12,320 sq. miles (31,910 sq. km) comprise 6 percent of Spain's share of the Iberian peninsula, and are divided into four provinces, Barcelona, Girona, Lleida and Tarragona, and 38 *comarques*, or counties. The simplest way to approach it, however, is to divide Catalonia into three basic elements: water, air and earth – or the Mediterranean, the Pyrenees and the interior.

The Costa Brava: The term *Costa Brava* (sheer, bold, rocky – or literally "brave" – coast) was originally coined by the Catalan journalist Ferran Agulló in 1905 and initially only referred to part of the rough coastline north of Barcelona. It is now taken to include all of the seafront which is in Girona Province, from **Blanes** all the way up to the French border.

A series of *cales* or inlets, with small, intimate beaches, restaurants, hotels and villas punctuate rocky cliffs rising out of the clear, blue-green Mediterranean. Passenger boats ply their way from one inlet to another, picking up and dropping off travellers.

The hermitage of **Santa Cristina** and the two beaches below are located between Blanes and **Lloret de Mar**. Santa Cristina is the closest Costa Brava inlet to the city of Barcelona – barely an hour by the coast road – and, though exquisite, can also be crowded. Above the populous and busy Lloret de Mar are the beaches at **Canyelles** and the **Morisca** inlets. Farther north are the extraordinarily wild and unspoiled *cales* of **Bona**, **Pola**, **Giverola**, **Sanlionç** and **Vallpregona**. The coast road from Lloret de Mar to **Sant Feliu de Guixols** or the local ferry boat are the best ways to see this breathtaking scenery.

Canyet de Mar is another important stop on the way to Sant Feliu de Guixols, a delicious inlet typical of this piney, rocky coastline. Further north are **S'Agaro**, the smart 1920s resort, and **Platja d'Aro**, with a big disco scene. North of **Palamós** are a series of lonely beaches and *cales* which rank among the simplest and purest stretches remaining on the Costa Brava. **S'Alguer** is a tiny fishing inlet with boat houses on the sand and natural rock jetties. **Tamariu** is a particularly cosy little *cala*. **Aiguablava's Parador Nacional** is just over the top from Tamariu, although many maps don't show this road. Aiguablava's sheer cliffs high over the water are among the Costa Brava's most spectacular sights.

Left, the Pyrenees at dawn. **Right**, fishing boats along the Costa Brava.

Inland are interesting things to do and places to visit. **La Bisbal**, the area's most important commercial centre, has held its Friday markets since 1322. Earthenware products of all kinds, as well as the School of Ceramics, are traditional specialities. Sunday markets at **Palafrugell** are always festive and refreshing. **Peratallada** and **Pals**, northeast of La Bisbal, are fine examples of medieval architecture.

Cultural centre: The city of **Girona** (Gerona in Castilian), originally a Roman settlement, is strategically located at the intersection of four rivers. Completely surrounded by walls up until modern times, Girona was so regularly besieged that it became known as "the city of a thousand sieges". Its famous Jewish quarter is one of Catalonia's most interesting examples of early Mediterranean architecture. The **Monastery of Sant Pere de Galligants**, **Sant Nicolau Church**, the **Arab baths** and the cloister and bell tower of the cathedral are the city's most important Romanesque structures. **La Seu de Girona** cathedral is famous for its Gothic nave, the widest in the world.

Begur is the nerve centre for another corner of the coastline which includes **Aiguablava**, **Fornells**, **Sa Tuna**, **Aiguafreda** and **Sa Riera**. All of this part of the Costa Brava seems to have been put together by teams of artists: olive trees, pines, oaks, rock cliffs and spires surrounded by the diaphanous softness of the Mediterranean.

Dalí Museum: The northernmost section of the Costa Brava stretches from the town of **l'Escala** across the **Gulf of Roses** and north to France. **Figueres** is the area's main town, known for its 18th-century **Sant Ferrán Castle**, its important role in the development of the *sardana* – Catalonia's national dance – and, more recently, for its **Dalí Museum**. This houses a startling collection of some of Catalan painter Salvador Dalí's most extraordinary creations.

North from l'Escala, the Greek ruins at **Empúries** are an impressive glimpse into the area's rich history. **Roses**, an important fishing port, and neighbour-

Catalan farmer.

ing **Empúria-brava** are busy resorts. **Cadaqués**, which was Dalí's home, is a sparkling, white port town heavily populated with artists and *literati*.

Cap de Creus, north of Cadaqués, is a wild and refreshing trip especially if the prevailing wind, known as the *Tramuntana*, is blowing. North still is the fishing town of **Port de la Selva**, much celebrated by Catalan poets. The mythical monastery of **Sant Pere de Rodes** overlooks the Gulf of La Selva, the ruins an eery testimony to bygone times set against the immense panorama of the bright coastal towns and the sweep of the Mediterranean below.

The Golden Coast: The coast south of Barcelona, known as the **Costa Daurada** or "Golden Coast", becomes progressively wider, wilder and lonelier. Even in August you can walk for miles over strands in the **Delta de l'Ebre** with barely a glimpse of another human. If the Costa Brava *cales* are intimate and cosy, the southern beaches of Catalonia are the opposite: vast and empty spaces of sand, sea, sky and sun.

Castelldefels and **Sitges** are the two beaches closest to Barcelona – good party value but slim on natural assets. Between Sitges and Tarragona, there are long, open beaches with fine sand, clear water and plenty of fresh seafood.

Tarragona itself is rich in Roman art and archaeology. It also has an impressive cathedral and a provincial freshness which, all together, create a unique blend of past and present, town and country. Roman remains of the **Centcelles Mausoleum**, the **Ferreres Aqueduct**, **Scipio's Tower** and the **Berá Arch** are all located on the city's outskirts. The **Passeig Arqueologic**, a walk through the city's ancient walls, including massive boulders set in place in the 3rd century BC, is one of Tarragona's most spectacular sights. The ruins of the arena, built near the beach in order to use the natural incline of the shore, are another point of interest. Tarragona's **Rambla**, an elegant, broad walkway down to the sea, is a key spot, particularly for restaurants.

South from Tarragona, there are

Cadaqués.

miles of sandy beaches – **Salou** is the most developed and best known. **Cambrils**, further south, is an excellent fishing port and marina, especially known for superb seafood served in the restaurants of the harbour. **L'Ametlla de Mar** and **L'Ampolla** are excellent beaches to the south, approaching the **Delta de l'Ebre**. In the Delta itself, known for its wildlife and rice padi, **El Trabucador** and **La Punta de la Banya** are two of the wildest, purest, most tourist-forsaken stretches of sand anywhere on the Iberian peninsula.

The Pyrenees: The Catalan Pyrenees are lush peaks and valleys where skiing, climbing, hunting, fishing and nature's full measure are surrounded by thousands of years of civilisation. Roman bridges span trout streams; there are restaurants at the foot of ski lifts.

The **Vall d'Arán** is Catalonia's northwest corner. "L'Aranes", the language of the valley, is another linguistic branch of the Langue d'Oc or Provençal root of Catalan. **Baqueira-Beret**, where Spain's royal family spends Easter Week, is one of the country's best ski resorts. There are mountain trails and superb views to be found on foot or horseback in the summer, on skis in the winter. The peculiar mountain architecture of the Vall d'Arán, like Alpine or Tyrolean high country design – steep, slate roofs – seems to reflect the stone *cordillera* which surround these Pyrenean dwellings.

The 12th-century church at **Bossost** is one of the most extraordinary religious monuments of the valley. The church at **Salardú** is another important structure, built in the 12th and 13th centuries. The crucifix, the "Sant Crist de Salardú", is one of the treasures of Pyrenean art.

The best route east from the Vall d'Arán would be to start south through the **Viella Tunnel** and drive down to the **Boí Valley**, which connects through to **Aigüestortes National Park** and Espot. The Boí Valley's set of churches is considered the most important collection of Romanesque architecture in the Pyrenees. Aigüestortes National Park,

Rice farmer in the Ebre Delta.

Lake Maurici and the Espot Valley are all spectacular, as is the **Assua Valley** and its Llessui ski area, accessible from the town of **Sort**. East from Sort is **La Seu d'Urgell** and its important cathedral, cloister and museum. Romanesque art is everywhere – each Pyrenean hamlet clustered around its tiny chapel.

The eastern Pyrenees extend almost to the Mediterranean sea. **La Cerdanya** is an especially luminous east–west running valley, which history has divided between France and Spain.

Sun and wild mushrooms: Solar energy projects, solar-powered bakeries, and year-round tennis are a few results of the Cerdanya's record number of annual sun-hours. About 45 minutes from **Puigcerdà** are a dozen ski resorts in three countries: Spain, France and Andorra. Boar, chamois and wild mushrooms are hunted in the fall, while in spring and summer the **Segre River** is considered one of Europe's premier trout streams. Hiking and camping in the upper reaches of the Pyrenees, which reach heights over 9,000 ft (2,700 metres), are superb. **Llivia**, a Spanish enclave within French territory – thanks to the wording of the Treaty of 1659 ceding certain "villages" to France (Llivia was a "town") – has ancient stone streets and buildings, Europe's oldest pharmacy, and the area's best restaurant (**Can Ventura**) located in a unique and antique village farmhouse in the centre of town. La Cerdanya abounds in terrific things to do: skiing, hiking, horseback riding, hunting, fishing or just browsing through tiny villages which have changed little in hundreds of years. **Guils**, **Aja**, **Vilallovent** and **Bellver de Cerdanya** have retained the rustic Pyrenean flavour of the early mountain towns. La Cerdanya is open and lush, brilliant and broad compared to the Vall d'Aran's steep, angular pitch.

East of La Cerdanya, the "*cremallera*" (zipper) or cogwheel train from **Ribes de Freser** up to **Núria**, one of Spain's earliest winter sports stations, is a spectacular excursion. The **Vall de**

Shepherds in Aigüestortes National Park.

Camprodón, the most eastern valley in the Pyrenees, can be reached via **Ripoll**, an important medieval capital known as the *bressol* or "cradle" of Catalonia. The portal of Ripoll's Santa María monastery church is among the best Romanesque works in Spain. The Vall de Camprodón, east of Ripoll, has a ski area at **Vallter** and two fine Romanesque churches at **Molló** and **Beget**.

La Garrotxa, east of Camprodón, is a volcanic Pyrenean area with the important medieval town of **Besalú**, **Castellfollit de la Roca** (perched on a cone of basalt rock) and **Olot**, known for its 19th-century school of landscape artists. From Olot to **Figueres**, past **Banyoles**' blue lake where the Olympic rowing events were held, the terrain smooths out into the moist and fertile lowlands of the **Empordà**.

The interior: Most Catalans take it for granted that one lifetime isn't enough to browse through everything the provincial towns of Catalonia have to offer.

Montseny, north from Barcelona, is a series of peaks – smooth, placid, massive heights from which there are excellent views out on to the coastal plain of Catalonia. *Seny* – "sense" or "calm" in Catalan – is a well-recognised quality of the Catalan personality (surprisingly, for a passionate Mediterranean people) and the Montseny massif is taken to represent that tranquility.

Rupit, northeast of Vic on the Olot road, is a stunning medieval town built over a clear stream. Well-populated with restaurants specialising in the renowned *Patata de Rupit*, a potato stuffed with herbs, duck, lamb and veal, Rupit is an architectural and gastronomic gem in a wild area.

Subtle satire: An hour north of Barcelona is the thriving provincial capital of **Vic** with a lovely central square, **La Plaça Major**, and a cathedral famous for the energetic murals of Catalan painter Josep María Sert. Sert's work was destroyed by anti-clerical vandals at the beginning of the Civil War in 1936, but was restored by the painter himself before his death in 1945. Many of the faces are said to be satirical repre-

The Pyrenees at Collegats Defile.

sentations of fascist leaders, although Franco failed to catch on when he toured the cathedral.

Cardona, to the west, is notable for its **Parador Nacional** at the site of the ancient castle and church which overlook the **Cardoner Valley**. The **Salt Mountain**, a 500-ft (150-metre) hill of almost pure salt, is one of the most extraordinary geological curiosities in Catalonia, a resource exploited by the Romans and still mined today.

Solsona, further west, a town steeped in medieval mystery – silence, stone, tiny streets – is known for its excellent **Cathedral**, its **Diocesan Museum** and its **Crafts Museum**. The two main squares are fine examples of early provincial architecture. Solsona's principal attraction, however, is the *feel* of the place – the sense of time, the depth of the serenity in that antique granite world. There's even a town crier.

Lleida (**Lérida** in Castilian) is an ancient city, perched on the edge of Spain's flat, central plateau, with an excellent cathedral and an elegant old section. **La Paería**, on the Carrer Major, and the Gothic **Hospital** are two of Lleida's best early structures. **Sant Llorenç church** is another important piece of architecture, particularly the delicate, octagonal bell tower.

Falset and the country around it, known as **El Priorat**, is a rugged, bitter, but beautiful combination of pine, olive, rock and Roman construction. The **Portal del Bou** (Doorway of the Ox) in Falset forms part of the remains of the ancient walled town. Wine in the *Priorat* region is the major product. These rough, dry wines are good company for hearty Catalan cuisine featuring rabbit, wild boar, duck, sausage, white beans, spinach dishes and typical potato omelettes.

The **Poblet monastery** north of Tarragona is the spiritual centre commemorating the reconquest of Catalonia from the Moors. Ramón Berenguer IV, Count of Barcelona, completed his drive from Lleida, via the Segre and then the Ebro, to the sea and made the initial donation for the founding of the monastery. Poblet, surrounded by rough, austere country, reflects this severity in its sober, powerful architecture. A self-sufficient unit, the monastery has controlled vast tracts of land down through its history.

Celebrate: The seat of Catalonia's famous *cava* industry is at **Vilafranca del Penedès**. *Cava* is a champagne-like bubbly white wine grown in the Penedès region – 90 percent of it in nearby **San Sadurni d'Anoia**. Vilafranca is the commercial centre at the eye of the grape hurricane. The arid agricultural panorama of the Penedès yields two crops: cereals and vines – bread and wine. A town with an aristocratic architectural presence, Vilafranca has plenty to offer: its **Museu del Vi** (Wine Museum), Romanesque ruins, **La Fira del Gall** (fowl market) just before Christmas, human architecture – *Els Castellers* – erected by teams of "castlers" who construct human towers, and *La Calçotada* in February – a feast of new onions and *romesco* sauce. All of it accompanied by plenty of good *cava*, of course.

Typical Pyrenean community.

THE BALEARIC ISLANDS

"I am now in Palma amidst palm trees, cedars, aloes, orange trees, lemon trees, fig trees, and pomegranates. The sky is turquoise, the sea is blue, and the mountains are emerald. The air? Well, the air is just as blue as the sky, and the sun shines all day and people wear summer clothes because it is hot... In a word, life here is delicious."
—Frédéric Chopin

In the 150 years since these words were written, millions of tourist postcards have echoed Chopin's view of life in Mallorca. With its approximately 1,400 sq. miles (3,600 sq. km), Mallorca is the largest of the Balearic Islands which begin some 57 miles (92 km) off the coast of Alicante and extend northeast into the Mediterranean Sea. Minorca is next in size, followed by Ibiza, the island closest to the Spanish mainland. The smallest, Formentera, which is visible from Ibiza, has just 30 sq. miles (82 sq. km).

Slingshots and *talyots*: These islands make up the autonomous region of the Balearics (Baleares) whose capital is Palma. Their name comes from the Greek word for sling, *ballo.* So famous were the ancient natives of the Balearics for their skill in hurling deadly lead pellets with slings that the Romans called the two larger islands *Balear Maior* and *Balear Minor.*

Skeletal remains indicate that the islands were inhabited as early as 4000 BC but the oldest architectural ruins date from the 3rd millennium BC. The Talyotic Age, which extended from 1000 BC to the Roman conquest, left the most archaeological testimonies; stone structures called *talyots,* believed to have been built by a people who came from the Eastern Mediterranean.

Strategic location and fertile soil made the Balearics coveted objects of conquest throughout the following centuries. The Carthaginians, whose occupation dated from the middle of the 7th century BC, recruited Balearic mercenaries whose slings were the terror of the Romans. It was not until 20 years after the destruction of Carthage (146 BC) that Rome was able to subjugate the islands.

Conquests: As the Roman Empire was falling apart, the Vandals swept into the islands in AD 426 and remained until they were driven out by the Byzantines some 100 years later. The three centuries of Muslim domination of the Balearics, made tributary to the Emirate of Córdoba in 848, left a heritage of Moorish place-names (beginning "Bin") and whitewashed architecture. The Christian religion survived and a large colony of Jews flourished under tolerant Arab rule.

The Christian Reconquest took place in Mallorca in 1229 under King James of Aragón. The event proved decisive in the final evolution of the islands' culture. They fell under the influence of Catalonia, and to this day each island has its own dialect of Catalan.

During the 13th century the Balearic Islands became important stops on the trade route between northern Italy and northern Europe. Mallorca produced great artists and craftsmen whose work may be admired in Palma's Cathedral and the Castle of Bellver. The island also produced during this time a genius with an encyclopedic mind named Ramon Llull. After a wild and lusty youth, Llull became a monk and scholar and produced some 500 books which include poetry, allegorical novels and works on mathematics, medicine and mysticism. He mastered Arabic and travelled throughout the Mediterranean in an effort to convert the Muslims; sadly, the latter stoned him to death at the age of 80.

With the rise of the Turkish Empire in the 16th century, the Balearic Islands became a bastion of the expanding Spanish Empire. There are many watchtowers or *atalayas* throughout the islands testifying to the constant need to keep watch against sudden raids of Muslim corsairs in search of booty and slaves. Ibiza city's magnificent walls date from this period.

With the resurgence of Mediterranean commerce in the middle of the 17th century, Mallorcan merchants once again began to benefit from the islands' strategic location. Many of the country mansions or *possessiós* which grace the countryside date from this period, and their Italian-inspired architecture illustrates the strong links between Mallorca and Italy.

In 1708 the British seized Minorca during the War of the Spanish Succession. They remained, except for a brief occupation by the French, until 1781.

Artist colony: In the mid-19th century, foreign tourists began to discover the delights of the Balearics. A five-month stay by Aurore Dupin, Baroness Dudevant, better known by her pen name of George Sand, and the pianist and composer, Frédéric Chopin, inaugurated a whole era of tourism.

George Sand's book, *A Winter in Majorca*, was the first of what is now an extensive travel literature on the islands. They were followed by writers such as Charles Wood, Gaston Vouillier and the eccentric Archduke Louis Salvador of Hapsburg Bourbon. This errant descendant of Europe's oldest royal families discovered Mallorca in 1867. He returned in his yacht five years later to settle down and acquired the estate of Miramar where in the 13th century Ramon Llull had founded a language school for missionaries. He maintained a large household presided over by the Mallorcan peasant girl, Catalina Homar, the great love of his life. Archduke Louis Salvador was not an idle aristocrat; he wrote more than 50 books headed by his seven-volume work, *The Baleares Described in Word and Picture.*

A steady stream of writers and artists looking for out-of-the-way picturesque places continued to visit Mallorca and Ibiza. Some, like Robert Graves, settled down to stay.

Mallorca: The tourist boom of the 1960s turned Mallorca into the most advanced holiday centre of the Mediterranean, providing accommodation and diversions for both monied jet-setters and economy-minded package-holiday

Typical Mallorca: Porto Cristo.

tourists from France and Germany. Each summer, members of the Spanish royal family spend their holidays in the Marivent Palace near Palma.

Capital city: The most impressive way to arrive at the island is by regularly scheduled boat service from either Barcelona or Valencia. From a distance **Palma's** medieval masterpiece of Gothic, its **Cathedral**, stands out like a huge, rose-coloured, craggy rock. As the boat draws closer the city's profile is crowned by other ancient monuments: **Bellver Castle**, perched on a high hill, the crenellated towers of **Sa Llotja** and the royal **Palace of Almudaina**, beside the Cathedral.

Work on the Cathedral was begun in the 13th century and completed in the 16th century. Because of the number and size of its windows, it is the most luminous of Mediterranean cathedrals.

The area around the Cathedral was the site of the Arab city known in the Muslim world as *Medina Mayurka*. The only architectural remnants are an arch on **Calle Alumudaina** and the **Arab baths** on **Calle Serra**. This neighbourhood is especially interesting for wandering about, poking into ancient churches and admiring the facades and courtyards of the house of wealthy noblemen and merchants. The 13th-century Almudaina Palace was built on the foundations of the original Arab *alcázar* or fortress.

The nearby streets of **Almudaina**, **Zanglada** and **Morey** have noble houses dating from the 16th through to the 18th century. On the **Plaça San Francesc** is a church of the same name built during the 14th century although its present facade dates from the end of the 18th century. One of its eight-sided chapels, all of which are decorated with Renaissance and baroque art, contains the 15th-century sarcophagus of Ramon Llull.

A symbol of Palma's prosperous past is the magnificent 15th-century building known as **Sa Llotja** which used to house the merchants' stock exchange. With its four crenellated, octagonal-cornered towers and galleried windows, it stands out as a counterweight to

the majestic Cathedral. Next door is the **Consolat de Mar** which was built in the 17th century and graced by an impressive Renaissance-style gallery.

Palma is also known for its nightlife, which centres around the modern west side of the city, especially the **Plaça Gomila** and the waterfront below.

Scenic drives: Inland, Mallorca divides into two: the **Tramuntana** mountains which run along the northern coast, and the fertile **plain** which makes up the bulk of the rest. The bays of **Alcudía** and **Pollença,** on the northern tip, are particularly attractive. Most heavy tourist urbanisation is within the Bay of Palma and out along the coves of the eastern coast.

The mountains are very rewarding for the visitor. If time is short, head straight toward **Valldemossa** to see the **Carthusian Monastery** where George Sand and Chopin spent a winter. In spite of having a rather primitive piano to work with, Chopin composed some of his most beautiful pieces here, including the *Raindrop Prelude*.

The monastery was originally built as a palace by the Mallorcan King Sanç over the site of a former Moorish one. The neoclassical monastery chapel has frescoes on the ceiling painted by Goya's brother-in-law, Fray Miguel Bayeu. The owners of the well-kept houses of this village make a point of keeping the curtains of their windows open for passers-by to admire the decor of their living rooms.

Closer to Palma, take the road to **Andratx**. This town's port is one of the most enchanting spots on the island. Despite tourist-oriented development, Port d'Andratx has kept its colour as a fishing village. Like many towns in the Balearics, the main town of Andratx was built some miles inland for protection from pirates and was surrounded by *atalayas* or watchtowers. The **fortified church**, typical of many on the islands, was once surrounded by a moat. It was the last refuge in the face of invaders.

From Andratx, you can head again toward the beach. The **Cala San Telm** affords a striking view of the island of **Sa Dragonera**. Nearby is the abandoned monastery of **Sa Trapa**. Local fishermen may be hired for a trip around Sa Dragonera, believed to be the beachhead of the Christian expedition which conquered Mallorca in 1229.

Scenic route: The coastal road follows one of the world's most breath-taking routes hugging the mountainside high above the sea. The village of **Estellencs** which steeply straddles the side of **Mount Galatzó** boasts a defensive tower used in the days when pirates were a menace.

Further down the road is the village of **Banyalbufar**, set amid terraced gardens which have been carved out of the mountain and shored up with meticulously set stone walls. The terraces are irrigated by a network of flowing and glistening canals. The town still has half of the dozen fortified towers built as a defence against the marauding Turks of the 16th and 17th centuries. Below, a stony beach is made especially inviting by a cascade.

A few miles past the Palma-Valldemossa road is the estate of **Miramar**,

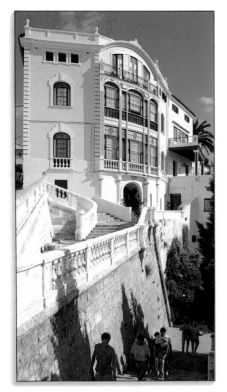

once the nucleus of various properties owned by the Archduke Louis Salvador. The most notable of these is the *possessió* **Son Marroig**, on the way to Deiá. This splendid mansion built around an ancient defensive tower has a museum of Mallorcan folklore and collections of the Archduke.

Deiá has kept much of its original architecture. It has resisted the ravages of hotel complexes and tourist shops thanks largely to the efforts of its artist colony led by Robert Graves, who was a resident here beginning in the early 1920s. The Archduke Louis Salvador set up an inn in Deiá called the CoMado Pilla where visitors were allowed to stay free of charge for three nights.

For additional rugged countryside next to the sea, visit the peninsula of **Formentor** in the northernmost part of the island. Nearby is the charming town of **Pollença** which has a **Roman bridge** in its outskirts.

The extensive **Caves of Drach** and **Artá** in the eastern part of the island are worth seeing. A chamber-music ensemble performs on a boat in the largest of the subterranean lakes of the Caves of Drach. Also in this part of the island is the town of **Capdepera** which has an impressive walled citadel.

Father Junípero Serra, the founder of California's first missions, was born in the town of **Petra**, located in the agricultural heartland of the island. The state of California has set up a museum here, and the house in which the missionary was born has been preserved and furnished much as it was.

A bit of England: The second island of **Minorca** stands out because of the abundance of prehistoric structures here and because its culture was influenced by British occupation in the 18th century. The people who built the three types of prehistoric constructions are believed responsible for similar works in Sardinia and for the monoliths of Stonehenge, England.

The first type are known as *talyots*. These are usually round, conical stone towers, two to three storeys high. Satisfactory explanations for the purpose of *talyots* have yet to be given although it

Minorcan style in Mahón.

is clear that they were useful for defence and as dwellings. Another construction, a *naveta*, has the shape of an upside-down hull of a ship and was used as a mausoleum.

The most fascinating and puzzling of the prehistoric monuments to be found in Minorca are called *taulas,* from the Catalan word for table. A *taula* is one multi-ton megalith balanced on top of another in the form of a "T". Of the some 30 that have been identified, seven are still standing. They were most likely religious in purpose.

Caves and mansions: Another prehistoric wonder can be seen in **Cales Coves**. Here is a network of some 140 man-made caves, most dating from the 9th century BC. In one of them may be seen Latin inscriptions from the 2nd century BC.

In the two main cities of Mahón and Ciutadella, bars and discotheques have been installed in caves. The most spectacular discotheque on the islands is located in **Cala'n Porter**, set in a series of natural caves overlooking the sea.

British influence on Minorca is most clearly seen in and around **Mahón**. This city, which the English made the island's capital, is situated at the end of a 3-mile (5-km) fjord, the only geological formation of its kind in the Balearics. Nowhere else in Spain are sash windows a regular feature of the architecture as they are here.

Outside the city are a number of Georgian mansions. At the seaside end of the fjord is the town of **Villa Carlos**, founded and named Georgetown by the British. Minorcan gin, introduced by Englishmen, has a distinctive taste and is popular throughout Spain. The Minorcan dialect has even assimilated a number of English words from that period of occupation.

Minorca's other large town, **Ciutadella**, is situated at the western extreme of the island. It was the capital under Muslim rule and after the Christian conquest. Its Gothic **Cathedral** has a tower built on the foundations of the minaret of a mosque which used to stand in the same place. The stately houses of the

Sunbathing at Cala Torado on Ibiza.

nobility, dating from the 16th to the 19th century, give Ciutadella a much more dignified air than that of Mahón.

Ciutadella comes alive during the annual fiesta of Sant Joan on 23 and 24 June. This celebration, which dates from the late-Middle Ages, features horsemen dressed to represent different social classes. They prance about the narrow streets of the old part of town while young men crowd around and make their horses rise on their hind legs.

Ibiza: Founded as *Ibosim* by the Carthaginians in the middle of the 7th century BC, **Ibiza** developed a flourishing economy, based on the export of salt, ceramics, glassware and agricultural products. Testimony of this prosperity are the Ibizan coins found throughout the Mediterranean.

There are archaeological relics of this period in Ibiza's two archaeological museums. One is in the plaza at the top of the oldest part of Ibiza city (often known as **Eivissa**). The museum has one of the best collections of Punic articles in the world. The other is on **Via Romana** at the foot of the hill, **Puig des Molins**, which is a huge necropolis with more than 400 tombs carved into the rock at various depths.

Jet-set destination: But if Ibiza had a flourishing ancient past, its present is no less prosperous. For some 20 years it has been a mecca for jet-setters and trendy young travellers in search of not only sun, sand and surf but of a highly sophisticated nightlife, a nightlife often beginning in fashionable bars near the port and ending up near dawn in some of the world's most exotic discotheques in the country.

In contrast to the hustle and bustle around the port is the dignified serenity of the oldest part of Eivissa called **D'Alt Villa**, enclosed within a complete ring of walls. The basic street plan of this part of Ibiza has changed little since it was first laid out by the Carthaginians.

A pair of the local rope-soled *alpargatas* are the best footwear for the irregular street surface of D'Alt Villa. A road winds from this gate up the steep hill to the citadel and Cathedral above. Midway up is a section of mansions of old Ibizan families. One house has been turned into a unique hotel and restaurant called the **Corsario**. Its name reflects an entire era in the island's history when Ibiza had its own fleet of corsairs which, in the 16th and 17th centuries, not only protected the island but attacked menacing privateers. In the Corsario's garden is the entrance to a cave that once connected to a cove below, either for escape or for counter-attacking invading pirates.

At the top of the hill of D'Alt Villa, the sombre-looking **Cathedral** is built on truly holy ground since its predecessors on the spot were a mosque, a palaeo-Christian church, a Roman temple dedicated to Mercury and a Carthaginian temple.

Formentera: The island of **Formentera** is separated from Ibiza by 4 miles (7 km) of straits and islets. A regular boat service links Ibiza's port to Formentera's port of **La Sabina**. This limited access is an advantage for those who want to get away from the hordes of tourists on Ibiza. Besides peace and quiet, Formentera offers the visitor the superb, long beaches of **Illetas** and **Mitjorn**, the package-tour-oriented beach of **Es Pujols** and a number of small *calas* or coves. The agricultural character of the island is reflected in its name, which is derived from the Latin word for grain.

The best way to get around the island is by motorscooter, which may be rented at La Sabina. On a scooter the island can be crossed in 40 minutes. Not to be missed is the drive up to the plateau on the far side of the island known as **La Mola**. The winding road to the top affords incomparable views of the island below and Ibiza at a distance. At the end of the road is a lighthouse presiding over sheer cliffs. A plaque commemorates the fact that Jules Verne chose this spot for the blast-off for his novel, *From the Earth to the Moon*.

During the summer Formentera attracts young people from all over Europe and North America. Since nightlife is limited to a few discotheques and clubs that open around midnight, it is a friendly and intimate island.

NAVARRE
AND ARAGON

In the year 778, the mighty Charlemagne, King of the Franks, decided to try his luck conquering the lands toward the south. It was an unsuccessful venture, and he headed home through the Pass of Roncesvalles with his tired army. There he was ambushed by Basques, who annihilated the rearguard, and there died Roland, later to be immortalised in the *Chanson de Roland*, with the Basques conveniently replaced by Moorish attackers.

Soon after Roncesvalles, a group of Basque warlords declared themselves independent. The state they founded was destined eventually to become the kingdom of Navarre.

Navarre was only finally demoted to the status of province in 1841. The greatest of its medieval kings was Sancho III, El Grande, one of a line of Sanchos that ran from the 10th to the 13th century. Sancho III doubled Navarre's territories through astute politics, military campaigns and marriages and introduced the beginnings of a modern legal system and a process of church reform.

***Fueros* and Carlism:** The period immediately following his death in 1035 marked an enormous advance for Navarre, as the prosperous and secure kingdom initiated the *fueros* system, or the guarantee by the monarchy that towns and cities could enjoy a certain autonomy with their customary laws. The *fuero general* was probably written in the 13th century, and applied to Navarre as a whole. Similar to the Magna Carta, it set down a comprehensive collection of precise and realistic laws in 508 chapters.

Beginning in the 13th century, Navarre was ruled by a succession of French dynasties. But due to a series of weak rulers, the Black Death of 1348, the loss of the important Jewish commercial class in pogroms and Navarre's unlucky geographical position, which put it in the midst of France and Castile's squabbles, the Duke of Alba was able to seize the kingdom in 1512 in the name of King Ferdinand.

Navarre was no longer independent but it did have its *fueros*, and the monarchs in Madrid were obliged to swear to uphold them, which they did until the rise of the Bourbon Dynasty in the 18th century. But until then, Navarre was incorporated in the Castilian Crown.

This system made Navarre into a very pro-monarchist region, and it is not surprising that the new ideas of liberalism, republicanism and anti-clericalism that penetrated Spain in the late-18th and 19th centuries were not well received in Navarre. The centralist tendencies these movements implied meant that Navarre's autonomy was threatened.

When Ferdinand VII died in 1833, there was some question as to who should succeed him, his daughter Isabella or his brother Carlos. Navarre threw in its lot with Carlos, in the hope that a strong ruler like him would restore its traditions. "*Dios, Patria y Rey*" (God, Fatherland and King) was the Carlist motto, however, making it clear that the religious fervour of traditional Navarre Catholicism was also in the forefront of the Carlist Wars.

The last of the wars ended in 1876. The Carlists resurfaced during the Civil War, when they actively participated with the Francoists and played a crucial role in fomenting the coup that began the war. Franco, in fact, praised Navarre after a visit in 1936 as "the cradle of the nationalist movement".

This position set Navarre off from the neighbouring Basque Country, with which it has so many ties. Even though they share a language to a certain extent, a common past and many customs, the more industrial provinces of Vizcaya, Alava and Guipúzcoa threw in their lot with the Republic, and lost.

As the Basque nationalist movement began to grow in the early 20th century, there were vain attempts to unite with Navarre. Today, there is little doubt that part of Navarre is Basque in everything but name, but the centuries-old *Navarrismo* of the more conservative sectors has impeded unity. After the death of Franco, Basque nationalist leaders drawing up their region's Statute of Autonomy tried to incorporate the people of Navarre into the project, but failed once again.

Pamplona: Known in Roman times as Pompaelo (the city of Pompey), **Pamplona** was from the 10th to the 16th century the capital of the kingdom of Navarre. Since the Civil War, the conservative, religious and hard-working Navarrese have transformed their ancient citadel into a prosperous industrial city. High-rise apartment blocks, manicured boulevards and factories form a protective and often ugly ring around the lovely old city which perches on the banks of the **Arga River**.

The centre of this area is the **Plaza del Castillo**, lined with outdoor cafés. Novelist Pío Baroja once said of the *paseo* in this plaza that the varying degrees of aristocracy were as evident as if they were separate floors of a building. Industry and democracy may have made a difference here, but the city's noble past is close at hand in the **Diputación Foral** at the western end of the plaza. The building contains a magnificent **Throne Room** decorated with portraits of the kings of Navarre.

Most of Pamplona's historical buildings are located north of the plaza. Near the old city walls is the 14th-century **cathedral**, with an 18th-century facade by the neoclassical architect Ventura Rodríguez. Inside are the lovely alabaster tombs of Charles the Noble of Navarre and his wife Leonor. The adjoining Gothic cloister is considered to be the best of its kind in Spain.

The **Museo de Navarra**, situated in a 16th-century hospital, has interesting pieces of Navarrese archaeology, frescoes taken from Romanesque churches around the province and Goya's portrait of the Marquis of San Adrián.

Beginning at the south end of the Plaza del Castillo, the tree-lined **Paseo de Sarasate**, named after the native violinist, is Pamplona's main promenade. It runs past the **Monument to the Fueros** and the 13th-century church of **San Nicolás**, skirting the grassy **Ciudadela**, a fortress built by Philip II

Running with the bulls in Pamplona.

and now the site of outdoor concerts in warm weather. The Paseo finishes in the **Parque de la Taconera**, a park resplendent with tame deer, fountains and monuments to Navarrese heroes. The church of **San Lorenzo**, located in the middle of the park, has a chapel dedicated to the city's world-famous saint, San Fermín.

The fiesta: There is a measured, middle-European air to Pamplona much of the time. Native *pamplonicas*, proud of their industriousness, look down upon such Spanish pastimes as flamenco, although the younger generation lead a fast and furious bar life.

But at noon on 6 July, the Eve of San Fermín, a *chupinazo* (rocket) fired from the balcony of the 16th-century **Ayuntamiento** puts an end to the order and tedium which have made the city flourish. For the next week, Pamplona becomes delirious.

It's been said that this wildest of wild fiestas is an extension, rather than an aberration, of the Navarrese personality. The festival isn't about flowers or gorgeously dressed Virgins but sheer endurance. It might be true that a certain amount of stoical Basque blood is necessary to produce a celebration where the idea is for revellers to drink, dance and sing without stopping for seven days, then, once worn down by exhaustion, to throw themselves in front of a herd of charging bulls.

The fiesta appealed to Ernest Hemingway and by making its particulars universal in *The Sun Also Rises*, he changed it for good. The thousands of foreigners who arrive in Pamplona every year to prove their mettle or his text are as much a permanent part of the fiesta's landscape as are the wineskins and drums and red sashes.

Since there's no place in the city where a visitor can merely stand and watch, everyone who arrives has no choice but to put together a semblance of the red and white costume and join in the dance.

Occasionally, the *Sanfermines* are the scene of human, as well as taurine mayhem, and by the end of the week the heat, filth and broken glass will make the merriment seem less like the pages of a children's storybook come to life.

The bulls: Lest you become too seduced by the prevailing fiesta mood, it ought to be pointed out that fatal gorings occur almost every year at the morning running of the bulls. If you decide to run, it's a good idea to watch one *encierro* from behind a grille. You may find that vicarious terror, or a confused bull charging the barricade you are peering through, is thrilling enough. Or you may choose to subscribe to the *pamplonica* theory that the large number of *encierro* survivors proves that a well-timed prayer to San Fermín is all one really needs.

With luck, in a few days you'll be singing "*pobre de mí*", with the rest of the fiesta stragglers; not without sincerity, but with part of your mind on showers, hot meals and the cool stone villages and sweet green of the rest of Navarre Province.

The southwest countryside: The province is enormously varied, ranging from the low western Pyrenees to vineyards

Dancing in front of Pamplona's city hall in the San Fermín festival.

near Rioja to the desert-like Bardenas Reales north of Tudela. Pilgrims on their way to Santiago from France were obliged to travel through Navarre, meaning that Romanesque churches abound. It is a province to take one's time in, drive slowly (or better yet, ride a bike) and allow plenty of time to sit down and eat, for among the many things that makes Navarre a Basque province is its fine cuisine.

Southwest of Pamplona is **Estella**, one of the province's most monumental cities and the closest thing to a holy city for the Carlists. Among the splendid Romanesque churches in Estella are **Santa María Jus del Castillo** (which used to be a synagogue), **San Pedro** and **San Miguel**, while the 12th-century **Royal Palace** is a rare example of secular Romanesque architecture.

At the foot of **Montejurra**, site of an historic Carlist victory over the Republican troops in 1873, is the **Irache Monastery**, which had its own university in the 16th century. And further down the N-111 highway is **Viana**, founded in 1219 by Sancho The Strong. The Crown Princes of Navarre held the title of Prince of Viana until they assumed the throne. In the **Santa María Church** you can see the tomb of Cesare Borgia, who died in battle here in 1507.

The C-132 road takes you to **Tafalla**, whose **Santa María Church** has a beautiful Renaissance altarpiece. But before reaching Tafalla, veer to the left to visit **Artajona**, a fortified town that rises up in the distance like a ghost from the Middle Ages.

Olite: South from Tafalla is **Olite**, the former residence of the kings of Navarre from the 15th century. Their castle has been restored – *too* restored, in the opinion of some – and is used for summer theatre and music festivals, as well as for a government-run *parador*.

Two side trips from Olite are well worth the time: **Ujué** is a village that has barely been touched since the Middle Ages and has miraculously survived intact; and the **Oliva Monastery**, used today by Trappist monks, was founded in 1134 by King García Ramírez.

Principe de Viana *parador* in Olite, Navarre.

Tudela: South of Olite on the A-15, **Tudela** is one of those remarkable Spanish cities that illustrate the harmony in which Christians, Moors and Jews lived for several centuries. It was founded in 802 by the Moors, the remains of whose mosque can be seen today inside the **cathedral**, a brilliant example of the transition from Romanesque to Gothic. The Last Judgement doorway in the main facade is a sculpted vision of the rewards and punishments supposedly awaiting us all.

Tudela's old Jewish district, or *aljama*, is one of the best known in Spain. It was situated between the cathedral and the **Queiles River** junction with the **Ebro**.

North of Xavier, above the Yesa Reservoir and surrounded by rugged mountains, is the **Leyre Monastery**, Navarre's spiritual centre in the 11th century and pantheon of Navarre kings. Consecrated in 1057, it features beautiful Romanesque architecture, including a magnificent vaulted crypt. Abandoned last century, the monastery has been restored by Benedictine monks and now includes a hotel for those in search of tranquilllity.

Moving north again, east of Tafalla, is **Sangüesa**, located at the start of the Navarre Pyrenees. This is another 11th-century town, founded by Alfonso I, The Warrior, with another **Santa María Church**. This one has Spain's most beautiful Romanesque porticoes.

Nearby is the 16th-century **Castle and Convent of Saint Francis Xavier**, the great Jesuit missionary who was born in a house on this site. Pilgrims still visit the castle to pay homage to Xavier, and they say that one of the crucifixes there bled the day the saint died in 1552.

North of Xavier, on the other side of the **Yesa Reservoir**, is the **Leyre Monastery**, a beautiful work of primitive Romanesque architecture which was mentioned in 848 by Saint Eulogio of Córdoba in a letter to the Bishop of Pamplona. However, it was only consecrated in 1057, and most of what is visible today dates from the 11th century, including its enormous crypt lined with columns. As an indication of the monastery's importance during the Middle Ages, the Bishops of Pamplona were almost always chosen from among the monks at Leyre.

The valleys: By this time the traveller is entering the **Roncal Valley**, one of a series of beautiful green valleys dotted with small villages that extend west to Guipúzcoa and east to Huesca and the High Pyrenees. These valleys have few monuments *per se* to offer, although there are isolated Romanesque churches and hermitages, but rather stand out more for their setting and traditional architecture. **Roncal** and **Isaba** are two of the major villages in the Roncal Valley, which is surrounded by peaks reaching as high as 6,500 ft (2,000 metres) or more.

North of Ochagavía in the **Salazar Valley** is the **Irati Forest**, one of Europe's densest and largest forests. It is said to be inhabited by witches, not an unusual occurrence in these parts.

Continuing west you reach **Roncesvalles**, where pilgrims coming from France would stop for the night at one of the most important hostelries along the road to Santiago. Today it is an **Au-**

The Navarrese are known for reserve and conservatism.

gustine monastery. Also in Roncesvalles you can see the **Royal Collegiate Church**, an overly restored Gothic construction in whose chapterhouse lies the enormous tomb of Sancho VII, The Strong (1154–1234), and his queen.

Smugglers and witches: Down the road from Roncesvalles to **Valcarlos** is the steep canyon where the famous ambush of 778 featured in the *Chanson de Roland* took place, and you can understand how Charlemagne's men didn't stand a chance against the Basque warriors perched high on either side. This is smugglers' country, and Valcarlos has not a few families who have made small fortunes carrying merchandise back and forth over the French border, as do all the mountain villages in this area.

The last of the valleys before entering Guipúzcoa is the beautiful **Baztán Valley**, with its 14 villages of stone houses, many of them with noble coats-of-arms. There are a good deal more heraldic crests in Navarre than most other provinces, where an estimated 20 percent of the population during the heyday of the kingdom belonged to a noble family.

The capital of the Baztán is **Elizondo**, a resort town and residence of many *indianos*, the name given to Basques who went off to the New World, made a lot of money and returned to live out their days comfortably in their villages. North of Elizondo is **Arizcun**, one of the villages partially inhabited by *agotes*, who suffered centuries of persecution due to their supposed descent from Jews, Moors, Visigoths or even Albigensians, depending upon the myth one chooses to believe. And further north is **Zugarramurdi**, where witches reputedly used to gather in caves to hold their *akelarres*, or covens. The caves were already inhabited in the Neolithic period, but their fame as the site of witches' gatherings arose from an Inquisition trial in Logroño in 1610, when 40 unfortunate women were accused of witchcraft and 12 of them were eventually burned at the stake.

Home of kings: Many Spaniards know **Aragón** only as the region one must

The lower gate of Daroca, Aragón.

drive through when going from Madrid to Barcelona, or the home of the *jota*, the country's best-known folkloric music and dance. In winter, skiers race up the region's major roads in search of the perfect slopes in the Pyrenees, passing by *mudéjar* and Romanesque churches, villages that are dying from lack of attention and walled cities that hide wonders of *mudéjar* architecture.

The Romans founded Caesaraugusta, which we know today as **Zaragoza**, in 25 BC. Not much evidence of their presence remains today.

Aragón was invaded along with the rest of Spain by the Moors in 714. Resistance to the occupation began around 100 years later; in 1035, Ramiro I, the bastard son of Sancho II of the neighbouring kingdom of Navarre, set up the kingdom of Aragón, which was to last until 1469. At its height it included parts of France, the Balearic Islands, Naples, Sicily and stretched as far south as the southeasterly region of Murcia.

Zaragoza was recaptured by the Christian armies at the orders of Al-

fonso I in 1118. But, despite the Reconquest, Christians and Moors lived well side-by-side for centuries. The word "*mudéjar*" comes from "*mudayyan*", Arabic for "subject". But these subjects were privileged and esteemed ones; at the beginning of the 16th century it is estimated the *moriscos*, or Moors living under Christian domination, comprised 16 percent of the region's population. But in 1525 all Moors were ordered to convert or leave, and the definitive expulsion order of 1611 put an end to the cohabitation.

Although King Ferdinand was from Aragón (his marriage to Isabella of Castile in 1469 marked the unification of Spain), he was not overly sensitive to the social realities of his home region. Ignoring the protests of his lords, he imposed the Inquisition, with the unpleasant result of having his Inquisitor-General murdered in the Seo Cathedral in Zaragoza in 1485. The swords supposedly used to commit the crime can be seen today next to the altar.

Geographically, Aragón is divided

At the festival of El Pilar in Zaragoza.

into three areas which roughly correspond to its three provinces: the Pyrenees (Huesca), the Ebro River Valley (Zaragoza) and the Iberian mountains (Teruel). It is the least densely populated of Spain's regions.

The capital of the region is **Zaragoza** with a population of around 700,000. The visitor will find few monuments indicating the city's past grandeur because time, neglect and two terrible sieges suffered during the Napoleonic Wars (1808–09) destroyed a great deal.

It has two cathedrals: the **Seo**, which was consecrated in 1119 on the site of the old mosque, and **El Pilar**, built in honour of Spain's patron saint, the Virgin of Pilar, who supposedly appeared there atop a pillar to St James in AD 40. The Parroquieta chapel's *mudéjar* wall and ceiling, the Gothic altarpiece and the baroque choir stalls are the Seo Cathedral's most outstanding features. The **Seo Cathedral Museum** contains one of the best tapestry collections in Spain as well as liturgical objects and some paintings.

The distinctive Basilica of El Pilar, with its 11 domes, is the oldest church in Christendom consecrated to the Virgin. The present building, dating from the 17th and 18th centuries, is the third on the site. Massive pillars split the church into three bays, some of the frescoes on the cupolas being the work of Goya. But the focal point is the Lady Chapel. There you will see the legendary marble pillar which supports the much-venerated Virgin, a tiny alabaster image whose rich mantle is changed every day. The day of El Pilar, 12 October, a national holiday, is attended by lavish celebrations in Zaragoza.

The **Aljafería** was first built in 1030 by the ruling Moorish king and could well have been taken from the *Arabian Nights*, according to testimonies of the time. But it has gone through hard times: the Catholic Monarchs transformed part of the palace into their headquarters it was later used by the Inquisition, and then as an army barracks in the 19th century. Ferdinand and Isabella's throne room, with its remarkable ceiling, and the Moorish chapel are the best-preserved parts of the palace.

The **Provincial Fine Arts Museum** has a small collection of paintings by Goya, who was born in the village of **Fuendetodos**, 31 miles (50 km) south of Zaragoza. The house in which he was born is now a museum after having been abandoned for years (open every day except Monday).

There are fine examples of *mudéjar* architecture throughout the province of Zaragoza. **Tarazona**, 45 miles (72 km) east of the capital, is known as "The *Mudéjar* City" and offers a spectacle of Moorish and Sephardic history. The 12th-century **cathedral**, the old Jewish district behind the **Episcopal Palace**, the 8th-century **Magdalena Church** and winding streets crossed by *mudéjar* arches make this town worth visiting.

Another town that is equally beautiful but much a victim of neglect is **Daroca**, in the southern part of the province. Surrounded by 8 miles (13 km) of walls with more than 100 towers, **The cathedral** Daroca appeared in the annals of the **in Jaca,** Greek voyagers. **Aragón.**

Also in southern Zaragoza is the **Monasterio de Piedra**, an oasis of gardens, lakes and waterfalls around a 12th-century Cistercian monastery.

Nearby is **Calatayud** with its famous *mudéjar* towers, the best example of which rises above the **Colegiata de Santa María**.

Visitors who want to understand Spain's more recent history would be well advised to visit **Belchite**, 25 miles (40 km) southeast of Zaragoza. This town was the site of one of the most ferocious battles of the Civil War, and its ruins have been preserved as a reminder of the horrors of war.

Romanesque region: If the dominant architectural or historical motif in Zaragoza is *mudéjar*, moving north to the province of **Huesca**, the traveller is surrounded by Romanesque constructions. The stream of pilgrims on their way to Santiago during the Middle Ages encouraged the construction of churches from Catalonia to Galicia, of which Jaca's cathedral is one of the most important. And in addition to of-fering literally hundreds of well-preserved examples of the Romanesque style, Huesca is a paradise for hikers, skiers, climbers and mountain lovers.

The capital of the province is **Huesca**, whose age of splendour was the 13th century. Peter IV founded the University of Huesca in the 14th century, but it was abolished in 1845, by which time the city had been reduced to the status of an unimportant provincial capital.

Huesca's **cathedral** was built in the 14th and 15th centuries on the site of the old mosque. Of particular interest is the alabaster Renaissance altarpiece by Damián Forment. Nearby is the **City Hall** (1577) with a mural depicting the story of "The Bell of Huesca", one of the typically bloody legends of Spanish history: Ramiro II, a former monk who ruled Aragón in the 12th century, was disturbed by his nobles' refusal to submit to his rule. After consulting with the abbot of his former monastery, Ramiro II hit upon a solution: he summoned his nobles one by one, had them each beheaded and piled up their heads in the

Tarazona's former bullring is converted to apartments.

form of a large bell. In this way discipline was restored.

The other major city in the province is **Jaca**, whose **cathedral** is one of Spain's treasures of Romanesque architecture. The beautifully restored Diocesan Museum contains a remarkable collection of Romanesque frescoes. **La Ciudadela**, a fortress built by Philip II, is currently under the jurisdiction of the army but is open for guided tours.

Soon after the kingdom of Aragón was established, King Sancho Ramirez founded the **Monastery of San Juan de la Peña**, which became the point of religious inspiration for the Christian Reconquest campaign. Located 17 miles (27 km) southwest of Jaca, the monastery is wedged between enormous boulders and under a sheer rock cliff. It contains an extraordinary Romanesque cloister and a 10th-century church, the monks' sleeping quarters and the **Nobles' Pantheon**.

West of Jaca are a series of valleys which eventually lead to Navarre and which maintain the old architectural, linguistic and cultural traditions of Aragón. The villages of **Hecho** and **Ansó** feature houses with odd-shaped chimneys which distinguish one town from another, and the windows are outlined in white.

Mountaineering: North of Hecho is the **Los Valles National Reserve**, and directly north of Jaca is the **Somport Pass**, marking the border with France and the starting point for many trails into the high country.

To the northeast of Jaca lies the **Vignemale National Reserve**. To get there you pass through the towns of **Sabiñánigo** and **Biescas**, as well as a host of tiny towns along the C-136 road that contain Romanesque churches and usually little else. Branching off the road leads you to the **Panticosa Spa**, with a lake, hotel facilities and stores where you can stock up on provisions, buy a trail map and head off into the wild. The highest peaks in this area are over 9,800 ft (3,000 metres).

Further to the east is one of Spain's most famous national parks, **Ordesa**,

Gardens at the Monastery of La Piedra.

which is actually part of a chain of reserve areas that can lead the hiker across the border to France or east into the Catalonian Pyrenees.

The Pyrenees in winter are, of course, taken over from the hikers by the skiers. **Candanchú** and **Canfranc**, on the road from Jaca to Somport, the town of **Panticosa** and **Formigal**, north of there, are all major ski resorts.

Of the three Aragonese provinces, **Teruel** is the least known, and the capital city of **Teruel** is the least populated of all Spain's provincial capitals. It is a province in which *mudéjar* architecture abounds, both in the capital itself and in towns so far off the beaten track that most Spaniards don't know they exist.

Lovers of Teruel: The **cathedral** is justly famous for its remarkable ceiling, a masterpiece of the 14th century in which daily life in the Middle Ages is portrayed in portraits painted on wood. Another outstanding church is **San Pedro** on the eastern side of the former Jewish quarter, which has a beautiful 16th century altarpiece. It is best known

Modern lovers of Teruel.

for housing the tombs of the Lovers of Teruel, a tragic couple immortalised in poems and plays, whose fame in Spain outdoes that of Romeo and Juliet. A relief by Juan de Avalos depicts the lovers and, if you peer into the tomb, you can see the mummified bodies.

Diego Marcilla and Isabel Segura were in love, the story goes, but their parents opposed the marriage. Diego was sent off to make his fortune, and thus endear himself to his lover's father.

He came home in 1217 a very rich man, only to find his beloved walking down the aisle with someone else. He died of heartbreak the next day and Isabel, still wearing her bridal dress, kissed the cadaver and passed on to a better world with her Diego.

The visitor should also stop to admire the twin *mudéjar* towers of **San Martín** and **El Salvador**, supposedly the result of a contest between two Moorish architects in love with the same woman. The winner won his love and the loser (who built San Martín) jumped off the tower.

Of all the mountain villages in Teruel, **Albarracín** is the best preserved, so much so that in the 1980s it won a European competition for historical preservation. It is a town to stroll through, admiring the city walls, the towers, the harmony between land and construction and the architectural magic of a fortified town rising high above a river.

Alcañiz, to the northeast of Teruel, is famed for its castle, with murals depicting the history of the Calatrava Order, and the **Colegiata de Santa María**, with its magnificent baroque portal. North of Alcañiz, towards Zaragoza, lies **Azaila**, which has been declared a national monument due to the discovery of buried Roman and Celtic cities.

Moving south of Teruel, to the harsh mountains of the Maestrazgo region, stop at **Mora de Rubielos** to see its immense castle, built between the 13th and 15th centuries, and the nearby **Rubielos de Mora** (they shouldn't be confused). The truth is that nearly any road through the mountains of Teruel will lead to *mudéjar* towers, castles, city walls or outstanding churches.

THE BASQUE COUNTRY

Mountain chains, like "bones showing through skin" as one historian has described them, extend along the Bay of Biscay west of the Pyrenees, separating much of the rolling farmland of the **Basque Country** from the rest of Spain. Peaceful green river valleys planted with grass, grain and fruit trees – or, more recently and controversially, with pines – against dour peaks in the distance form the contrasting backdrop of lively fishing ports, resorts and sandy beaches. In this clearly defined geographical area, known locally as Euzkadi, the Basques and their shadowy ancestors have lived since the end of the last Ice Age.

A world apart: Basques live on either side of the Pyrenees; in the French region of Pyrénées-Atlantiques, Spanish Navarre and the three Spanish provinces which have made up the autonomous Basque community since 1980:

Guipúzcoa and Vizcaya on the coast and Álava on the plateau.

In addition to possessing physical characteristics which have led some anthropologists to believe they are directly descended from Cro-Magnon Europeans, the Basque language, *Euskera*, sets this people apart from their French and Spanish countrymen.

Of Western Europe's living languages, only *Euskera* does not belong to the Indo-European family. It has fascinated linguists since the Middle Ages, when scholars traced it to Tubal, the grandson of Noah who settled the peninsula after The Flood. More recently, philologists comparing the Basque words for axe, *aitzor*, and stone, *aitz* have raised the possibility that the language dates from a time when tools were made of stone.

Basque was mostly preserved among rural families during the Franco years and possesses a very small written literature. It is now taught along with Castilian in Basque schools and at popular adult night courses, although it takes the average adult some 500 hours of study to be able to carry on a conversation. Road signs in Basque can confuse visitors, thus Donostia stands for San Sebastián, Bilbo for Bilbao, and Gasteiz (actually of Visigothic origin) for Vitoria.

Fiercely proud of their unbroken ancient past, Basques like to say they have never submitted to outside conquerors, including the Romans. Guipúzcoa and Vizcaya possess a number of prehistoric caves and dolmens, but are notably lacking in Roman and early-Christian remains. However, both the Romans and Christianity made inroads into the mountain strongholds, and the Basques' Catholicism has stood firm ever since. They are considered the most religious people in Spain. Appropriately, Ignacio de Loyola, the warrior who founded the influential Society of Jesus or Jesuits, was born in this region, near Azpeitia, 32 miles (52 km) from San Sebastián. On his saint's day, 31 July, large crowds flock to the massive monastery with its basilica topped by a lofty cupola.

A *boina*, or beret, is everyday wear for older Basques.

To a certain extent it was religious feeling which brought the Basques into the 19th-century Carlist Wars. But, ironically, it was mainly to protect their *fueros* that they chose what turned out to be the losing side in both the Carlist and the Civil Wars, thus losing their independence.

The terrorist incidents for which the Basque Country has become known since the 1970s – seen by radical separatists as a continuation of the struggle for the restoration of self-rule – have not generally been directed at tourists.

Relatively few non-Basques make a comprehensive tour of the interior of the region. Visitors typically spend the summer on the mild and misty Basque coast, as Spaniards and an increasing number of French have done since the 19th century, when the point of resort life was to rest in the shade.

Guipúzcoa: The smallest province on the peninsula and one of the most densely populated corners of Europe, **Guipúzcoa** has had close cultural connections with the other side of the Pyre-nees since prehistoric times. More recently, the fortified Basque ports a few miles from the frontier have been easy targets for the French in wartime.

Eugenie de Montijo, the beautiful daughter of a Spanish nobleman who fought on the French side in the Peninsular War and the Empress of Napoleon III, is credited with setting the style for summering on the Basque coast. Soon after she introduced the Emperor to Biarritz in the French Basque Country, other royals, including Queen Victoria, arrived. By the end of the 19th century, the Spanish and South American aristocracy had made **San Sebastián** their favourite summer watering place.

From this period date the **Casa Consistorial** (town hall), formerly the Gran Casino, the royal family's Tudor-style **Miramar Palace**, dividing the two long curving beaches, and the high-style **Zurriola Bridge** over the canalised **Urumea River**. Casino gambling is now confined to the **Hotel Londres y Inglaterra** nearby.

Although it is now a city of 200,000

View of San Sebastián's beautiful bay.

with a diverse economy, San Sebastián is still one of the most beautiful resorts in Europe: elegant and cosmopolitan during the jazz and film festivals, favoured by the Spanish aristocracy – including the king – during the warm autumn months, but still humming with street life in the old town. If you happen to arrive in the morning, proceed to the efficient tourist bureau by the **Alderdi Eder Park** south of the Casa Consistorial. The beaches lying beyond a windbreak of tamarisks on the elegant **Paseo de la Concha** will rarely be full. This would be a good time to take the inexpensive funicular to the top of **Monte Igueldo**, the westernmost of the wooded promontories overlooking the Bay of La Concha.

On 31 August, as the summer ends, a torchlight procession in the **Parte Vieja**, or Old Quarter, at the foot of Monte Urgull commemorates the virtual destruction of San Sebastián during the Peninsular War. Among the surviving structures belonging to the old walled port, you can still visit the cavernous 18th-century **Basilica of Santa María del Coro**, with its apsidal portal deeply recessed to protect the sculptures from hard winters and its graceful statue of the city's namesake in a niche, and the 16th-century Dominican monastery of **San Telmo** in the **Plaza de Zuloaga**, converted into a wonderful Basque museum.

Part of the ethnographic collection in San Telmo is devoted to the history of the seafaring Basques. The Spanish colonisation of America depended on the skills of Basque navigators and shipbuilders with their experience in deep-sea fishing. Other exhibits in the San Telmo museum introduce *pelota*, the Basque national sport, and traditional Basque cuisine, costume and customs. In this traditionally rainy country, the matriarchal kitchen and adjoining stable, reconstructed in the museum, became the most important rooms of the Basque farmhouse, the stone-and-timber *caserío*.

The Fine Arts collection ranges from Hispano-Flemish to contemporary. **Balconies in Pasaje de San Juan.**

Occupying a place of honour, the Basque painter Ignacio Zuloaga's best-known work shows three hearty Basque men enjoying a meal.

Eating clubs: Private, men-only gastronomic societies *(txokes)* were founded here in the Parte Vieja in the 1870s. Basque cookery, with its fresh vegetables, dairy products and fish from the Bay of Biscay, seasoned with subtle sauces, is generally acknowledged to be the best on the peninsula.

The neoclassical **Pescadería** (fish market), a few hundred yards south of the **Plaza de Zuloaga** near the arcaded **Plaza de la Constitución**, has, appropriately, one of the grandest facades in the Parte Vieja. At the nearby market ask for Idiazabel, cheese from the long-haired Laxa sheep which has been cured and smoked, and *txakoli*, the thin white Basque wine drunk with shellfish.

The Basque coast: It is possible to drive west from San Sebastián all along the hilly coast of Guipúzcoa and Vizcaya, stopping whenever you feel like visiting one of the family beaches or enjoying a freshly caught fish dinner. Typical port resorts have at least one old church near the water, several good restaurants and sandy beaches.

Zarauz, with its nice long beach, and **Guetaria**, which has a smaller one, are two of the best-known producers of *txakoli*. This part of the coast may be the best place in Spain to order *chipirones en su tinta* (squid in its own ink).

In Guetaria, formerly a whaling port, is a monument to Magellan's Basque navigator, Juan Sebastián Elcano, who was born here. The man who may prove to be the 20th century's greatest couturier, Cristobal Balenciaga (1895–1972), was also born in Guetaria.

Past Guetaria, the craggy shoreline of the **Cornisa Cantábrica** begins. Although it does not look far on the map, **Lequeitio**, one of the most interesting ports on the Basque coast, is a full half-day's drive from San Sebastián. The painter Zuloaga's summer villa and studio in a former convent at the well-heeled resort of **Zumaya** was turned into a good museum after his death.

The Basque country benefits from summer rain.

Zuloaga was an important collector, and the **Museo Zuloaga's** collection includes one of El Greco's many versions of Saint Francis receiving the stigmata, a painting by Morales il Divino and two paintings by Zurbarán, who came from a Basque family.

The 15th-century church at Lequeitio with its flying buttresses and baroque tower is a few yards from a pretty beach where, in the morning, you may see fishermen painting their boats, or groups of children being given swimming lessons. From Lequeitio it is only a short drive south to Guernica.

Guernica: The bustling modern market town of **Guernica** is sacred to the Basques for its associations with their ancient tradition of self-government. At least since the early Middle Ages, their representatives met at Guernica to elect a council of leaders and witness the titular monarch's oath to uphold their *fueros*. An event of enormous consequence for today's Basques, the election of José Antonio Aguirre at the **Casa de Juntas**, the parliament building, in the 1936 election, revived this tradition. Members of his government were sworn in under the **Guernikako Arbola**, the symbolic oak of Guernica. (The original oak which had stood for centuries was evidently destroyed by the French in the Peninsular War. The present one, it is claimed, grew from the original tree's acorn or sapling.)

The declaration of an independent Basque state was met with swift retribution by the Nationalists under General Mola. Miraculously, the Casa de Juntas, the oak and the neighbouring **Church of Santa María** (begun in the 15th century) survived the almost total destruction of Guernica on Monday 26 April 1937, the most infamous episode of the Civil War.

Mondays, then as now, were market days and the narrow streets were crowded with farm families and refugees. A third of the civilian population was killed in the attack, and many more were wounded, when German aircraft dropped 100,000 pounds of bombs, then flew low to shoot at the Basques

The sacred tree of Guernica, symbol of Basque independence.

fleeing into the fields. *Caseríos* in the hills were also bombed. "In the night these burned like candles", one of the dazed correspondents covering the war wrote in *The Times* of London. International outrage probably discouraged the use of such air attacks again in Spain.

The very word "Guernica" became synonymous with the horrors of war, symbolised in Picasso's famous painting with this title, which now hangs in Madrid's Reina Sofia Museum.

"General Franco's aeroplanes burned Guernica and the Basques will never forget it", predicted *The Times* correspondent. Repression under the Franco regime only stiffened resistance to domination by the central government and on the night of the dictator's death Basques danced in the streets. The 1979 Statute of Guernica finally gave the 2 million Basques autonomous government, although significant pressure continues for a greater degree of self-rule. Oddly enough, some of the most fervent Basque nationalists are young descendants of non-Basques who migrated to the region's industrial cities in Franco's time.

The rebuilt town of Guernica is not handsome. However, be sure to notice the murals with their tranquil scenes of Basques at work, under the eaves of the **Casa de Ahorros Municipal de Bilbao** at the intersection of the **Gran Vía** and the **Calle Adolfo Urioste** between the tourist bureau and the Casa de Juntas. The castellated country house at **Arteaga**, 5 miles (8 km) to the north of Guernica, where the Empress Eugenie spent part of her early life, is seen in one of them. Eugenie's castle is visible from the highway, but the principal attraction on the outskirts of Guernica are the nearby **Santimamiñe Caves** and their prehistoric wall paintings, first discovered in 1916.

Northern port: In 1300 the fishing and ironmongering village of **Bilbao** received *villa* status from Diego López de Haro. His statue stands on a high plinth sometimes hung with the *Ikurrina*, the red, white and green Basque flag inspired by the Union Jack, at the foot of the pink and black **Banco de Vizcaya**

tower in the **Plaza Circular** near the **Puente de la Victoria**. The Puente is the main bridge joining old Bilbao on the east bank of the **Nervión River** and the newer bourgeois quarter which grew up on the west bank in the 19th century. Once you locate the **Gran Vía de López de Haro**, the main traffic artery running east to west from the Plaza Circular to the large **Parque de Doña Casilda Iturriza**, or the smart new Metro designed by Norman Foster, it is easy to get around this industrial centre, which is Spain's largest port.

There are long, sandy beaches at **El Abro**, about 12 miles (19 km) northwest on the Nervión estuary, and a Basque theme park, the **Parque de Atracciones de Vizcaya**, to the east near **Galdacano**. But the city itself, despite the air pollution and a wide ring of discouraging working-class apartment blocks, has a good deal to offer visitors.

The earliest settlements here are said to have been made near the present 15th-century **Church of San Antón** in the **Atxuri** district along the Ribera east of the **Siete Calles**, the "Seven streets" of the **Casco Viejo**, or Old Town.

The prosperous Casco Viejo was pillaged by the French during the Peninsular War, and much of it was destroyed in the Carlist Wars. But narrow streets and a number of pre-19th-century structures remain. The **Museum of Archaeology, Ethnology and History of Vizcaya** is in a converted Jesuit monastery in the **Calle de la Cruz** which was once attached to the baroque **Church of los Santos Juanes**. Along with prehistoric exhibits, it contains a copy of an important piece of Basque folk art, the Kurutziaga Cross from Durango.

You can look down on the Casco Viejo from the terrace of the **Sanctuary of Nuestra Señora de Begoña** (*circa* 1511 and later). To get there, take the elevator in the **Calle Esperanza Ascoa** behind the 15th and 18th-century **Church of San Nicolás de Bari**, the original Father Christmas and patron saint of Bilbao's children, sailors, prisoners and prostitutes, on the **Arenal**, the promenade at the east end of the Puente de la Victoria.

Industry and art: In the 1870s, at the end of the Second Carlist War, Bilbao began to exploit its natural iron deposits and industrialise in a big way. By the end of the century, half the Spanish merchant fleet came from Basque shipyards, much of its steel industry was located near Bilbao, and Basque bankers and businessmen wielded great financial power. The **Teatro de Arriaga** (1890) on the Paseo del Arenal, the **Ayuntamiento** (1892) at the bend in the river north of the Puente de la Victoria, and the **Palacio de la Diputación** (1897) were built, and a ground-swell of popular sentiment for going it alone and declaring a Basque State developed.

The wealthy, cosmopolitan aspect of Bilbao is reflected in the **Museum of Fine Arts'** presence in Iturriza Park. It contains the most important collection of paintings in northern Spain. In addition to its Flemish, Catalan and classical Spanish holdings, it has a modern wing with some pieces showing the influence of various international art movements on the generation of artists who grew up under Franco, including Isabel Baquenado, Juan José Arqueretta, Andrés Nagel and Javier Morras.

The graffiti and other forms of *ad hoc* wall art, especially in Bilbao and San Sebastián where there are a large number of politicised young Basques of all classes, were probably the most interesting in Europe in the 1980s, drawing upon virtually every counterculture movement of the 20th century for style and iconography.

Elements of the traditional Basque costume – white canvas and rope shoes called *alpargatas*, the crimson sash, the *makila* (walking stick) – are in evidence at the many Basque festivals. There are week-long festivals in each of the three provincial capitals in August. The *Semana Grande* in Bilbao is the biggest. The events usually range from heavy culture to heavy metal to Basque folk music and traditional contests of stamina and strength in which both men and women participate.

Old town: The capital of Álava, **Vitoria** is the largest and least Bascophone of the three Basque provinces and the seat of the autonomous Basque government. While Vitoria is best known for the bloody battle of 1813 in which Wellington defeated the French general Jourdan, it received its name as early as 1181 when Sancho the Wise founded a walled city here.

The **Feria de la Virgen Blanca** in August pays homage to the "White Virgin", standing in her jasper niche in the porch facade of the 14th-century **Church of San Miguel**. The city's protector, she overlooks the miradors of the busy **Plaza de la Virgen Blanca** and the monument erected in 1917 to commemorate the Battle of Vitoria.

The narrow, concentric alleyways of the **Old Town**, some named for the crafts which flourished here – Zapatería, Cuchillería, Pintorería, Herrería – underwent a certain amount of urban renewal in the mid-19th century when medieval arcades were demolished and all the widening and airing-out possible performed to make them salubrious. But this quarter, with its three Gothic churches, town-houses

Basque fisherman.

decorated with escutcheons and carved doorways, and shops and cafés, still imparts an authentic feeling of the prospering commercial town of the Middle Ages and Renaissance.

The Gothic sculpture in the porch of the church of **San Miguel** is of high quality. Inside is a retable by Gregorio Fernández, an important Golden Age sculptor. Notice the bagpipe player in his *Adoration of the Shepherds.*

The adjacent **Plaza del Machete**, named for the large knife on which oaths to uphold the town's *fueros* were sworn, marks the southern end of the Old Town. Walk north, stopping to admire the sculpture in the porch and on the column capitals of the **Cathedral of Santa María**, to the **Archaeological Museum**. This well-designed small museum, in a 15th-century merchants' house in the **Correría**, distinguished by half-timbering and horizontal brickwork, is a sensitive adaptation of an historic structure. The tens of thousands of years of local history to which it is devoted range from the Lower Paleolithic era through to the Middle Ages.

Art and wine: To the south, in a neighbourhood of large private houses between the **Jardines de la Florida** park and the 19th-century park called El Prado, is the **Provincial Museum of Fine Arts**. Its varied holdings include a Crucifixion by José de Ribera and a Virgin by the irascible Sevillan painter and sculptor Alonso Cano (1601–67), one of the most picaresque personalities in Spanish art. There are paintings and sculptures by Basque artists and a growing modern collection featuring the work of Miró, Picasso and Antonio Tápies (born 1923), the best-known Spanish abstract painter.

A small part of the Rioja winegrowing district lies inside the Basque Country. Drive into the **Rioja Alavesa** to the fortified village of **Laguardia**. The view of the Ebro Valley alone is worth the trip. Laguardia's dark, narrow streets and the cellars opening into them smelling of farm animals and wine suggest what a promenade of Vitoria's Old Town might once have been like.

Bilbao.

CANTABRIA AND ASTURIAS

The autonomous regions of Cantabria and Asturias lie between the Basque Country and Galicia along the Bay of Biscay or *Mar Cantábrico*. Each region consists of one narrow province: **Santander** and **Asturias**, respectively. A formidable mountain chain, the **Cordillera Cantábrica**, separates the coast and its narrow strip of fertile valleys from the *meseta*.

Few parts of Spain have greater natural beauty. There are 72 beaches in Cantabria, stretching east to west from Castro de Urdiales to San Vicente de la Barquera. The 180 miles (290 km) of coastline in Asturias is a succession of beaches, estuaries and promontories. From the 300-ft (91-metre) **Cabo de Penas**, north of Gijón and Áviles, you can see a large part of it.

In summer the soft greys and greens of the rugged landscape are scattered with bright red, blue, yellow and green tents, flags and cars in the beautifully sited camping areas. On rainy days you may see the tiny figure of a solitary fisherman on a long stretch of sand at the foot of an immense weatherbeaten cliff. On a sunny day, the same spot will be filled with bathers and beach tents.

Even in summer there is snow on the **Picos de Europa**, which rise to over 8,660 ft (2,640 metres). The highest mountains in the Cordillera, they begin in Cantabria and almost completely cover Asturias. They are made up of the Cornión, Urrieles and Andorra massifs. The region containing the mountains which are the source of the rivers flowing into the Cantabrian Sea has long been called *La Montaña*.

History: Small nomadic bands of hunters and food-gatherers belonging to the Stone Age cultures decorated the walls and ceilings of the limestone caves in this region with pictures of the migratory animals they followed.

The similarity between the decorated prehistoric caves in the limestone area of southern France and those of northern Spain led to the designation of a pre-

historic "Franco-Cantabrian" cultural area, which includes a number of sites in the foothills of the Pyrenees in the Basque Country and in Asturias.

Castro Urdiales and Laredo: Castro Urdiales, the old Roman settlement of Flavio Briga, is the easternmost and one of the oldest ports on the coast of Cantabria. The **Playa de Brazomar** and the **Playa de Oriñón** at the mouth of the **Agüera River** are characteristically long, sandy Cantabrian beaches, a short walk from both summer resort facilities and an old quarter with medieval remains.

From the small fortified peninsula, a ruined Templars' hostel, the "**Castle** " **of Santa Ana** and the Gothic **Church of Santa María**, with French sculptures, flying buttresses and uncompleted towers reminiscent of Notre Dame in Paris, overlook the photogenic harbour filled with fishing boats.

The most important medieval pilgrimage trails led to Santiago de Compostela and, in the opposite direction, to Rome and on to Jerusalem. The

Left, verdant Cantabria. Right, farmer in *comillas*, special clogs for walking in mud.

rich, powerful military Order of Knights Templars, ascetic monks in arms distinguished by their white habits embroidered with the red Crusaders' cross, was founded in 1120 to protect pilgrims on their way to Palestine. At Castro Urdiales the Templars ministered to the pilgrims of Saint James and recruited suitable members for their main work in the Holy Land.

At **Laredo**, **Salvé Beach** attracts so many summer visitors that the off-season population of something over 10,000 will have multiplied by a factor of 10 by mid-August. This explains the highrises and summer houses that follow the curve of the beautiful beach.

In the Castilian Golden Age that followed the Reconquest, this part of the coast was the administrative centre of Cantabria, and Old Castile's only outlet to the sea. The size of the Cantabrian fleet which operated here increased dramatically in the 16th century. The ports on the Bay of Biscay were, according to a contemporary Venetian, the jewels in the Spanish emperor's crown. They were the basis of Spain's superior maritime capability. Ships carrying Spanish wine and wool sailed from San Sebastián, Laredo, Santander and La Coruña to Flanders and England, or into the Mediterranean through the Straits of Gibraltar. All along this coast churches were enhanced by the massive building campaign of the Catholic Monarchs as well as from their location on the pilgrim trail. In Laredo, for example, a 16th-century doorway was added to the 13th-century Gothic **Church of Nuestra Señora de la Asunción**.

In 1556 Charles V, having abdicated in favour of his son Philip II, sailed into Laredo from Flanders on the way to his Hieronymite monastery in Extremadura. With him arrived his sister, Mary of Hungary, ruler of the Netherlands, and the art treasures accumulated by both these great Hapsburg collectors. The Spanish public collections still hold most of the priceless works of Flemish art carried across Spain from Laredo more than 400 years ago.

Across **Santoña Bay** from Laredo is

El Sardinero Casino in Santander.

the port and resort of **Santoña**. It has another church begun in the 13th century and several beaches, including the mile-long (2-km) **Playa de Berria**.

Castilian summer retreat: The important modern port of **Santander** has been the provincial capital since the 18th century, when the French depredated the coastal area to the east. The city centre, rebuilt after much of it was destroyed by a fire in 1941, looks south across a beautiful protected bay. On a clear day you can see the Cordillera Cantabrica from the busy quay.

There are nice beaches (**El Camella, La Concha, La Primera** and **La Segunda,** all joined at low tide) facing out to sea in the older residential and resort quarter, **El Sardinero**. Here, too, are the **Gran Casino del Sardinero**, the **International Menéndez Pelayo University**, which offers summer courses to foreign students, and the large old-fashioned resort hotel, the **Hotel Real**. July and August are particularly lively in Santander, with an international festival of music, dance and drama. On the

Península de La Magdalena is the neo-Gothic summer palace of the royal family, an imitation of Balmoral built by Alfonso XIII in 1912 for his English queen. It is now part of the International University.

On a rainy day, visit the **Municipal Museum of Fine Arts** on the **Calle Rubio** west of the **Plaza Porticada**. It shares a building with the library donated by the Santander writer, Marcelino Menéndez y Pelayo (1856–1912), whose statue is in the garden leading to the house. The museum has an interesting small collection ranging from Zurbarán to contemporary Cantabrian artists and roomy galleries for temporary exhibitions. Here hang portraits of three of Spain's less-beloved rulers: Ferdinand VII, Isabella II, deposed in 1868 while summering in the Basque Country, and General Franco. The portrait of Ferdinand, one of several painted by Goya of this weak and cruel king, is believed to have been commissioned by the city of Santander.

Nearby Goya's four famous series of

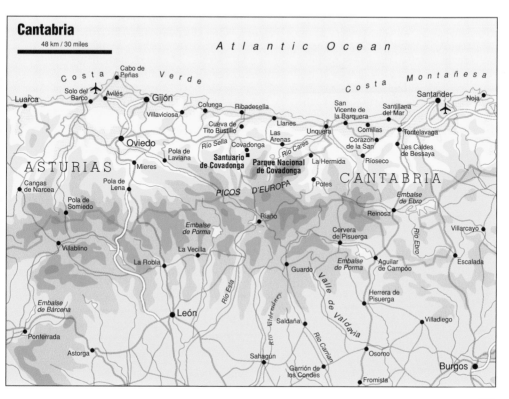

Cantabria

48 km / 30 miles

A t l a n t i c   O c e a n

Costa Verde · Cabo de Peñas · Luarca · Solo del Barco · Avilés · Gijón · Villaviciosa · Colunga · Ribadesella · Cueva de Tito Bustillo · Llanes · Las Arenas · Unquera · San Vicente de la Barquera · Santillana del Mar · Comillas · Tontelavaga · Costa Montañesa · Santander · Noja · Oviedo · Pola de Laviana · Río Sella · Covadonga · Río Cares · Corazón de la San · Les Caldes de Bessaya · **ASTURIAS** · Mieres · **Santuario de Covadonga** · **Parque Nacional de Covadonga** · La Hermida · Rioseco · **CANTABRIA** · Cangas de Narcea · Pola de Lena · *PICOS D'EUROPA* · Pótes · Embalse de Ebro · Pola de Somiedo · Riaño · Reinosa · Embalse de Porma · Cervera de Pisuerga · Villarcayo · Villablino · La Vecilla · La Robla · Río Esla · Guardo · Embalse de Porma · Aguilar de Campóo · Escalada · Herrera de Pisuerga · Embalse de Bárcena · Valle de Valdavia · Río Carrión · Río Esla · Saldaña · Villadiego · León · Ponferrada · Astorga · Sahagún · Garrión de los Condes · Osorno · Fromista · **Burgos** · Río Ebro

etchings are displayed: the *Caprichos*, the *Disasters of War*, the *Tauromaquía* and the *Disparates* or *Proverbios*.

The **Provincial Museum of Prehistory and Archaeology** in the **Diputación Provincial** near the **Puerto Chico**, where fishing boats are moored, provides an introduction to the Late-Paleolithic cave art found in this region.

The resorts of **Suanes**, **Santillana del Mar** and **Comillas** on the coast west of Santander are crowded in summer with well-heeled Spaniards from further south. This is an agreeable area of first-rate beaches, pretty farms overlooking the sea, medieval and Renaissance churches and balconied, galleried and escutcheoned granite Golden Age palaces or townhouses.

Santillana is an amazingly well-preserved medieval village, with fine stone mansions and cobbled streets. The 12th to 13th-century Romanesque **Collegiate church** contains the bones of one of the virgin saints, the 4th-century Saint Juliana. "Santillana" is derived from the Latin *Sancta Juliana*. The Colegiata itself, like many other churches in the French-influenced Romanesque style, was designed to serve as a roomy reliquary entered through the elegant round-arched west portal.

Despite the cosmopolitanism it has acquired over a thousand years or so, Santillana has been able to preserve the character of a market town. The **Parador Nacional Gil Blas** on the main square, one of the most popular *paradors* in Spain, is named for the picaresque hero of *Gil Blas de Santillane*, a novel by the 18th-century French satirist Alain-Rene Le Sage, and later a verse play by Victor Hugo. Both attacked social problems in France while pretending to write about Spain.

In Comillas, follow the signs to **El Capricho**, the summer house built to the designs of the Catalan architect Gaudí in 1883–85. At El Capricho, Gaudí combined references to the squat Romanesque columns, the minaret, *mudéjar* brickwork, the traditional Spanish iron balcony, the pink neo-Gothic **Sobrellano Palace** adjacent to it, and – most imaginatively of all – the

shapes and colours of the Cantabrian countryside and seashore.

Cave art: Altamira is about a mile (1.5 km) south of Santillana del Mar. The "Sistine Chapel" of cave art was the first, and arguably is still the finest, Palaeolithic-decorated cave identified. In 1879 Don Marcelino de Sautuola, who lived in a villa nearby and had seen some small engraved Palaeolithic art objects which were accepted as genuine at the Universal Exposition in Paris the year before, realised by their similarity that the paintings at Altamira were prehistoric.

The bison, hinds, wild boar, horses and other animals on the ceiling at Altamira are the largest known group of "polychromes", that is, figures which were painted using several colours of pigment (ochres, manganese oxides, charcoal, iron carbonate). The three most important polychrome sites in the world are Altamira, Tito Bustillo (in Asturias) and Lascaux in Perigord, France (the last of which can no longer be visited).

Altamira's authenticity was not generally accepted until the turn of the century, when other caves to which the entrances had been blocked, so there was no possibility of a hoax, were discovered. The quality and precise detail of figures such as the pregnant bison were the greatest impediment to Altamira's acceptance.

Some of these sophisticated figures of 15,000 years ago are large – over 6 ft (2 metres) long, while the ceiling is low (5 to 6 ft high). The best way to see them is by lying on your back.

As visitor numbers are strictly controlled, you must book at least 10 months ahead. Write to Museo de Altamira, 39330 Santillana del Mar, Santander, specifying the number in your party and naming a date. But no reservation is needed to visit the museum and the Cave of Stalactites. Seeping groundwater formed stalactites, which covered the paintings at several sites, actually protecting them.

The Costa Verde: Looking down for a change instead of up, the view of **San Vicente de la Barquera**, 6 miles (10 km) west of Comillas, is one of the nicest surprises on the Cantabrian coast. As you travel west, the little harbours on which the old ports were built become wider, the river valleys look greener and the mountains are higher. The fortified walls and castle, and the 13th to 16th-century **Church of Santa María de los Angeles** on the piney headland, are reflected in the inlet spanned by the 17th-century **Puente de la Maza**, a stone bridge with 28 arches. The beach, the **Sable de Merón**, is almost 2 miles (3 km) long and as much as 328 ft (100 metres) wide when the tide is out.

Mozarabic art: Leave the coast at San Vicente and take the road that follows the **Deva River** valley to **Unquera, Panes**, and then up into the eastern end of the Picos de Europa in the direction of the village of **Potes**. The narrow **Desfiladero de la Hermida** may be slow going as it criss-crosses the Santander-Asturias border, but it widens north of Potes to form the austere mountain setting for one of the jewels of *mozarabic* architecture, the **Church of Santa**

María de Lebeña. Founded by Alfonso, Count of Liebana (924–63), and his wife Justa, possibly immigrants from Andalusia, it combines the architectural concepts of the mosque with the forms of local pre-Romanesque Asturian churches, with its small agglomerative compartments and tunnel vaults, which had developed independently north of the Cordillera Cantabrica from the 8th century, based to some degree on Visigothic prototypes. Like the Asturian churches, Santa María was completely vaulted over.

Entered by a side door, the church has the feeling of a mosque, due in part to its horseshoe arches. Its 15th-century red, white and blue Virgin of the Good Milk is now part of an 18th-century retable. A stone stele re-used by a 9th-century builder is carved with Visigothic designs in roundels. A primitive human figure in the lower left corner of the stele was painted, it is said, with a mixture of blood and ashes.

At the time Santa María was built, this remote area had been a centre of

monastic culture for several centuries. It was in the monastery of **Santo Toribio**, a few miles south, that the 8th-century monk Beatus wrote his commentaries on the Apocalypse and the Book of Daniel. The *Beatos*, as they were called, were illuminated in the scriptoria of various monasteries in the following centuries. As examples of *mozarabic* art, they are as important as Santa María. Santo Toribio also possesses what is claimed to be the entire right arm of Christ's wooden cross.

The **Fuente Dé Parador** west of Potes is located at the source of the Deva River and surrounded by high peaks. It is open all year, and climbers use it as a base. The view from the **Mirador del Cable**, reached by a cable car which runs all year from Fuente Dé, takes in Potes, the Deva Valley, the nearby wildlife reserves and the mountains.

Asturias: Returning to the coast and entering the kingdom of Asturias, you will find yourself on an increasingly irregular shoreline. Sandy beaches and port resorts lie between high promonto-ries. Pretty **Llánes** has a cliff walk, the **Paseo de San Pedro**, and 30 small beaches. Ask when the charming Asturian folk dance called *El Pericote* is to be performed. A prehistoric menhir carved with an anthropomorphic figure called **Peña Tu** is at **Vidiago** close by; at **Colombres** is one of the more important decorated caves, **El Pindal**.

Ribadesella occupies the east bank of the estuary of the **Ría Sella**. One of the most important Franco-Cantabrian caves, **Tito Bustillo**, is west of the port across the bridge over the estuary. The original entrance has been lost, so that it is uncertain whether the paintings here were exposed to daylight. On a red ochre-painted wall overhanging the habitation site, more than 20 animals were painted in other colours and then engraved with flint tools. The size of these well-observed animals is considerable, averaging over 6 ft (2 metres). They include at least one reindeer, a species rarely encountered in Cantabrian Palaeolithic art. Tito Bustillo is easier to visit than Altamira, but the **Boat painter in Gijón.**

number of visitors per day is limited.

Sea and cider: An overwhelming mural painting by the Uria Aza brothers, depicting the horrors of modern war in the church at Ribadesella, is worth a sobering look, as is the view of mountains and port life from the quay.

In any of the fishing villages, you can eat excellent *caldereta* (fish stew), hake in cider or locally caught shellfish such as sea urchins.

Cider, the traditional Asturian drink, is aerated by being poured from a bottle held some distance from the glass. Visitors tend to spill a lot, but it does not seem to matter. You may be treated to the local folk songs; Asturian voices are said to have both the depth of the mountain valleys and the lilt of the sea.

From Ribadesella it is a pleasant excursion to Covadonga National Park in the Picos de Europa. In a green, tree-shaded valley lies the important national shrine of Covadonga, where in the 8th century Pelayo, an Asturian warrior, crushed a Moorish force, thus becoming a symbol of Christian resistance to the invaders. A statue of Pelayo stands near a neo-Romanesque church. Continuing into the park, you reach two glacier-formed lakes, Enol and La Ercina. In the background are the snow-capped peaks of the Picos.

Oviedo: Unless you are able to make an extended visit to Asturias, you should go first to **Oviedo** (population about 200,000), the provincial capital of the kingdom of Asturias. It is on a plain of meadows, surrounded by fields of maize, apple orchards and small prosperous towns. The fishing-port resorts around **Gijón** with their folkloric festivals, all of the pre-Romanesque churches in the area and **Covadonga** are within easy driving distance.

Orient yourself by the large park in the city centre, the **Parque de San Francisco**. With the tall grey post office tower on your left, walk straight ahead to the old ecclesiastical district much damaged in the anti-Fascist uprising of working-class parties led by the miners in 1934 and in the Civil War soon afterward. The tourist bureau with its models of Asturian churches is on the **Plaza**

Alfonso II El Casto, next to the remains of the pre-Romanesque **Church of San Tirso** built by that king. The flamboyant Gothic cathedral, the **Basilica del Salvador**, its perforated spire damaged in the 1930s and subsequently restored, contains the **Pantheon of the Asturian Kings** and the **Cámara Santa**, their reliquary chapel. Behind the cathedral is a burial ground for pilgrims to Santiago de Compostela and a superb archaeological museum in the **Convent of San Vicente**.

Several of the finest pre-Romanesque Asturian buildings can be found in Oviedo, including the basilican church of **San Julián de los Prados** (*circa* 830) with illusionistic wall paintings. It was built in the reign of Alfonso II to adjoin one of the king's palaces. On **Mount Naranco** the barrel-vaulted **Santa María de Naranco**, originally a royal hall built for Ramiro I in the mid-9th century, and the incomplete **San Miguel de Lillo** of the same period, are close together on the same hillside.

Oviedo is one of the best places to try the local specialities of Asturian cookery. The classic dish is *fabada*, the rich stew made with a buttery white bean only grown here, pork and various types of sausage. You might also like to try one of the 20 types of cheese made around Asturias, such as the pungent *Cabrales*, made from cow, goat and ewe milk, or spicy *Los Beyos*.

Mountain view: It is only an hour's drive directly south to **Puerto de Pajares** (4,460 ft/1,360 metres), a pass in the Picos on the border between Asturias and León. At **Mieres**, a steel-workers' town along the way, the Socialist Republic was proclaimed on 5 October 1934. Past Mieres, and accessible only by doubling back through **Pola de Lena**, the single-naved early 10th-century pre-Romanesque **Church of Santa Cristina** is perched on a hill and visible from the highway.

There is a winter sports centre and an incomparable view at Pajares. To the pilgrims, soldiers and refugees of Asturian history, it must have been an unforgettable experience to cross the mountains here, especially in winter.

GALICIA

Criss-crossed by myriad rivers and mountain ranges, the northwestern region of **Galicia** is a land of unforgettable vistas and pristine, ocean-chiselled coastline. Across this nature-blessed region can be found treasures that are a legacy of the Celts, the Seubi, the Romans and the Visigoths who conquered and settled it. Isolated from the rest of Spain by a bulwark of mountains on the east and south and bounded to the north and west by the tumultuous North Atlantic, Galicia's natural formations include craggy mountains, long, loping valleys and distinctive *rías* or estuaries.

Half of its area lies between altitudes of 1,300 and 2,000 ft (400 to 600 metres) and less than one-fifth at altitudes lower than 1,300 ft. Mountains ring the interior, separating the region from the Spanish provinces of Asturias, León and Zamora to the east and Portugal to the south. Galicia is a *Finisterre*, or Land's End, as the Romans named its westernmost point. Despite occasional blasts from Atlantic storms and an average rainfall of 40 inches (102 cm), Galicia's winters are mild enough for residents of the regional capital, Santiago de Compostela, to term their city "the place where rain is art".

In spring and summer a striking palette of colours – deep green, yellow and orange – blooms, attracting thousands of tourists. Lining the 240 miles (380 km) of its bold, indented coastline are dainty towns and postcard-pretty fishing villages. The *rías* in the north are known as the **Rías Altas** and those along the southwest as the **Rías Bajas**.

Celtic roots: Galicia and its people retain many traces of the passage of the Celts, who swept through around 1000 BC and established a hold on this windswept, rain-soaked land that they did not relinquish until the arrival of the Romans in 137 BC. The region's name is derived from the word "Gallaeci", the name by which the Celtic tribes were known to the Romans.

Centuries before the Celts invaded, the indigenous people lived in *pallozas*, conical-shaped stone houses with thatched roofs. In impoverished areas, such as Las Ancares in Orense Province and parts of Lugo Province, some peasants lived in *pallozas* together with their animals until recently, but now Las Ancares is a tourist sight. Indeed the people of Galicia have never lived in large numbers in towns and even today many of the 3 million Galicians live in small, secluded hamlets.

As a result of a shared heritage, Galicians, like the Irish, Welsh and Bretons, are known for the characteristics associated with the Celtic races. They have a passion and some genius for poetry and music, a melancholic and pessimistic outlook on life, a fascination with death and a deep love of what they affectionately call "*Terra Nosa*" (Our Land). Historian Luis Moure Mariño has written that "the sentiment of the land as part of one's flesh and blood and a pantheistic vision of the world has always been a part of the Galician soul". As in Scotland and Ireland, bagpipes, or *gaitas*, are traditional in Galicia.

Isolation: Galicia remained relatively free of Muslim influence during Spain's Moorish period despite occasional attacks by Moorish forces. Its mountains and distance from the rest of the peninsula permitted the region to develop a distinct cultural personality. The Roman era ended in the mid-5th century with the arrival of the Seubi, a rugged people from northern Europe who organised the remains of the Roman territory into an independent kingdom that lasted through the 6th century.

In the 8th, 9th and 10th centuries Galicia came under the power of the Asturian monarchs and later those of León. Linguists place the beginning of the Galician language in the early 11th century. The Galician culture showed greater affinity for Portuguese culture than for that of Spain until the final separation of the two countries in 1668. But by the time Galicia came under the rule of the Catholic Monarchs, who established the *Junta* of the kingdom of Galicia in 1495, the region had firm economic and religious ties to the cen-

Left, Galician *gaitas* are similar to bagpipes.

tral kingdom because of the importance of its shrine of St James at Santiago de Compostela.

Abundant rainfall gives Galicia the appearance of a bucolic paradise, but it is not so much the agricultural blessing one might suppose. Excessive rain causes severe erosion and the soil retains little moisture. Another impediment to agricultural development is the uneven terrain, making the mechanisation of farming nearly impossible in large parts of the region. The division of the land into small family farms, known as *minifundio*, effectively stymies political attempts to bring about reforms leading to industrial-type farming. Everyone has some land and no one wants to give up his small parcels, which are not usually together, but spread apart, because of the way land has been passed down through inheritance.

Recent government efforts to join plots belonging to different families have failed, largely because of suspicions that the new plans would benefit the investors rather than the locals.

La Coruña: A good point of departure for travellers planning to tour the Rías Altas is the port city of **La Coruña** in the very northwestern corner of Spain. It has been a key shipping centre for nearly 2,000 years. Julius Caesar entered it by way of Gaul (France) in AD 60 to re-establish Roman rule in several rebellious towns nearby. The old part of the city (La Ciudad Vieja) rises from a narrow strip of land pointing out into the Atlantic, while the new section (La Pescadería) rests on the edge of the mainland and an isthmus.

The city's showpiece is its **Tower of Hercules**, the world's only existing and working Roman-era lighthouse, which stands on the northernmost edge of the isthmus, 10 minutes by car from the city centre. It dates from the time of the Celtic chieftain Breogan, who built it to commemorate the departure of an expedition to Ireland, and was rebuilt during the reign of Trajan, the Roman Emperor born in Spain in AD 98. Because of its position near a great sea route between northern Europe and South and Central

The harbour at Betanzos, Galicia.

America, La Coruña continues to play an important role and is one of Spain's biggest fishing ports.

The characteristic enclosed glass balconies (*miradores*) of the pretty white buildings in the new section permit residents to admire the bay while protecting them from stiff ocean winds. The open nature of its people have made La Coruña known as "the city where no one is a stranger".

To take in the sun, cross the old city and stop at the downtown beach, **Riazor**, or take a short cab ride toward the mainland and swim at **Santa Cristina** beach on the isthmus. In the old section, pass along the gardens lining **Avenida de la Marina** and then walk over to the **Plaza de María Pita**, named after the heroine who courageously gave the alarm alerting citizens of an attack by the English admiral, Francis Drake in 1589. The spacious square is dominated by the impressive 19th-century Ayuntamiento (City Hall) building. A few streets south is the **Castillo de San Antón**, once a prison and now an archaeological museum.

The churches of **Santiago** (12th century), **María del Campo** (13th century) and **Santo Domingo** (17th century) are in the city's old section. Just south of the latter and overlooking the harbour is the **Jardín de San Carlos**, an enclosed garden containing the granite tomb of Sir John Moore, the Englishman who died in 1809 while helping to defend the city against the French during the Peninsular War.

Franco's birthplace: An hour's drive east along the coast from La Coruña leads to the major upper *ría* on whose edge lies the city of **El Ferrol**, founded during the Middle Ages. The large estuary forms a near-perfect, protected deep-water port where one of Spain's principal naval bases has existed since the 18th century. Kings Ferdinand VI and Charles III developed strongholds at the head of the channel, which is 4 miles (6 km) wide at the *ría's* mouth. It remains a key shipbuilding centre.

General Francisco Franco was born and grew up here, the son of a navy

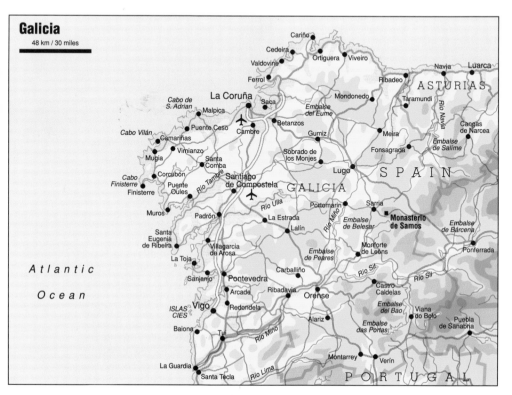

supply clerk. During his rule the city was officially known as *El Ferrol del Caudillo* (of the Leader). A huge equestrian statue of Franco still dominates the **Plaza de España**. One might think a native son of Galicia might have used his power to develop his home region economically. Franco, however, like other Galicians who held important national posts before him, identified more with Spain than with Galicia. Unlike politicians from the Basque Country and Catalonia, he viewed strong regional loyalty as anti-Spanish, and also prohibited the teaching and official use of the Galician language.

Among Spaniards, Galicians are known as a conservative, cautious, but above all, cunning people. It is said that if a Galician is seen on a staircase it is hard to determine whether he is going up or down. Franco was famous for making ambiguous statements on policy and letting his ministers argue before he made his own views known.

Another *ría* easily reached (20 minutes east by car) from La Coruña is **Betanzos**, with a city of the same name. It reached its apogee in the 14th and 15th centuries when the nearby **Las Marinas Valley** provided wheat for the entire La Coruña province. Three impressive but small Gothic churches, **Santa María del Azogue** (founded late 1300s), **San Francisco** (1387) and **Santiago**, have been well-preserved and serve as an illustration of the town's best moments.

In the heart of the country: An hour's drive south from La Coruña through high mountain passes on the smooth A-9 toll highway is a panorama of rustic Galician beauty. A feeling of entering the heart of this country is confirmed by the sight of the twin baroque towers of Galicia's pride, the **Cathedral of Santiago de Compostela**, which shelters the tomb of St James, patron of Spain.

According to legend, a peasant led to a field by the light of a shining star discovered the tomb of the Apostle of Jesus. Saint James was martyred in Jerusalem in AD 44 but his remains returned by boat with his followers to Spain, where he was said to have trav-

elled and evangelised. The discovery occurred between AD 812 and 814 and became a focus of unity for Christians who were then separated politically and spread across a narrow strip of northern Spain. It inspired Christian efforts to carry out the Reconquest which would eventually force the Moors off the Iberian peninsula.

Although contemporary historians dispute whether St James ever visited Spain, at the time the idea of the possession of the sacred remains of the saint aroused tremendous passion and pride, and emboldened the Christians.

Historians have passed on numerous testimonies by Spanish champions – men who won battles in the Mediterranean and in America against great odds – who said they were spurred on to victory by "visions of a white knight on horseback brandishing a fear-inspiring sword and wearing a vengeful grimace". As a battle cry, Christian soldiers shouted *"Santiago y cierre España!"* ("St James, and close Spain!") to urge their brethren to defeat the Moors. Christian fighters gave their patron the name of *Matamoros* (Slayer of Moors).

The road to Santiago: After the discovery, immediate support from the Asturian king and his successors and later the offering – *voto de Santiago* – of the Spanish monarchs created within an otherwise turbulent province a bustling town and then a cosmopolitan city that eventually became the "light of the Christian world in the Middle Ages". Over the saint's tomb, King Alfonso II of Asturias ordered the erection of an earthen temple, later replaced by a stone church under the rule of Alfonso III. In 997, al-Mansur Abu Jafar (military commander of the Moorish Caliphate of Córdoba) destroyed the entire town except for the tomb. But in 1075 work began on the present **cathedral** by order of King Alfonso VI of León and Castile.

The Romanesque building (consecrated in 1211) occupies the east end of the **Plaza del Obradoiro**. Its baroque facade by Fernando Casas y Novoa has graced the entrance to the cathedral since 1750. The interplay of curved and straight lines on the carvings appears to culminate in flickers of flame at the height of the two slender towers. Inside the facade is *El Pórtico de la Gloria*, the tripartite porch depicting the Last Judgment, the masterpiece of Maestro Mateo, considered the world's greatest example of the Romanesque style.

The well-travelled path of thousands of pilgrims through Navarre and Galicia became known as *El Camino de Santiago* (Road to Santiago). The number of pilgrims increased dramatically after Pope Calixto II conceded the Roman Catholic Church's greatest privileges to the See of Santiago de Compostela and designated as holy years those in which the day of St James fell on a Sunday. Pilgrims who reached Santiago in those years obtained a plenary indulgence and absolution for one year.

The shrine became the greatest place of Christian pilgrimage after Rome and Jerusalem. The cathedral inspired the design of numerous others. The city itself emerged as one of Europe's most brilliant, attracting outstanding artists, sculptors, scholars and silver and gold-smiths. Noted Spanish historian Americo Castro wrote that "the Christian Spain of the 9th century, united by the banner of St James that represented its ancient beliefs, emerged from the Galician corner with a new strength" to combat the Moors. Today, thousands of tourists visit the cathedral, which is unique in Spain in that it can be seen from plazas on all sides. A formidable fireworks display at midnight on 25 July of each year initiates the week-long festivities dedicated to Santiago.

The cathedral: Inside the cathedral, the high altar is dominated by a sumptuously attired 13th-century statue of St James. Some pilgrims mount the stairs behind the altar to kiss the saint's mantle. Below the altar, a crypt constructed in the foundations of the 9th-century church holds the remains of the saint and two of his disciples, St Theodore and St Athanasius. Other obligatory stops include the *Puerta de las Platerías* (Silversmith's Door), a Romanesque doorway so named because it led outside on to a plaza lined by silversmith shops, and the *Puerta Santa* (Holy Door), which is only opened during holy years.

Across the Plaza del Obradoiro from the cathedral stairs, the **Rajoy Palace**, a severe but impressive 18th-century mansion designed by French architect Charles Lemaur, serves as City Hall. It is capped by a bronze sculpture of Santiago the Moor Slayer in battle gear, riding a charging stallion. At the plaza's south end is the **Colegio de San Jerónimo**, a 17th-century building attractive for its 15th-century-style gateway. The north side of the plaza is occupied by the **Hostal de los Reyes Católicos**, begun in 1501 under orders of Ferdinand and Isabella as an inn and hospital for pilgrims. It is now a very luxurious hotel, forming part of the state-run *parador* chain. The building's facade features an ornate Plateresque doorway of great beauty and the wrought-iron work and carved columns in a chapel inside are of exceptional artistic merit.

Tourists and pilgrims: Heading out of the plaza between the cathedral and the

The Hostal de los Reyes Católicos, Santiago de Compostela.

Colegio de San Jerónimo, turn into the **Calle del Franco**. University of Santiago students, tourists and pilgrims mingle on this street among bars and shops. The street is lined with colleges, the Colegio de Fonseca (finished in 1530) being a required stopping point because of its remarkable Renaissance doorway. While in the old section of the city, visit the **Colegio de San Clemente** (1601) and the **Monastery of San Francisco**, said to have been founded by St Francis of Assisi in 1214 when he made a pilgrimage. The **Monastery of San Martín Pinario**, now a seminary, was founded in the 10th century and rebuilt in the 17th century.

To tour the **University of Santiago de Compostela**, walk west from the Plaza del Obradoiro along descending cobblestoned streets. The university was established in 1532, although its present building dates from 1750. Before leaving Santiago, stroll out to the **Paseo de la Herradura**, once a fairground and now a park set on a wooded hill not far from the university. The view of the cathedral's facade enveloped in the green mantle of surrounding hills is magnificent.

Lugo is 59 miles (95 km) east of Santiago on a highway that twists and turns through jagged mountains. The drive is worth the effort, for circling this former Roman capital in the region is one of the best-preserved Roman walls to be found anywhere in the world. The massive schist walls are 1 mile (2 km) long and 33 ft (10 metres) high and date from the 3rd century when the town was known as Lucas Augusti.

"Virgin of the Big Eyes": Lugo's position on the French road to Santiago explains the strong French influence in the Romanesque parts of its **cathedral**, begun in the 12th century. It was expanded in the Gothic period and enlarged in the 18th century. The **Capilla de la Virgen de los Ojos Grandes**, a chapel at its east end, containing the pre-Christian figure of the Virgin, features an exquisite baroque rotunda, which contrasts with the north door where a Romanesque Christ in Majesty is ensconced within a 15th-century porch.

Across from the north door on the lovely **Plaza de Santa María** is an 18th-century **Bishop's Palace**, a typical *pazo*, or Galician manorhouse, one storey high with stone walls and elaborate iron balconies. The **Provincial Museum** houses artifacts representing provincial history and a country cottage kitchen along with Roman coins.

Heading southwest towards Orense, the other inland provincial capital, a good choice for a brief stop is **Santa Eulalia de Bóveda**, a palaeo-Christian monument unearthed early this century, which consists of a vestibule open to the sky and a rectangular chamber with a basin and round-arched niche. Lovely frescoes of birds and leaves of early Christian origin remain intact here.

Feudal remnants: The 59 miles (95 km) of highway south from Lugo to Orense provide an insight into Galician history. Old men with weatherbeaten and wrinkled faces plough, with the help of a pair of oxen, small plots bordered by stone walls. Old women in the rigorous black of widowhood trudge

The cult of St James brought thousands of pilgrims to Galicia.

along roads, their long-handled scythes on their shoulders as they follow carts piled high with long grass.

Farming methods here vary little from the strip farming done in the Middle Ages. In fact, a semi-feudal society continues to exist. Dominant *caciques* (bosses) maintain great influence and power over peasants in villages in many areas where communication by road off the major highways remains difficult despite recent improvements. The provinces of Lugo and Orense have the lowest income per capita in all Spain.

Orense is said to have received its name because of the gold that legend says was mined in the hills of the **Miño Valley** and culled from the river of the same name that runs alongside the city. Although it is now a busy commercial town, Orense retains some wonders of its Roman origin, including the **Roman bridge** over the Miño that was rebuilt on its Roman foundations in the 13th century. In its **Archaeological and Fine Arts Museum**, once a bishop's palace, a large number of prehistoric,

pre-Roman and Roman-era specimens of great interest are kept. The Fine Art departments hold Romanesque Virgins and crucifixes, baroque altarpieces and a 17th-century woodcarving of the Stations of the Cross.

Orense has attracted visitors for hundreds of years because of Las Burgas mineral waters that emerge from three springs at a temperature of 153°Fahrenheit (67°Celsius).

"Cradle of Sailors": From the ancient city of **Pontevedra**, located 65 miles (105 km) east of Orense, you can visit most of the impressive Rías Bajas on the western coast with relative ease by car. According to legend, the town that sits at the point where the **Lerez River** flows out to the Ría de Pontevedra and the Atlantic was founded by Teucer, son of Telamon, half-brother of Ajax. But historians say the town probably dates from the Roman period and its name from the Latin *"Pons Vetus"* (or Old Bridge) that described the 11-arch span over the Leréz. Pontevedra is the birthplace of great sailors, including the ex-

Santiago Cathedral.

plorer Pedro Sarmiento de Gamboa, a skilled 16th-century navigator and cosmographer who wrote *Voyage to the Straits of Magellan*. Some local historians even claim Christopher Columbus as a native son.

The trading port had a brilliant life during the Middle Ages and Columbus' "*Santa María*" was built in its shipyards. But after the port at the innermost point of the Ría de Pontevedra silted up, a new port built at **Marín** surpassed it in importance. The small port town of Marín is today home to the Spanish Naval Academy and a small fishing community.

The new town of Pontevedra preserves the charm of the old in a section near the river and the **Puente del Burgo** bridge where the townspeople live in quaint stone houses with tall windowed balconies looking out over the river. The **Santa María La Mayor** Plateresque church, nestled among the alleyways and gardens in the fishermen's quarter, was built late in the 15th century by the mariners' guild. Its interior features an impressive mix of Gothic notched arches, Isabelline twisted columns and ribbed vaulting in the Renaissance style. Two other churches within walking distance are **La Vírgen Peregrina** (a cult to the Virgin of the Pilgrimage began here in the 17th century) and **San Francisco**.

Witchcraft: Galicians are notorious in the rest of Spain for their belief in magic, witches and superstition. In some cases this shows as an almost pagan belief in the spirit world; in others, it has grafted itself on to Christianity. At one fiesta held in the central Pontevedra Province town of **Corpiño** late in June, people who believe themselves possessed by evil spirits gather near the town's small church (**Our Lady of Corpiño**) and shout, scream and blaspheme until they liberate themselves from the spirit's spell. Others make offerings, such as circling the church on their knees 20 times, in a sacrifice to please the patron saint.

In the municipality of **Nieves** in southern Pontevedra Province, every

Galician ladies prepare octopus.

year on 29 July, people whose lives have been saved in one manner or another during the previous year gather to thank St Marta for her saving grace by taking part in what is known as "the Procession of Coffins". In this exotic exhibition of the Galician fascination with death, the "saved" people dress up in funeral clothes and get inside coffins which are then paraded around the church of **Ribarteme** by their families.

Water and wine: The coastal highway C-550 zigzags north from Pontevedra. In the traditional fishing villages of **Moaña** and **Sangenjo** a great variety of fish and shellfish changes hands at morning auctions on local wharves and a number of excellent seafood restaurants line the coast. Round a cape on the southern side of the **Ría de Arosa** is the extraordinary **La Lanzada beach**. In summer hundreds camp out on this long, picturesque strand which shines like a white clam shell. Further north is the island of **La Toja**. A sick donkey abandoned on the island by his owner and later found cured was the first living

The *horreo*, or Galician granary, is built on stilts to keep out vermin.

creature to benefit from the mineral waters of a spring here. Today an elegant luxury hotel offers everything from blackjack to beauty treatment.

A satisfying stop on this highway cruise is the town of **Cambados**. Savour the strong white Albariño wine produced nearby which goes so well with seafood. A 17th-century church and the adjoining **Fenfiñanes Pazo** (mansion), along with a row of arcaded houses, form the attractive **Plaza de Fenfiñanes** at the town's north entrance. A bit further down the highway is a lovely promenade overlooking the bay and bordered by gardens in the fishing village of **Villagarcía de Arosa**. The **Convent of Vista Alegre**, dating from the 17th century, lies between Villagarcía and **Padrón**.

Rosalía de Castro: Padrón is said to be the town where the boat bearing the body of St James arrived in Spain. The boat's mooring stone can be seen under the altar in the local church beneath the bridge over the **Sar River**. Galicia's most famous poet, Rosalía de Castro

(1837–85) lived for many years in a stone house near the Sar that is now a museum. Her penetrating and sympathetic studies into the suffering of country folk and their love of the land won widespread acclaim and sparked a new interest in Galician culture. She and her husband, the historian Manuel Murguía, formed the nucleus of a group of enthusiastic poets and writers who stimulated a *Rexurdimento* (renaissance) in Galician letters. Her *Cantares Gallegos* (Galician Songs, 1863) is one of the great works of Spanish literature. The *Rexurdimento* stirred latent nationalist sentiment, and by the early 20th century several nationalist parties had been formed.

Rosalía de Castro identified with the tribulations of the poor of rural Galicia because of the pain in her own life. The illegitimate daughter of a priest, she was rejected by family and society, lived for many years in an unhappy marriage and in old age was racked by cancer. She is somewhat of a mother figure for Galicians, who know her poetry well.

More recently, Padrón was the birthplace of the Nobel-prizewinning novelist Camilo José Cela.

Jewel of Galicia: On the northern side of the Ría de Arosa is the flower-bedecked town of **Puebla del Caramiñal**, with its exquisitely kept stone houses and majestic view of the *ría*.

Vigo, one of Galicia's largest and most industrialised cities, lies on the southern flank of the *ría*. Although Vigo dates back to Roman times, almost no buildings from that era remain. The major landmark is the **Castillo del Castro** built on a commanding hill above the city. After feasting on local seafood in the excellent **Restaurante El Castro** on the hill, tour the castle walls and enjoy the magnificent view.

Vigo became a rich port after Charles V authorised it to begin commercial trade with America in 1529. In the 15th and 16th centuries English pirates frequently raided the harbour, hoping to loot Spanish galleons returning from the Americas laden with riches.

English naval forces led by Drake

View of Galicia's Rías Bajas.

sacked the town in 1589. Queen Elizabeth of England had sent Drake and 30 ships and 15,000 men to attack Spain and Portugal in an attempt to establish the Portuguese pretender Dom Antonio. In 1701 English and French corsairs fired on ships bringing treasures from the colonies to Philip V of Spain, grandson of Louis XIV. Attacks on Spanish ships worsened the next year and when a convoy of Spanish ships returned in 1702 they were intercepted by a British fleet. The galleons were destroyed as they sought shelter in Vigo Bay. To this day it's believed that tons of gold lie at the bottom of the bay in the holds of lost galleons.

Enjoy the sun at one of several sparkling beaches, including **Samil, Alcabre** and **Canido**. Or take a ferry ride from the port to the charming fishing village of **Cangas** on the north side of the *ría* or to the **Islas Cíes**, small isles in the mouth of Vigo Bay. The Cíes break the violence of the Atlantic and serve to keep bay waters calm. During World War II submarines of Nazi Germany found refuge and supplies there. Vigo is Spain's key fishing port. It is home to one-half of Spain's fishing fleet, the fourth largest in the world.

Fish feast: Seafood is abundant, inexpensive and delicious. Local delicacies include boiled octopus, stuffed squid boiled in its ink, fried shrimp with cloves of garlic, fried hake, raw oysters with lemon, boiled lobster and baked clams. Several large fish-processing and canning factories and two shipyards employ many locals.

To see the port where Columbus's *"Pinta"* docked in 1493 with news of the discovery of the New World, drive south for an hour on coastal highway C-550 to **Bayona**.

An obligatory and satisfying stop is **Monte Real**. A massive castle fortress with a long defence wall was built on this promontory rock about 1500. It later became the governor's residence and has now been converted to the *parador* **Conde de Gondomar**. It is surrounded by pine and eucalyptus woods, and has a commanding vista of the Atlantic, the **Estelas Islands** in the mouth of the bay and the coast south to **Cape Silleiro**.

Emigration: Vigo was also the port of departure for the Galicians who sought a better life in Latin America. Underemployment in the agricultural sector and low incomes were primary motives for emigration. Historians have estimated that during the last 500 years one out of every three Galician males left his homeland.

In the mid-18th century Spain ended restrictions on settlement in Spanish America. Most Galicians made their way to Argentina, Cuba, Uruguay and Venezuela. In much of Latin America, the native-born call Spaniards – regardless of what part of Spain they come from – *gallegos* (Galicians).

Emigration was especially strong between 1911 and 1965 when almost 1 million Galicians, mostly men, left. Perhaps the most famous immigrant's son is Cuban President Fidel Castro, the son of a Galician veteran of the Spanish-American War who became a prosperous sugar-cane plantation owner.

Sardines in a Galician fish market.

INSIGHT GUIDES
Travel Tips

So, you're getting away from it all.

Just make sure you can get back.

AT&T Access Numbers

Dial the number of the country you're in to reach AT&T.

*AUSTRIA†††	022-903-011	***GREECE**	00-800-1311	NORWAY	800-190-11
*BELGIUM	0800-100-10	***HUNGARY**	00◇-800-01111	POLAND¹◆³	0◇010-480-0111
BULGARIA	00-1800-0010	*ICELAND	999-001	PORTUGAL¹	05017-1-288
CANADA	1-800-575-2222	**IRELAND**	1-800-550-D00	ROMANIA	01-800-4288
CROATIA¹◆	99-38-0011	**ISRAEL**	177-100-2727	***RUSSIA¹ (MOSCOW)**	155-5042
*CYPRUS	080-90010	***ITALY**	172-1011	SLOVAKIA	00-420-00101
CZECH REPUBLIC	00-420-00101	KENYA¹	0800-10	SOUTH AFRICA	0-800-99-0123
*DENMARK	8001-0010	***LIECHTENSTEIN**	155-00-11	SPAIN•	900-99-00-11
*EGYPT¹ (CAIRO)	510-0200	**LITHUANIA◆**	8◇196	***SWEDEN**	020-795-611
*FINLAND	9800-100-10	LUXEMBOURG	0-800-0111	***SWITZERLAND**	155-00-11
FRANCE	19◇-0011	F.Y.R. MACEDONIA	99-800-4288	***TURKEY**	00-800-12277
*GAMBIA	00111	***MALTA**	0800-890-110	UK	0500-89-0011
GERMANY	0130-0010	***NETHERLANDS**	06-022-9111	**UKRAINE†**	8◇100-11

Countries in bold face permit country-to-country calling in addition to calls to the U.S. **World Connect**℠ prices consist of **USADirect**® rates plus an additional charge based on the country you are calling. Collect calling available to the U.S. only. *Public phones require deposit of coin or phone card. ◇ Await second dial tone. ¹May not be available from every phone. †††Public phones require local coin payment through the call duration. ◆ Not available from public phones. • Calling available to most European countries. ¹Dial "02" first. outside Cairo. ³Dial 010-480-0111 from major Warsaw hotels. ©1994 AT&T.

Here's a travel tip that will make it easy to call back to the States. Dial the access number for the country you're in to get English-speaking AT&T operators or voice prompts. Minimize hotel telephone surcharges too.

If all the countries you're visiting aren't listed above, call **1 800 241-5555** for a free wallet card with all AT&T access numbers. Easy international calling from AT&T. **TrueWorld Connections.**

AT&T

TRAVEL TIPS

GETTING THERE

BY AIR

Madrid's Barajas airport, located just 10 miles (16 km) out of the city, is one of Europe's six leading airports for passenger traffic. There are direct flights to England via BTA and Iberia (the official Spanish airline) and service to the United States by Iberia, TWA, Delta, United and American Airlines.

Iberia, whose main offices in Madrid are at Calle Velázquez, 130, operates all regular Spanish carrier flights abroad and domestic connections, the latter jointly with its subsidiaries Aviaco (headquarters at Maudes, 51) and Viva Air (Zurbano, 41). **Tickets** can be purchased at Iberia's local ticket offices or any travel agency. Iberia **information**, tel: 411 2545; reservations, tel: 411 1011 or 411 2011.

To get into the city from the airport, there is a regular **bus service** which runs every 12 to 20 minutes (depending on the time of day) into the heart of town, to the underground bus terminal at the Plaza Colón. The Aeropuerto-Colón bus operates from 4.45am through the day until 1.40am. (For bus information, tel: 401 9900.) Easy connections can be made at Colón to the Madrid Metro (or Underground), a variety of bus lines and taxis. The bus fare is 300 pesetas; **foreign currency** can be exchanged into pesetas by the airport tellers of the Banco Exterior de España.

If taking a **taxi** from the airport into Madrid, avoid unofficial cab drivers. Official Madrid taxis are white with red stripes painted transversally across the doors. An additional 300 pesetas will be added to the fare shown on the meter as an airport surcharge, and 50 pesetas more can be included for each large piece of luggage. On Sunday, holidays and after 11pm, there is a further 150 peseta surcharge.

There is a **Left Luggage** Service in the International Arrivals Section and in the Plaza Colón Bus Terminal. Cars can be rented at the Atesa, Avis, Europcar and Hertz agencies, with service counters in both the National and International Arrivals terminals.

For flight information, tel: 305 8344/45/46.

BY RAIL

Madrid's most modern railway station, Chamartín, at Avda Pio XII in the north of the city, handles 80 percent of the city's rail traffic at the moment, while the recently modernised Atocha station will gradually be taking over trains travelling to the South, to Extremadura and Levante.

Arriving at the **Spanish border** on an international train, you may have to wait some time while trains are changed, due to the difference in Spanish and European rail gauges. This inconvenience will eventually be resolved when the Spanish government finally undertakes to unify their railway system with that of the rest of the continent.

BY BUS

The Estación del Sur de Autobuses at Calle Canarias, 17, (tel: 468 4200) is Madrid's main bus station and most of the major bus companies covering the long-distance routes use this terminal.

BY CAR

Foreign motorists in Spain must have either an international driving licence or a valid licence from their country of origin, the car's registration papers and valid insurance. Those who are not nationals of a European Community country will also require a *Carta Verde* or Green Card, which can be purchased at the border.

TRAVEL ESSENTIALS

VISAS & PASSPORTS

Visitors from EC countries require only a valid National Identity Card from their home state to enter Spain. Citizens of Andorra, Austria, Liechtenstein, Monaco and Switzerland enjoy a similar privilege.

US citizens, Australians and New Zealanders require a valid passport and are automatically authorised for a three-month stay, which can be renewed for another three. Visitors from elsewhere must obtain a visa from the Spanish Consulate in their respective country before setting off.

Europeans can prolong a three-month stay for an additional three-month period by applying for a *permanencia* in Madrid at the Comisaría de Policía, Sección de Extranjería, Calle Los Madrazo, 9. Tel: 521 9350.

However, in order to reside in Spain for any extended period of time a *Residencia* (*Visado de Residencia Serie V*) must be applied for in one's

A Wise Man Never Thinks How Far He's Come. He Thinks How Far He Can Still Travel.

REMY XO BECAUSE LIFE IS WHAT YOU MAKE IT

Swatch. The others just watch.

seahorse/fall winter 94-95

shockproof
splashproof
priceproof
boreproof
swiss made

swatch✚

SCUBA 200

country of origin. As of 1992 these laborious formalities do not apply to members of the European Community who are allowed to live and work freely in Spain.

A *Tarjeta de Estudiante* or Student Card can be applied for at District Police Stations or at Calle Los Madrazo, 9, by presenting a valid passport, an ordinary visa (*Series y Calve 4*, issued by the Spanish Consulate in the country of origin), proof of financial means to cover one's stay, medical insurance and proof of enrolment in an officially recognised school.

All official documents must be accompanied by a corresponding photocopy (two photocopies are necessary if a work permit is also requested). Three passport-size photographs are required for each application.

MONEY MATTERS

The peseta is the official Spanish currency. It comes in coins of 1, 5, 10 (not too common), 25, 50, 100, 200 (rare as well because it is a hexagonal silver coin, but easily confused with the round 5-peseta coin, nicknamed a *duro*) and 500 (a gold septagonal coin) and notes of 200 (rare, too), 500, 1,000, 5,000 and 10,000 denominations.

Best rates for travellers' cheques and foreign currency are obtained at banks (*see Banking below*), but you can also change money in Madrid at currency exchange shops (*Cambios*, of which one is at Calle Alcalá, 20), the American Express Office (Plaza de las Cortes, 2), hotels (where the rates are lower), major department stores and shops frequented by tourists.

BANKING

Practically all Spanish banks will change foreign currency and travellers' cheques, for a small fee. It is also possible to obtain pesetas in cash at any bank against your Visa or Mastercard credit card. However, visitors should be aware that **personal cheques** are not readily accepted in shops or other establishments as they are in other countries, even though they may be drawn on local banks.

Banking hours vary slightly from one bank to another. Most are open 9am (although some open at 8.30am) to 2pm weekdays and 9am–12.30 or 1pm on Saturday. All are closed on Sunday and holidays. Several banks keep their major branches in the business districts open until 4.30pm.

VALUE ADDED TAX

In order to be eligible, as a tourist, for a refund of the Spanish IVA (Value Added Tax), you must spend 15,000 pesetas or more on one item. This tax can range from 6 to 12 percent on the item, although on certain luxury goods it may be as high as 33 percent. The refund procedure is awkward and there

are usually long waits at the department store offices which process the requests.

In any event, this is how it is done: first, you must obtain a triplicate form from the shop, indicating your purchase, its cost and the incorporated tax. If you are a citizen of the EC, show all copies of the form to your local customs, together with the goods, and in due course you should receive a cheque from the shop for the amount of the tax.

If you are not an EC citizen, turn the form over to Customs officials before you leave Spain. If you go from Madrid Barajas or any of the other major international airports, you can present the validated blue copy of the form at the Banco Exterior de España and they will refund the sum of the tax to you in the currency you wish. If you leave the country from another Customs post, get them to validate your form and then send the blue copy back to the shop. The discounted sum should be forwarded to you by cheque in due course.

HEALTH PRECAUTIONS

No special innoculations are required for entering Spain, unless the visitor comes from an area where there has been a recent outbreak of smallpox, cholera or yellow fever.

Tap water can be drunk without reservations except in regard to taste, but bottled water is available in every bar, restaurant and hotel. The same applies to the water in the towns surrounding Madrid.

Unfortunately the phrase "Spanish tummy" can still prove accurate: food hygiene has improved enormously in recent years but you should nevertheless be a little cautious. In modest establishments avoid seafood on Sunday and Monday (it may not be as fresh as it should be) and be wary too of dishes containing raw egg, such as mayonnaise.

In summer come prepared with a sun hat and protective suncreams if you plan to be out in the open air a lot.

Bring with you any prescription medicine you require. Although Spanish pharmacies are amply stocked with medicines made by international companies and many drugs can be purchased over-the-counter without prescription, your particular medication may not be available. Chemists in Spain do not honour foreign prescriptions.

WHAT TO WEAR

Spaniards tend to judge a person by the way he or she dresses, ascribing importance to smart clothes and well-shined shoes. Shorts and miniskirts are acceptable and considered fashionable for young women, though they may stop you from being admitted to churches and religious sites: the Ecumenical Council requires that shoulders be covered. (Gone are the days of Francoist Spain when bikinis were outlawed – nowadays, topless sunbathing is quite usual in the coastal areas.) However, Spaniards still like to dress up and men do not eschew suits, jackets and ties when going out for dinner or to a top nightclub.

CUSTOMS

Visitors can bring the following items into the country duty-free: Any personal effects, such as jewellery, a typewriter, cameras, film, portable video and sound equipment, musical instruments, sports equipment, camping material, etc., plus reasonable quantities of cigarettes (300 cigarettes for EC residents, 200 for the rest of Europe and 400 for non-Europeans), and limited amounts of alcoholic beverages, perfumes, coffee and tea. If your camera, typewriter or whatever is new and you do not have the purchase receipt, it would be wise to ask a Customs official to certify that you brought it into the country with you.

Pets may be brought with you as long as you have a suitable Health Certificate for the animal signed by an officially recognised vet from the country of origin, which indicates the dates of the last vaccines and, in particular, that of an anti-rabies shot.

Not all Spanish hotels admit pets so do check before making reservations; nor are animals accepted in restaurants, cafeterias and food shops.

GETTING ACQUAINTED

GOVERNMENT & ECONOMY

Spain is a constitutional monarchy under King Juan Carlos I, who has ruled since the death in 1975 of dictator General Franco. He had ruled the country for almost 40 years following the end of the Spanish Civil War in 1939. Parliament currently has a Socialist majority. It is made up of a Congress of Deputies and Senate. Spain is a member of the European Community, the North Atlantic Treaty Organisation and the OECD.

Spain's economy has slowed in recent years. Nevertheless, optimism reigns as the country entered full-status membership of the European Community in 1992. Madrid is at the very heart of the country and of the Iberian Peninsula which Spain shares with Portugal. It is located on the flat central plateau, 2,200 ft (670 metres) above sea level, surrounded by mountain ranges.

While the city itself has well over 3 million inhabitants, the greater metropolitan area, which includes the suburban communities of Alcobendas, Alcorcón, Fuenlabrada, Getafe, Leganés, Majadahonda, Móstoles, Pozuelo, Las Rozas and San Sebastián de los Reyes, is inhabited by close to 4 million.

TIME ZONE

Spain is 1 hour ahead of Greenwich Mean Time, while the Canary Islands coincide with GMT. Consequently, when not on Daylight Saving Time, if it is noon in Madrid, it is also noon in Paris, Rome and Bonn; 11am in London and the Canary Islands; 6am in New York, Montreal and Boston; 5am in Chicago; 3am in Los Angeles and San Francisco; and 9pm in Sydney.

CLIMATE ·

Madrid has a relatively temperate climate. In autumn and spring, both extremely pleasant seasons, average temperatures range from 54°F to 60°F (12°C to 15°C), with a spread of 43°F (6°C) minimum to 70°F (21°C) maximum.

Summer and winter are more extreme. In summer, the thermometer can rise as high as 102°F (39°C) although breezes from the mountains can make the evenings slightly cooler. It is essential to dress accordingly, in light cotton clothing, sun hat or visor and comfortable shoes. Espadrilles are the ideal footwear, and are inexpensive, plentiful and available in many colours.

The average winter temperature is 41°F (5°C), although it can drop below 32°F (0°C) in January, the most unsettled month of the year. You'll need to bring your winter coat and although it does not rain often (with a total annual rainfall of about 438 mm per year), the wettest months are usually January, March and April. Most of the year, however, the sun shines amidst a clear, blue sky.

TIPPING & ETIQUETTE

Service is presumed to be included in restaurants and hotels, but it is customary to leave the spare change (50–100 pesetas per person) in the dish when eating at a modest restaurant and a few *duros* (5-peseta coins) at a bar. When dining at an averagely-smart restaurant, 10 percent of the bill is appropriate. A 25-peseta tip is fine for an average taxi ride, and bathroom attendants and movie-ushers will expect at least 10 pesetas per person.

WEIGHTS & MEASURES

Spain, like most of Europe, uses the metric system. One kilogram is equal to approximately 2.2 lbs, 1 litre is approximately 1.76 pints, 1 metre is about a yard or 3 feet and 1 kilometre is equal to five-eighths of a mile.

ELECTRICITY & VOLTAGE

The electrical voltage is 220 volts so US appliances which work on 110 volts will require a transformer, otherwise they will burn out. Some hotels, however, do have specially marked sockets with a built-in transformer for using 110-volt shavers and hairdriers. The flat-pronged American plugs require round-pronged converters in order to fit the Spanish sockets. British plugs also need adaptors.

BUSINESS HOURS

Although some offices are adopting a standard 8 or 9am–5pm work day, shops usually have a morning and afternoon schedule, with a break at midday for the long lunch and siesta which are still very much a part of Spanish life, especially in summer. As a result, many Spaniards return home for lunch, which is the major meal of the day, while supper is light.

Shops are open 9.30 or 10am–1.30 or 2pm and then reopen again in the afternoon from 4.30 or 5–8pm, or a little later in summer. Most are closed on Saturday afternoons and all of Sunday. However, the major department stores like El Corte Inglés and Galerías Preciados are open without interruption six days a week, 10am–9pm, and frequently on Sunday, despite the protests of small shopkeepers.

Panaderías (bakeries) open on Sunday mornings and usually well stocked with other food staples and canned items which can prove useful at weekends.

HOLIDAYS

The following are national holidays:
1 January; 6 January (Epiphany); Holy Thursday and Good Friday; 1 May (Labour Day); Corpus Christi Day (a Thursday in late May or early June); 25 July (St James' Day, the Patron Saint of Spain); 15 August (Assumption Day); 12 October (Columbus Day or *Día de la Hispanidad*); 1 November (All Saint's Day); 6 December (Constitution Day); 8 December (Immaculate Conception) and 25 December (Christmas).

Each town is also entitled to two local holidays in honour of its patron saints. Madrid celebrates 15 May, *Día de San Isidro*, and 9 November, *Día de la Almudena*. There are actually so many holidays, what with national and local fiestas, that it's said there is no one week in the whole year when all of Spain is working.

RELIGIOUS SERVICES

As a Roman Catholic country, Madrid has a great number of historic and contemporary churches, along with one synagogue, a large, modern Islamic Centre and churches of other denominations.
British Embassy Church of St George, Anglican/Episcopalian. Nuñez de Balboa, 43. Tel: 576 5109. Reverend Henry Scriven. Sunday services at 8.30, 10

and 11.15am and Friday at 10.30am.
Catholic Masses held in English at 10.30am. Father Sullivant. Alfonso XIII, 165. Tel: 533 2032.
Christian Science Church, C/Pinilla del Valle, 5 (entry through Horcajvelo). Tel: 359 2135.
Community Church, Protestant/Inter-denominational. Pastor Richard Wilcox. Sunday, 11am at the Colegio de los Sagrados Corazones, Padre Damián, 34. Tel: 858 5557.
Synagogue, Balmes, 3. Tel: 445 9835. Friday night service 7.30pm.
Church of Christ, Gran Vía, 24–2nd floor. Tel: 705 0978. Services Thursday and Sunday 6pm.
Islamic-Christian Centre, Alonso Cano, 3. Tel: 448 0554 and 448 4357.
The **Centro Cultural Islámico** (Islamic Mosque), rising above the M-30 highway on Calle Salvador de Madariaga, is a splendid building of Moorish architecture, featuring a large auditorium, library and several exhibition halls. Tel: 326 0480.

For further information about religious services Tel: 541 4804.

COMMUNICATIONS

TELEVISION & RADIO

There are two nationwide television channels in Spain, TVE 1 and TVE 2, and each region has one or more local stations. In Madrid, you can also watch Telemadrid which is run by the local Autonomous Community, and three recently-authorized private networks: Antena 3, Tele 5 and Canal Plus.

Most of the programmes are in Spanish with the occasional late-night film in the original language and a 1pm news programme, "Eurodiario", in English, French and German, on the second national channel, TVE 2, during the summer months. Local stations in Catalonia (TV3 and Canal 33), the Basque country (ETB–1 and ETB–2), Galicia (TVG) and Valencia (Canal 9) have programming in the regional languages, while Canal Sur is the local Andalusian network.

The better hotels have access to satellite programming which includes a variety of channels, several of which broadcast in English (Super Channel, Sky Movies, Eurosport, BBC, CNN, Lifestyle etc.).

MAGAZINES & NEWSPAPERS

The Spanish daily papers are *El País*, *ABC*, *Ya*, *Diario 16* and *El Mundo* and they provide full local information on cinema, theatre, regular and satellite television programming, and which chemist shops are open late at night. *El País*, *El Mundo* and *Diario 16* put out very handy supplements with their Friday editions, which give complete listings on all the activities, exhibitions, art shows and movie schedules being presented in Madrid that week, along with lists of restaurants, entertainment, television, etc. They are much on the lines of the weekly, all-encompassing *Guía del Ocio* (Guide to Leisure).

You will also be able to find the *International Herald Tribune* and *Time* and *Newsweek* magazines at major newsstands in most major cities and other papers such as the *The Times* and the *Wall Street Journal* can be purchased at larger stands.

There are three magazines about Spain, printed in English, which you can buy: *Lookout*, *In Spain*, both published monthly and the Madrid weekly, *Guidepost*. The major newspapers also have regional editions, and some regions have their own dailies.

POSTAL SERVICES

The few existing district post offices are only open 9am–2pm on weekdays, 9am–1pm Saturday and closed Sunday. Principal post offices are open 9am–2pm and 4–7pm for general services, including preparation and postage of packages. Stamps can be purchased from 9am–10pm every day and telex and telefax services are also available within these hours.

Stamps can also be bought in *estancos* or tobacconists, which are distinguishable by their deep red and gold sign with the word *Tabacos*. The *estancos* are useful establishments, for in addition to selling tobacco, they can provide you with everything you need for writing home – paper, pens, envelopes and postcards – and will even weigh your letter to tell you what postage it requires.

TELEPHONES

Coin operated telephone booths are everywhere, though it seems that more than half either don't work or have been vandalised. Assuming that they do function, wait for the tone, deposit either 3 *duros* (silver 5-peseta coins) or a 25-peseta piece and dial the number. It is possible to place a long-distance call by depositing a handful of 25-peseta coins. Most bars have coin-operated or meter telephones available for public use as well. You can also purchase a phone card for 1,000 pesetas at any tobacconists for use in the newer public phones.

For overseas calls, it's probably better to go to the offices of Telefónica (the Spanish telephone company), or to privately-run telephone shops where one can talk first and pay later and not have to worry about having enough coins. (Although it is conven-

ient to ring from your hotel room, and all top hotels have direct-dialling facilities, you will be charged much more than you would on a public phone.)

To make a direct overseas call, first dial 07 and then wait for another dial tone before dialling the country and city codes. It is cheaper to call before 8am and after 10pm. There are no additional discounts at weekends.

If you need operator assistance or wish to reverse the charges, tel: 008 (for Europe) or 005 (for the rest of the world).

The following numbers may be helpful – though in some cases you'll need good Spanish.

003 Telephone information (Spain)
008 Telephone information (Europe)
089 Telephone information (the rest of the world)
005 Operator Assistance for international calls
091 Police
080 Fire Department
092 Municipal Police
093 The Time
094 The Weather
095 News in Spanish
096 Wake-up service
061 Emergency medical attention
097 Sports Information
098 General Information about city streets, bus service, chemist shops which are on duty round-the-clock, etc.
010 Citizen's Information. Every thing you need to know about the city and its government.
002 Telephone company offices

EMERGENCIES

SECURITY & CRIME

Spain these days is no more dangerous than any other cosmopolitan community, but it is no longer the haven of peace and safety it used to be. A high unemployment rate, an increasingly alarming drug problem and perhaps even freedom from authoritarian rule have changed all this, so it makes sense to take a few elementary precautions.

Bag-snatching and pick-pocketing are probably the worst problems, so don't allow yourself to be distracted and take care in crowds and busy tourist areas. Avoid ostentation with money. Keep valuables in the hotel safe and don't carry large sums of money or your passport (take a photocopy instead), unless you are going to exchange money.

Should you have the misfortune to be robbed, contact the local Police Station or telephone Police Emergency at 091.

Useful Emergency Numbers:
Police: Tel: 091
Municipal Police: Tel: 092
Emergency Medical Care: Tel: 061
Fire Department: Tel: 080 or 532 3232 in Madrid.
Red Cross Emergency: Tel: 522 2222 in Madrid.

For lost or stolen Credit Cards:
American Express: Tel: 579 6200 or 572 0320
Diner's Club: Tel: 547 4000
Eurocard, Mastercard: Tel: 435 3040
Visa: Tel: 519 2100
Tarjeta 4B: Tel: 555 2400

MEDICAL CARE & CHEMISTS

Should you become seriously ill, go to the nearest major hospital. In Madrid, all of the following have 24-hour emergency rooms: La Paz Hospital in the north, Doce de Octubre in the south and the Gregorio Marañón Hospital in the centre of the city, on Calle Dr Esquerdo.

If you are an EC national, your state health insurance will cover your care. There is also a reciprocal arrangement with many foreign medical insurance companies.

Also available is a Spanish insurance policy, ASTES, which will cover any medical or hospital care if you fall ill or have an accident during your stay in Spain. This Spanish Tourist Insurance, created and promoted by the Spanish state and backed by a group of 80 private insurance companies, covers full medical and hospital care, hotel lodging if an extension of your stay is recommended by a physician, repatriation and even lost luggage. The ASTES Insurance Group is located at Núñez de Balboa, 101, PO Box 6175, 28006 Madrid. Tel: 562 2087.

The Official Association of Dentists has opened a 24-hour, seven-day-a-week Dental Clinic for emergency dental care, at Calle Juan Bravo, 44 – 6th Floor. Tel: 402 6421 or 402 6422.

Spain has countless chemist shops or *farmacias*, each identifiable by a big, white sign with a flashing green cross. They are open from approximately 9.30am–1.30pm and 5–8pm Monday–Friday; 9am–1.30pm Saturday mornings. In most towns an effective system of rotation operates whereby there is always one chemist open round the clock in each area. An illuminated sign posted in front of each should indicate which chemists are on duty from 10pm–10am that day, and which is closest to where you are.

You can also consult the daily newspapers for a list of chemists on duty outside normal hours or telephone 098. Most chemist shops also have a list of the nearest clinics and hospitals for obtaining emergency medical attention posted in their windows.

GETTING AROUND

BEYOND MADRID – BY AIR

Iberia is Spain's national airline, servicing both national and international routes. Its main offices are at Calle Velázquez, 130, 28006 Madrid. Flight information, tel: 411 2545; reservations, tel: 411 1011 or 411 2011. Iberia has ticket offices at Calle Velázquez 130; and in the Hotel Eurobuilding (Padre Damián) or you can purchase an air ticket at any travel agency.

Aviaco, Iberia's subsidiary airline, only services domestic flights, while Viva Air covers international routes. The planes are generally older and smaller and fly less-frequented routes. Aviaco is at Maudes, 51 in Madrid, tel: 554 3600; and Viva Air at Zurbano, 41, tel: 349 0600.

No point on mainland Spain is more than 55 minutes flying time from Madrid, though travelling to and from airports can be quite time-consuming in the big cities. Approximate flying times are as follows:
Madrid–Barcelona: 55 minutes.
Madrid–Valencia: 30 minutes.
Madrid–Bilbao: 50 minutes.
Madrid–Seville: 50 minutes.
Madrid–Palma de Mallorca: 1 hour.
Madrid–the Canary Islands: 2 hours and 30 minutes.

BY TRAIN

With the exception of the AVE (High speed trains connecting Madrid with Seville), the track gauge of the Spanish national railway system still does not conform with that of the rest of Europe.

Madrid's main train station is Chamartín in the north of Madrid. This is an entire complex featuring the station itself, amply furnished with bars, restaurants, a self-service cafeteria and a shopping area and, across the driveway, a car park, cinemas, bowling alley, skating rink and discotheque.

However, the *Cercanías* lines which go to Avila, Sigüenza, El Escorial, Soria, Toledo, Segovia, Cercedilla, Navacerrada and Avila still go from Atocha. When work is completed on this station, it will not only be converted into a modern commercial complex, but will again handle all the rail traffic to the south (Andalusia, Extremadura, as well as Levante). It also houses the terminal for the new, superfast AVE trains, put into service in time for

Expo 92 in Seville. The AVE connects Madrid with Seville in a little over 3 hours.

The Estación del Norte "Príncipe Pío" previously handled all traffic to the north of the country but now it only services Alcalá de Henares.

You can obtain train information from RENFE, the state-owned Spanish railway system, tel: 563 0202. Reservations, tel: 562 3333 and then, for a small fee, tickets can be delivered to you. They can also be purchased at the RENFE offices (Alcalá, 44; and at the Paseo de Recoletos; and Nuevos Ministerios underground stations), the stations themselves or from most travel agencies.

Spanish trains have two classes: First (*Primera* or 1ª) and Second (*Segunda* or 2ª), and a variety of train categories which vary considerably in terms of comfort. The *Talgo* is a fast, comfortable train with video entertainment to while away the hours; the *TERS* and *Electrotrens* also have similar distractions. The *Expresos* are the night trains, on which one can usually get a *cama* (small, private compartment) or an inexpensive *litera* (a couchette in a compartment shared with five other passengers). The *Rapidos* are local day trains, which should be avoided other than for short journeys.

There are many ways to save money on rail travel in Spain. The first is to buy a Eurailpass which allows for free, unlimited, first-class travel throughout Spain and most Western European countries as well. Eurailpasses *must* be purchased in your own country before leaving for Spain. When travelling with one of these passes it is usually advisable to make reservations in advance in peak season, although first class is hardly ever full. Eurail/passes can be purchased for 15, 25, 30, 60 or 90 days, according to the traveller's needs, and become effective as of the first day of use.

If you did not purchase a Eurailpass before leaving home, you can buy a *Tarjeta Turistica* in Spain, as long as you are not a local resident, and it will entitle you to free and unlimited travel on Spanish trains without paying any supplements. You can purchase one for first or second class, its price varying according to whether the card is valid for 8, 15, or 22 days.

Ask the RENFE office for a calendar of Blue Days (*Días Azules*), days which are neither holidays nor immediately prior to them. If you travel return on these, you are entitled to a 25 percent discount on tickets. If travelling on Blue Days, look into other possible discounts: *Tarjeta Familiar* for families, 50 to 75 percent discount; *Tarjeta Dorada* for senior citizens, 50 percent; *Tarjeta Joven* for young people between 12 and 25 years of age, 50 percent; Groups, 20 to 30 percent; Auto-Express, where you transport your car with you, 20 to 100 percent depending on the number of people in your group. There is also a big discount for couples travelling in *Coche Cama*.

If you pay for your tickets with *Chequetren* cheques, which can be purchased for varying amounts, you obtain an additional 15 percent discount.

A lovely trip, if you are planning a jaunt to Aranjuez, is to take the antiquated, coal-burning *Tren de la Fresa* which leaves at 10 in the morning from the old Delicias Station (also the setting of the Railway Museum). It operates on Saturday, Sunday and holidays during the months of May, June, July, September and the first half of October, and includes a tourist visit to the city and free time for lunch. Traditionally-dressed stewardesses present travellers with souvenirs of their journey, and the famous fare of Aranjuez: *fresas* (strawberries).

Other train excursions are organised every year to the North or South of Spain, Wine Routes, Pilgrimage to Santiago de Compostela, etc. For further information, tel: IBERAIL 571 5815.

BY BUS

Bus travel has improved considerably in Spain. Buses covering the longer, inter-city routes are air-conditioned, with video entertainment to pass the time and sometimes restrooms. Buses may take longer but are usually cheaper than trains and a better way to see the country. They make frequent stops at rest areas, giving passengers a chance to freshen up, have a bite to eat and stretch their legs.

There are several bus companies in Madrid which service specific areas of the country. Most leave from the Estación Sur de Autobuses, at Palos de Moguer (near the Metro stop): Calle Canarias. For information, tel: 468 4200.

Auto Res, Calle Fernández Shaw, 1, near Plaza Conde de Casal. Has a large network of bus lines which includes the entire Levante coast (Valencia and Castellón), Extremadura (Badajoz and Cáceres), Zamora, Cuenca, Valladolid, Salamanca and Palencia. For information, tel: 551 7200.

The **Continental** bus line at Calle Alenza, 20, tel: 533 0400, 533 3711 or 356 2307, covers local routes, including Alcalá de Henares, Torrejón de Ardoz, Guadalajara, and also Burgos, San Sebastián, Vitoria, Santander, Soria, Logroño and Pamplona. Buses for Toledo leave from the Estación Sur, Canarias, 17. Tel: 527 2961.

Enatcar buses leave from the Estación Sur de Autobuses (Canarias, 17), for Orense, Pontevedra, Barcelona, Alicante and Levante, Granada, Algeciras, Huelva and the Costa del Sol. For information, tel: 467 3577 or 527 2927.

CAR RENTAL

To rent a car in Spain, you have to be at least 19 years of age with either an international driving licence or a valid licence from your own country.

It is usually necessary to pay for the car rental with a major credit card such as Visa, Mastercard, American Express, Diner's Club, etc., or you might be obliged to leave a large deposit. You are also required to take out insurance.

Cars can be rented per day with an additional fee

according to mileage, or in package deals, available for a set number of days, at unlimited mileage; consider which will be most advantageous for your purpose. You might also be interested in picking the car up in Madrid and leaving it in another city.

Renting a car for use in Madrid is *not* recommended. The traffic can be a bore at best, and a nightmare at worst.

MAJOR CAR RENTAL AGENCIES IN MADRID

American Express, Plaza de las Cortes, 2, tel: 429 5775.
Atesa, Gran Vía, 59, tel: 547 0202; and Rosario Pino, 18, tel: 571 3294 and 522 0159.
Avis, Gran Vía, 60, tel: 547 2048; Padre Damián, 23, Hotel Eurobuilding, tel: 345 3120.
Europcar, Calle Orense, 29, tel: 555 9930/1.
Hertz, Gran Vía, 88, tel: 548 5805/542 1000; Dr Fleming, 46, tel: 457 8819.

MOTORING ADVICE

Spain has 196,850 miles (317,000 km) of highway but only a few thousand miles are fast, convenient and relatively safe motorways. Toll fees are payable on the modern motorways, which have rest areas, bars and service stations. Roadside telephones are also placed at convenient intervals, to call for assistance in case of emergency or breakdown.

The speed limit is 75mph (120kph) on motorways, 60mph (100kph) on all other roads and 35mph (60kph) going through cities and towns. Seat belts must be worn by the driver and front-seat passenger, and the car should be equipped with a spare set of head and rear-light bulbs or you could be fined.

All motorcycle riders must wear helmets and ride with their headlights on, even during the day.

LANGUAGE

USEFUL WORDS & PHRASES

Good morning	*Buenos días*
Good afternoon	*Buenas tardes*
(after lunch, until about 9pm.)	
Good evening	*Buenas noches*
Hello	*Hola*
Goodbye	*Adiós*
See you!	*Hasta luego*

Please	*Por favor*
Thank you	*Gracias*
Not at all, you're welcome	*De nada*
Excuse me	*Perdón*
Yes/No	*Sí/No*
Do you speak English?	*¿Habla inglés?*
I don't speak Spanish	*No hablo español*
I'm sorry	*Lo siento*
I don't understand	*No entiendo*
The menu, please	*La carta, por favor*
The bill	*La cuenta*
What time is it?	*¿Qué hora es?*
It is one o'clock, two o'clock	*Es la una, Son las dos…*
How are you?	*¿Cómo está?*
Fine, thank you. And you?	*Bien, gracias. ¿Y usted?*
Is it ready?	*¿Está listo/a?*
Where is?	*¿Dónde está?*
What do you want?	*¿Qué desea/quiere usted?*
I want	*Yo quiero*
With pleasure	*Con mucho gusto*
No smoking	*Se prohibe fumar*
Do you have a room for one/two?	*¿Tiene una habitación para una/dos?*
How much does it cost?	*¿Cuánto cuesta?*
I like it	*Me gusta*
I don't like it	*No me gusta*
I am in a hurry	*Tengo prisa*
It is very important	*Es muy importante*
Which way is?	*¿Cómo se va a?*
Straight ahead	*Todo seguido*
To the right	*a la derecha*
To the left	*a la izquierda*
Breakfast, lunch, dinner	*Desayuno, almuerzo, cena*
Today	*Hoy*
Yesterday	*Ayer*
Tomorrow	*Mañana*
Day, week, month, year	*Día, semana, mes, año*
When? Where? How?	*¿Cuándo? ¿Dónde? ¿Cómo?*
How long?	*¿Cuánto tiempo?*
How far?	*¿Cuánto lejos? ¿A qué distancia está?*
How much is it?	*¿Cuánto vale?*
Big, bigger	*Grande, más grande*
Small, smaller	*Pequeño, más pequeño*
Cheap, expensive	*Barato, caro*
Hot, cold	*Caliente, frío*
Old, new	*Viejo, nuevo*
Open, closed	*Abierto, cerrado*
Free, occupied	*Libre, ocupado*
Early, late	*Pronto, tarde*
Easy, difficult	*Facil, difícil*
Please help me	*Por favor, ayúdame*

DAYS

Days of the week	*Días de la semana*
Sunday	*Domingo*
Monday	*Lunes*

Tuesday	*Martes*
Wednesday	*Miércoles*
Thursday	*Jueves*
Friday	*Viernes*
Saturday	*Sábado*

NUMBERS

1	*Uno*
2	*Dos*
3	*Tres*
4	*Cuatro*
5	*Cinco*
6	*Seis*
7	*Siete*
8	*Ocho*
9	*Nueve*
10	*Diez*
11	*Once*
12	*Doce*
13	*Trece*
14	*Catorce*
15	*Quince*
16	*Dieciseis*
17	*Diecisiete*
18	*Dieciocho*
19	*Diecinueve*
20	*Veinte*
21	*Veintiuno*
22	*Veintidos*
30	*Treinta*
40	*Cuarenta*
50	*Cincuenta*
60	*Sesenta*
70	*Setenta*
80	*Ochenta*
90	*Noventa*
100	*Cien*
1,000	*Mil*
1,000,000	*Millón*

FURTHER READING

Although Spain did not figure in the Grand Tour of the early tourists, from the 19th century it attracted a succession of foreign travellers in search of the "exotic". Andalusia in particular awakened their interest. Théophile Gautier, Hans Christian Andersen and Washington Irving were among those to visit the region and their comments make fascinating reading.

Ian Robertson aptly titled his book on the succession of English travellers *Los Curiosos Impertinentes* (the impertinent inquisitive ones). These impertinent English included Henry Swinburne, Joseph Townsend, and Richard Ford. Ford did the most to awaken interest in the region with witty and shrewdly-observed accounts of his travels between 1830 and 1833. This century Gerald Brenan, who lived much of his life in Andalusia, stands out as a writer whose great affection for the region did not diminish his critical faculties.

Los Andaluces. Madrid: Ediciones Istmo, 1980. Collection of wide-ranging essays on the people, their history, economy and culture to the present day.

The Art of Flamenco, by D.E. Pohren. Musical New Services Ltd, 1984. The *aficionado's* bible; and *A Way of Life.* Madrid: Society of Spanish Studies, 1980. Colourful, humorous account of a disappearing Andalusian lifestyle.

As I Walked Out One Midsummer Morning, by Laurie Lee. Penguin, 1983. Heady, romantic young man's vision of pre-Civil War Spain; *A Rose for Winter.* Penguin, 1983. Lee's post-war return to Andalusia.

The Assassination of Federico García Lorca, by Ian Gibson. Penguin, 1983. Banned in Franco's Spain because it revealed the truth about Lorca's death; *Federico García Lorca: A Life.* Faber & Faber, 1989. Award-winning, deeply researched biography.

The Bible in Spain, by George Borrow. First published 1842. Eccentric, opinionated and entertaining.

La Civilización hispano-árabe by Titus Burckhardt. (Original title: *Die maurische Kultur in Spanien.* Munich: Verlag Georg D.W. Callwey, 1970.) Madrid: Alianza Editorial, 1977. Examination of Moorish culture.

Cooking in Spain, by Janet Mendel. Fuengirola, Málaga: Lookout Publications. Details of many typical Andalusian dishes.

Los Curiosos Impertinentes, by Ian Robertson. Published in Spanish by Serbal, 1988. English travellers' adventures in and comments on Spain between 1760 and 1855.

Death's Other Kingdom, by Gamel Woolsey. Virago Press, 1988. Vivid account of outbreak of Civil War by this American poet, the wife of Gerald Brenan.

Handbook for Travellers in Spain, by Richard Ford. Centaur Press, 1966; and *Gatherings from Spain.* Dent Everyman, 1970. Classic accounts of Spanish travels last century.

Here in Spain, by David Mitchell. Fuengirola, Málaga: Lookout Publications. The country viewed through the eyes of foreign travellers through the centuries.

Histoire de l'Espagne Musulmane, by Evariste Lévi-Provencale. III volumes. Erudite history of Spain under the Moors.

Inside Andalusia – A Travel Adventure in Southern Spain, by David Baird. Fuengirola, Málaga: Lookout Publications, 1988. Informative account of Andalusia and its people, profusely illustrated.

Los Moriscos del Reino de Granada, by Julio Caro Baroja. Madrid: Ediciones Istmo, 1985. One of Spain's foremost historians relates the last days of the Moors of Granada.

Or I'll Dress You in Mourning, by Larry Collins and Dominique Lapierre. Simon & Schuster. Brilliantly documented insights into Spain's post-Civil War hardships which moulded the Andalusian matador El Cordobés.

The People of the Sierra, by Julian A. Pitt-Rivers. Weidenfield & Nicolson, 1954. Social anthropologist's dissection of a remote mountain community.

The Pueblo: *A Mountain Village in Spain*, by Ronald Fraser. Pantheon. Villagers of Mijas tell their own story. *In Hiding*: *The Life of Manuel Cortes*. Penguin, 1982. How a village mayor stayed hidden for 30 years for fear of execution.

The Road from Ronda, by Alastair Boyd. Collins, 1969. Vivid account of a horse-ride through the Serranía de Ronda.

South from Granada, by Gerald Brenan. Cambridge University Press, 1988. Classic account of life in a remote Granada village; *The Face of Spain*. Penguin, 1987. Brenan's grim view of an impoverished post-war Spain.

Tales of the Alhambra, by Washington Irving. Granada: Miguel Sánchez. Legends and colourful view of Granada's last century.

Tartessos, by Adolph Schulten. Madrid: Espasa-Calpe. Controversial attempt to establish the site of Tartessos near the mouth of the Guadalquivir.

Teoría de Andalucía, Sueño y Realidad, by José Ortega y Gasset and María Zambrano. Editoriales Andaluzas Unidas. Insights into the Andalusian character by a distinguished thinker.

Los Toros en Andalucía. Málaga: Arguval. Large format, for bullfight *aficionados*, history, statistics, personalities, superstitions of the *corrida*.

White Wall of Spain, by Allen Josephs. Iowa State University Press. Fascinating examination of Andalusia's roots and the creation of a unique culture.

OTHER SOURCES

A Romantic in Spain, by Théophile Gautier. (1926, first published 1845 as *Voyage en Espagne*).

A Spanish Raggle-Taggle, by Walter Starkie. *(1934)*.

Death in the Afternoon, by Ernest Hemingway. (1932).

In All Countries, by John Dos Passos. (1934).

Instructions for Forrein Travel, by James Howell. (1642).

Letters Concerning the Spanish Nation, by Reverend E. Clarke. (1763).

Letters Written during a Journey in Spain, by Robert Southey. (1808).

Lettres de la Cour d'Espagne, by Marquise de Villars. (1868 edition).

Life, Letters and Journals, by George Ticknor. Vol. I (1876).

The Modern State of Spain, by J.-F. Bourgoing. (1808).

The Presence of Spain, by James Morris. (1964, reissued as *Spain* by Jan Morris).

Spain in 1830, by Henry Inglis. (1831).

Spain Revisited, by Slidell Mackenzie. (1836).

The Spaniards: A Portrait of the New Spain, by John Hooper. (1986).

Travels into Spain, Mme d'Aulnoy. (1930, first published 1691).

Travels Through Spain and Portugal in 1774, by Major William Dalrymple. (1777).

For *Insight Guides* which highlight other destinations in this region *see page* 396.

USEFUL ADDRESSES

TOURIST INFORMATION

Tourist information covering all of Spain is available at the Madrid Community Tourist offices in the Torre de Madrid at:

Princesa, 1. Tel: 541 2325. Open: 10am–7pm.

Barajas airport. Tel: 305 8656.

Duque de Medinaceli, 2. Tel: 429 4951.

Chamartín Station, Door 14, in the Main Hall. Tel: 315 9976.

Information on Madrid itself is available at Plaza Mayor, 3. Tel: 566 5477.

The Patronato Municipal de Turismo (Municipal Tourism Board) is at Calle Mayor, 69 (near the City Hall on the Plaza de la Villa). The Patronato organises tours of the city and the province. Open to the public: 9am–2pm, Saturday 9am–noon. Tel: 588 2906/7.

TOURIST OFFICES ABROAD

If you want to stock up on information before you leave home, here are a few of the Tourist Information Offices (with international dialling codes) which Spain has set up abroad.

New York: 665 Fifth Avenue, New York, New York 10022. Tel: (1-212) 759 8822/28.

Chicago: 845 N. Michigan Avenue, Suite 915, Chicago, Illinois 60611. Tel: (1-312) 944 0215/16.
Los Angeles: 8383 Wilshire Blvd, Suite 960, 90211 Beverly Hills, California. Tel: (1-213) 658 7188/93.
Houston: 5085 Westheimer, Suite 4800, 77056 Houston, Texas. Tel: (1-713) 840 7412/13.
Toronto: 60 Bloor Street West, Suite 201, Toronto, Ontario M4W3B8. Tel: (1-416) 961 3131.
London: 57 St James's Street, London SW1. Tel: (44-71) 499 0901 or 499 1169.

USEFUL NUMBERS

American Express, Plaza de las Cortes, 2. Tel: 322 5500. You can buy and exchange traveller's cheques here, book tours, rent cars and use it as a postal address.
British Chamber of Commerce, Marqués de Valdeiglesias, 3, Madrid. Tel: 521 7922.
US Chamber of Commerce, Padre Damián, 23, Eurobuilding, Madrid. Tel: 458 6559.
Chamber of Commerce and Industry of Spain, Claudio Coello, 19, Madrid. Tel: 575 3400.
Royal Automobile Club of Spain (RACE), General Sanjurjo, 10, Madrid. Tel: 593 3333.

EMBASSIES IN MADRID

Australia: Paseo de la Castellana, 143. Tel: 579 8504.
Austria: Paseo de la Castellana, 91. Tel: 345 6718.
Belgium: Paseo de la Castellana, 18. Tel: 577 6300.

Canada: Núñez de Balboa, 35. Tel: 431 4300.
Denmark: Claudio Coello, 91. Tel: 431 8445.
France: Salustiano Olozaga, 9. Tel: 435 5560.
Germany: Fortuny, 8. Tel: 319 9100.
Greece: Dr Arce, 24. Tel: 564 4653.
Ireland: Claudio Coello, 73. Tel: 576 3500.
Israel: Velázquez, 50. Tel: 411 1357.
Italy: Lagasca, 98. Tel: 402 5436.
Japan: Joaquín Costa, 29. Tel: 562 5546.
Mexico: Paseo de la Castellana, 93. Tel: 556 1263.
Morocco: Serrano, 179. Tel: 563 1090.
Netherlands: Paseo de la Castellana, 178. Tel: 359 0914.
Portugal: Pinar, 1. Tel: 561 7800.
Soviet Union: Calle Velázquez, 155. Tel: 411 0807 or 562 2264.
Sweden: Zurbano, 27. Tel: 308 1540.
Switzerland: Núñez de Balboa, 35. Tel: 431 3400.
United Kingdom: Fernando el Santo, 16. Tel: 319 0200.
United States: Calle Serrano, 75. Tel: 577 4000.

GETTING AROUND MADRID

METRO SYSTEM

The Madrid underground or Metro system is the fastest, cheapest and most efficient way of getting around the city. (If you are claustrophobic, avoid rush hours: 8–9.30am, 1.30–2.30pm and 8–9pm).

The Metro is the second oldest in Europe – it was opened by King Alfonso XIII in 1919, and today has 115 stations, which will take you to just about every corner of the city. It operates from 6am–1.30am in the morning and is used by over 1 million people daily, but it has the considerable inconvenience, in summer, of not being air-conditioned. It costs 125 pesetas for one journey regardless of where you go and you can buy a *Bono* (blue ticket) good for 10 trips for only 550 pesetas.

For Metro information, tel: 435 2266.

CITY BUSES

The Madrid bus system might not be as fast or as comfortable as one would like, due to traffic conditions, but then again, Madrid is a small, rather compact city. Tickets cost 125 pesetas regardless of length of journey or whether the bus is red or yellow. You enter from the front and pay the driver with change or a note, preferably of no more than 500 pesetas. Press the buzzer to tell him to let you out at the stop you want and leave by the rear door.

A *Bonobus*, good for 10 journeys, can be purchased from the bus information booths at Puerta del Sol, Plaza Callao, Plaza Cibeles, Plaza de Castilla, etc., as well as at the Caja de Madrid Savings Banks, all newspaper stands and *Estancos* for 550 pesetas. There is a slotted box behind the driver and when you insert your *Bonobus* it automatically registers your journey.

Buses are in service 6am–midnight. For municipal bus information, tel: 401 9900.

If you are planning an extended period of time in Madrid and doing a lot of bus and Metro travelling, it might be a good idea to purchase an *Abono*. This card can be applied for at any *estanco* by filling out a form and providing a passport-size photograph and a photocopy of your passport or national identity document. A month's travel in the central area of Madrid costs 3,450 pesetas; 2,350 pesetas for those under 21 years of age and 1,100 pesetas for senior citizens over 65.

TAXIS

Compared with those of other cities, taxis in Madrid are an inexpensive way of getting around and are plentiful (except when it is raining). They are white, bear a transversal red stripe on the sides and the Madrid coat of arms. They are available if they are displaying a green *libre* ("Free") sign on the windscreen or at night have a little green light on. If a red sign with the name of a Madrid neighbourhood is displayed, it means they are on their way home and are not obliged to pick you up unless you are on their route.

A meter on the dashboard will indicate the fare. When you flag a taxi, the meter starts off at 150 pesetas (1993 prices), and automatically chalks up 70 pesetas for every kilometre. If you ask the driver to wait, he can charge you 1,500 pesetas an hour. Additional supplements can be added to the meter price, so don't think the driver is trying to "take you for a ride". Prices are also constantly going up.

If you have serious reason to believe that the driver is over-charging you, ask for a receipt from his official note pad, which is perforated with his taxi licence number. Ask him to write down the starting point of the journey, the conclusion, date and time (there are spaces for these on the receipt) and sign it. Then send or present the receipt to: Area de Circulación y Transportes, Plaza de la Villa, 4, 28005 Madrid.

Taxis can be hailed with relative ease in main thoroughfares, found at a *Parada de Taxi* (taxi stand, indicated by a large white "T" against a dark blue background) or requested by phone. For taxi pick-up, call Radio-Teléfono Taxi, tel: 547 8200; Radio-Taxi Independiente, tel: 405 1213 or 405 5500; or Teletaxi, tel: 445 9008 and 448 4259.

ACCOMMODATION

With over 50,000 beds, Madrid has accommodation to meet every need and wallet. *Hoteles* are classified in to five categories, reflected in the number of stars they have been awarded. *Hoteles-residencias* are also classified according to quality and services. These do not have a restaurant, but often have bar and cafeteria facilities. *Hostales* are more modest, and classified according to only 1, 2 or 3 stars.

Pensiones or guesthouses are also useful for those on limited budgets. Most *pensiones* are run by a family. Rooms can be rented with home cooking included, and there is usually a family room which is shared with the other guests for watching television or reading.

An official notice should be posted behind the door, indicating the daily price of the room, although the rate can vary according to season. Breakfast is not included in the room rate and is often continental: coffee, tea or hot chocolate and toast or buns. Remember that 6 percent VAT will be added to your bill, except for those of the Grand

Luxury category, which charge 15 percent VAT.

Another possibility for longer stays is to rent a furnished apartment, an increasingly popular idea.

If planning excursions out of Madrid, probably your best bet would be to make a reservation at any of the *paradors* (state-run inns) on your route. The *parador* system, first planned in 1926, was started in the 1970s by the Ministry of Information and Tourism. Run-down castles and palaces were taken over and converted into charming and luxurious hotels.

Paradors relatively close to Madrid are: the Parador of Chinchón, Parador Conde de Orgaz of Toledo, Parador Raimundo de Borgoña of Avila, Parador of Salamanca, San Marcos Parador of León, Parador of Segovia, Zurbarán Parador of Guadalupe, Castle Parador of Sigüenza, Parador of Oropesa and the Parador of Gredos (which is noted for its magnificent natural mountain setting). Reservations can be made at the central office: Calle Velázquez, 18. Tel: 435 9700/435 9744. Monday–Thursday 9.30am–1.30pm, 3.30–5.30pm; Friday 9am–2pm.

Note: s/n in an address signifies *sin número* (no number); ctra means *carretera* (highway).

The prices given below are for a standard double room. (They may have changed since this book went to press.)

HOTELS

Price guide: *5-star Luxe = up to 60,000 pesetas; 5-star = over 20,000 pesetas; 4-star = over 15,000 pesetas; 3-star = 5,000–15,000 pesetas.*

Ritz ☆☆☆☆☆ Luxe, Plaza de la Lealtad, 5. Tel: 521 2857. One block away from the Prado Museum, offers luxury in the old style.
Santa Mauro ☆☆☆☆☆ Luxe, Zurbano, 36. Tel: 319 6900. An old palace converted into a posh hotel with a quiet atmosphere.
Villamagna ☆☆☆☆☆ Luxe, Paseo de la Castellana, 22. Tel: 576 7500. Grand luxury in modern style.
Barajas ☆☆☆☆☆, Avda Logroño, 305. Tel: 747 7700. Nine miles (14 km) from the capital and close to the airport, ideal for those seeking a quiet ambience. Swimming pool and gym.
Eurobuilding ☆☆☆☆☆, Padre Damián, 23. Tel: 345 4500. In the heart of the business district of northern Madrid. Has many facilities including shops, restaurants, swimming pool.
Melia Castilla ☆☆☆☆☆, Capitán Haya, 43. Tel: 571 2211. Well suited for those on a business trip.
Palace ☆☆☆☆☆, Plaza de las Cortes, 7. Tel: 429 7551. A comfortable, classic hotel, with a fine cultural/political/international ambience, across the street from the Parliament.
Wellington ☆☆☆☆☆, Velázquez, 8. Tel: 575 4400. An old-fashioned, stylish hotel. Traditional meeting place for the bullfighting crowd. Close to good shops. Small outdoor swimming pool and a fine restaurant.

Alameda ☆☆☆☆, Avda Logroño, 100. Tel: 747 4800. Near the airport, 9 miles (14 km) from the city. Courtesy service for clients to the airport. Swimming pool.
Alcalá ☆☆☆☆, Alcalá, 66. Tel: 435 1060. Across the street from the Retiro Park and near good shops. It has a fine Basque restaurant.
Castellana Intercontinental ☆☆☆☆, Paseo de la Castellana, 49. Tel: 410 0200. A fine classic hotel and a frequent meeting place for international businessmen.
Chamartín ☆☆☆☆, Agustín de Foxá, s/n. Tel: 323 3087. Situated near the Chamartín railway station.
Colón ☆☆☆☆, Dr Esquerdo, 117. Tel: 573 5900. In a residential area. Rooftop pool.
Emperador ☆☆☆☆, Gran Vía, 53. Tel: 547 2800. Rooftop pool.
Gran Hotel Conde Duque ☆☆☆☆, Plaza Conde del Valle Suchil, 5. Tel: 447 7000. In the Argüelles area.
Gran Hotel Reina Victoria ☆☆☆☆, Plaza del Angel, 7. Tel: 531 4500. Remodelled and upgraded hotel which maintains its old-world atmosphere.
Holiday Inn Madrid ☆☆☆☆, Avda General Perón. Tel: 597 0102. It is representative of the US chain. Swimming pool. Fine restaurant, which serves brunch on Sunday.
Suecia ☆☆☆☆, Marqués de Casa Riera, 4. Tel: 531 6900. Centrally located beside the Fine Arts Circle. Its restaurant is noted for the typical Swedish smorgasbord served on Thursday and Friday evenings.
Las Alondras Sol ☆☆☆, José Abascal, 8. Tel: 447 4000. A comfortable hotel.
Claridge ☆☆☆, Plaza Conde de Casal, 6. Tel: 551 9400. On the outskirts of the city at the start of the Madrid–Valencia highway.
Inglés ☆☆☆, Echegaray, 10. Tel: 429 6551. A small, cosy hotel in a busy area, close to the Puerta del Sol and a good value.
Madrid ☆☆☆, Carretas, 10. Tel: 521 6520. An older hotel, a block away from the Puerta del Sol.
Prado ☆☆☆, Prado, 11. Tel: 369 0234. Recently remodelled and centrally located hotel.
Puerta de Toledo ☆☆☆, Glorieta Puerta de Toledo, 4. Tel: 474 7100. Located in old Madrid, near the Rastro flea market and the Puerta de Toledo Market complex.
Regina ☆☆☆, Alcalá, 19. Tel: 521 4725. Very centrally located.

PENSIONES

Alburquerque, León, 11. Tel: 429 5157. (2,400 pesetas, room with wash basin only).
Avenida, Gran Vía, 15. Tel: 522 6360. (4,800 ptas).
Continental, Gran Vía, 44. Tel: 521 4640. (5,000 pesetas).
Fuente Sol, Victoria 2, 3rd floor left. Tel: 521 6674. Just off the Puerta del Sol. (4,500–8,500 pesetas with bath).

Gravina, Gravina, 4. Tel: 522 3862. (1,700 pesetas).
Los Angeles, Artistas, 18. Tel: 233 0375. Near the Plaza Tirso de Molina. (2,600–5,000 pesetas).
Persal, Plaza del Angel, 12. Tel: 369 4643. (6,000 pesetas).
San Jerónimo, Carrera de San Jerónimo, 32. Tel 429 6780. Across the street from the Palace Hotel and the Parliament building. (3,200 pesetas).

FLATS

Centro Colón, Marqués de la Ensenada, 16. Tel: 310 4600.
Foxá 25/32, Agustín de Foxa, 25 and 32. Tel: 323 1119 and 733 1060, respectively.
Goya 75, Goya, 75. Tel: 435 6346.
Habana 73, Paseo de la Habana, 73. Tel: 345 8755.
Los Jerónimos, Moreto, 9. Tel: 228 1001.
Muralto, Tutor, 37. Tel: 542 4400.
Recoletos, Villanueva, 2. Tel: 431 9640.

WHAT TO EAT

In Spain restaurants, like hotels, are classified into five categories, this time symbolised with forks. In addition to *restaurantes*, there are *bares*, or all-purpose drinking establishments, where one can have anything from a coffee or a coke to a whisky and a *bocadillo* (a sandwich on crusty fresh bread) or a *sandwich* (on toasted white bread); *mesones*, which are typical taverns with appropriate fare; modern cafeterias or coffee shops where you can get toasted "sandwiches", or meals throughout the day; and of course, the "imported" hamburger and pizza parlours.

Spanish eating hours are different, the main meal being a hearty, three-course affair served between 2 and 4pm, while dinner is light and eaten after 10pm.

Tapas are also an important part of the programme. These small, varied snacks help one get through the long gaps between meals.

Spaniards tend to have a light breakfast before going to work and then a coffee break at mid-morning when they indulge in pastries, *churros* (fried dough rings) or a *pincho de tortilla* (a wedge of potato omelette served with crusty bread). One o'clock is aperitive time, when a vast array of *tapas* are laid out along the bar counters. It is *tapa* time again at 8pm and the idea is to go from one bar to the next, sampling the specialities proffered at each.

Spaniards usually wash down their *tapas* with draught beer (*una caña de cerveza*), a *botellín* (a small bottle of beer), or a small glass of wine (*un chato de vino*), *tinto* being red and *blanco*, white. One should sample the dry sherry, *vino fino* or simply *fino* or *jerez*, which comes from the southern grape-growing region around Jerez de la Frontera.

Spanish wine, like the food, is reasonable in price and very good besides. The country is particularly proud of its Riojas from the north, the different varieties of sherry from Jerez, and the champagnes or *cavas* (sparkling wines) from Catalonia. Inexpen-sively-priced, ordinary table wines from the Valdepeñas region can also be pleasant.

Although you can find just about every alcoholic beverage in Madrid, the country also has an interesting selection of after-dinner drinks: the famous *anisette* of Chinchón, the *pacharán* of Pamplona, the herbal brandies of Galicia and assorted *eaux de vie* and *ponches* from diverse regions of the country.

Despite the wide availability of alcohol in Spain and its relatively low price, you will rarely see anyone drunk.

Should you have any serious problems with the food, service or bill in a restaurant request the *hojas de reclamación*, the complaint forms. When they are filled out, the proprietor is obliged to send one copy to the local Police Station, which will look into the complaint.

WHERE TO EAT

The approximate cost per person, including house wine, is coded in the following way: Inexpensive = less than 1,500; Moderate = between 1,500 and 4,500 pesetas; Expensive = over 4,500 pesetas.

SPANISH

Alkalde, Jorge Juan, 10. Tel: 576 3359. Basque cooking. A charming, cosy restaurant, offering traditional specialities, located off the Calle Serrano. Moderate

Artemisa (Vegetarian restaurant), Ventura de la Vega, 4. Tel: 429 5092. Tres Cruces, 4. Tel: 521 8721. Good, imaginative cooking. Closed: Sunday evening. Moderate

La Bola, Bola, 5 (Centre). Tel: 547 6930. Home cooking and famous for its Madrid *cocido* (stew). Closed: Sunday, Christmas Eve, the month of July and Saturday evenings in August. Moderate

Boñar, Cruz Verde, 16 (Centre). Tel: 531 0030. Cooking from León, fine meats and fish. Open: until 3am. Moderate

Botín, Cuchilleros, 17 (Plaza Mayor). Tel: 366 4217. Famous for its roast pig and lamb prepared in an old wood-burning oven. Moderate

Brasserie de Lista, José Ortega y Gasset, 6. Tel: 435 2818. A charming, old-fashioned restaurant with a turn-of-the-century flavour, though it is fairly new. Moderate

Casa Lucío, Cava Baja, 35. Tel: 365 3252. Good food, wine, service and frequented by top celebrities including the Spanish royal family. Closed: August. Expensive

Casa Paco, Puerta Cerrada, 11 (Plaza Mayor). Tel: 266 3166. Fine sirloin steaks, among the best in the city. Closed: Sunday. Moderate

Casa Patas, Cañizares, 10. Tel: 528 5027. Home cooking and evening flamenco performances. Moderate

Casa Ricardo, Fernando el Católico, 31. Tel: 447 6119. Typical Madrid cooking including *callos* (tripe), squid in its own ink and home-made sausage. Closed: Sunday. Moderate

Las Cuevas de Luis Candelas, Cuchilleros, 1 (Plaza Mayor). Tel: 366 5428. A typical restaurant located below the Plaza Mayor. Famous for its roasts and as the erstwhile hideaway of a legendary "Robin Hood" style bandit, Luis Candelas. Moderate

Hogar Gallego, Plaza del Comandante de las Morenas, 3. Tel: 559 6404. Galician cooking and seafood, and outdoor tables in summer. Closed: Sunday nights. Moderate

Horcher, Alfonso XII, 6. Tel: 522 0731. International and Central European cuisine, specialising in game. Considered one of the best restaurants in Madrid. Closed: Saturday midday and Sunday. Expensive

Horno de Santa Teresa, Santa Teresa, 12. Tel: 319 1061. Asturian cooking, including *fabada* stew and fresh salmon. Closed: all day Saturday, Sunday and August. Moderate

Malacatín, Ruda, 5. Tel: 265 5241. Typical cooking in a tavern-style restaurant, located in the Rastro flea market. Speciality: Madrid *cocido* stew. Closed: Sunday and holidays. Inexpensive

Taberna del Alabardero, Felipe V, 6. Tel: 547 2577. Basque cooking. Near the Royal Palace. It now has a branch in Washington, DC. Moderate

La Trainera, Lagasca, 60. Tel: 576 8035. Specialises in seafood. One Michelin star. Closed: Sunday. Expensive

Zalacaín, Alvarez de Baena, 4. Tel: 561 5935. Specialises in Basque cooking. One of the best restaurants in Madrid. Three Michelin stars. Expensive

AMERICAN

Hollywood, Magallanes, 1, tel: 448 9165; Apolonio Morales, 3, tel: 457 7911; Tamayo y Baus, 1, tel: 531 5115; Velázquez, 80, tel: 435 6128; Plaza del Sagrado Corazón de Jesús, 2, tel: 411 4125; Princesa, 13, tel: 559 1914. Hamburger haven.

Rancho Texano, Ctra de Barcelona, Km 12. Tel: 747 4736/44. Nice steaks and all the trimmings. Expensive

FRENCH

Le Bistroquet, Conde, 4. Tel: 547 1045.

La Botella de Pepe, Padre Damián, 47. Tel: 350 7255. Pretty interior, outdoor tables in summer.

GERMAN

Edelweiss, Jovellanos, 7. Tel: 521 0326. Very popular so you might have to wait for a table. Closed: Sunday evenings. Moderate

INDIAN

Annapurna, Zurbano, 5. Tel: 319 8716 and 308 3249. Elegant interior and fine cooking. Closed: Sunday and holidays. Expensive

Ganges, Bolivia, 11. Tel: 457 2779. Charmingly decorated and good value. Moderate

ITALIAN

La Dolce Vita, Cardenal Cisneros, 58. Tel: 445 0436. Moderate

Nabucco, Hortaleza, 108. Tel: 410 0611. Inexpensive

LEBANESE

Baalbeck, Orense, 70. Tel: 572 0786/7. Stylish belly-dancing while you dine. Expensive

NOUVELLE CUISINE

El Cenador del Prado, Prado, 4. Tel: 429 1561. Considered one of the best restaurants in Madrid. One Michelin star. Expensive

Las Cuatro Estaciones, General Ibáñez Ibero, 5. Tel: 553 6305. Gourmet dining and seasonal dishes. Closed: Saturday, Sunday and August. Parking. Expensive

Viridiana, Juan de Mena, 14. Tel: 523 4478. Very imaginative dishes. Closed: Sunday and August. Expensive

THINGS TO DO

SIGHTSEEING TOURS

As Madrid is the capital, it has a rich cultural heritage and endless possibilities for entertainment. Perhaps the best way to get to know it is to start off with a general city tour to get your bearings. Tours are available through the local tourist agencies, and the Tourist Board of the Madrid Town Council occasionally organises walking tours and excursions out of the city. For further information, contact the Patronato Municipal de Turismo at Calle Mayor, 69. Tel: 588 2906/07. Open: 9am–2pm.

Among local tour companies are:

Pullmantur, Plaza de Oriente, 8 (Metro: Opera). Tel: 541 1805.

Trapsatur, San Bernardo, 23 (Metro: Santo Domingo). Tel: 542 6666.

Juliatours, Gran Vía, 68 (Metro: Santo Domingo). Tel: 548 9605.

EXCURSIONS OUT OF MADRID

Alcalá de Henares, a university town, 20 miles (30 km) east of Madrid. You can see the Renaissance university founded by Cardinal Cisneros, Cervantes' House, the Santa María Collegiate Church and the Hostelería del Estudiante.

Avila, a totally walled-in city, 70 miles (115 km) northwest of Madrid with ramparts dating back to the year 1100. Its Romanesque cathedral is one of the oldest in Spain and the city has an important religious background, as the birthplace of St Teresa.

Chinchón, a charming, picturesque town, 30 miles (50 km) south of Madrid. Its typical main square has been the colourful backdrop for bullfights and cultural events since 1502, towered over by the Church of the Assumption, and close to a charming 17th-century convent-turned-*parador* and a 15th-century Gothic castle. Its old-fashioned tavern-restaurants offer the best in typical Castilian fare, including garlic soup, roast pig and lamb. The town is also famous for the aniseed spirit which bears its name.

Cuenca, 100 miles (165 km) east of Madrid. Cuenca is famous for its *Casas Colgadas*, houses hanging over the cliff, one of which contains the Contemporary Art Museum. Nearby is the Ciudad Encantada

of rock formations eroded into intriguing shapes.
El Valle de Los Caídos (Valley of the Fallen), an impressive architectural monument, this huge cross, visible from the La Coruña highway near El Escorial, crowns a mountain with a basilica carved out of its interior. It is the burial place of José Antonio Primo de Rivera and Francisco Franco.
Segovia, 55 miles (85 km) north of Madrid. Segovia has many exceptional monuments including its Roman aqueduct built by Augustus, its Gothic cathedral, many Romanesque churches and the 11th-century fairy tale castle of El Alcázar. It is famous for its excellent roast suckling pig.
Toledo, certainly one of the most picturesque cities in the world, has many monuments worth visiting along its ancient, cobblestone streets. They include the home of El Greco, the Synagogues of the Tránsito and Santa María la Blanca, the Cathedral, the Alcázar fortress, the Palace of Fuensalida, the Museum of Tavera, the Church of Santa Tomé and the Mosque of Cristo de la Luz.

MUSEUMS, ART GALLERIES & PALACES

Casón del Buen Retiro, Alfonso XII, 28. Tel: 530 9114. This annex of the Prado features 19th-century Spanish paintings. Open: Saturday 9am–7pm, Sunday and holidays 9am–2pm. Closed: Monday.
Monasterio de las Descalzas Reales, Plaza de las Descalzas, 3. Tel: 521 2779. Rich in works of art, it was awarded the distinction "European Museum of the Year" in 1987. Open: Tuesday, Wednesday, Thursday and Saturday 10.30am–12.30pm and 4–5.30pm, Friday 10.30am–12.30pm, Sunday and holidays 11am–1.30pm. Closed: Monday.
Museo Arqueológico National (National Archaeological Museum), Serrano, 13. Tel: 577 7915. Collections of archaeological objects, dating back to Prehistoric, Classic and Middle Ages. Numismatic and ceramic collections and classic sculptures, including the famous Dama de Elche. A life-size reproduction of the prehistoric Altamira Cave paintings has been re-created in the garden. Open: Tuesday–Saturday 9.30am–8.30pm, Sunday 9.30am–2.30pm; July and August 9.30am–6.30pm. Closed: Monday.
Museo de Artes y Tradiciones Populares (Popular Art and Traditions Museum), located in the Philosophy and Letters Faculty of the Autonomous University of Canto Blanco. Tel: 397 4270. Open: weekdays 11am–2pm. Closed: Saturday, Sunday, holidays and 15 July–31 August.
Museo Nacional de Reproducciones Artísticas (Museum of Artistic Reproductions), Avda de Juan de Herrera, 2 (Ciudad Universitaria). Tel: 549 7150. Reproductions of Greek sculptures and travelling exhibitions. Open: Tuesday–Saturday 10am–6pm, Sunday 10am–2pm. Closed: Monday.
Museo Municipal (Municipal Museum), Fuencarral, 78. Tel: 522 5732. The history of Madrid from

prehistoric times to date. Open: Tuesday–Saturday 10am–9pm, Sunday 10am–2.30pm. Closed: Monday and holidays.
Museo Nacional de Antropología, Avda de Juan de Herrera, 2 (Ciudad Universitaria). Tel: 549 7150. Anthropology exhibitions. To be opened in early 1995.
Museo Nacional de Artes Decorativas, Montalbán, 12. Tel: 521 3440 or 521 5732. Its 62 rooms contain ceramics, furniture and other decorative items, brought from all over Spain. Open: Tuesday–Friday 9.30am–2.30pm, Saturday and Sunday 10am–2pm. Closed: Monday and holidays.
Museo Nacional del Prado (The Prado), Paseo del Prado. Tel: 420 2836. One of the outstanding art collections of the world. Open: daily except Monday 9am–7pm, Sunday and holidays 9am–2pm.
Museo Romántico, San Mateo, 13. Tel: 448 1045 or 448 1071. A charming museum featuring collections of paintings and furniture, arranged in a typical 18th-century domestic setting. Open: weekdays 10am–2pm. Closed: Monday, holidays and August.
Museo Sorolla, General Martínez Campos, 37. Tel: 310 1584. This is the delightful home of the painter Joaquín Sorolla, now used to display his work. Open: daily except Monday, 10am–3pm. Closed: August.
Museo Taurino (Bullfighting Museum), Alcalá, 237 (in the bullring). Tel: 725 1857. Paintings and sculptures relating to bullfighting, old "suits of lights", swords, etc. Open: 9am–2.30pm. Closed: Monday and Saturday.
Planetario de Madrid (Planetarium), Parque de Tierno Galván. Méndez Alvaro. Tel: 467 3461 and 467 3898. Shows start at 5.30 and 7pm during the week and at 11.30am, 12.45, 5.30, 6.45 and 8pm on Saturday, Sunday and holidays. Closed: Monday.
Museo de Escultura al Aire Libre (Open-Air Sculpture Museum), on the Paseo de la Castellana, under the Eduardo Dato overpass, and features works by contemporary sculptors.
Biblioteca Nacional (National Library), Paseo de Recoletos, 20. Tel: 575 6800. The library, which is back-to-back with the Archaeological Museum, was founded in 1711 and contains valuable manuscripts, including a first printing of Cervantes' *Don Quijote*.
Real Fábrica de Tapices (Royal Tapestry Factory), Fuenterrabia, 2. Tel: 551 3400. This is still in operation, and you can see how tapestries and rugs are produced on old-fashioned looms. It has a museum of 18th and 19th-century tapestries. Open: Monday–Friday 9.30am–12.30pm. Closed: Saturday, Sunday and August.
Ermita de San Antonio de la Florida (Sanctuary of San Antonio de la Florida), Glorieta de San Antonio de la Florida, 5. Tel: 542 0722. Built in 1792 and magnificently decorated by Goya, whose (headless) body is buried here. Open: Tuesday–Friday 10am–2pm and 4–8pm, Saturday and Sunday 10am–2pm. Closed: Monday and holidays. (Admission free Wed.)

Museo Nacional Ferroviario (National Railway Museum), Paseo de las Delicias, 61. Tel: 527 3121. The evolution of the train, from steam engines to modern locomotives. Open: 9am–3pm in summer; 10am–5.30pm in winter; Sunday and holidays 10am–2pm. Closed: Monday.

Museo de Cera (Wax Museum), Paseo de Recoletos, 41. Tel: 308 0825. It features over 400 famous Spanish and international figures in wax, some in animated settings. Open: 10am–2pm and 4–8.30pm.

Centro Reina Sofía, Santa Isabel, 52. Tel: 467 5062. Contemporary art and important exhibitions. Now housing Picasso's famed canvas, *Guernica*. Originally designed in 1756 by Sabatini as the Gran Hospital of Madrid, the building was converted into a cultural and artistic centre in 1986. Open: daily except Tuesday 10am–9pm, Sunday 10am–2pm.

El Escorial. Open: Tuesday–Sunday 10am–6pm. Closed: 25 December, 1 January and 10 August. Getting there by train: from Atocha or Chamartín stations, 24 to 27 departures daily; by bus: (Autocares Herranz, at Calle Isaac Peral 10, by the Moncloa Metro stop) every 30 minutes except from noon–3pm. Either way, allow for at least an hour's travel time to this grand and austere palace. The site is 30 miles (49 km) from Madrid. Combined admission: 500 pesetas.

CONCERTS, BALLET, OPERA

Concerts and recitals can be enjoyed throughout the year in Madrid. Main venues are the new Auditorio Nacional de Música (Príncipe de Vergara, 136, tel: 337 0100 or 337 0321), the home of the National Orchestra; the Teatro Monumental (Atocha, 65, tel: 527 1214), the official concert hall for the National Radio and Television Orchestra; the Teatro de la Zarzuela (Jovellanos 4, tel: 429 8225) and the Centro Cultural de la Villa (Plaza Colón, tel: 575 6080).

Despite the fact that the Teatro Real was scheduled to reopen as an opera house in October 1992, renovations have still not been completed. For the moment, opera is performed in the Teatro de la Zarzuela from January to July and *zarzuela* (Spanish light operetta) from October to December, alternating with National Ballet Company performances. Other ballet, concert and opera performances are presented in the Centro Cultural de la Villa in the Plaza Colón, along with an extensive theatre programme. Occasionally, original works in English by touring foreign companies are put on at the Teatro Español (Príncipe, 25, in the Plaza de Santa Ana, tel: 429 6297).

There are relatively few ticket agencies in Madrid. However, tickets for plays, concerts, films, bullfights and soccer matches can be purchased at Galicia, Plaza del Carmen 7, tel: 531 2732 or 531 9131. Tickets for bullfights and soccer games only are sold at the small stores and booths set up along Calle Victoria, a small street off the Puerta del Sol.

NIGHTLIFE

FLAMENCO

You can watch the experts at a *Tablao Flamenco* or join in yourself at a *Sala Rociera*. But be warned that prices will probably be high.

Tablao Flamenco shows:

Café de Chinitas, Torija, 7. Tel: 548 5135.

Corral de la Pacheca, Juan Ramón Jimenez, 26. Tel: 458 1113 or 438 2672.

Corral de la Moreria, Morería, 17. Tel: 265 1137.

Torres Bermejas, Mesoneros Romanos, 11. Tel: 532 3222.

Salas Rocieras (Do-it-yourself flamenco):

Faralaes, Orense, 68. Tel: 571 2671.

El Portón, López de Hoyos, 25.

Zambra, Velázquez, 8 (Wellington Hotel). Tel: 435 5164. Flamenco shows every night.

CLUBS WITH LIVE MUSIC

Café Central, Plaza del Angel, 10. Tel: 369 4143. Open: 1pm–1.30am.

Café Jazz Populart, Huertas, 22. Tel: 429 8407. Open: 6pm until the early morning.

Cafe Libertad, 8, Libertad, 8. Tel: 532 1150. Classical music and exhibitions.

Honky Tonk, Covarrubias, 24. Tel: 445 6886. Open: 8.30pm–4am. Wednesday night is Magic Night.

Torero, Cruz, 26. Tel: 523 1129. Open: Wednesday–Sunday 10pm–6am.

Whisky Jazz Club, Diego de León, 7. Tel: 261 1165. Open: 7pm–3.30am.

DISCOTHEQUES

Archy, Marqués de Riscal, 11. Tel: 308 3162. Open: midnight–4am.

Bocaccio, Marqués de la Ensenada, 16. Tel: 319 9329. Open: 7pm–4.30am.

Joy Eslava, Arenal, 11. Tel: 266 3733. Open: weekdays at 11.30pm Thursday evening, the Chattanooga Orchestra plays old dance favourites from the 1940s.

Pacha, Barceló, 11. Tel: 446 0137. Open: midnight–5am.

Stella, Arlabán, 7. Tel: 531 0192. Open: daily except Monday, 10pm–4am.

Villa Rosa, Plaza de Santa Ana, 15. Tel: 521 3689.

NIGHTCLUBS WITH SHOWS

Cleofás, Goya, 7. Tel: 576 4523 or 576 3678. Discotheque in the afternoon, a show featuring a top singer or performer is put on at 1am.

Florida Park, Avda de Menéndez Pelayo (Retiro Park). Tel: 573 7805. Dinner is also served.

La Scala Meliá Castilla, Capitán Haya, 43. Tel: 571 4411. A fine Las Vegas-style show.

GAMBLING

Spaniards are among the world's most enthusiastic gamblers. The Madrid **Casino** is at Ctra de La Coruña, Km 28.3 near the town of Torrelodones (tel: 859 0312 and 856 1100). To be admitted, you have to be over 18, carry proper identification and be correctly dressed (for men this means a tie, except in the month of August). A free bus service is provided from Plaza de España, 6.

SHOPPING

Madrid, as the capital, offers the visitor the whole range of shopping possibilities found in the different regions of Spain.

Spain has always been noted for the variety and quality of its craft work from colourful hand-sewn, embroidered Manila shawls, leather and suede goods, to its internationally exported footwear and furniture. You'll find a fine selection of the latter at the state-run Artespaña shops (Velázquez, 140; Hermosilla, 14; Ramón de la Cruz, 33; and at the La Vaguada shopping centre in the north of Madrid).

The major department stores and tourist shops are to be found in the centre of Madrid between the Puerta del Sol and the Plaza Callao, and along the Gran Vía. The more select shops and international boutiques line Calle Serrano and its adjoining streets in the Salamanca area, while the most avant-garde designers have their shops in Calle Almirante, just off the Paseo de Recoletos. (Beware of the streets directly to the west of Almirante, as they lead into one of Madrid's worst drug and crime zones.)

There are also possibilities for antique shopping in Madrid: the Calle del Prado is a good hunting ground. The Madrid Rastro, the open-air flea market, operates on Saturday, Sunday and holiday mornings, and you can find everything and anything there from valuable antiques, second-hand clothing and old books, to souvenirs, toilet articles and live canaries. Watch out for pickpockets.

The two major department-store chains are El Corte Inglés (branches at Preciados, 3; Princesa, 41; Goya, 76; and Raimundo Fernández Villaverde, 1), and Galerías Preciados (Plaza Callao, 1; Arapiles, 10; Serrano, 47).

Over the last five years several **shopping centres** have been built. Among them are:
Madrid 2, La Vaguada, Avda Monforte de Lemos, s/n, Barrio del Pilar, in the north of Madrid. An ultra-modern, multi-level shopping centre with shops, supermarkets, bars, restaurants and cinemas.
Mercado Puerta de Toledo, Ronda de Toledo, 1. A former fish market transformed into a bright, spacious shopping centre where the best shops in town are to be found alongside exhibition and cultural areas, restaurants and bars.
Multicentros, Serrano, 88 (the smallest of the Multicentros with 30 top boutiques); Princesa, 47 (due to its location in the university quarter of Argüelles, this offers the best in youthful trends); and Orense, 6.
Moda Shopping, in the Azca complex off the Paseo de La Castellana, is one of the newest centres with 100 shops and an atmosphere designed to induce a feeling of relaxation.
Galería del Prado, Plaza de las Cortes, 7, is probably the most elegant of the Madrid shopping complexes. On the ground floor of the Palace Hotel, with its main entrance on the Carrera de San Jerónimo, this lavishly decorated centre contains 38 exclusive shops and boutiques, together with a very pleasant, stylish restaurant.

SPORTS

GOLF
Madrid's golf courses include:
Somosaguas Club, Somosaguas. Tel: 316 1647. 18 holes.
Nuevo Club de Golf de Madrid, Las Matas. Ctra de La Coruña, 26. Tel: 630 0820.
Club de Golf de Puerta de Hierro, Km 4. Madrid–La Coruña highway. Tel: 316 1745. 36 holes.

TENNIS
Tennis can be played at:
Club de Campo, Ctra de Castilla, s/n. Tel: 307 0629.
Club de Tenis Chamartín, F. Salmón, 2. Tel: 345 2500.
Club Internacional de Tenís, Ctra de El Plantío a Majadahonda, no. 3.
The Real Club Puerta de Hierro, Ciudad de Puerta de Hierro, s/n. Tel: 316 1635.

SKIING
The nearest ski slopes are found at:
Navacerrada, only 30 miles (50 km) from Madrid along the N-6012 highway. Information in Madrid from Casado del Alisal, 7, tel: 530 5572; or from the resort itself, tel: 852 1435/32. It has five ski-chairs and six ski-lifts.
The **Valcotos** ski resort is 40 miles (65 km) along the N-601 road and has two ski-chairs and four ski-lifts. (Address in Madrid: Felipe IV, 12, tel: 539 7503 or 852 0857.)
Valdesquí is 40 miles (70 km) further on and has six ski-lifts and a ski tow. Information in Madrid from San Ramón Nonato, 1. Tel: 315 5939 or from the resort, tel: 852 0416.
The **La Pinilla** resort, 70 miles (120 km) from Madrid, at Cerezo de Arriba in the province of Segovia, has one ski-chair, six ski-lifts, one ski tow and two cable cars. Information in Madrid from Paseo de la Castellana, 173, tel: 570 6731 and from the resort, tel: (911) 550304.

BOWLING
AMF Bowling, Castellana, 77. Tel: 555 7626. Sixteen lanes. Open: Sunday–Thursday 10am–1.30am. Friday and Saturday 10am–3am.
Chamartín, Chamartín Train Station. Twenty lanes.

Open: Monday–Friday 10am–2am, Saturday–Sunday 10am–4am. Tel: 315 7119.
Club Stela, Arlabán, 7. Tel: 531 0192.
Recreativos Princesa, Princesa, 5. Tel: 559 9802.

HORSE RIDING
Stables are located at:
Club de Campo, Ctra de Castilla, s/n.
Tel: 307 0395.
Club Hípico El Trébol, Calle Rosas, 15, Ctra de Humera-Pozuelo de Alarcón. Tel: 218 3001.
Escuela Española de Equitación, Avda de la Iglesia, 9, Pozuelo. Tel: 218 1247.

SQUASH
There are courts at:
Squash Abascal, José Abascal, 46. Tel: 442 7900.
Gimnasio Argüelles, Andrés Mellado, 21.
Tel: 549 0040.
Mr Gym, Comandante Zorita, 49. Tel: 572 1935/6.
Motel Avión, Ctra Barcelona, Km 14.
Tel: 747 6222.

SKATING
There is an ice skating rink at **Ciudad Deportiva del Real Madrid**, Paseo de la Castellana, 259, tel: 315 0046, and a roller skating rink at **Chamartín Station**.

SPECTATOR

SOCCER
Madrid has several soccer stadiums, the most important being the Estadio Santiago Bernabéu (Paseo de la Castellana, 140, tel: 344 0052. Metro: Cuzco) in the north of the city, home of the Real Madrid team; and the Estadio Vicente Calderón (Paseo de los Melancólicos, s/n, tel: 266 2867), in the south beside the Manzanares river, belonging to the Atlético de Madrid team. These are, for the moment, Madrid's two First Division teams.

BASKETBALL
Is becoming increasingly popular and games are held in the Real Madrid Baloncesto installations, north of the Plaza de Castilla, or in the Palacio de Deportes on Avda Felipe II.

RACING
Can be enjoyed at the Hipódromo de la Zarzuela, Avda del Padre Huidobro (Ctra de La Coruña, Km 7.8, tel: 307 0140). Admission: adults 500 pesetas, children under 15 and adults over 65 are admitted free. Buses leave for the racetrack from the Plaza de España.

JAI-ALAI
This fast and exciting Basque sport can be seen at the following *frontones* (Jai-alai courts):
Frontón Madrid: Dr Cortezo, 10. Tel: 539 1037.
Frontón Reyzabal: Avda Moratalaz, 40.
Tel: 439 9131.
Frontón Recoletos: Villanueva, 2. Tel: 576 0148.

CAR & MOTORCYCLE RACES
These are held out at the Circuito de Jarama Racetrack, Ctra N-1 de Burgos, Km 27. Tel: 447 3200 and 652 2744.

BULLFIGHTS
These are held in the Las Ventas bullring, Calle Alcalá, 237 (Metro stop: Las Ventas on Line 5). The season begins in mid-March and ends in mid-October, with bullfights scheduled for every Sunday and holiday, and on Thursday evenings during the summer months.

The big **San Isidro Festival**, over three weeks of daily bullfights featuring top matadors and bulls from the best ranches, starts on 14 May. The **autumn fair** is held at the end of September.

During San Isidro, the corrals at El Batán in the Casa de Campo park exhibit the bulls due to be fought and for a modest admission fee you can get a close look at these impressive animals. There is also a pleasant outdoor bar and restaurant overlooking the corrals.

Tickets for the bullfights can be purchased a day in advance of the actual fight at Las Ventas.

Bullfights start at different times, so check local listings. In March, April and October, they start at 4.30–5pm, while May–August they begin at 7pm.

SPECIAL INFORMATION

CHILDREN
Spaniards love children and on the whole won't frown at their presence, which is fortunate considering the problems involved in finding baby-sitters. Some suggestions for family entertainment:

The **Casa de Campo Park** has a swimming pool at the El Lago Metro stop, near the lake, where boats and canoes can be rented.

The park is also the setting for the modern **Madrid Zoo** (tel: 711 9950 or 711 5416) with its Children's Zoo, where it is possible to feed and pet the goats, sheep, deer, squirrels and pigeons. The zoo, home to over 3,000 animals, is located near the Batán Metro stop. Open: 10am–sunset. The Dolphin show in the *Delfinario* is worth seeing. Admission: Adults 800 pesetas, children under 8 years old 500 pesetas. Dolphin show times: Monday 1pm, Tuesday–Friday 12.30 and 5pm, Saturday and Sunday 12.30, 2 and 5pm.

Also in the Casa de Campo is the **Parque de Atracciones** or Amusement Park (tel: 463 2900) with a wide variety of rides and, in summer, performances by top Spanish and international singers. It is also near the Batán Metro stop and can be reached by buses 33 and 65. Open: Monday, Tuesday and Wednesday 5pm–3am, Saturday noon–3am, Sunday and holidays noon–1am. Admission: Adults 300 pesetas.

The Casa de Campo can also be reached by way of a soaring cross-town ride on the *Teleférico* **Cable Car** which can be boarded at the Paseo Pintor Rosales (Tel: 541 7222). Return trip: 400 pesetas; one-way: 250 pesetas.

There are **marionette shows** at noon and Sunday morning **concerts** (for adults) in Retiro Park, where children can also enjoy the many playgrounds or go boating on the artificial lake.

Short trips through Retiro Park in a *calesa* (**horse–drawn carriage**) cost between 500 and 1,000 pesetas, depending upon the length of the ride. The carriages can be found near the *Estanque* (lake), 10am–6pm.

Travelling **circuses** come to Madrid in the months of January, May and December. See newspapers for details.

Other possibilities are the **Aquarium** at Calle Maestro Vitoria, 8, off the Plaza de Callao (tel: 531 8172) and the **Minigolf course** at Calle Montesa, 11. Open: 3–8pm.

Museo Interactivo de la Ciencia (Interactive Science Museum), Pintor Murillo, s/n, Parque de Andalucía, Alcobendas. Tel: 661 3909. Chemistry, optics, paleontology, energy… exhibitions in which children can participate are staged in this new museum. Open: daily. Admission: 600 pesetas.

The **Planetarium** in the Tierno Galván Park. Tel: 476 5731. (Metro: Méndez Alvaro.) Open: Tuesday–Friday in the afternoon, Saturday and Sunday all day. Closed: Monday. Admission: Adults 375 pesetas, children and senior citizens 185 pesetas.

Safari Park is a wild animal reserve located in the town of Aldea del Fresno, on National Highway V near Navalcarnero. Open: March–November. It also has a museum, trained animal shows, a boating lake, miniature golf, swimming pools and restaurants. Tel: 862 0811.

And finally to the latest craze, the **Aquaparks**: **Aquapalace**: A year-round aquapark. Paseo de la Ermita del Santo, 40. Tel: 526 1779. Open: Thursday–Friday 10am–9pm; Saturday, Sunday and holidays 11am–7pm.

Aquopolis: In the town of Villanueva de la Cañada, Km 30, on the La Coruña Highway (N–VI). Open: 10am–8pm. Free buses leave from the Plaza de España. Tel: 815 6911 or 815 6986.

Aquapark: Ctra de Andalucía, Km 44, on the way to Aranjuez. Tel: 891 0641.

NORTHERN SPAIN

Northern, or Green, Spain is perhaps the region least known to the tourist. Technically it comprises the Basque Country, Galicia, Cantabria and Asturias, although for convenience we have also included regions closer to Madrid.

ACCOMMODATION

Following is our selection of hotels in the Northern Spanish provinces of Aragón, Asturias, Cantabria, the Basque Country, Galicia, Navarre, and León-Castile. **Price guide**: *5-star = over 20,000 pesetas; 4-star = over 15,000 pesetas; 3-star = 5,000–15,000 pesetas.*

AVILA

Avila is the highest provincial capital in Spain, situated 3,700 ft (1,127 metres) above sea-level. It is most noted for its impressive ramparts, dating back to the 12th century, which are in an excellent state of restoration. It is also famous as the birthplace of the illustrious St Theresa, and features many noteworthy religious monuments, such as the 12th-century Cathedral; the Royal Monastery of Santo Tomás; the Romanesque Hermitages of San Segundo, San Nicolás and San José; the Mudejar tower of San Martín; and a host of interesting churches, convents and aristocratic mansions. Tourism Office: Plaza de la Catedral, 4. Tel: 211 387. Area code: 918.

Palacio de Valderrábanos ☆☆☆☆, Plaza de la Catedral, 9. Tel: 211 023. It has a good restaurant.
Parador de Turismo Rainmundo de Borgoña ☆☆☆, Marqués Canales de Chozas, 2. Tel: 211 340. A very charming hotel set in the 15th-century Palacio de Benavides.

SEGOVIA

Segovia is a provincial capital, boasting a wealth of interesting towns and good eating. Its most awesome monument is the Roman Aqueduct dating back to the 1st or 2nd century AD, along with the impressive Alcazar castle, the 15th-century Gothic Cathedral, several Romanesque churches, etc. Not to be missed is the region's culinary speciality, the roast suckling pig. Tourism office: Plaza Mayor, 1. Tel: 430 328. Area code: 911.

Parador Nacional of Segovia ☆☆☆☆, Apartado de Correos, 106. Tel: 443 737. A grand view of the city, with indoor and outdoor swimming pools, suites and a gymnasium.
Acueducto ☆☆☆, Padre Claret, 10. Tel: 424 800. Close to Segovia's main attractions.
Infanta Isabel ☆☆☆, Isabel la Católica, 1. Tel: 443 105. A comfortable, centrally located hotel.
Los Linajes ☆☆☆, Dr Velasco, 9. Tel: 415 578. In a nice area, with garden.

SALAMANCA

Salamanca, situated on the banks of the Tormes river, was known as "Little Rome" due to its large number of monuments, many of which were constructed from the unique "golden" stone of the region and of typical Plateresque style. The most noteworthy monument is the University, one of the oldest in Europe, along with the Old (21st-century) and New (15th-century) Cathedrals, the Church of San Esteban, the College of the Archbishop Fonseca, the Palace of Monterrey, the House of Shells and the harmonious 17th century Plaza Mayor. Salamanca is also one of the most important breeding areas for the brave fighting bull. Tourism Office: Gran Vía, 39. Tel: 268 571 and Plaza Mayor. Tel: 218 342. Area code: 923.

Monterrey ☆☆☆☆, Primo de Rivera, 13. Tel: 214 400. With garden and restaurant in a scenic area.
Parador Nacional of Salamanca ☆☆☆☆, Teso de la Feria, 2. Tel: 228 700. This modern building is located on the Tormes River and offers a spectacular panorama of the city and especially of the Cathedral.
Gran Hotel ☆☆☆☆, Plaza del Poeta Iglesias, 3-5. Tel: 213 500. A classic hotel, popular with the bullfighting crowd and complete with a "feudal restaurant".
Alfonso X ☆☆☆, Toro, 64. Tel: 214 401.
Las Torres ☆☆☆, Plaza Mayor, 26. Tel: 212 100.

LEÓN

León is particularly famous for the 13th-century Cathedral, with its magnificent stained-glass windows; the 11th-century Romanesque Basilica of San Isidoro, with its Pantheon of the Kings of León; the old *Hospedería* (Hospice) and Hospital of San Marcos, converted into a luxurious National Parador; the Palace of Los Guzmanes, the Casa de Botines (built by Catalan architect Gaudí) and the ramparts, among other places of interest. The region is noted for its trout rivers, which has led to the annual celebration of International Trout Week. Tourism Office: Plaza de la Regla, 3. Tel: 237 082. Area Code: 987.

Parador San Marcos ☆☆☆☆☆, Plaza de San Marcos, 7. Tel: 237 300. Suites available. The Rey Don Sancho restaurant is well known for its cuisine.

Conde Luna ☆☆☆☆, Independencia, 5. Tel: 206 512. With a garden and pool.

Quindos ☆☆, Avda Jose Antonio, 24. Tel: 236 200. A picturesque location with swimming pool and garden.

PALENCIA

Palencia is a relatively small provincial capital which nevertheless offers a certain tranquillity, good cooking based on the local produce of its fertile valley, and several monuments such as the Cathedral, nicknamed the "Unknown Beauty", the Monastery of Santa Clara, the Churches of San Miguel, San Pablo and San Francisco and the Archaeological and Sacred Art Museums. Tourism Office: Mayor, 105. Tel: 740 068. Area code: 988.

Europa Centro ☆☆☆☆, Magaz de Pisuerga. Tel: 784 000. In the Magaz castle.

Castilla la Vieja ☆☆☆☆, Casado del Alisal, 26. Tel: 749 044. Centrally located.

HUSA Rey Sancho de Castilla ☆☆☆, Avda Ponce de León, s/n. Tel: 725 300. A comfortable hotel with a large garden, pool and tennis court.

VALLADOLID

This region is rich in cities and villages with monuments in Romanesque, Mudéjar and Gothic styles. The capital of the province is a more modern city, although it still conserves its traditional Plaza Mayor (Main Square), the Sculpture Museum, the Cathedral, the Convent of Las Huelgas and a series of interesting churches. Its Easter Week celebrations, with its particularly moving Good Friday processions, are particularly worth a visit. Tourism Office: Plaza de Zorrilla, 3. Area Code: 983.

Olid Meliá ☆☆☆☆, Plaza San Miguel, 10. Tel: 357 200. This hotel, with modern installations, is nicely situated in the old part of town.

Felipe IV ☆☆☆, Gamazo, 16. Tel: 307 000. A comfortable, centrally located hotel.

Lasa ☆☆☆, Acera de Recoletos, 21. Tel: 390 255.

Meliá Parque ☆☆☆, García Morato, 17 bis. Tel: 470 100. With a restaurant.

ZAMORA

Situated in a province of varied topography, Zamora is mainly noted for the remains of its medieval ramparts, its Cathedral with a magnificent Byzantine dome and several 12th-century Romanesque temples. Tourism Office: Santa Clara, 20. Tel: 533 813. Area code: 988.

Parador de Turismo Condes de Alba de Aliste ☆☆☆☆, Plaza Viriato, 5. Tel: 514 497. Installed in a 15th century palace with a splendid Renaissance cloister, situated in the heart of town.

Hostería Real de Zamora ☆☆☆, Cuesta de Pizarro, 7. Tel: 534 545. An attractive hotel also with a beautiful cloister.

Hostal Rey Don Sancho, Ctra Villacastín-Vigo, Km 276. Tel: 523 400. With a restaurant.

ZARAGOZA

Zaragoza, situated beside the Ebro, features remnants of the diverse cultures which inhabited Spain: the Roman ramparts, the Arab Aljafería Palace, built in 1030, the Cathedral of El Pilar, dating back to the reign of Carlos II, and the 12th-century Seo Cathedral, among many other interesting monuments. Tourism Office: Don Jaime, 6, bajos. Tel: 297 582. Area code: 976.

Meliá Zaragoza Corona ☆☆☆☆☆, Avda César Augusto, 13. Tel: 430 100. A luxurious hotel in the centre of the city with a good restaurant.

Hotel Don Yo ☆☆☆☆, Bruil 4 and 6. Tel: 226 741. Very nice hotel with pleasant staff.

El Cisne ☆☆☆, Ctra Madrid-Barcelona, Km 309. Tel: 332 000. On the outskirts of the city, with a golf course and a swimming pool in a pretty setting.

Hotel Palafox ☆☆☆, Casa Jiménez, s/n. Tel: 237 700. A modern hotel with a rooftop pool.

Conde Blanco ☆☆, Predicadores, 84. Tel: 441 411. In a pretty area.

Ceylan ☆☆, San Juan de la Cruz, 7. Tel: 212 603. Centrally located.

HUESCA

The province of Huesca is set in a very scenic, mountainous area, featuring a number of popular ski resorts. The city itself has an old quarter containing a Gothic Cathedral, with an interesting museum, the Old University with its Provincial Archaeological Museum and the Cloister of San Pedro el Viejo. Tourism Office: Coso Alto, 23. **Jaca**, on the Pilgrims Road to Santiago de Compostela, features an important Romanesque Cathedral and the Museum of Romanesque Painting. Area code: 974.

Pedro I de Aragón ☆☆☆, Del Parque, 34. Tel: 220 300. Located in the province of Aragón, in the foothills of the Pyrenees.

Sancho Abarca ☆☆, Plaza de Lizana, 15. Tel: 220 650. Situated in the centre of town, with a restaurant.

JACA

Gran Hotel ☆☆☆, Paseo General Franco, 2. Tel: 360 900. Has its own restaurant.

La Paz ☆☆, Mayor, 41. Tel: 360 700. A small hotel right in the centre of this little mountain town.

PAMPLONA

Pamplona has earned international fame for its tumultuous week-long festivities in honour of its patron saint, San Fermin, which begin on 7 July. Brave fighting bulls are run through the streets in the early morning hours and an atmosphere of joyous celebration envelops the city round the clock. Pamplona also has Cathedral with a 14th-century cloister, several churches, the Cámara de los Comptos, the Diocesan Museum, the Citadel and the old ramparts. Furthermore, this region is especially noted for its excellent cuisine. Tourism Office: Duque de Ahumada, 2. Tel: 220 741. Area code: 948.

Husa Iruña Park ☆☆☆☆, Ronda de Ermitagaña, s/n. Tel: 173 200. A large hotel with restaurant.

Iruña Palace-Los Tres Reyes ☆☆☆☆, Jardines de la Taconera. Tel: 226 600. A beautiful hotel in a scenic area. Includes gardens, a swimming pool and restaurants.

Ciudad Pamplona ☆☆☆, Iturrama, 21. Tel: 266 011. Medium-sized hotel in the heart of the city.

Maisonnave ☆☆☆, Nueva, 20. Tel: 222 600. A centrally located hotel with pleasant service.

NH El Toro ☆☆☆, Ctra Guipúzcoa, Km 5. Tel: 302 211. Located a few miles outside of town, with a swimming pool.

Orhi ☆☆☆, Leyre, 7. Tel: 228 500. Centrally located and one of the city's classics.

Yoldi ☆☆, Avda de San Ignacio, 11. Tel: 224 800. Has its own restaurant.

La Perla ☆☆, Plaza del Castillo, 1. Tel: 227 706. In the main square.

SAN SEBASTIÁN/DONOSTIA

(Guipúzcoa)

San Sebastián (Donostia, to the locals) has always been a popular seaside resort on the Cantabrian Sea. In addition to its beautiful La Concha beach, visits should be made to the Church of Santa María, the Church of San Vicente, the Cathedral del Buen Pastor, the Museum of San Telmo and the Oceanographic Museum, as well as the scenic views from Monte Igueldo. The city also offers many gourmet restaurants. Tourism Office: Fueros, 1. Tel: 426 282. Area code: 943.

María Cristina ☆☆☆☆, Plaza República Argentina, 4. Tel: 424 900. Originally opened in 1912, it has been entirely remodelled and redecorated and is once again the top hotel in the city.

Londres y de Inglaterra ☆☆☆☆, Zubieta, 2. Tel: 426 989. A lovely hotel very close to the beach and the city's famous old section.

Monte Igueldo ☆☆☆☆, Monte Igueldo, s/n. Tel: 210 211. With a scenic view.

Avenida ☆☆☆, Paseo de Igueldo, 55. Tel: 212 022. On the road up to one of San Sebastian's mountains overlooking the sea.

Niza ☆☆☆, Zubieta, 56. Tel: 426 663. A centrally located hotel with a scenic view. Coffee-shop.

Parma ☆☆, General Jauregui, 11. Tel: 428 893. In the city's old section.

BILBAO

Bilbao is the capital of one of the smallest provinces in Spain, although it can boast of the highest population density and income per capita. The city is an important industrial centre, with an interesting old quarter, scenic surroundings and an excellent cuisine. Tourism Office: Plaza Arriaga, s/n. Tel: 416 0022 and 416 0288. Area code: 94.

Villa de Bilbao ☆☆☆☆☆, Gran Vía, 87. Tel: 441 6000. Centrally located with excellent service.

Carlton ☆☆☆☆, Plaza Federico Moyúa, 2. Tel: 416 2200. A traditional, centrally located hotel.

Ercilla ☆☆☆☆, Ercilla, 37–39. Tel: 443 8800. A highly popular hotel and the centre of bullfighting and theatrical activity of the city. A fine restaurant, the Bermeo.

Nervión ☆☆☆, Paseo Campo Volantí, 11. Tel: 445 4700. Located beside the estuary.

SANTANDER

Santander has a busy port area and is surrounded by a dozen beaches. Sixteen miles (26 km) away is the medieval city of Santillana del Mar and the famous prehistoric Caves of Altamira, with their Rupestrian paintings. Tourism Office: Plaza Velard, 1. Tel: 310 708. Municipal information: Jardines de Pereda. Tel: 216 120. Area code: 942.

Real ☆☆☆☆☆, Perez Galdos, 28. Tel: 272 550. An elegant hotel very close to Santander's beaches. It dates back to the beginning of the century.

Bahia ☆☆☆☆, Alfonso XIII, 6. Tel: 221 700. Close to the picturesque port area.

Santemar ☆☆☆☆, Joaquín Costa, 28. Tel: 272 900. Centrally located.

Sardinero ☆☆☆, Plaza de Italia, 1. Tel: 271 100. Right on Sardinero beach.

NH Ciudad de Santander ☆☆☆, Menéndez Pelayo, 13-15. Tel: 227 965. Centrally located with parking.

Rhin ☆☆, Avda Reina Victoria, 155. Tel: 274 300. In a pretty area close to the sea.

LA CORUÑA

La Coruña, capital of the seaboard province bathed by the Atlantic and the Cantabrian seas, and consequently famous for its seafood dishes, is set in very scenic surroundings. Of special interest in Coruña is the Roman Tower of Hercules, the oldest working lighthouse in the world. The city also has an interesting old quarter and the Provincial Museum and House of Sciences. Not far away is the monumental city of Santiago de Compostela, whose magnificent Cathedral has been for centuries the destination for pilgrimages to the tomb of St James Apostle. Also worthy of a visit are the Hotel-Parador of the Reyes Católicos, the Fonseca Palace, housing the city's University and many other interesting sites. Tourism Office in La Coruña: Dársena de la Marina, s/n. Tel: 221 822. Tourism Office in Santiago de Compostela: Rúa del Villar, 43. Tel: 584 081. Area code: 981.

Atlántico ☆☆☆☆, Jardines de Mendez Nuñez. Tel: 226 500.

Finisterre ☆☆☆☆, Paseo del Parrote, 22. Tel: 205 400. A fine, centrally located hotel.

Sol Coruña ☆☆☆☆, Ramón y Cajal, 53. Tel: 242 711. A very modern hotel on the Paseo Marítimo.
Riazor ☆☆☆, Avda Barrié de la Maza, 29. Tel: 253 400.

SANTIAGO DE COMPOSTELA

Parador Los Reyes Católicos ☆☆☆☆☆, Plaza de Obradoiro, 1. Tel: 582 200. A luxury hotel a short distance from the mighty Cathedral of Santiago, with all the creature comforts a weary pilgrim deserves.
Compostela ☆☆☆☆, General Franco, 1. Tel: 585 700. With its own restaurant.
Gelmírez ☆☆☆, General Franco, 9. Tel: 561 100. A large hotel with a coffee-shop.
Peregrino ☆☆☆, Rosalia de Castro. Tel: 591 850. With a pool, gardens and a restaurant.

VIGO

Set on a picturesque estuary, Vigo is the busiest fishing port in the country. A visit to the city should include the dock area, with the Puerta del Sol, the Parque de Castro with its fortress and the neoclassic Collegiate Church. Tourism Office: Las Avenidas, s/n. Tel: 430 577. Area code: 986.
Bahia de Vigo ☆☆☆☆, Canovas del Castillo, 5. Tel: 226 700. Suites available. In-house restaurant.
Ciudad de Vigo ☆☆☆☆, Concepción Arenal, 5. Tel: 435 233. Centrally located.
Ensenada ☆☆☆, Alfonso XIII, 35. Tel: 226 100.

WHERE TO EAT

A city-by-city guide to eating out in the provinces of Northern Spain.

AVILA

El Molino de la Losa, Bajada de la Losa, 12. Tel: 211 101. Two forks. Housed in a 15th-century mill, the restaurant offers classic Castilian cuisine, including homemade sausage, roast pig and lamb, as well as salmon and hake. Closed: Monday from 15 October–15 March.
La Hostería de Bracamonte, Bracamonte, 6. Tel: 251 280. Two forks. A 16th-century mansion-cum-restaurant with typical decor. Its specialities are stuffed prickly pears, roast lamb, pheasant with mushrooms and a variety of cakes. Closed: Tuesday.

SEGOVIA

Casa Amado, Fernandez Ladreda, 9. Tel: 432 077. Two forks, Castilian cuisine. Frequented by the locals, good quality *casera*. Specialities include garlic soup, fried hake, frogs legs, lamb, suckling pig. Closed: Wednesday, and October.
Mesón de Cándido, Azoguejo, 5. Tel: 425 911. Three forks, Castilian cuisine. Always crowded, and full of ambience. This establishment's speciality is its collection of photos of famous people tasting the suckling pig.

SALAMANCA

Chez Victor, Espoz y Mina, 16. Tel: 213 123. Three forks, Nouveau cuisine. Specialities include leek and eggplant mousse, duck and, for dessert, crepes.
El Candil Nuevo, Plaza de la Reina, 2. Tel: 217 239. Three forks. Castilian cuisine. Specialities include roast piglet and flan. Closed: Thursday, and June–August.
Rio de la Plata, Plaza del Peso, 1. Tel: 219 005. Two forks. Castilian cuisine. Specialities include clams, the meats and fish of the region, and rice pudding. Closed: Monday, and July.

PALENCIA

Casa Damián, Ignacio Martínez de Azcoitia, 9. Tel: 764 628. Two forks. Specialities include vegetable stew, fried hake and cooked partridge, followed by home-made desserts. Closed: Monday and from 25 July–25 August.
Lorenzo, Avda Casado del Alisal, 10. Tel: 743 545. Two forks. A popular restaurant of the city offering simple dishes and special desserts. Closed: Sunday, and 7 September–7 October.

VALLADOLID

La Fragua, Paseo de Zorrilla, 10. Tel: 337 102. Three forks. A culinary institution of the city, this restaurant's dishes rely on quality local produce and excellent meat and fish. Closed: Sunday evening.
Mesón Cervantes, Del Rastro, 6. Tel: 306 138. A family-run establishment, it specialises in rice with hare, fresh vegetable stew, stuffed partridge, venison with sweet and sour sauce and roast pig and lamb, among other succulent dishes. Closed: Sunday, and August.

ZAMORA

Hostería Real de Zamora, Cuesta de Pizarro, 7. Tel: 534 545. Two forks. Housed in a 16th-century mansion, it features both Castilian and Basque cooking.
París, Avda de Portugal, 14. Tel: 514 325. Two forks. Typical Castilian cuisine including ox-tail stew.

LEÓN

Novelty, Independencia, 4. Tel: 254 752. Three forks, international cuisine. Specialities include veal and grilled fish. Closed: Sunday nights, and Monday.
Casa Pozo, Plaza de San Marcos, 15. Tel: 223 039. Two forks. Specialities include crayfish with clams, *morcilla* (blood pudding made with rice and onions),

and San Marcos pie. Closed: Sunday, July, and Christmas.

Casa Teo, Avda de Castilla, 17. Tel: 223 005. One fork. *Cocina casera* (home cooking). Tiny restaurant known for its spinach soup and *cocido* (vegetable and sausage stew). Closed: Monday, and March.

ZARAGONA

Los Borrachos, Paseo de Segasta, 64. Tel: 275 036. Four forks. Specialities include patés, fresh fish, wild boar, venison and homemade ice-cream and sherbert. Closed: Sunday, and August.

Mesón del Carmen, Hernán Cortes, 4. Tel: 211 151. Three forks. Aragonese cuisine. Specialities include chicken in *chilindrón* (tomato-based sauce), lamb, cod and, for dessert, peaches with wine.

HUESCA

Las Torres, María Auxiliadora, 3. Tel: 228 213. Three forks. Imaginative cooking, including cod with black noodles, hake *al chilindrón*, pig's feet, and licorice ice cream. Closed: Sunday, and 16–30 August.

Navas, San Lorenzo, 15. Tel: 224 738. Three forks. Traditional dishes which feature brains with thyme, tuna with herbs, cod with red peppers and a variety of home-made desserts.

JACA

El Parque, General Franco, 1. Three forks. Aragonese cuisine. Dishes typical of the region, such as chicken *chilindrón*, *magras con tomate* (ham with tomato) and peaches in wine. Closed: November.

PAMPLONA

Josetxo, Estafeta, 73. Tel: 222 097. Three forks, Navarrese cuisine. Located on the street where the running of the bulls takes place, the restaurant's specialities are dishes typical of the region: artichokes and asparagus of Tudela, cod, lamb *al chilindrón*, and flounder in champagne. Closed: Sunday, and August.

Rodero, Arrieta, 3. Tel: 228 035. Three forks. Navarrese cuisine. Specialities include croquettes, mixed vegetables in the spring, jewfish *a la donostiarra*, and hake *a la navarra*.

SAN SEBASTIÁN

Akelarre, Paseo Padre Orcolaga, 56. Tel: 212 052. Barrio Igueldo. Three forks. Basque cuisine. Specialities include asparagus spears in hollandaise sauce, endive salad with apples and walnuts, sea bass with green pepper, flounder, and for dessert strawberry cake. Closed: Sunday, Monday afternoons, and during the first two weeks of October.

Arzak, Alto del Miracruz, 21. Tel: 278 465. Four forks, Basque cuisine. Specialities include baby squid in their ink, flounder in champagne, and exceptional vegetable dishes. Closed: Sunday, and Monday afternoons, and during the first two weeks of June.

BILBAO

Garrotxa, Alameda Urquijo, 30 (Gallery). Tel: 443 4937. Three forks. Exquisite cuisine featuring *vieiras* (local shellfish) with mushrooms, foie gras pastry with peregourdine sauce, lobster, turbot with onions and *chacolí* wine, steak Wellington, and excellent desserts. Closed: Sunday, and 25 July–15 August.

Guria, Gran Vía, 66. Tel: 441 0543. Four forks. This restaurant is known as the home of the Codfish Wizard, although it offers many other interesting dishes. Closed: Sunday.

SANTANDER

Gran Casino del Sardinero, Plaza de Italia. Tel: 276 054. Five forks, international cuisine. Specialities include cream of vegetable soup, hake, filet mignon and apple tart.

Chiqui, Avda de García Lago. Tel: 282 700. Four forks, Cantabrian cuisine. Specialities include mixed vegetables, roasted brill, *tocino del cielo* (a sweet flan) and an excellent wine list.

El Molino, En Puente Arce, Ctra N-611, Km 12. Tel: 575 055. Two forks, Cantabrian cuisine. Specialities include *pastel de setas* (a pastry with wild mushrooms), sea bass salad, and between courses, celery sherbert. Closed: Monday.

LA CORUÑA

Duna-2, Estrella, 2 y 4. Tel: 221 082. Three forks, Galician cuisine. Specialities include octopus, brill with clams, angler with cheese, and for dessert *filloas*, cream-filled crepes. Closed: Sunday.

Coral, Estrella, 5. Two forks. Tel: 224 221. Galician cuisine. Specialities include hake, seafood soup, filet mignon and *bonito* in tomato sauce.

O'Piote, Avda de la Marina, 10. Tel: 221 782. Two forks. Good Galician food at very reasonable prices. Closed: Wednesday.

SANTIAGO DE COMPOSTELA

Chiton, Rua Nueva, 40. Two forks, Galician cuisine. Specialities include flounder stuffed with seafood, seafood brochette, hake in cider, *caldo gallego* (a light broth), and cream-filled crepes.

Casa Vilas, Rosalia de Castro, 88. Tel: 591 000. Two forks. Galician cuisine. Specialities include octopus with potatoes, lamprey in red wine, and the native *tarta de Santiago*, a moist almond cake. Closed: Sunday.

VIGO

El Mosquito, Plaza Villavicencio, 4. Tel: 433 570. Three forks. Galician cuisine. Specialities include excellent flounder, roasted kid and grilled meats. Closed: Sunday, and August.

Puesto Piloto Alcabre, Avda Atlantida, 98. Tel: 297 975. Three forks. Galician cuisine. Specialities include *arroz de vieiras* rice with a shellfish typical of the region, angler in seafood sauce, ham with turnip tops, and for dessert, *tarta de yema*, a sweet cake made with egg yolk.

PONTEVEDRA

Calixto, Benito Crobal, 14. Two forks. Galician cuisine. Specialities include mixed vegetables, fresh fish and different meats of the region.

Casa Solla, Ctra La Toja, Km 4. Tel: 852 678. Two forks, Galician cuisine. Specialities include flounder with clams and shellfish in a light butter sauce, seafood omelette, and fruit tart. Closed: Thursday, and Sunday nights.

Eastern Spain comprises Catalonia, Valencia and Murcia. Most of this section deals with Catalonia, the most popular of the regions, although the restaurant recommendations cover the whole area. For further regional detail, contact the local tourist office. Area code: 93

GOVERNMENT & ECONOMY

Catalonia, the most unified region of Eastern Spain, is a self-governing community within the country, governed by the Generalitat in Barcelona, an institution which originated in the Corts Catalanes in the Middle Ages.

Since it gained its autonomous status in 1977, the Convergencia i Unió (centre-right) party has been in power. There is a strong socialist opposition. The president of the Generalitat is Jordi Pujol. Catalonia's four provinces – Barcelona, Girona, Lleida and Tarragona – are divided into 41 *comarques*, each with its own local administration.

Catalonia is one of the most prosperous regions of Spain with a relatively high standard of living. Some 25 percent of Spain's industry is located in Catalonia, mainly textiles, chemicals and mechanical equipment. Thirty-five percent of the population is engaged in industry, 60 percent in services and only 5 percent in agriculture, which nevertheless flourishes, with olives, grapes, apples and pears as the basic crops. The Olympic Games in Barcelona in 1992 were also a benefit to the economy.

GEOGRAPHY & POPULATION

Catalonia, in the extreme northeast corner of Spain, covers an area of approximately 12,355 sq. miles (32,000 sq. km), somewhere between the sizes of Wales and Scotland. The Catalan Pyrenees boast impressive peaks, snow-covered for many months of the year, some up to 9,700 ft (2,950 metres) high.

The Vall d'Aran in Lleida and the Cerdanya in Girona are typified by brown, rolling foothills and broad, fertile valleys; the *comarca* of La Garrotxa is a volcanic region and a swathe of wooded hills follows the coast down to Barcelona. To the north of the capital is the spectacular massif of Montserrat, on which the monastery of the Black Virgin stands.

The coast is more than 350 miles (580 km) long and is divided into four main parts: the Costa Brava, from the border to Blanes, mainly an area of attractive rocky coves; the Costa del Maresme, to the north of Barcelona, its long sandy beaches protected from wind by the hills behind; the shorter expanse of the Costa Garraf, which reaches as far south as Cubelles and is often included in the Costa Daurada (Dorada) which stretches the length of Tarragona province.

In the Empordà, in the province of Girona, and the Ebre delta, in Tarragona, there are extensive marshlands, important reserves for migratory birds and areas of rice cultivation. The Alt Penedès, in Tarragona, is one of the biggest wine-producing regions in Spain and the plain of Alcanar at the southern end of the Costa Daurada is covered with citrus groves.

Catalonia has a population of just over 6 million, of which 1.7 million live in the city of Barcelona and almost 1 million more in the industrial towns and suburbs surrounding it.

CLIMATE

For a relatively small area, Catalonia has a climate as varied as its geography. In Andorra and the Pyrenees the temperature can drop to below freezing in winter and in the foothills nights can be quite cool even after days of warm summer sun.

In the north of the Costa Brava spectacular cloud formations can appear quite suddenly above the mountains, and winds, of which the Tramuntana is the most fierce, whip up apparently out of nowhere and can last for several days. But a little further south the climate is more reliable: there is very little rain from June to September and what there is is usually concentrated in short, heavy showers.

The average temperature in coastal resorts is 77°F (25°C) in summer and 52°F (11°C) in winter. Inland, away from cooling sea breezes, it can be much hotter and the mild, sunny seasons of spring and autumn may be preferred for serious sight-seeing or long-distance walking.

FESTIVALS

There are numerous colourful national and local festivals, especially in spring and early summer. Important ones are:

Carnival: on Shrove Tuesday, celebrated everywhere, particularly in Roses, Sitges and Vilanova i la Geltrú.

Semana Santa: Holy Week, religious processions in most towns.

Festival of the Virgin of Montserrat: 27 April, at the monastery.

Corpus Christi: flower carpets in several towns, including Sitges.

St John's Eve: 23 June, bonfires and other pyrotechnics.

Vendimia: the wine harvest festivals are in mid-September.

24 September: the Verge Mercè festival is Barcelona's biggest.

MEDIA

Television: There are seven television channels. TVE 1 and TVE 2 are national, the first broadcasting almost exclusively in Castilian, the second mostly in Catalan. The two Catalan channels supported by the Generalitat are TV3, a popular channel, and Canal 33, which is slightly more high-brow, covering the arts, sports and minority interests. There are three private channels: Antena 3 and Tele 5, both Madrid based, and Canal Plus, a subscription-only channel linked to its French counterpart. French television can be seen in some northern areas and people in Tarragona can pick up Valencian television, which is on the same wavelength as Canal 33. There is also a useful device available which allows viewers the choice of watching some films either in their dubbed version or in their original language.

Radio: Between 9.30am and 4.30pm on weekdays during July and August Radio Associò de Catalunya broadcasts an hour each of Catalan, English, German, Italian and French (105 MHZ on FM). There are local radios in every town and in summer foreign languages burst through the Catalan to advertise shops, discos and events. The most popular radio station is Cadena SER, a national radio with high local input (828 KHZ MW). Radio 2 national radio is a very good classical music station.

Print: Catalonia's two main daily newspapers are *El Periódico* and *La Vanguardia*, both in Castilian. The popular Madrid daily, *El País*, has a large Barcelona staff producing a Catalonia edition which alters about six news and features pages plus the sport. *Avui* (Today) is the only Catalan region-wide daily, but there are a number of local daily papers such as the *Diari de Barcelona*, *El Nou* in Vic, and the *Diari de Girona*.

GETTING AROUND

Barcelona is the only Catalan city with an underground railway – and the only city large enough to need one. In all other towns and cities, even Lleida, Girona and Tarragona, you can explore and shop on foot or on frequent and inexpensive buses. If footsore and in need of a taxi, there are prominently marked ranks in central areas and fares are very reasonable (a 10 percent tip is usual). Although public transport is adequate and you won't need a car for visiting any of the major towns, to make the most of the country you really do need private transport.

BY RAIL

There are four main rail links in and out of Barcelona:

R1: Portbou-Girona-Barcelona. This is the main line down from Paris. An additional line operates north of Barcelona in summer: the Vapor de la Costa goes up the Maresme coast to Blanes then picks up the R1 at Massanet.

R2: Puigcerdà-Ripoll-Vic-Barcelona. This is the link-up to Toulouse in France, and a good way into the Pyrenees.

R3: Barcelona-Manresa/Reus/Valls-Lleida. This line continues to Zaragoza, and Madrid. From Lleida a line goes up to Pobla de Segur, half way to the Aigüestortes national park.

R4: Barcelona-Tarragona. The Costa Daurada train continues down the coast to Valencia.

Trains to the northeast resorts use the Cercanías station behind the Estació de França, near the harbour, refurbished in the late 1980s as a major national and international terminus. Trains to the southeast run from the Passeig de Gràcia and from the central station, Sants, in Plaça Països Catalans, from which connections can be made to any part of Spain or Europe. Stations are prominently marked with the national railways acronym RENFE (Red Nacional de Ferrocarriles Españoles).

Further information: RENFE, Estació Central Barcelona de Sants, Plaça Països Catalans s/n, 08014 Barcelona. Tel: (93) 322 4141.

Barcelona also has a suburban line, run by the Ferrrocarils de la Generalitat de Catalunya. Tel: (93) 205 1515. From Estació Plaça d'Espanya trains go to Montserrat, Igualada and Manresa. Get off at Santa Coloma de Cervelló to see Gaudí's Colònia Güell. From Plaça Catalunya they go to Sabadell, Terrassa and Sant Cugat.

BY CAR

Catalonia is well served by motorways: the A7 runs from the border towards Valencia, becoming the A17 briefly before it reaches Barcelona, and the A2 for a short while to the south of the city. A brief stretch of motorway, the A19, runs north from Barcelona to Mataró, and a new ring road, known as the "Olympic belt", should greatly improve the city's severe traffic problems.

The N11 (N roads are main, single-lane, national highways) shadows the motorway from the border down to Exit 9. It then follows the coast down to Barcelona, emerging to the south of the city and turning inland towards Lleida. For much of its length the N11 has a fairly light traffic flow, although its coastal stretch becomes horribly congested in the summer months and should be avoided if possible. From Barcelona the Autovia 152 (a two-lane highway) goes to Vic and on to Puigcerdà; the 240 links Tarragona and Lleida; and the 141 goes from Lleida to join the 152 just below Vic.

In between these main routes, Catalonia is criss-crossed by a network of regional and local roads, mainly going north-south, following the rivers coming down from the Pyrenees and making hard work of east-west journeys. The roads themselves are of varying quality, some of which more than compensate, by scenery and lack of traffic, for what they may lack in width or smoothness.

HITCHHIKING

There are two organisations in Barcelona which organise lifts at low prices. These are: Barnastop, Pintor Fortuny, 21, 08001 Barcelona, tel: (93) 3182 731; and Comparco, Ribes, 31, 08013 Barcelona, tel: (93) 246 69 08.

HOTELS & RESTAURANTS

Price guide: *5-star = over 20,000 pesetas; 4-star = over 15,000 pesetas; 3-star = 5,000–15,000 pesetas.*

LLEIDA/LÉRIDA PROVINCE

LLEIDA
Residència Principal ☆☆, Plaça de la Paeria, 8, 25007 Lleida. Tel: (973) 240 900. A comfortable, medium-priced hotel in the heart of the old town.

For good value, typical Lleidan food and wines try **La Huerta restaurant**, Avinguda de Tortosa, 9. Tel: (973) 242 413.

SOLSONA
Gran Sol ☆☆☆, Ctra Manresa s/n, 25280 Solsona. Tel: (973) 480 975.

Local cheeses, wines and dishes can be found at the **Sant Roc restaurant**, Plaça de Sant Roc, 2. Tel: (973) 811 006.

CELLERS (Selles)
Hostal del Lago ☆☆, Ctra C147 s/n (the main Balaguer-Tremp road) 25631 Cellers. Tel: (973) 650 350. Beautifully set by a lake. It also has a good, inexpensive restaurant serving local dishes as well as a surprisingly good *paella*.

AIGÜESTORTES PARK
Hotel Saurat ☆☆, Sant Martí s/n, 25597 Espot, (on the Val d'Espot side). Tel: (973) 635 063.
Hotel Manantial PPPP, 25528 Caldes de Boi, (on the Val de Boí side). Tel: (973) 690 191. This spa hotel is worth the extra for a luxury stay and has a good restaurant.

LA SEU D'URGELL
Parador Nacional ☆☆☆, Carrer Sant Domènec s/n, 25700 La Seu d'Urgell. Tel: (973) 352 000. Has 3-stars but should have more. The menu is excellent.

For half the price there is the comfortable **Hotel Andria** P, Passeig Joan Brudieu, 24, 25700 La Seu d'Urgell. Tel: (973) 350 300.
Can Ton restaurant in Carrer de la Font is ridiculously cheap and very popular.

VALL D'ARAN

ARTIES
Parador Nacional Gaspar de Pórtola, Carrer Afores s/n, 25599 Arties. Tel: (973) 640 881. A 16th-century house, once home to an explorer who went to California, now converted into an intimate inn which caters for skiiers.
Hostal Valarties, Carrer Major, 3, 25599 Arties. Tel: (973) 640 900. Has a dozen rooms and a lounge with open fireplace and is attached to the renowned restaurant run by Irene España Plagues.

Exceptional cooking can be found at **Casa Irene**, Carrer Major, 3. Tel: (973) 640 900. Dishes include home-smoked salmon with crab sauce, duck with truffles; green walnut liqueur is the house speciality.

GIRONA PROVINCE

CERDANYA
María Victoria Hotel ☆☆, Carrer Florença, 9, 17520 Puigcerdà. Tel: (972) 880 300. Has a good restaurant and a fine view over the Cerdanya plain.

Cosier, and cheaper, is the **Internacional**, Carrer La Baronia s/n, 17520 Puigcerdà. Tel: (972) 880 158. On the edge of town on the road to Alp, it has the advantage of easy access and parking.

The most famous restaurant of the region is **Can Borell** high in the hills at Meranges, for many years in the vanguard of Catalan nouvelle cuisine. The restaurant is pretty, the portions are small, the prices are high, but it's worth the experience, just once.

OLOT
Mulleras, Can Mulleras s/n, 17176 Sant Privat d'En Bas. Tel: (972) 693 257. Pretty country *pensió* only a couple of miles outside Olot in the Val d'En Bas. Its walls are covered with local paintings. Bread and tomato with ham for breakfast and an inexpensive evening set menu includes local trout.

CAMPRODÓN
Güell ☆, Plaça Espanya, 8, 17867 Camprodón. Tel: (972) 740 011. An elegant and inexpensive hotel that deserves more than its one-star.

You will eat heartily, especially meat dishes such as beef with prunes, at any of the restaurants in the rural village of **Setcases**, 8 miles to the north.

FIGUERES
Durán ☆☆☆, Lasauca, 5, 17600 Figueres. Tel: (972) 501 250. Has a traditional interior of tiles and high-backed chairs and a *purró* of Muscatel does the rounds at the end of the meal of Empordà dishes.
Hotel Ampurdán ☆☆☆, Ctra Nacional N11, Km 763. Tel: (972) 500 562. Was one of Josep Pla's favourites, and is often credited as the birthplace of the "new" Catalan cuisine.

GIRONA
Peninsular, Carrer Nou, 3, 17001 Girona. Tel: (972) 203 800. Well-established hotel, just over on the new side of town.
Reyma ☆☆, Pujada del Rei Martí, 15, 17004 Girona. Tel: (972) 200 228. Relatively inexpensive.

Centro ☆☆, Carrer Ciutadans, 4, 17004 Girona. Tel: (972) 201 493. A hotel with large rooms which has seen grander days; in the heart of the old town, it is taken over by university students in term time.

COSTA BRAVA

PORTLLIGAT
Hotel Portlligat, 17488 Portlligat. Tel: (972) 258 162. The only commercial establishment in Dalí's bay, with a salt-water swimming pool alongside it. The sort of place one might go for a treat, either staying overnight or just for a meal in the well-appointed dining room overlooking the bay.

EMPÚRIES
Hotel Ampurias ☆, 17130 L'Escala. Tel: (972) 770 207. Out of town, right by the ruins and right on the beach.

AIGUABLAVA
Aiguablava Hotel ☆☆☆☆, 17255 Platja de Fornells. Tel: (972) 622 058. Is the classic Costa Brava hotel, beautifully situated in Fornells Bay and presided over by one of the coast's characters, Xiquet Sabater, who chooses his guests so that no one nationality dominates. A much more human-looking place than the modern *parador* opposite, though these national hotels have an excellent reputation for good local dishes: **Parador Nacional Costa Brava**, 17255 Platja d'Aiguablava. Tel: (972) 622 058.

PALAFRUGELL
Cypsele ☆, Carrer Ample, 30, Palafrugell. Tel: (972) 300 192. Has a restaurant with a good reputation. One of the few places where you can try the classic local dish, *el niu*, a huge stew based around cod's tripe, but this must be ordered in advance.
Sant Sebastià, Santuari de Sant Sebastià s/n, 17200 Palafrugell. Tel: (972) 300 586. An unusual hotel spectacularly placed above a lighthouse at the top of cliffs. The hotel, built around a courtyard, has character and there is a bar and restaurant attached.

PALAMÓS
Trias ☆☆☆, Passeig del Mar s/n 17230. Tel: (972) 314 100. Rather pricey, but another of the coast's well-known hotels which has been going for years.

There are a number of good fish restaurants around the port, such as:
Maria de Cadaqués, Notaries, 39. Also serves Empordà dishes.
Xivarri, Reuda, 22. Where pork and prawns are mixed together.

S'AGARÓ
La Gavina ☆☆☆☆☆, Plaça de la Roselada s/n, S'Agaró. Tel: (972) 321 100. Is the only 5-star hotel on the coast. If you are not super-rich, drop in for a coffee and stay instead at the nearby **Ancla** ☆, Ctra Sant Feliu-Palamós, Km 2, S'Agaró. Tel: (972) 320 128. Or you could simply splash out on a pot of fish (*olla pescadors*) at the up-market beach café, the **Taverna del Mar**.

COSTA DEL MARESME

CALDES D'ESTRAC
Hotel Colón ☆☆☆☆, Ciutat de la Paz, 16, 08393 Caldes d'Estrac, (at the end of its *passeig marítim*). Tel: (93) 791 0500. There is also a very pleasant and slightly cheaper hotel, the **Racó de Peix**, Passeig dels Anglesos, 3, 08393 Caldetes. Tel: (93) 791 0144. This small, grand house on the seafront has large rooms and bathrooms and a restaurant with terrace attached.

ARENYS DE MAR
There are good fish restaurants in the port, such as the **Posit de Pescador**. The **Hispania** in Ctra Reial, 54 is celebrated for its Catalan cuisine. Counter the effects of a large restaurant bill by staying at the **Los Angeles** *pensió*, Carrer Margarides, 8, 08350 Arenys de Mat. Tel: (93) 792 3849.

COSTA DAURADA

CASTELLDEFELS
Rey Don Jaime ☆☆☆☆, Avinguda de l'Hotel s/n, 08860 Castelldefels. Tel: (93) 665 1300. Expensive, but it is worth it for the beautiful hilltop view of the *costa* as far as Barcelona. Fine food.
Rancho, Passeig de la Marina, 212, 08860 Castelldefels. Tel: (93) 665 1900. Quieter than the beach-front hotels and has good quality cuisine and service.
Nàutic, Passeig Marítim, 374. Tel: (93) 665 0174. Facing the beach, serves superior seafood in quaint surroundings.
Las Botas, Autovía de Castelldefels. Tel: (93) 665 4096. A busy restaurant right on the main road serving traditional Catalan dishes; grilled meats a speciality.

SITGES
Calípolis ☆☆☆☆, Passeig Marítim s/n, 08870 Sitges. Tel: (93) 894 1500. A fairly large hotel just a few hundred metres from the church and museums on the seafront.
Terramar ☆☆☆☆, Passeig Marítim s/n, 08870 Sitges. Tel: (93) 894 0054. An older style establishment facing the beach with gardens and sports facilities.
Vivero, Platja de Sant Sebastià. Tel: (93) 894 2149. A basic place with tables outside overlooking the small beach and serving mainly seafood.
Els 4 Gats, Carrer Sant Pau, 13. Tel: (93) 894 1915. A reasonably priced, quality restaurant on a narrow street descending to the sea.

CAMBRILS
Can Gatell, Carrer Miramar, 27. Tel: (977) 36 0106. One of three restaurants in the town owned by the Gatell family. All are famous for their classic Tarragona fish dishes (*romesco*, *àrros a banda*, *suquet*, etc.) but this one is the most traditional.

TARRAGONA PROVINCE

TARRAGONA

España, Rambla Nova, 49, 43003 Tarragona. Tel: (977) 23 2712. A small, old-fashioned hotel right in the middle of town, reasonably priced. **Restaurant Les Coques,** Baixada del Patriarca, 2. Tel: (977) 22 8300. Serves good regional dishes.

El Tiberí, Carrer Martí Ardenys, 5. Tel: (977) 23 5403. Isn't much to look at but its buffet food is Catalan, cheap and cooked by one of the best local chefs.

La Rambla, Rambla Nova, 10. Tel: (977) 23 8729. Rather smart and it serves what some consider to be the best and most authentic *romesco* with two courses of different kinds of fish; Pau Aquilo is an old-fashioned owner, always around and running everything with precision.

EL VENDRELL

Restaurant Pi, Rambla, 2. Tel: (977) 66 0022. A café-restaurant done in a rather overblown Modernist style. It serves good local dishes such as *xató* salad and their own version of *calçots*.

VALLS

Although Valls makes a good base there are only a couple of places to stay one of which is:

Torreblanca ☆☆ *pensió*, Carrer Josep M Fàbregas, 1, 43800 Valls. Tel: (977) 60 1022. Attractive.

Restaurant Masía Bou, Ctra de Lleida s/n. Tel: (972) 60 0427. *The* place to eat *calçots*. There are countless photos of celebrities, from Dalí to Suarez, wearing bibs and wolfing down their onions. It is smart and on the pricey side, but the *calçots* are the real thing, grown at the back of the restaurant, cooked in the backyard and followed by the traditional meal of spicy sausage and lamb.

PRIORAT

Residència-Casa de Pàges, Carrer Carrerada, 8, 43739 Porrera. Tel: (977) 82 8021. One of the first of several *casas de pàges* supported by the Generalitat to supply accommodation on a small scale. It is an old house, beautifully converted in a modern abstract style, and designed for only a dozen guests. **Restaurant Piro,** Carrer Piro, 21, Gratallops. Tel: (977) 83 9004. Serves really good *platos típicos* with a menu which changes daily according to local ingredients (they collect their own *rovellon* mushrooms).

VALENCIA

Valencia is surrounded by beautiful beaches and fertile farmland, which contribute to the region's excellent culinary offerings. Among the city's monuments are the 15th century *Lonja* (Commodity Exchange), the Cathedral and its Miguelete Tower, the Generalidad Palace, the Serranos and De Cuarte Gateways and a series of interesting museums. Nearby are the Roman ruins of Sagunto. Municipal Tourism Office: Plaza Ayuntamiento, 1. Tel: 351 0417. Area code: 96.

Sidi Saler Palace ☆☆☆☆☆, Playa del Saler. Tel: 161 0411. A very comfortable hotel, situated on the beach a few miles outside the city.

Astoria Palace ☆☆☆☆, Plaza Rodrigo Botet, 5. Tel: 352 6737. Centrally located, luxury hotel with good service.

Meliá Valencia Rey Don Jaime ☆☆☆☆, Avda Baleares, 2. Tel: 360 7300. A modern hotel, complete with swimming pool.

Expo Hotel ☆☆☆, Avda Pío XII, 4. Tel: 347 0909. A new hotel with a swimming pool.

ALICANTE

Alicante is another popular Mediterranean resort area with lovely beaches and modern hotel installations. The city's touristic attractions include the Castle of Santa Barbara, the Monastery of Santa Faz, the Cathedral, the Archaeological Musseum, the Church of Santa María and the Modern Art Museum. Tourism Office: Explanada de España, 2. Tel: 521 2285. Area code: 96.

Hotel Sidi San Juan ☆☆☆☆☆, Plaza de San Juan. Tel: 516 1300. A fine hotel with excellent installations, restaurants, swimming pools, etc., situated on the beach.

Meliá Alicante ☆☆☆☆, Playa Postiguet. Tel: 520 5000. A very comfortable hotel with a swimming pool and restaurant.

Leuka ☆☆☆, Segura, 23. Tel: 520 2744. Centrally located and reasonably priced.

MURCIA

Murcia also boasts of lovely beaches and the very popular Mar Menor, a large, natural salt water lake, ideal for practising all water sports. The capital city features many monuments of baroque, rococo and Churrigueresque styles, including the cathedral, the museum of the famous sculptor Salzillo and the Archaeological Museum. Tourism Office: Alejandro Seiquer, 4. Tel: 362 000. Area code: 968.

Meliá Siete Coronas ☆☆☆☆, Paseo de Garay, 5. Tel: 217 771. A comfortable hotel.

Rincón de Pepe ☆☆☆☆, Apóstoles, 34. Tel: 212 239. Centrally located, with an excellent restaurant.

BARCELONA CITY HOTELS

The capital does not have an abundance of accommodation and better class hotels should be booked, as conventions and can fill them up. Middle-priced hotels are particularly in short supply.

Two good hotels towards the top of the range are: **Comtes de Barcelona** ☆☆☆☆, Passeig de Gràcia, 75, 08008 Barcelona. Tel: (93) 215 0616. In a converted Modernist mansion, and the slightly cheaper **Colón** ☆☆☆☆, Avinguda Catedral, 7, 08002 Barcelona. Tel: (93) 301 1404. In the Gothic quarter, though the cathedral bells may keep you awake.

There are two palatial hotels which are not sky-high in price:

Hotel Gran ☆☆☆, Gran Viá de les Corts Catalanes, 642, 08007 Barcelona. Tel: (93) 318 1900. Near the Plaça Catalunya and has a brocaded, Regency feel. **Hotel España** ☆☆, Sant Pau, 9 i 11, 08001 Barcelona. Tel: (93) 318 1758. A Modernist extravaganza from Domènech i Montaner and though the bedrooms are plain, its public rooms maintain a sense of the *belle époque*.

There are a clutch of pleasant, middle-priced hotels by the Rambla de Catalunya, such as: **Windsor** ☆☆, Rambla de Catalunya, 84, 0800 Barcelona. Tel: (93) 215 1198. **Neutral**, Rambla de Catalunya, 42, 08007 Barcelona. Tel: (93) 318 7370.

Most of the hotels are on or near the main Rambla. There are lots of inexpensive places on the roads and lanes leading off both sides of the street, and they become progressively more seedy towards the port. Near the Plaça Catalunya at the top there are 1 and 2-star hotels on Carrer de Santa Anna: the **Catalunya**, tel: (93) 301 9150; **Cortes**, tel: (93) 317 9112; and the **Nouvel**, tel: (93) 301 8274. Further down on Carrer del Carme, there are four *pensiós*: the **Carmen**, tel: (93) 317 1076; **Aneto**, tel: (93) 318 4083; **Selecta**, tel: (93) 209 1930; and the **Mare Nostrum**, tel: (93) 318 5340. The **Sant Agustí** ☆☆, Plaça Sant Agustí, 3, 08001 Barcelona, tel: (93) 317 2882, is pleasantly situated in a quiet square behind the market, and on the opposite side of Rambla the **Hotel Jardí**, Plaça St Josep Oriol, 1, 08001 Barcelona, tel: (93) 301 5900, overlooks two attractive squares.

BARCELONA PROVINCE

CALDES DE MONTBUI

Balneario Termes Victòria, Carrer Barcelona, 12, 08140 Caldes de Montbui. Tel: (93) 865 0150. A spa hotel which is now becoming trendy.

MONTSENY

Sant Bernat, Finca el Cot, 08460 Montseny. Tel: (930) 847 3011. A pleasant small hotel situated near the forest and mountains of the natural park.

VIC

Parador Nacional, 08500 Vic, 10 miles (15 km) northeast of Vic off the N153. Tel: (93) 888 7211. Very popular and very beautiful. A relatively new building for a *parador*, it is wonderfully set in a pine forest overlooking the Sau reservoir. The restaurant serves good traditional Vic dishes.

MONISTROL DE MONTSERRAT

Monistrol ☆☆, Ctra Abrera-Manresa (C1411), Km 13. Tel: (93) 835 0477. Overshadowed by mountains and an is an alternative to a cell in the monastery.

EL BRUC

El Bruc ☆☆☆, Ctra Nacional 11, Km 574, 08194 El Bruc. Tel: (93) 771 0061. A well-appointed hotel set in this legendary valley. It also has a good restaurant: listen out for the mythical drummer boy as you eat traditional Catalan cuisine.

CARDONA

Parador Nacional Duques de Cardona, 08261 Cardona. Tel: (93) 869 1275. A hilltop castle overlooking the town and salt mines, authentically complete with squeaking floorboards. The restaurant in the baronial hall is pricey but the food is fine and the portions large.

BARCELONA CITY RESTAURANTS

As one might expect, the city's restaurants cater to all tastes. These are just a small flavour.

Eldorado Petit, Carrer Dolors Monserdá, 51. Tel: (93) 204 5153. Is the younger sister of the famous Sant Feliu de Guíxols restaurant. You get the extra you pay for here, in the best modern Catalan cuisine, and there is a fine garden and terrace, plus parking. Also at the top of the bill is **BotaFumeiro**, Carrer Gran de Grácia, 81. Tel: (93) 218 4230. The seafood restaurant and oyster bar which also serves Galician dishes.

Passadís de'n Pep, Plaça de Palau, 2. Tel: (93) 310 1021. A small but "in" restaurant, where most diners are happy to eat what they are given. **El Raïm**, Carrer Pescadería, 6. Tel: (93) 319 2998. Has been "in" for bygone literati and is still a pleasant, informal place. To get an artistic flavour, visit **Els Quatre Gats**, Carrer Montsío, 3. Tel: (93) 302 4140. It is a shadow of its former self, and the paintings on the walls are copies, but one really does have to sit in the same place that Rusiñol, Casas, Picasso and the rest did, even if the idea of such smart food in a once-bohemian atmosphere is hard to digest. There is a reasonable lunchtime set menu.

Other characterful spots include **El Gran Café**, Carrer de Avinyó, 9. Tel: (93) 318 7986. A turn-of-the-century sewing machine premises, which nostalgically retains its decor and serves good Catalan dishes bistro style. An inexpensive restaurant is the **Estevet**, Carrer Valldonzella, 46. Tel: (93) 302 4186. Try also one of the **Eqipto** "chain", the latest opened in the Rambla; the one at the back of the market is fun: Carrer Jerusalem, 12. Tel: (93) 317 7480.

RESTAURANTS IN
MURCIA, ALICANTE & VALENCIA

ALCANTARILLA

Mesón de la Huerta, Ctra Murcia-Lorca s/n. Tel: 802 390. Echoing a traditional inn next door to the Museo de la Huerta with excellent *tapas* and full meals based on the surrounding *huerta's* vegetable produce. Desserts include *papajarotes*, double-sized pancakes fried on lemon leaves, with a sweet liqueur sauce.

ALCOY/ALCOT

Vente del Pilar, Ctra Alcoy-Valenciana s/n, Termino de Cocentaina. Tel: 559 2325. Closed: August. Renowned 18th-century coaching inn. Classics are *olleta*, roast lamb. Orange tart and home-made *aguardiences* (lethal *eaux-de-vie*).

ALICANTE/ALACANT

Dársena, Club Nautico, Muelle del Puerto. Tel: 520 7589. Unbeatable for rice dishes – over 20 on the menu – and also good for fish. More relaxed at dinner than lunch. Closed: Sunday evenings, and Monday in summer.

BENIDORM

Casa L'Esclau, Panaderos. Tel: 585 6415. Excellent city-centre fish restaurant with largely local clientele. Photos of old Benidorm on the walls set the atmosphere.

La Rana, Costera del Barco 6. Casa Antig (or smaller branch at La Raneta, Martinez Oriola, 25). The Arroyos owned the first eating house before tourism hit. Now they concentrate on *tapas*. Quality produce. Very central.

CABO DE PALOS

La Tana, Patio Le Barra, 33. Cabo is the place to eat *caldero*, the local answer to *paella*, and sea-bass (or more traditionally mullet) in salt.

DENIA

El Peqoli, Baret de Les Rotes. Tel: 578 1035. Memorable family restaurant worth a special expedition. The formula is a set menu of giant prawns from the bay, *arroz abanda* and fresh fruit, or fish and shellfish paid for by weight.

ELCHE/ELX

Els Capellans, Porta de la Morera, 8. Tel: 454 8040. One of three restaurants within the Hort del Cura Hotel. Gracious and very smart, surrounded by the famous palm-trees. The menu is an imaginative hybrid of international and local – as in palm-heart salad and sweet date omelette. Expensive

JUMILLA

Casa Sebastián, Mercado de Abastos, Avda de Levante. Highly recommended market restaurant serving breakfast and lunch till 4.15pm. Solidly provincial cooking with big rounded flavours to match local wines (18,000 bottles in the cellar). Closed: for two weeks in August.

MONOVAR/MONOVER

La Pedrera, Cami La Pedrera NH 59. Tel: 547 1206. Kitchen open until 7pm except June–September when it is open until 10pm. (Found down a signed track at the junction with Pinoso in a low white house.) Good local *gazpachos*, *gachas* and *migas* and other country dishes. Inexpensive

MORAIRA

El Giraso, Ctra Moraria-Calpe, Km 1.5. Tel: 574 4373. Star-chef cooking aiming at Parisian standards. Falls slightly short but Heinz Orth's central European style adapted to local products is interesting. Tables must be reserved. Gastronomic menu. Expensive

MURCIA

Rincón de Pepe, Apóstoles, 32. Tel: 212 239. Two forks. Highly recommended, with an extremely varied menu. Closed: Sunday.

Hispano, Radio Murcia, 4. Tel: 216 152. Two forks. A classic restaurant serving local cuisine.

PINOSO

Alfonso, Plaza Espana, 4. Tel: 547 7828. Country restaurant known for its *arroz serrano*, with local white snails and roast garlic. Moderate

SANTA POLA

Mesón del Puerto, Astilleros, 2. Tel: 541 1289. Cheaper and more local than most of the fish restaurants, with *gazpacho de mero* – a fish stew served on flatbread – and *caldero*. Or, in the centre of town near the fortress/museum, try **La Naveta**. Tel: 541 6765.

VALENCIA

Eladio, Chiva, 40. Tel: 384 2244. Three forks. A classic restaurant in Valencia, particularly noted for its fish dishes and desserts. Closed: Sunday, and August.

Galbís, Marva, 28-30. Tel: 380 9473. Two forks. It specialises in typical Valencian cooking, especially rice dishes. Closed: Saturday mid-day, Sunday, and 1 August–5 September.

La Hacienda, Navarro Reverter, 12. Tel: 373 1859. Three forks. A traditional and popular restaurant in the city with a *belle epoque* decor.

THINGS TO DO

NATURAL PARKS

There are more than 30 conservation areas in Catalonia alone and visitors are encouraged to enjoy many of them. The parks are not fenced off and access is easy.

Aigüestortes and Lake Sant Maurici: The region's only National Park is in the mountainous northwest and covers 38 sq. miles (100 sq. km). It has to be approached in one of two completely different directions: the western part from the Boí Valley, off the N230 from Lleida; the eastern part, which includes the Sant Maurici lake, from Espot via the C147 from Balaguer to La Pobla de Segur. There are information centres at both villages as well as in Lleida: Carrer Camp de Mart, 35, 25004 Lleida, tel: (973) 246 650.

Cadí-Moixeró: There are a number of access points into this 160 sq. mile (415 sq. km) natural park covering the Cadí and Moixeró mountain ranges. It is probably best approached from the Cerdanya plain on the north side of the range where the tourist offices in Puigcerdà and Bellver de Cerdanya, tel: (973) 510 016, can provide maps and guides.

Garrotxa Volcanic Zone: The natural park based on the defunct cones of this curious volcanic area occupies 46 sq. miles (120 sq. km) and includes the towns of Castellfollit, Sant Joan les Fonts, Santa Pau and Olot. There is a tourist office at both but the Casal dels Volcans on the Santa Coloma road out of Olot, Avinguda de Santa Coloma s/n, 1700 Olot, tel: (972) 266 202, is more likely to be open.

Aiguamolls de l'Empordà: The natural park covers 18½ sq. miles (48 sq. km) and is in two parts, divided by the resort of Empúria-brava, which has destroyed much of the natural wetlands the birds here once enjoyed. The northern half is between Castelló d'Empúries and the village of Palau Saverdera and includes a couple of hides. But the main reserve is signposted half way along the road between Castelló and Sant Pere Pescador. Here is the information centre, Els Cortalet, which supplies maps to the hides and trails which go down to the sea. Tel: (972) 451 231.

Delta de l'Ebre: A wetland park particularly noted for its birdlife. For any further information contact El Centro de Recepció del Parque Natural del Delta del Ebre, Plaça del 20 de Maig s/n, Deltebre. Tel: (977) 489 511.

WINE ROUTES

Wine producers, co-operatives and *bodeges* are hospitable places, and at most of them you will be able to taste the wine before buying.

Empordà-Costa Brava: In the most northeasterly corner of the region, this stretches between Figueres and the French border to the sea. There are co-operatives at Roses, Pau, Vilajuïga, Garriguella, Mollet de Peralada, Capmany, Sant Climent Sescebes, Rabós and Espolla, a village whose wines Catalan writer Josep Pla thought the best. The centre for the local *cava* industry is Peralada, a delightful medieval town worth a visit.

Penedès: Catalonia's largest and best-known wine region, just west of Barcelona, centres on the towns of Vilafranca del Penedès and Sant Sadurní d'Anoia. The famous high-tech Torres Bodega is in Carrer Comercio, Vilafranca (closed: August). There is a good selection of the local producers' wines in the shops, plus the excellent Museu del Vi (closed: Sunday).

Sant Sadurní is the *cava* town, home of Catalonia's two top producers of this *méthode champenoise* wine, Codorníu and Freixenet. Caves Codorníu on the edge of the town is a fine Modernist building restored by Puig i Cadafalch and worth a visit.

Priorat: Perhaps the most charming of the regions, where small villages make wine in small quantities. The precipitous slopes are attractive to look at but hard to work, and few young people remain at home to help out on the land. There are co-operatives at Bellmunt del Priorat, Lloà, Gratallops, Porrera, Torroja del Priorat, La Viella Alta, La Viella Baixa, Pobleda and La Morera de Montsant. The most modern wine makers are at Scala Dei.

Tarragona: De Müller, supplier of altar wine to the Vatican, is the surviving grand old wine maker in Tarragona, in the Carrer Reial, open during weekday office hours. There are several cavernous *bodeges* in the town. Outside Tarragona, on the N240 towards Valls, there is the modern Lopez Bertrán wine producer.

MUSEUMS

Catalonia is rich in museums of all kinds, from the Museu Picasso in Barcelona to the local museums in the capital towns of each *comarca*, called "*comarcal*" museums. The following is but a brief selection.

Museums change their opening times, and sometimes even their locality, with great alacrity, but generally opening hours are 9am–1pm and 4–7pm, although the Picasso Museum in Barcelona and the Dalí in Figueres are both open all day. The Dalí Museum, the second most popular in Spain after the Prado in Madrid, is also the exception to the rule that museums close on Monday. Addresses are given only for those in large cities; those in smaller places will be easily located. Entrance fees are usually a few hundred pesetas.

BARCELONA CITY

Museu Arqueològic, Passeig Santa Madrona, Parc de Montjuïc. Tel: 423 2149. Archaeology.

Museu d'Art de Catalunya, Palau Nacional, Parc de Montjuïc. Tel: 423 1824. The place to go to understand what Romanesque art is all about.

Museu d'Art Modern, Plaça d'Armes, Parc de la Ciutadella. Tel: 319 5728. Catalonia's artists, from the 19th century until today.

Museu Frederic Marès, Carrer Comtes de Barcelona, 10. Tel: 310 5800. Idiosyncratic collection of Romanesque, Gothic, Renaissance and baroque sculpture.

Museu d'Historia de la Ciutat, Plaça del Rei. Tel: 315 1111. City history with Roman basement.

Museu Marítim, Plaça Portal de la Pau, 1. Tel: 318 3245. Maritime museum in the extraordinary Drassanes docks.

Fundació Joan Miró, Plaça Neptu, Parc de Montjuïc. Tel: 329 1908. Miró's work and that of other contemporary artists.

Museu Picasso, Montcada 14–19. Mostly early work, donated by the artist and his widow.

Museu Tèxtil i d'Indumentària, Montcada 12–14. Tel: 310 4516. Textiles and costumes. Opposite the Picasso Museum, it's worth seeing both.

BARCELONA PROVINCE

Museu del Monastir de Montserrat, archaeology and paintings. The monastery, 32 miles (50 km) from Barcelona, is an important spiritual centre, home of the Black Virgin, La Mare de Deu de Montserrat. The mountain itself is a popular area for walking and rock climbing. Access from exit 25 on A2/A7 motorway from Barcelona to Tarragona, or by train from Barcelona's Plaça Espanya.

Museu-Institut de Paleontologia in Sabadell is one of Spain's most important palaeontological museums.

Museu Episcopal in Vic is second only to Barcelona's Museu d'Art de Catalunya for Romanesque and Gothic art.

Museu de Vilafranca, housed in 12th-century Palau de Comtes-Reis in Vilafranca de Penedès. Comprises six separate museums, among which is the Museu del Vi, Spain's only museum devoted to wine and viniculture. Art, geology, archaeology and ornithology are in the other five.

GIRONA CITY

Museu Arqueològic de Sant Pere de Galligants, Plaça de Santa Lucia. Archaeology in fine Romanesque monastery.

Museu Capitular i Claustres del Catedral, Plaça de la Catedral. Contains the wonderful 12th-century *Tapestry of the Creation*.

Museu d'Art, Palau Episcopal, Pujada de la Catedral. From Romanesque to modern art.

GIRONA PROVINCE

Museu Arqueològic Comarcal in Banyoles. Prehistoric finds including the famous Neanderthal jaw.

Museu Darder in Banyoles. Anthropology and ethnology, including some grotesque mummies.

Teatro-Museu Dalí in Figueres. Designed by Dalí as well as containing many of his works.

Museu de Joguets, Figueres. Private museum with huge collection of old toys.

Museu Comarcal. Housed in an ancient Olot hospice. Paintings by Olot School and exhibition of work from local saint-making industry. Open: Monday. Closed: Tuesday.

Arxiu-Museu Folklòric, Ripoll. Famous Catalan forges, armaments, pottery and shepherds' artefacts.

TARRAGONA CITY

Museu d'Història de Tarragona, Escales de Sant Hermenegild. Roman and medieval artefacts. Housed in the Roman Pilatus Castle.

Museu Nacional Arqueològic, Plaça del Rei. Most important Roman collection in Catalonia.

Museu de la Necròpolis, Passeig de la Independencia. Mosaics and sarcophagi from important early Christian necropolis.

TARRAGONA PROVINCE

Museu del Monestir de Santa Mariá in Poblet. Archaeology and fine art.

Museu Comarcal, Reus. Paintings by Fortuny, sculpture by Rebull, plus Romanesque and Gothic remains. Museu Arqueologìa Salvador Vilasec, important prehistoric remains.

CLUBS & DISCOS

The brightest night spots tend to be in the kind of crowded resorts one wants to avoid: the spectacular razzmatazz of the Grand Palace in Lloret de Mar or the Galas in Salou; or the laser shows of La Platja d'Aro, which boasts the greatest concentration of discos on the coast.

In the summer months discos spring up in all the resorts, charging perhaps 2–3,000 pesetas to get in and adding several hundred pesetas to the price of a drink. With meals eaten late, nightlife doesn't begin to get going until after midnight, continuing until around 5am when the tradition in some resorts is to have fresh *churros* (doughnuts) dunked in hot chocolate.

Many of the late drinking places in Barcelona, like the Zsa Zsa, have no entrance fee: they just demand a lot of money for their drinks. Others, such as Otto Zutz, like you to queue up so they can then refuse you entrance because they don't like your face. It is hard to recommend any of these, not least because they come in and out of fashion so fast.

CASINOS

Public gambling is a relatively new experience in Spain, as it was banned under Franco. There are three casinos in Catalonia and they are open from about 7pm–4am. There is a small entry fee of around 600 pesetas and you will need to take your passport.

Peraleda. The casino is part of the castle in this medieval, sparkling-wine village. Though the gaming rooms are tastefully hung with tapestries, the hostesses in glittering top hats and tails look quite out of place. Tel: (972) 50 3162.

Lloret de Mar, part of the modern Hotel Casino de Lloret, it has all the usual games, plus a slot machine room, restaurant, disco and swimming pool. Carrer de Tossa s/n. Tel: (972) 36 6512.

Sant Pere de Ribes, called the Gran Casino de Barcelona, this is actually 26 miles (42 km) from the city on the outskirts of Sitges. There is a dance hall with an orchestra on Friday and an open-air concert theatre. Tel: (93) 893 3666.

SHOPPING

Leather goods are very good value, from belts and purses to jackets, boots and shoes. There is a wonderful and inexpensive range of kitchen, garden and decorative **ceramics** available in small shops, at markets and in huge roadside emporiums. La Bisbal is the largest Catalan ceramic centre with nearly 100 shops in the town. Miravet, in Tarragona is also an important pottery town, as is Verdu in the Urgell (Lleida) where most of the ceramic ware is black. **Hand-made lace** can be bought, especially in L'Arboc in Baix Penedès, Tarragona.

Olive oil and wine vinegar (*aceite de oliva* and *vinagre de vino*) are good value. Wine and spirits are still ridiculously cheap. Table wine can cost as little as 90 pesetas a litre and a good quality Rioja or Valdepeñas can be had for less than 300 pesetas. There are some very good Spanish brandies costing about 850 pesetas a litre.

SPORTS

SAILING

There are 36 marinas along the 360 miles (580 km) of Catalonia's coast. Even though facilities have been expanding rapidly since the mid-1980s, berths can still be hard to come by in summer. For most of the summer all club berths are accounted for. There are some anchorage points along the rockier northern coast, and temporary berths on public jetties or in harbours are either very cheap or free. See the port authorities on arrival. A helmsman's certificate is required for any boating activity.

DIVING

Anyone wishing to dive in Spanish waters must have a diving permit. Permits cannot be obtained by post. It is best to get one of the reputable diving centres or schools to organise a permit on your behalf from the local marine commandant. They are only issued for the period of your stay and they cost around 1,000 pesetas.

GOLF

Club de Golf Costa Brava, La Masía, 17246 Santa Cristina d'Aro, province of Girona. Tel: (972) 83 7150. Open: all year round. Closed: Wednesday October–May. Just inland between Sant Feliu de Guíxols and La Platja d'Aro, this course has some narrow doglegs. The clubhouse is a fine traditional *masía*.

Club de Golf Pals, Platja de Pals, 17256 Pals, province of Girona. Tel: (972) 63 6006. Open: all year round. Closed: Tuesday between 1 September and 30 June. Finely set among pine woods beside the beach at Pals, the main hazard is the Tramuntana wind. The most expensive of Catalonia's clubs.

Reial Club de Golf de Cerdanya, Apartat de Correus, 63, 17520 Puigcerdà, province of Girona. Tel: (972) 88 1338. Open: all year unless snowed off. The Cerdanya Valley is a beautiful setting for a golf course, and this club makes the most of it, among poplars and oaks. The green fees are modest, but the course has many championships, particularly in August and September as well as at Easter. The club house complex includes a hotel.

Club de Golf Sant Cugat, 08190 Sant Cugat del Vallès, province of Barcelona. Tel: (93) 674 3958. Open: all year except Monday. Just inland from Barcelona city, the pre-war course here was built by English expatriates. It has since been re-laid out, and this is where Severiano Ballesteros made his professional debut.

Club de Golf Vallromanes, Apartat de Correus, 43, 08170 Montornès del Vallès, province of Barcelona.

Tel: (93) 568 0362. Open: all year round. Closed: Tuesday. Behind Mataró on the Maresme coast, the first half of the course is flat, the second half on a hilly slope.

Reial Club de Golf El Prat, Apartat de Correus, 10, 08820 El Prat de Llobregat, province of Barcelona. Tel: (93) 379 0278. Open: all year round. Visitors arriving by air fly over this course just before touchdown at Barcelona's El Prat airport.

WALKING

You can walk your boots off in Catalonia. Some 1,875 miles (3,000 km) of footpaths have been mapped out by trail-blazing Catalans.

It is, however, crucial not to get lost, so most of these are marked with parallel red-and-white stripes painted on rocks and trees. If they are accompanied by an arrow it shows a change of direction. If the two lines are crossed it shows you where not to go. If there are several paths and they cross each other, as they do in parts of the Volcanic Park in Garrotxa, each one is separately colour coded in yellow or green instead of red.

There are some long-distance "GR" routes, which have small signposts with the numbers of the routes and the names of the next village. These are ambitious walks. The GR 92 stretches the whole length of the coast from Portbou to Ulldecona; the GR 1 covers the entire Catalan Pyrenees, from Cap de Creus to Aragón.

Two useful Barcelona addresses are: Centre d' Excursionisme de Catalunya, Paradís, 10, tel: (93) 315 3972; and a good bookshop, Llibrería Quera, Carrer Peritxol, 2, in the *barri* Gòtic just off the Plaça del Pi.

SKIING

There are 12 resorts in the region, all in the Pyrenees. Their season extends from the beginning of December to the end of April.

Baqueira-Beret, 43 pistes from 4,820–8,200 ft (1,500–2,500 metres). The "in" place where the royal family go.

Tuca-Mall Blanc, 20 pistes from 3,280–7,380 ft (1,000–2,250 metres). Also in the Vall d'Aran, this is a mile (2 km) from the region's main town of Vielha. It has some tricky trails and a slalom stadium.

Boí-Taüll, 14 pistes from 6,685–8,060 ft (2,040–2,455 metres). Its lack of sophistication is compensated for by the fine Romanesque villages.

Super Espot, 24 pistes from 4,890–7,610 ft (1,490–2,320 metres). At the entrance to the Aigüestortes Park, Espot is a popular holiday centre in both summer and winter and is surrounded by magnificent scenery.

Llesui, 22 pistes from 4,740–7,970 ft (1,445–2,430 metres). A resort just north of Sort. The bare slopes of the mountains around it make it obstacle-free.

Port Ainé, 18 pistes from 5,410–8,000 ft (1,650–2,440 metres). Begun in 1986, this resort is also near Sort, 4 miles north of Rialp. It has slopes suitable for beginners.

Port del Comte, 31 pistes from 5,545–7,870 ft (1,690–2,400 metres). This most southerly resort is actually in the pre-Pyrenees. There are meadow and woodland trails and a slalom stadium.

Rasos de Peguera, 9 pistes from 6,215–6,725 ft (1,895–2,050 metres). South of the great Cadí range and 8 miles (13 km) north of Berga, this is Barcelona's closest resort.

La Molina, 29 pistes from 5,215–8,085 ft (1,590–2,465 metres). One of the longest established resorts, on the eastern edge of the Cerdanya Valley, La Molina is always popular, and sometimes very full.

Masella, 88 pistes from 5,248–8,300 ft (1,600–2,530 metres). Next to La Molina, on the north face of Tossa d'Alp. Most of its 40 miles (62 km) of trails go through pine woods.

Vall de Núria, 9 pistes from 6,440–7,440 ft (1,965–2,270 metres). Inaccessible by road, skiers must take the "zip" train up the Freser Valley from Ribes. Uncomplicated slopes, plus ice skating on the lake in front of the large sanctuary.

Vallter 2000, 16 pistes from 6,595–8,201 ft (2,010–2,500 metres). The most easterly resort, from here on a clear day you can see the Bay of Roses.

LANGUAGE

Catalonia, and to a much lesser extent Valencia, is bilingual in Castilian (Spanish) and Catalan. Everybody speaks Spanish, although some older people in rural areas do so with difficulty, and Catalans much prefer to speak Catalan.

Catalan is a separate language, not a dialect. Its teaching and publication were banned during the Franco era and it has since undergone a great resurgence. It is used in conversation, in schools, in businesses, on radio and television and in newspapers. Most books, including guide books, are in Catalan. All street and place names have been changed and any remaining notice in Spanish may well have *En Català* scrawled across it, for language is a vital part of Catalan nationalism. Nobody, however, expects foreigners to speak the language, though efforts are appreciated. Most people will be very pleased to talk to you in Spanish.

Here are a few basic words and phrases, in both Catalan (first) and then Spanish:

Good morning	*Bon dia*	*Buenos días*
Good evening	*Bona tarda*	*Buenos tardes*
Hello/Goodbye	*Hola/Adéu*	*Hola/Adiós*
Please	*Si us plau*	*Por favor*
Thank you	*Gracie/Merci*	*Gracias*
You're welcome	*De res*	*De nada*
How much is?	*Quant val?*	*Cuanto es?*
Where is?	*On es?*	*Donde está?*
At what time?	*A quina hora?*	*A que hora?*
How do you say?	*Com es diu?*	*Como se dice?*
Open/Closed	*Obert/Tancat*	*Abierto/Cerrado*

Where can I change money?
On pue canviar moneda?
Donde se puede cambiar dinero?

USEFUL ADDRESSES

TOURIST OFFICES

The addresses of a few main offices are as follows:

Lleida: Oficina d'Informació Turistica, Arc del Pont, 25007. Tel: 248 120.

Andorra: Sindicat d'Iniciativa, Carrer Dr Vilanova, Andorra La Vella, tel: (9738) 20214; Oficina de Turisme del Principat d'Andorra, Carrer Marià Cubí, 159, 08021 Barcelona.

Puigcerdà: Oficina de Turisme del C.I.T., Carrer Querol. Tel: 880 542.

La Jonquera: Oficina de Turisme, Porta Catalana, A7 motorway. Tel: 554 354.

Portbou: Oficina d'Informació Turistica, Estació RENFE, 17497. Tel: 390 284.

Girona: Oficina de Turisme, Rambla Libertat, 1, 17004; Oficina Municipal de Turisme, Estació (Station) RENFE, 17007. Tel: 419 419.

Barcelona: Patronat Municipal de Turisme, Estació (Station) de Rodales, 08003; Oficina de Turisme, Gran Via de les Corts Catalanes, 658, 08010, tel: 301 7443; Patronat Municipal de Turisme, Passeig de Gràcia, 35, 08007, tel: 215 4477; Patronat Municipal de Turisme, Estació (Station) de Sants, 08014, tel: 257 331.

Reus: Oficina de Turisme, Aeroport de Reus, 43204. Tel: 257 331.

Tarragona: Oficina de Turisme, Carrer Fortuny, 4, 43001; Patronat Municipal de Turisme, Carrer Major, 39, 43003. Tel: 230 312.

Government regional tourist services (Servei Territorial de Comerç, Consum i Turisme): for registering complaints, etc.

Lleida: Avinguda Prat de la Riba, 76, 25004.

Girona: Travessia de la Creu, 1, 17002.

Barcelona: Avinguda Diagonal 431 bis, 5a, planta, 08071.

Tarragona: Rambla Vella, 7, 43003.

BALEARIC ISLANDS
GETTING THERE

The Balearic islands of Mallorca, Menorca and Ibiza, off the eastern coast of Spain, have modern airports and are served regularly by both scheduled international and charter flights. Scheduled services operate from several Spanish mainland cities, and these are flown by both Iberia and Aviaco.

Visitors to the fourth largest Balearic island, Formentera, can make their connections in Ibiza, from where frequent ferries, including car-ferries, cross to the port of La Savina. Ferries also operate to Formentera from Denia and Alicante on the Spanish mainland.

BY AIR

Services by sea to the Balearic Islands are provided by convenient ferry routes, primarily from Barcelona and Valencia, with summer operation from the French port of Sète and from Genoa and Algiers. In summer, there are also services to Alcudia, in Mallorca. Ferries operate from Alicante and Denia to Ibiza and Formentera. There are also regular inter-island ferries, and a fast hydrojet (2 hours) runs between Palma and Ibiza.

The principal operator of these ferry services is a publicly-owned line called Trasmediterranea, popularly known as La Tras.

GETTING ACQUAINTED

GEOGRAPHY & POPULATION

The Balearic archipelago, located between the mainland of Spain and the North African coast, consists of the principal islands of Mallorca, Menorca, Ibiza and Formentera, with surrounding and outlying smaller islands, very few of them populated.

The islands have a population of some 800,000, in a combined area of 1,936 sq. miles (5,000 sq. km). Palma de Mallorca is 132 nautical miles from Barcelona, 172 from Algiers and 287 from Marseilles. The islanders are far outnumbered by the invasion of foreign visitors, as follows:

Formentera: With a pop. of 5,000, covers 31 sq. miles (82 sq. km), receives 15,000 visitors annually.
Ibiza: With a total of over 60,000 residents (about 5,000 are foreigners) and an area of 220 sq. miles (572 sq. km), receives over 1 million annual visitors.
Menorca: With 62,000 residents and 270 sq. miles (699 sq. km), gets visited annually by some 600,000 people.
Mallorca: With near to 600,000 residents and a surface of 1,405 sq. miles (3,640 sq. km), receives over 5,600,000 annual visitors.

In total, the Balearics receive in excess of 7 million mainland Spanish and foreign visitors annually.

The three main islands enjoy more or less the same weather conditions, with local variations caused by phenomena such as Mallorca's mountain ranges.

The Balearics' average high temperature annually is 70°F (21.2°C), average low 57°F (13.8°C) and the sun shines annually to an average 59 percent. Rainfall in Mahon (Menorca) is 580 mm a year, while that in Palma (Mallorca) only reaches 480 mm.

BUSINESS HOURS

The islands have traditionally observed the noon-time siesta, with businesses and shops generally open from 8.30 or 9am–1 or 1.30pm, and 4 or 4.30pm–7 or 7.30pm. As an exception, shops and businesses in Menorca tend to re-open after lunch at a later hour, around 5pm.

In certain sectors of business, these traditional hours are changing. For example the big department stores such as Galerias Preciados, and the out-of-town hypermarkets generally open all day, from 10am–9pm, but close on Sunday. Other businesses, related to businesses in other countries and different time-zones, will also sometimes have differing hours.

MEDIA

Newspapers: There are several excellent Spanish-language newspapers published in the islands. Some of these are the *Diario de Ibiza, Diario de Mallorca, Ultima Hora,* and *Diario Insular de Menorca.* In addition, all of the major mainland newspapers such as *El País, Vanguardia* and *Ya* are available at most kiosks.

English-speakers in Mallorca have their own peculiar love-hate relationship with the *Majorca Daily Bulletin.* Otherwise known as the *Daily Bee,* the newspaper has something for everyone. Feature articles, many from the wire services, goofy photos ("crocodile breast-feeds abandoned puppy..."), and entertaining local columnists. World news sometimes appears with a delay of a day or so, as it often needs to be translated from Spanish parent-paper *Ultima Hora.* Nobody publicly admits to buying the *Daily Bee,* but everybody seems to have read it, and many people quote from it.

Radio stations are varied in both quality and content, and more than one of the Spanish stations broadcast continuous music. The English-speaking station in Palma is worth listening to, and offers a variety of local personalities, each of whom present their own individual type of show, with local news, music, interviews, quizzes and other items. Radio 103.2 FM, as it is called, also carries advertising and is a very good source of information about the island.

In Ibiza, two local stations carry about one hour a day of English broadcasting, one being on Radio Popular on FM 89.1.

In Menorca, there is also an English programme on the local station.

EMERGENCIES

The local emergency number to call the **police** (*Policia Nacional*) in Palma, Ibiza and in Mahon is 091. In Ciudadela (Menorca), tel: 381 095 and in Manacor, Mallorca, tel: 550 044.

The **Fire Service** has local numbers everywhere (consult the directory) except in Palma, where 080 is their emergency number.

Ambulances are operated by the Spanish Red Cross as well as by private operators. For the **Red Cross**, in Mallorca tel: 200 102; Ibiza tel: 301 214; and Mahon (Menorca) tel: 361 180 or 365 400. All the emergency numbers are easily found in the first few (green) pages of the telephone directory.

For emergency ambulance service:
Palma – Tel: 200 102.
Ibiza – Tel: 301 214.
Mahon (Menorca) – Tel: 361 180.
Ciudadela (Menorca) – Tel: 381 993.

ACCOMMODATION

Selected recommendations from all four islands. **Price guide**: *5-star = over 20,000 pesetas; 4-star = over 15,000 pesetas; 3-star = 5,000–15,000 pesetas.*

MALLORCA: PALMA

Son Vida Sheraton Hotel ☆☆☆☆☆, Urbanización Son Vida. Tel: 451 011. Overlooking Palma and its Bay. Grand Luxe. One golf-course, another under construction, tennis, many other facilities.

Valparaíso Palace ☆☆☆☆☆, Francisco Vidal, La Bonanova. Tel: 400 411. Overlooking Palma, views of harbour and Bay, set in lush gardens. Indoor and outdoor pools, separate health clubs for men and women.

Meliá Victoria ☆☆☆☆☆, Joan Miró, 21, Palma. Tel: 234 342. Reigning over the Palma harbour front, the Meliá Victoria has its main entrance close to the nightlife around Plaza Gomila, and its lower, harbour exit leads directly to the centre of the night's activities on the Paseo Marítimo.

Sol Bellver ☆☆☆☆, Paseo Marítimo, 11, Palma. Tel: 238 008. Faces out over the harbour front, close to the centre of town. One of the more than 100 Sol hotels, the number one chain in Spain, now expanding internationally.

Nixe Palace Hotel ☆☆☆☆, Joan Miró, 269, Palma. Tel: 403 811. A seaside hotel, the Nixe Palace has a small beach, sun-terraces and other facilities. A good hotel for the business traveller who wants to be away (10 minutes) from downtown.

Costa Azul ☆☆☆, Paseo Marítimo, 7, Palma. Tel: 231 940. Although only a 3-star, the Costa Azul is listed as an old favourite with families and business travellers over the years. Right on the harbour front.

Saratoga ☆☆☆, Paseo de Mallorca, 6, Palma. Tel: 727 240. The Saratoga is convenient for the business traveller on a tight budget, close enough to be able to walk to most lawyers, banks, businesses and shops downtown.

OUTSIDE PALMA

Hotel Formentor ☆☆☆☆☆, Playa de Formentor. Tel: 531 300. Overlooking the beach, this peaceful traditional hotel is family-run and many of the staff have spent their entire career here. Surrounded by pine trees and gardens.

Maricel ☆☆☆☆, Ctra de Andraitx, Km 7, Ca's Catalá. Tel: 402 712. The Maricel is in a category all its own, being one of the original hotels along the coast road near Illetas, 15 minutes from Palma centre. Old world courtesy and charm from the employees, many of them with long-service with the hotel. Seaside, pool, quiet.

La Residencia ☆☆☆☆, Son Moragues, Deyá. Tel: 639 011. Individually designed and decorated rooms, quiet luxury in this hill town, home to artists and poets. Famous for excellent cuisine.

Bonanza Playa ☆☆☆☆, Ctra de Illetas. Tel: 401 112. Built into a cliff at the sea's edge, the lobby area is at street level on the top floor, with rooms and extensive facilities below. Family run with year-after-year repeat clients.

The Villamil ☆☆☆☆, Ctra de Andraitx, Km 22, Paguera. Tel: 686 050. A member of the Forte Group chain. Overlooks the beach, and has gardens and sun-terraces to relax in.

Hotel Bendinat ☆☆☆, Urb. Bendinat. Tel: 675 254. A family run hotel. Only some 30 rooms, ensuring individual attention for clients. Located on a small point, with good sea swimming right at the end of the garden.

MENORCA

Port Mahón Hotel ☆☆☆☆, Paseo Marítimo, Mahón. Tel: 362 600. The Port Mahón overlooks the fjord-like port, once the Mediterranean base for Nelson's Royal Navy. Quiet, almost sedate, it makes a good base for a business or holiday visit.

The Hotel del Almirante ☆☆☆☆, Ctra Villacarlos, near Mahón. Tel: 362 700. Interesting and sympathetic conversion of British admiral Collingwood's residence, good views of Mahón harbour, hacienda-style accommodation around swimming pool.

The Almirante Farragut ☆☆☆, Avda de los Delfines, Ciudadela. Tel: 382 800. A very large hotel, built on a promontory over the sea, with a small beach on one side. In summer, tour-operators from all over Europe keep the Farragut fully-booked.

IBIZA

Although there are city-centre hotels in Eivissa (Ibiza town), the level of activity and noise is high. As distances around the island are relatively short, it is best to stay outside and make trips into town for shopping or nightlife.

Anchorage Hotel ☆☆☆☆, Puerto Deportivo Marina Botafoch, Paseo Marítimo, Ibiza. Tel: 311 711. Right in the newest marina in town, with views across the harbour of Ibiza town and its citadel. A variety of shops and restaurants surround the hotel, which is 5 minutes from downtown. There is no pool, but Talamanca beach is an 8-minute walk away.

Pike's, Ctra Sa Vorera, Km 12, C'an Pep Toniet. Tel: 342 222. Classified as a 2-star *pension*, Pike's is really difficult to grade, being nearly unique. Owned and run by Australian yachtsman Tony Pikes, the hotel has less than 10 rooms, and provides a relaxing retreat for jet-setters and well-known actors and singers, etc. Set in a restored farmhouse, there is a pool and garden, and a good restaurant. Children aren't welcome.

Les Jardins de Palerm, near Es Cubells. Tel: 342 293. In the same genre as Pike's, Les Jardins is unclassifiable although listed as a *pension*. Self-described as "a little piece of Paradise", it is the ideal hideaway for lovers or honeymooners, and children aren't encouraged. Operated by jack-of-all-trades René Wilhelm, a Swiss former Formula III driver, decorator, fashion designer, boutique owner, etc. Excellent *nouvelle cuisine* restaurant, pool, gardens, in this 10-room retreat.

Hotel Club Village, Urb. Caló den Real, San José. Tel: 344 561. This hotel perches high over the sea, surrounded by pine forest and gardens, with a stairway down to the beach. A tennis-players' paradise, with four courts and professional coaching. Pool, sauna and whirlpool and a good restaurant make this a favourite new place, particularly in the German market.

Ca's Catalá, Calle del Sol, Santa Eulalia. Tel: 331 006. Classified as a Residence Hostal, the Ca's Catalá offers nicely-furnished single and double rooms, a swimming pool and garden. Breakfast only is served, but non-residents drop in for this and also for midmorning coffee and pastries.

FORMENTERA

Club La Mola ☆☆☆☆, Playa de Mitjorn. Tel: 320 050. In a picturesque setting, with a swimming pool, tennis, mini-golf, children's playground and cafeteria.

Hotel Formentera Playa ☆☆☆, Playa de Mitjorn. Tel: 320 000. Located in a scenic area, with a pool, playground and cafeteria.

Hotel Roca Bella P, Playa Es Pujols. Tel: 320 185. Situated near the beach, with a swimming pool.

WHAT TO EAT

Although there is no menu visible at local bars, you can generally ask what they have to eat and you could be pleasantly surprised with a thick homemade stew or a fresh salad with grilled seafood.

There are all sorts of typical foods on the islands, from *paella* and *arroz brut*, through suckling pig and tender lamb, to *caldereta de langosta* and *tumbet*, or elvers in garlic-oil, or *calamares en su tinta* (squid in inky sauce – it sounds better in Spanish, and tastes great).

WHERE TO EAT

Three categories of price-level have been used in this selection: Inexpensive = less than 1,500 pesetas; Moderate = between 1,500 and 4,500 pesetas; Expensive = over 4,500 pesetas.

SPANISH/SEAFOOD

Honoris, Camino Viejo de Buñola, Palma. Tel: 203 212. Stylish ambience, good cuisine. On the edge of town. Expensive

Porto Pi, Joan Miró, 174, Palma. Tel: 400 087. Near Club de Mar and Rififi seafood restaurant. Serves gourmet Basque and nouvelle cuisine. Expensive

Bodega Santurce, Concepción, 34, Palma. Basque food in this family-run hole in the wall. No reservations, no coffee, open only lunchtime, uncomfortable seating, but unbeatable value. Moderate

Caballito de Mar, Paseo Sagrera, 5, Palma. Tel: 721 074. Fish cooked in sea-salt, expensive and takes time to cook, but must be tried once, with al-i-oli. Moderate

Casa Gallega, Pueyo, 2, Palma. Tel. 714366. Try the *salpicón*, *pulpo a banda* or fresh salmon. Moderate

Mesón Tio Pepe, Pont d'Inca, Palma. Tel: 680 880. *Bodega* atmosphere, enormous T-bones, selected suckling pig and a mixed-grill so big you'll have a problem finishing it. Avoid Sunday lunchtime. Moderate

Punta de Son Gual, Ctra Palma-Manacor Km 11. Tel: 490 484. Excellent shoulder or leg of lamb, other choices. Avoid Sunday lunchtimes. Moderate

Rancho Picadero, Flamenco, 1, Ca'n Pastilla. Tel: 261 002. Indoor barbecue. Suckling pig, other choices. Moderate

Bar Carlos, Joan Miró, Palma. Opposite Hotel Borenco. Typical Mallorquín food by Rafa Bonet, smoky and crowded, evenings only, good value. Inexpensive

Celler Montenegro, Calle Montenegro, Palma. Behind Plaza de la Reina, downtown Palma. Good Mallorquín home cooking. Inexpensive

Es Salé, Joan Miró, Palma. Near Plaza Gomila. No reservations. Inexpensive

IBIZA

El Brasero, Barcelona, 4, Eivissa. Duck, salmon. German owned.
El Shogun, Pasadis, 5, Eivissa. Sushi, Sashimi, Sukiyaki.
Es Pi D'or, Cala Gració, San Antonio. Salmon, fish soup and more.
Helmut's, Ctra a San José. German home-cooking.
Mr Pickwick's, San Vicente, 47, Santa Eulalia. Steak and kidney pie and more.
Pike's, C'an Pep Toniet, San Antonio. Salmon-stuffed hake and more.
Rincón de Pepe, San Vicente, 53, Santa Eulalia. *Tapas*, snacks.
Sa Capella, Ctra a C'an Germá, San Antonio. Pork of all kinds.
Sa Soca, Ctra a San Antonio. Ibicenco cooking.
Sausalito, Plaza Sa Riba, Eivissa. Swordfish, lamb. French owner.

MENORCA

Cap Roig, Near San Mezquida. No phone. Great view, seafood. Moderate
Cas Quintu, Plaza Alfonso III, 4, Ĉiudadela. Tel: 381 002. Menorquín and other dishes. Moderate
Pan Y Vino, Torret. Small, atmospheric restaurant popular with the resident population of expatriates. Moderate
Pilar, Cardona y Orfila, 61, Mahón. Tel: 366 817. Local Menorquín cuisine, evenings only. Moderate
La Tropical, Luna, 36, Mahón. Tel: 360 556. Budget-priced Menorquin food. Inexpensive

FORMENTERA

Bergantín, Port de la Sabina. Tel: 321 040. International menu. Moderate
Capri, Es Pujols. Tel: 321 118. Seafood. Moderate
Taberna La Formentereña, Playa Mitjorn, Km 9. Excellent *Espinacas Balear*, seafood, meats with irresistible sauces in this beach restaurant. Moderate
Truy, Es Pujols. International menu. Moderate

SHOPPING

The islands all produce good leatherware, with footwear factories in Mallorca and Menorca, and nicely-designed leather clothing everywhere.

Mallorca has artificial pearl and glass-blowing factories. Menorca has a well-developed costume jewellery industry, and produces excellent cheeses and gin. Ibiza is known for its Ad Lib fashion, an attractive mix-and-match approach to creating an ensemble, and has a large cottage-industry making bangles, jewellery, etc. The three main islands have branches or franchises of the standing of Benetton, Bally, Loewe, Charles Jourdan, etc.

Locally produced pottery and ceramics, particularly cooking-vessels, are a good buy on all islands,

and there is a choice of good embroidery and basketwork. Paintings by local artists are also worth looking at, and these can be seen in galleries, or at lower prices in the flea and hippy markets.

LANGUAGE

Although Spanish (or Castillian) is the national language, the Balearic people also use a vernacular language, which in Mallorca is known as Mallorquin, in Menorca, Menorquín, and in Ibiza, Ibiçenco. All three local languages are similar in vocabulary with component words having their origin in Italian, Latin, French, Portuguese and Arabic.

Interesting left-overs from the time when Britain's Royal Navy had its Mediterranean base in Menorca are words and expressions used by modern-day Menorquines in every day conversation. Examples:
A bow-window is called a *boinder*
A screwdriver is a *tornescru*
A bottle becomes *botil*
Marbles are *mervils*
A leg of pork (shank) is *un xenc*
A black eye is *un ull blec* (*ull* is eye in Menorquin)
To rap a door with your knuckles is to *toc de necles*

USEFUL ADDRESSES

TOURIST INFORMATION OFFICES

MALLORCA
Consell de Mallorca, at airport Arrivals building. Tel: 260 803.
Gobern Balear Tourist Office, Jaime III, 10, Palma. Tel: 712 216 and 712 744.
Fomento del Turismo de Mallorca, Constitución, 1, 1st floor, Palma. Tel: 715 135 and 725 396.
Palma Municipal Tourist Offices are at Santo Domingo, 11, tel: 724 090 and Plaza España, in Palma, tel: 711 527.

Other municipalities, such as Calviá, have local offices. Some are seasonal, mounted on trailers, and located strategically.

MENORCA
Consell de Menorca, Cami del Castell, 28, Mahón, and on the central Plaza Esplanada, 40, Mahón. Tel: 363 790.

IBIZA
Consell de Ibiza, Vara de Rey, 13, Eivissa (Ibiza town). Tel: 301 900.
Fomento de Turismo de Ibiza, Historiador José Clapés, 4, Ibiza town. Tel: 302 490.
Municipality of San Antonio, Passeig des Fonts, San Antonio. Tel: 343 363.
Municipality of Santa Eulalia, Mariano Riquer Wallis, Santa Eulalia. Tel: 330 728.
FORMENTERA
Municipality of San Francisco Javier, Port de la Sabina. (At the ferry terminal). Tel: 322 057.

WESTERN SPAIN
EXTREMADURA

Western Spain is a little-explored region of castles and hills between Madrid and the Portuguese border.

ACCOMMODATION

Price guide: *5-star = over 20,000 pesetas; 4-star = over 15,000 pesetas; 3-star = 5,000–15,000 pesetas.*

CÁCERES

Cáceres province has a mild climate and a very scenic, varied countryside. Cáceres proper features a well-restored monumental centre with fine palaces and mansions and the interesting Provincial Museum. A short trip away are the Monastery of Yuste, in a rustic setting, where Emperor Carlos V chose to spend the last days of his life dedicated to meditation and prayer, the magnificent Monastery and historic town of Guadalupe and Trujillo, with its beautiful main square, palatial mansions and Arab castle. Tourism Office in Cáceres: Plaza Mayor, 33. Tel: 246 347. Area code: 927.

Parador de Turismo de Cáceres ☆☆☆☆, Ancha, 6. Tel: 211 759. Installed in the 14th century Palacio del Comendador, it is situated in the heart of the restored monumental quarter.

Meliá Cáceres ☆☆☆☆, Plaza San Juan, 11-13. Tel: 215 800. A rehabilitated 16th-century palace, located beside the Arab ramparts.

Extremadura ☆☆☆, Avda de Virgen de Guadalupe, 5. Tel: 221 600. A reasonably priced, comfortable hotel, with a swimming pool and garden.

BADAJOZ

Badajoz, just 4 miles (7 km) from the Portuguese border, can boast of a long history dating back to prehistoric times. Its most important monuments are the *Alcazaba*, a Moorish citadel, the Cathedral, the Puerta de las Palmas Gateway (the symbol of the city), the Archaeological Museum and the Provincial Fine Arts Museum.

Extremadura, the largest of the Spanish provinces, features many historically and artistically noteworthy towns, the most important of which is Mérida with its magnificent Roman ruins. Tourism Office: Plaza de la Libertad, 3. Tel: 222 763. Area code: 924.

Gran Hotel Zurbarán ☆☆☆☆, Paseo de Castelar, s/n. Tel: 223 741. A classic, centrally located hotel with a swimming pool and fine restaurant.

Río ☆☆☆, Avda Adolfo Díaz Ambrona, 13. Tel: 272 600. Centrally located with a restaurant and swimming pool.

Conde Duque ☆☆, Muñoz Torrero, 27. Tel: 224 641. Reasonably priced and centrally located.

WHERE TO EAT

CÁCERES

Atrio, Avda de España, 30. Tel: 242 928. Three forks. Imaginative cooking based on regional specialities. Excellent desserts. Closed: Sunday evening.

Figón de Eustaquio, Plaza de San Juan, 12-14. Tel: 248 194. Two forks. Regional cooking.

BADAJOZ

Los Monjes, Paseo de Castelar, s/n. Tel: 223 741. Two forks. Situated in the Hotel Zurbarán. Typical cuisine, including partridge salad, pork sirloin, lamb stew and an excellent selection of cheeses.

Mesón El Tronco, Muñoz Torrero, 16. Tel: 222 076. Local dishes, with an excellent selection of cured hams and cheeses, typical *caldereta* lamb stew and walnut croquettes. Closed: Wednesday night, and Sunday.

BY AIR

Southern Spain has frequent air links with the rest of Europe and North Africa, as well as direct flights to North America. It is within two-and-a-half hours' flying time of London. Málaga and Seville airports have daily scheduled connections with international destinations, but in addition large numbers of visitors arrive by charter flights. Almería and Gibraltar are also important entry points.

The colossal growth of the Costa del Sol tourist industry has converted Málaga into Spain's sixth busiest airport, with 5 million passenger arrivals annually. Scheduled services are available from the major airlines, including Iberia, British Airways, KLM, Lufthansa, Sabena, SAS, and Royal Air Maroc.

BY SEA

Few liners call at Southern Spain ports, apart from those on cruises. Trasmediterránea vessels, carrying passengers and vehicles, ply between Almería, Málaga, Algeciras, Cádiz and Seville and ports on the African coast and on the Canary Islands.

There are frequent services across the Straits of Gibraltar, both by ferry and hydrofoil, from Algeciras to Ceuta and Tangier. There is also a Hovercraft service between Málaga and Ceuta.

BY RAIL

In 1992, a new high-speed rail service, the AVE, linked Seville to Madrid, and will eventually connect with Málaga to the South and with similar services in France. The new trains have halved travel time between these two cities, to just 3 hours. Up to now train services between Barcelona and Madrid and Southern Spain have often been slow, partly due to the inadequate tracks. The most comfortable way to travel south is by Talgo trains, smooth-running expresses which travel from Madrid to major Andalusian cities.

BY ROAD

Road access to Southern Spain has improved dramatically in the past few years, as the network of four-lane routes has been extended. The *Autopista del*

Mediterráneo (toll) runs all the way from the French border at La Junquera along the coast to Alicante.

Major roadworks improved connections between that city and Granada and Seville to create the so-called *Autovía de 92*. Completion of the *Autovía de Andalusia*, which follows the old N1V route to Córdoba and Seville, has slashed driving time between Madrid and the region.

An international bridge across the Guadíana river at Ayamonte was completed in 1991, allowing easy access to Andalusia from Portugal's Algarve coast.

GETTING ACQUAINTED

GOVERNMENT & ECONOMY

Andalusia is Spain's most important agricultural region and agriculture continues to play a vital part in the economy. Traditional products such as olive oil, cereals and grapes have lost ground to new crops and methods. Irrigation has been extended.

Cotton, sunflowers, citrus fruits, sugar beet and rice are major crops. Strawberries have become a money-spinning export from Huelva and along the sheltered Mediterranean coast avocadoes, sweet potatoes, kiwi fruit and custard apples flourish. Fish-farming is also expanding fast.

Mining of copper, lead, silver and gold, which dates from ancient times, is declining but service industries are growing and the regional authorities are striving to attract high-tech industry.

Since 1960 there has been phenomenal growth in tourism, which has brought undreamed-of wealth to one of Spain's poorest areas. Apart from the annual influx of package-tour visitors, several hundred thousand North Europeans have permanent or semi-permanent residences on or near the Mediterranean coast. Foreigners have invested heavily in hotels and thousands of apartments and villas.

GEOGRAPHY & POPULATION

Andalusia covers 34,700 sq. miles (87,000 sq. km), 17 percent of Spain's total area. Most of the 6.5 million inhabitants live on the coast or along the Guadalquivir river valley. The 410-mile (660-km) long Guadalquivir is the backbone of the region, draining a vast basin and providing water for power, irrigation and drinking. The alluvial sediments bordering the river provide fertile soil for crops.

North of the Guadalquivir, the hills of the Sierra Morena are a barrier to easy communication between Andalusia and the rest of Spain. To the south, the Cordillera Baetica runs from Gibraltar to Murcia, forming another higher barrier between the Guadalquivir basin and the Mediterranean coast. Mulhacén in the Sierra Nevada is the peninsula's highest mountain at 11,402 ft (3,478 metres) and the ranges bristle with dramatic crags. These sierras shield the coasts of Almería, Granada and Málaga from frost and snow.

CLIMATE

Andalusia's position at the southern edge of Europe gives it a privileged climate. Summers are hot and winters generally mild. However, there are considerable variations due to the size of the region, its mountainous character and the fact that it is bordered by both the Atlantic and Mediterranean.

Summers can be extremely hot in the interior with temperatures rising to 113°F (45°C) and even higher in the provinces of Seville and Córdoba. Almería has an extremely arid, desert-like climate. Snow covers the Sierra Nevada from November to June and frost is common in upland areas.

Weather in coastal areas is moderated by the sea and offshore breezes so that neither extremes of heat nor cold are experienced, except for a few weeks at the height of summer. Strawberries ripen in Huelva and Málaga in early February. Tropical fruits can be grown along the Mediterranean without the aid of greenhouses. The Levante wind has considerable influence, often blowing hard for days on the Cádiz coast and creating a persistent cloud over the Rock of Gibraltar. June to October are usually dry, except for sporadic torrential downpours. Heavy rain in the winter months is usually interspersed with brilliant sunshine. The best months to tour the region are in spring and autumn, when there are no climatic extremes.

MEDIA & COMMUNICATIONS

Media: A number of English-language publications serve the large number of expatriates living along the Mediterranean coast.

Of the magazines, the longest established and most respected is *Lookout*, a glossy, Fuengirola-based monthly featuring practical information and well-researched articles about life in Spain. *Costagolf* is a monthly magazine devoted to the golfing scene. Several free papers come out weekly, with details of doings in the expatriate community. They include *Sur* in English and *The Entertainer*. German publications include the monthly *Aktuelle* and the monthly *Solkysten* caters for Scandinavians.

Telephone: In tourist areas in season you will find temporary structures housing small telephone exchanges. These are handy for long-distance calls as instead of fumbling with change you pay the operator afterwards. Restrict your calls from hotels as they often treble the charge.

Note: Seville numbers are switching to seven digits, but are still often listed with only six digits. For local calls within the province, convert these numbers to seven digits by placing a 4 in front. Thus, if you want to call 61 01 22, you should dial 461 01 22.

EMERGENCIES

SECURITY & CRIME

Thefts from tourists and their cars have become common in recent years. Commonsense precautions should prevent your holiday being spoiled in this way. Cities, particularly Málaga and Seville, are black spots. Never leave anything of value in your car, including when parking near a beach. Don't leave cash or valuables unattended while you are swimming. When staying overnight, take all baggage into the hotel. If possible, park your car in a garage or a guarded car-park.

Particularly when driving into Seville, do not leave anything of value within sight. A favourite trick is to smash the windows of cars stopping at traffic lights, seize handbags and cameras and then take off on a motorbicycle. When walking, women should keep shoulder bags out of view if possible. Avoid badly-lit back streets at night in such quarters as Santa Cruz in Seville. Police patrols have been stepped up, but this area is a magnet for muggers, often working in twos and threes. Carry photocopies of your passport and other documents and leave the originals in the hotel safe.

If confronted do not resist, as thieves often carry knives. If robbed, remember thieves usually want easily disposable cash. Check the nearest gutters, rubbish containers, toilets for your personal possessions; thieves swiftly dispose of unwanted items.

EMERGENCY PHONE NUMBERS

Dial 091 for the Policía Nacional emergency 24-hour service.

ALMERIA
Municipal police: Tel: 092.
Ambulance: Tel: 234 879.
First aid: Tel: 230 712.
Red Cross: Parque Nicolas Salmerón 14. Tel: 257 367.

CADIZ
Municipal police: Tel: 226 710.
First aid: Tel: 211 053.
Hospital Provincial: Campo del Sur, s/n. Tel: 212 351.
Red Cross: Santa María de la Soledad, 10. Tel: 277 670.

CORDOBA
Municipal police: Tel: 472 000.
First aid post: Tel: 234 646.
Ambulance: Tel: 295 570.
General Hospital: Tel: 297 122.
Red Cross: Paseo de la Victoria, 4. Tel: 293 411.

GRANADA
Municipal police: Tel: 092.
Civil Guard: Tel: 062.
Ambulance: Tel: 202 024.
First aid: Tel: 221 263.
Red Cross: Cuesta Escoriaza, 8. Tel: 222 166.

Municipal police: Tel: 245 135.

First Aid: Tel: 253 800.

Red Cross & Ambulance: Avda Suroeste s/n. Tel: 261 211.

JAEN
Civil Guard: Tel: 221 100.

Municipal police: Tel: 258 011.

First aid: Tel: 259 031.

Red Cross: Carmelo Torres, 1. Tel: 251 540.

Jaén Provincial Hospital. Tel: 222 650.

MALAGA
Municipal police: Tel: 092.

Civil Guard: Tel: 391 900.

First aid: Tel: 290 340.

Red Cross: Fernando Camino, 2–4. Tel: 217 631.

Carlos Haya Hospital. Tel: 390 400.

Fire: Tel: 306 060.

Estepona

National police: Tel: 800 291.

Municipal police: Tel: 800 243.

Civil Guard: Tel: 801 087.

First aid: Tel: 800 683.

Fuengirola

Ambulance: Tel: 473 157.

First aid: Tel: 473 157.

Municipal police: Tel: 473 157.

Mijas

Ambulance: Tel: 485900.

Municipal police: Tel: 485067.

Marbella

Municipal police: Tel: 092 (for emergencies), and 773 194.

Civil Guard: Tel: 771 944; San Pedro Tel: 780 037.

First aid: Tel: 772 949.

Marbella Clinic: Tel: 774 282.

Nerja

Municipal police: Tel: 521 545.

Civil Guard: Tel: 520 091.

First aid: Tel: 520 935.

Ronda

Civil Guard: Tel: 871 461.

Municipal police: Tel: 871 369.

First aid: Tel: 871 540.

Hospital: Tel: 876 628.

Torremolinos

Municipal police: María Barrabino, 16. Tel: 381 422.

National police: Calle Skal. Tel: 389 999.

Ambulance: Tel: 386 266.

First aid: Ctra. de Benalmadena. Tel: 386 484.

SEVILLE
For calls within the province, place 4 in front of six-digit numbers.

Municipal police: Tel: 092.

First aid: Casa de Socorro, Jesús del Gran Poder, 34. Tel: 382 461.

Ambulance: 330 933.

Hospital Universitario: Avda Dr Fedriani. Tel: 378 400.

Lost property: Almansa, 21. Tel: 212 628.

GETTING AROUND

BY TRAIN

A train ride in the grand style of the Orient Express is offered by the Al-Andalus Expreso. Operating May–October, this de luxe train visits Seville, Córdoba, Granada and Málaga, with option of a visit to Jerez (from 150,000 pesetas).

CAR RENTAL

International chains such as Avis, Europcar and Hertz have airport offices, and offer collect and deliver services. A guide to price rates (1993): Ford Fiesta, one week, unlimited mileage, 7,500 pesetas a day. Smaller local companies are much cheaper and will arrange to meet you on arrival if you book.

Avis airport offices

Almería: Tel: (951) 224 126/221 954.

Córdoba: Tel: (957) 476 862.

Granada: Tel: (958) 446 455.

Jerez de la Frontera, Cádiz: Tel: (956) 344 311/335 284.

Málaga: Tel: (952) 313 943/326 227.

Seville: Tel: (954) 514 315.

Europcar airport offices

Almería: Tel: (951) 234 966.

Córdoba: Tel: (957) 233 460.

Granada: Tel: (958) 295 065/257 017.

Jerez de la Frontera: Tel: (956) 334 856/334 355.

Málaga: Tel: (952) 351 403/311 638.

Seville: Tel: (954) 673 839.

Hertz airport offices

Almería: Tel: (951) 221 954 ext. 125.

Córdoba: Tel: (957) 477 243.

Granada: Tel: (958) 446 411 ext. 40.

Jerez de la Frontera: Tel: (956) 351 153/347 467.

Málaga: Tel: (952) 318 740/326 187.

Seville: Tel: (954) 514 720.

ACCOMMODATION

Price guide, Southern Spain: *In a pensión, expect to pay about 3,000 pesetas for a double room. In 1 and 2-star hostales, prices will range from 3,000 to 7,000 pesetas. Hotel prices run roughly from 4,000 pesetas for a 1-star establishment to 15,000 for a 4-star. A double in a 5-star hotel is usually in the 15,000 to 25,000-peseta bracket. Paradors charge 10,000 to 12,000 pesetas a double room.*

ALMERÍA
Playaluz ☆☆☆☆, Bahía el Palmeral s/n, (4 miles/6 km from Almería). Tel: 340 504. On edge of the sea. Sports facilities.

NEAR EL EJIDO
Golf Hotel Almerimar ☆☆☆☆, Urb Almerimar. Tel: 480 950. Comfortable and tranquil. Golf, marina.

MOJÁCAR
Parador Reyes Católicos ☆☆☆☆, Playa de Mojácar. Tel: 478 250. A modern building, near beach.

SAN JOSÉ
Hotel San José ☆, Barriada San José, Níjar. Tel: 366 974. Overlooks the sea on pleasant bay. Closed: 15 January–15 February.

ALHAMA DE ALMERÍA
Hotel San Nicolas, Calle Banos s/n. Tel: 100 101. Medium priced, smart, old-fashioned spa hotel by hot thermal springs.

CÁDIZ

Atlántico ☆☆☆, Parque Genovés, 9. Tel: 212 301. State-run. On the bay. Swimming pool.

ALGECIRAS
Reina Cristina ☆☆☆☆, Paseo de la Conferencia. Tel: 602 622. Stately old hotel with tropical gardens.

ARCOS DE LA FRONTERA
Parador Casa del Corregidor, Plaza de España s/n. Tel: 700 500. Splendid views.
Los Olivos ☆☆☆, San Miguel, 2. Tel: 700 811. Beautiful old Andalusian house. Good value.

GRAZALEMA
Grazalema ☆☆, Ctra Olivar. Tel: 141 162. Hostal. Modern. Mountain views.

JEREZ DE LA FRONTERA
Jerez ☆☆☆☆☆, Avda Alvaro Domecq, 35. Tel: 300 600. Tennis courts. Near the fairground.

CÓRDOBA

Parador Nacional Arruzafa, Avda de la Arruzafa, 33. Tel: 275 900. Fine views.
Maimónides ☆☆☆, Torrijos, 4. Tel: 471 500. Near mosque.

MONTILLA
Don Gonzalo ☆☆☆, Ctra Madrid–Málaga Km 447. Tel: 650 658. Convenient, modern highway hotel.

PALMA DEL RÍO
Hospedería San Francisco ☆☆☆, Avda Pío X11, 35. Tel: 644 185. Hostal in a historic, converted monastery.

GRANADA

Parador Nacional de San Francisco, Recinto de la Alhambra. Tel: 221 440. Within the Alhambra. Once a Franciscan convent. Reservations essential.
Alhambra Palace ☆☆☆☆, Peña Partida, 2. Tel: 221 468. Elaborate Moorish-style decor. Views over city.
Washington Irving ☆☆☆, Paseo Generalife, 2. Tel: 227 550. Dignified old style.
Hostal América ☆, Real de la Alhambra, 53. Tel: 227 471. Intimate, within the Alhambra walls. Closed: November–February.

BUBIÓN (Alpujarras)
Villa Turística ☆☆☆, Barrio Alto. Tel: 763 111. Apartment hotel. Modern facilities in a village complex built in traditional Alpujarras style.

LOJA
Finca La Bobadilla ☆☆☆☆☆, Ctra Loja–Seville. Tel: 321 861. Luxury hotel with all facilities, in the heart of the countryside. Top-rated restaurant. Champagne for breakfast and prices to match.

SIERRA NEVADA SKI AREA
Parador Nacional Sierra Nevada ☆☆☆, Ctra S. Nevada, Km 35. Tel: 480 200.
Nevasur, Urb Sol y Nieve. Tel: 480 350. Closed: September–November.

HUELVA

Tartessos ☆☆☆, Avda Martín Alonso Pinzón, 13. Tel: 245 611. Centrally located.

AYAMONTE
Parador Costa de la Luz, El Castillito. Tel: 320 700. Looks over the Guadiana estuary towards Portugal.

MAZAGÓN
Parador Cristobal Colón, Ctra Matalascañas. Tel: 376 000. Recently renovated. In a tranquil, pine-shaded spot near sandy beach.

JAÉN

Parador Castillo de Santa Catalina. Tel: 264 411. Castle with magnificent views over the city and the sierra.

CAZORLA
Parador El Adelantado, 16 miles (26 km) from town. Tel: 721 075. In the heart of the sierra and park.

UBEDA
Parador Condestable Dávalos, Plaza Vázquez Molina, 1. Tel: 750 345. In a 16th-century palace.

BAEZA
Casa Juanito, Avda Arca del Agua, s/n. Tel: 740 040. Plain, cheap and on the main road; central position for the whole province. Good regional cooking.

La Iruela (SIERRA DE CAZORLA)
Río, Ctra del Tranco, 8. Tel: 720 211. Idyllically quiet and cheap country *pension* close to Cazorla.

BELMEZ DE LA MORALEDA
Hostal La Chopera, Ctra 325, Km 42. Tel: 394 006. Small, cheap and down to earth, one of the few places to stay in the Sierra Magina.

MÁLAGA

Parador Nacional Gibralfaro, Monte de Gibralfaro. Tel: 221 902. Overlooking old fortress and city.
Las Vegas ☆☆☆, Paseo de Sancha, 22. Tel: 217 712. Pool. Near bullring.
Derby ☆☆, San Juan de Dios, 1. Tel: 221 301. Hostal. Central.

ANTEQUERA
Parador, Paseo Garcia del Olmo, s/n. Tel: 840 261. Swimming pool, bar.

BENALMÁDENA COSTA
Hotel Torrequemada ✫✫✫✫✫, Ctra de Cádiz, Km 220. Swimming pool, golf, tennis, restaurants and one of the largest casinos in Europe.

CARRATRACA
Hostal El Principe ✫, Antonio Riobóo, 9. Tel: 458 020. Characterful old building.

ESTEPONA
Stakis Paraíso ✫✫✫✫, Urb El Paraiso, Ctra N340, Km 167. Tel: 783 000. Between sea and mountain.

Caracas ✫✫, Avda San Lorenzo, 50. Tel: 800 800. Modern. Comfortable.

FUENGIROLA
Las Palmeras Sol ✫✫✫✫, Paseo Marítimo, s/n. Tel: 472 700.

MIJAS
Byblos Andaluz ✫✫✫✫✫, Mijas Golf, Apartado, 138 (near Fuengirola). Tel: 473 050. Luxury. On golf course.

Hotel Mijas ✫✫✫✫, Avda de Mexico s/n, Urb. Tamisa, s/n. Tel: 485 800. Fine views.

MARBELLA
Los Monteros ✫✫✫✫✫, Ctra N340, Km 187. Tel: 771 700. Luxury. Golf course, riding.

Puente Romano ✫✫✫✫✫, Ctra N340, Km 176,7. Tel: 770 100. *Pueblo* style luxury.

Marbella Club ✫✫✫✫✫, Ctra N340, Km 1178,2. Tel: 771 300. Gardens, private beach.

NERJA
Parador Nacional, Almuñécar, 8. Tel: 520 050. Pool. Overlooking beach.

Las Chinas ✫✫, Plaza Capitán Cortés, 14. Frigiliana, near Nerja. Tel: 533 073. Immaculate hotel in picturesque village.

RONDA
Reina Victoria ✫✫✫✫, Jerez 25. Tel: 871 240. Spacious old hotel. Majestic views.

TORREMOLINOS
Meliá Torremolinos ✫✫✫✫, Avda Carlofa Alessandri, 109. Tel: 380 500. Pools, restaurant.

Don Pedro ✫✫✫, Avda Lido, s/n. Tel: 386 844. Amid gardens by the main beach.

SEVILLE
Alfonso XIII ✫✫✫✫✫, San Fernando, 2. Tel: 222 850. Neo-Mudéjar decor.

Doña María ✫✫✫✫, Don Remondo, 19. Tel: 224 990. Antiques and iron balconies. Opposite cathedral.

Fernando III ✫✫✫, San José, 21. Tel: 217 307. Near Santa Cruz quarter. Spacious, modern.

Murillo ✫✫, Lope de Rueda, 7. Tel: 216 095. In the heart of Santa Cruz.

Simon ✫, García de Vinuesa, 19. Tel: 226 660. Central location, in 18th-century house with Andalusian patio.

Goya ✫✫, Mateos Gago, 31. Tel: 211 170. Hostal. Budget bargain near main sights.

Parador Alcazar del Rey Don Pedro, Carmona (20 miles/33 km east of Seville). Tel: 141 010. Tranquil, Mudéjar-style building.

WHERE TO EAT

It is not necessary to step into a restaurant to eat well in Andalusia. Fast food was a part of Spanish culture when the hot dog was hardly more than a puppy. *Tapas*, tasty snacks varying from grilled birds to stewed tripe and chick peas, are served in thousands of bars. Sometimes they come automatically with the drink. Sometimes you have to order them and pay extra. If you want more, you can ask for a *ración* (plateful), or *media ración* (half plateful).

In many bars calling themselves cafeterias, you can order a *combinado*. This is usually a variation on pork chop, fried eggs, ham, salad and chips. Even the smallest village usually has a bar serving *tapas* or a *fonda* (inn) serving simple set meals at budget prices.

Restaurants usually offer a *menú del día*, a three-course meal, including wine, at an economical price. Note also that on the Atlantic and Mediterranean coasts you can eat well on the beaches in restaurants known as *chiringuitos* and *merenderos*. Some of these have become quite sophisticated, with prices to match. Others remain simple, with the best bet probably being "fish of the day".

Price guide: Inexpensive = under 1,500 pesetas per person for a three course meal, not including wine; Moderate = 1,500–3,500 pesetas; Expensive = more than 3,500 pesetas. Moderate to Expensive restaurants usually accept at least one of the credit cards. Cheaper establishments prefer cash.

ALMERÍA
Anfora, González Galbín, 25. Tel: 231 374. Imaginative cooking, international dishes in a pleasant setting. Closed: Sunday, holidays, and 17–31 July. CC: Amex, Master, Visa. Moderate

AGUADULCE
Mesón El Abuelo, Del Alamo. Tel: 341 653. Closed: Tuesday (winter). CC: Eurocard, Visa. Traditional Spanish. Moderate

MOJÁCAR
El Palacio, Plaza del Caño s/n. Tel: 478 279. International, national dishes. Closed: Thursday; November and February. CC: Master, Visa. Moderate

---

CÁDIZ
El Faro, San Felix, 15. Tel: 211 068. Recommended for its quality seafood. CC: Amex, Master, Visa. Moderate

Ventorillo del Chato, Ctra de San Fernando, Km 647. Tel: 250 025. Bull's tail is the speciality. Closed: Sunday, and in winter Sunday night. CC: Amex, Master, Visa. Moderate

ALGECIRAS
Los Remos, Finca Villa Victoria, Ramal La Linea-Gibraltar Km 2, Campamento San Roque. Tel: 760 812. Delicious seafood served in style in a magnificent colonial house. Closed: Sunday night, except August. CC: Amex, Master, Visa. Expensive

ARCOS DE LA FRONTERA
El Convento, Maldonado, 2. Tel: 702 333. Pleasant, family-run. Near top of the town adjoining a convent. CC: Master, Visa. Moderate

JEREZ DE LA FRONTERA
La Mesa Redonda, Manuel de la Quintana, 3. Tel: 340 069. Impeccably served regional dishes in a comfortable location. Closed: Sunday, holidays, and August. CC: Amex, Visa. Moderate–Expensive

PUERTO DE SANTA MARÍA
Alboronia, Santo Domingo, 24. Tel: 851 609. Imaginative cuisine in an old Andalusian house with garden. Dinner only in summer. Closed: Saturday lunch, Sunday, and January. CC: Amex, Master, Visa. Moderate

CÓRDOBA
El Caballo Rojo, Cardenal Herrero, 28. Tel: 475 375. Classic Córdoban and Mozarabic dishes in heart of the old quarter. CC: Amex, Diners, Master, 6,000, Visa. Expensive

Castillo de Albaida, Ctra de Trassierra, Km 4.5. Tel: 273 493. Old castle-style building outside city. Regional dishes. Closed: 24 December. CC: Amex, Diners, Master, 6,000, Visa. Moderate

PALMA DEL RÍO
Hospedería San Francisco, Avda Pío X11, 35. Tel: 644 185. Basque, Moorish dishes in restored monastery. Closed: Sunday evenings, and 1–15 August. CC: Amex, Master, Visa. Moderate

MONTILLA
Las Camachas. An old rambling, roadside restaurant where the landed gentry of the wine district dine out. Sturdy, good food. Montilla wines on sale.

GRANADA
Mesón Antonio, Ecce Homo, 6. Tel: 229 599. Home cooking in an intimate atmosphere. Closed: Sunday, and July–August. Moderate

Mirador de Morayma, Callejón de las Vacas 2, Albaicín (opposite road to Sacromonte). Tel: 228 290. Local dishes. Views of Alhambra. Summer dining in patio. Closed: Sunday night, and Monday. CC: Amex, Visa. Expensive

ALMUÑÉCAR
Cotobro, Bajada del Mar, 1 Playa del Cotobro. Tel: 631 802. French and international cuisine. Best to reserve. In summer dinner only. Closed: Monday, and mid-November to 6 December. Moderate

DÚRCAL
El Molino, Camino de las Fuentes, Paraje de la Isla, Durcal (15 miles/25 km, from Granada, off Motril road). Tel: 780 247. Andalusian Gastronomic

Research Centre and cooking school. Gastronomic adventures in a 200-year-old mill. Traditional Andalusian dishes. Closed: Monday, and Sunday and holiday evenings. Moderate

GUALCHOS
(17 km from Motril)
La Posada, Plaza Constitución, 9. Tel: 646 034. Located in a fine old house in small village. Tastefully prepared imaginative food. In the same building is a small, tranquil hotel. Closed: Monday, and November–February. Moderate

Riofrió, on the Málaga-Granada road N342, 3 miles (5 km) west of Loja: several restaurants serving fresh trout from adjacent hatchery. Inexpensive

HUELVA
Las Candelas, Ctra Punta Umbria, Aljaraque crossroads. Tel: 318 301. Good value and quality fresh seafood and meat dishes. Closed: Sunday. CC: Amex, Master, Visa. Moderate

ARACENA
Casas, Colmenitas 41. Tel: 110 044. Famed for its regional ham and pork dishes. CC: Visa. Moderate

EL ROMPIDO
El Caribe 11, Virgen del Carmen, 18. In the heart of a fishing community. Ultra-fresh seafood at very reasonable prices. Inexpensive–Moderate

JAÉN
Mesón Vicente, Arco del Consuelo, 1. Tel: 262 816. Closed: Sunday. CC: Visa. Popular for its tasty regional food. Moderate

ANDÚJAR
Don Pedro, Gabriel Zamora, 5. Tel: 501 274. Game, in season. Reasonably priced. CC: Amex, Master, Visa. Moderate

BAEZA
Juanito, Paseo Arca del Agua, s/n. Tel: 270 909. Regional dishes are a speciality. Closed: Sunday night, and the last fortnight in November. CC: Amex, Master, Visa. Moderate

CAZORLA
Cueva de Juan Pedro, near Santa María Church. Tel: 721 225. Meat grilled on an open fire in a traditional setting. Inexpensive

MALAGA
Thousands of restaurants cater to the millions of tourists annually visiting the Costa del Sol. New ones open as fast as old ones close. This is only a small selection of those which have showed stamina as well as quality.

El Cabra, Copo, 21 (Pedragalejo). Tel: 291 595. By the sea. Fish. CC: Visa. Moderate

Casa Pedro, Playa de El Palo. Tel: 290 013. Popular beach eating place. *Paella*, sardines. Closed: Monday night, and November. CC: Amex, Master, Visa. Moderate

Refectorium, Cervantes, 8. Tel: 218 990. Also in Avda Juan Sebastián Elcano, El Palo. Tel: 294 593. Traditional dishes. Closed: Sunday (El Palo-Monday). CC: Amex, Visa. Moderate

Tormes, San José, 2. Solid, simple fare. Inexpensive

ANTEQUERA

Chaplin, San Agustín, 3. Tel: 843 034. Regional. CC: Amex, Master, Visa. Inexpensive

EL CHORRO AREA

El Oasis. Overlooking one of Guadalhorce reservoirs. Barbecued meat. Inexpensive

RONDA

Don Miguel, Villanueva, 4, Ronda. Tel: 871 090. National and regional cooking, spectacular views over the gorge. Closed: Tuesday pm, also Sunday June–September; Tuesday night, and Wednesday October–May; 15 January–15 February. CC: Amex, Master, Visa. Moderate

ON THE COAST

ESTEPONA

Costa del Sol, Calle San Roque. Tel: 801 101. A French bistro offering excellent value. Closed: Sunday. CC: Amex, Visa, Master. Moderate

FUENGIROLA

La Baraka, Edificio Saturno, Paseo Marítimo, 10. Tel: 471 495. French specialities and pizza. Closed: Wednesday (winter). All credit cards. Moderate

Méson El Castellano, Camino de Coín, 5. Tel: 462 736. Authentic Castilian roasts. Closed: Saturday lunch. CC: Amex, Master, Visa. Moderate

MARBELLA

Hostería del Mar, Avda de Canovas del Castillo, 1A. Tel: 775 581. Dine on Spanish-international food in an intimate villa atmosphere. Closed: Sunday. CC: Amex, Master, Visa. Expensive

La Freiduría, Trapiche, 24. Tel: 772 681. Good seafood at reasonable prices. Closed: Wednesday. Inexpensive

La Meridiana, Camino de la Cruz, near mosque. Tel: 776 190. Stylish, sophisticated. One of Marbella's top eating spots. Expensive

NERJA

Casa Luque, Plaza Cabana, 2. Tel: 521 004. National, international dishes. Closed: Thursday. CC: Visa, Master. Moderate

Haveli, Almirante Ferrándiz, 44. Tel: 522 292. Indian Tandoori. CC: Visa, Master. Moderate

TORREMOLINOS

Frutos, Ctra de Cádiz, Km 235 (next to Los Alamos petrol station). Tel: 381 450. Hearty helpings in traditional Spanish style. Closed: Sunday pm in winter. CC: Amex, Master, Visa. Moderate

Marrakech, Ctra de Benalmádena. Tel: 382 169. Moroccan food in an exotic setting. Closed: Sunday, and Tuesday. Moderate

El Roqueo, Carmen, 35, La Carihuela. Tel: 384 946. Justifiably popular, possibly the best of the many seafood establishments on the Carihuela beach. Closed: Tuesday, and November. CC: Amex. Master, Visa. Moderate

SEVILLE

(Convert phone numbers to seven digits by placing the figure 4 in front when dialling within the province. Dial 954 from outside the province).

La Dorada, Virgen de Aguasantas, 6. Tel: 455 100. Fish specialities. Closed: Sunday, and August. CC: Amex, Visa. Expensive

El Ancora, Virgen de la Huerta, s/n, Los Remedios. Tel: 273 849. Fresh fish. CC: Amex, Master, Visa. Moderate

Don Raimundo, Argote de Molina, 26. Tel: 223 355. Andalusia food, decor. Closed: Sunday nights. CC: Amex, Diners, Master, Visa. Moderate

Río Grande, Betis 70. Tel: 273 956. Terrace on river. CC: Amex, Master, Visa. Moderate

El 3 de Oro, Sta María de la Blanca, 34. Tel: 222 759. Self service. Mecca for budget travellers. Closed: Saturday. Inexpensive

THINGS TO DO

ALMERÍA

Alcazaba built by the caliph of Córdoba Abd-er-Rahman II. Open: 10am–2pm and 4–8pm summer, 9am-1pm and 3-7pm winter.

Centro de Rescate de Fauna Sahariana (rescue centre for endangered Sahara species), this is located near the gypsy quarter, at the rear of the Alcazaba. Visits by prior arrangement.

From Almería, visit the filmsets in desert scenery near Tabernas (20 miles/33 km), where spaghetti Westerns were once churned out. Stuntmen put on special performances at Mini Hollywood. The Plataforma Solar (solar energy research station), near Tabernas, can also be visited, tel: (951) 365 015 for times. Níjar (17 miles/28 km) is a centre for pottery and blanket weaving, not far from the rocky, little-developed coast east of Cabo de Gata. The hilltop resort of Mojácar is growing fast. Castle connoisseurs should visit Vélez Blanco (100 miles/ 167 km from Almería), where there is an impressive 16th-century fortress.

CÁDIZ

Cathedral: Composer Manuel de Falla is buried in this neoclassic structure. Open: 5.30–7.30pm, Sat 9.30–10.30am and 5.30–8pm, Sunday 11am–1pm.

San Felipe Neri church: Spain's first constitution was signed here in 1812. Open: noon–2pm and 5–9pm. Closed: fiestas and July.

Jerez floats on sherry. Visit the bodeges, open mornings during the week. The dancing horses of Andalusia of the Escuela Andaluza del Arte Ecuestre, Recreo de las Cadenas, Avda Duque de Abrantes, train every morning and give public performances on Thursday at 11am.

Arcos de la Frontera is a superbly situated medieval town, atop a hill overlooking the Guadalete river.

Worth seeing are the town hall and the church of San Pedro Apostol with works by Zurbarán, Pacheco and Rivera.

Tarifa offers Europe's finest windsurfing beaches and a hydrofoil service across the Straits of Gibraltar to Tangier.

CÓRDOBA

Mosque: One of the great architectural treasures left by the Moors. A 16th-century cathedral stands at its centre. Open: 10.30am–1.30pm (all year) and 3.30–5.30pm (winter), 5–7pm (summer).

Alcázar of the Christian Kings: A 14th-century palace-fortress. Open: 9am–1.30pm and 5–8pm. Gardens floodlit May–September, 10pm–midnight. Closed: Monday.

Synagogue: Calle Judío. Open: 10am–2pm and 6–8pm May–September, 5–7pm October–April; Sunday and holidays 10am–1.30pm. Closed: Monday.

Museo Municipal del Arte Taurino (bullfight museum): In the Judería (old Jewish quarter). Open: 9.30am–1.30pm and 4–7pm. Closed: Monday.

Medina Azahara: On the edge of the Sierra Morena, overlooking the Guadalquivir valley (6 miles/9 km west of Córdoba) the splendours of this palace city of the Caliphs are being restored. Open: May–September 10am–1pm and 6–8pm; October–April 10am–2pm and 4–6pm; Sunday and holidays 10am–1.30pm. Closed: Monday.

GRANADA

Alhambra and Generalife: Largely dating from the 14th century, the Alhambra marks the peak of sophisticated Moslem architecture in Spain. The Generalife with its terraced water gardens was the summer palace. Open: summer 9am–6pm; winter 10.30am–8.30pm. Interior floodlit, summer Tuesday, Thursday and Saturday 10pm–midnight, winter Saturday 8–10pm.

Cathedral and Royal Chapel (tombs of the Catholic Monarchs): Open: 10.30–1.30pm (all year) and 4–7pm summer, 3.30–6pm winter.

Albaicín (Arabic for "Falconers' Quarter"): The old Moorish quarter, straggling over a hill opposite the Alhambra. For the finest views of Alhambra and the Sierra Nevada, visit the terrace of San Nicolas Church.

Casa-Museo Federico García Lorca: Poeta García Lorca, 4, in the village of Fuentevaqueros (12 miles/ 20 km, from Granada, north of the Málaga highway). Birthplace of the poet converted into a museum. Guided visits: 10am–1pm, on the hour, and at 4, 5 and 6pm (later in summer). Closed: Monday.

Sierra Nevada: Solynieve ski resort, 20 miles (33 km) from Granada. Season December–May, 31 miles (50 km) of marked runs, cross country routes, ski school. Cable car to top of Veleta peak (11,130 ft/ 3,395 metres), magnificent views of sierras and towards Mediterranean. Paved road, highest in Europe, open in summer to Veleta from where the track continues south to the Alpujarras.

HUELVA

Monument to Christopher Columbus: Punta del Sebo. Gift from the United States in honour of the discoverers of America, sculpture by Gertrude Vanderbilt Whitney.

Coto Doñana: Guided visits to the park interior are by four-wheel-drive vehicle, twice daily and last four hours – places reserved at Parque Nacional Doñana, Reception Centre, Acebuche, near park entrance on Ayamonte-Matalascañas road (Huelva 32 miles/51 km), tel: (955) 430 432. Open: 8am–7pm, except Monday. Information centres at La Rocina, near El Rocío, tel: (955) 406 140. Open: 9.30am–1.30pm and 4–7pm; and the Palacio del Acebrón (4 miles/ 6 km from the Rocina centre). Open: 8am–7pm.

JAÉN

Santa Catalina castle (housing a *parador*): Commands impressive views of town and surrounding olive groves. Cathedral, main chapel holds the relics of the Santo Rostro. Open: 8.30am–1.30pm and 4.30–7pm.

Arab baths: In the Palacio de Villardompardo, the most important Arab baths surviving in Spain. Tel: (953) 262 111 for visit.

MÁLAGA

Cathedral: A 16th-century building with baroque choir, the work of Pedro de Mena. Open: 10am–1pm and 4–5.50pm.

Alcazaba: Moorish fortress with Archaeological Museum. Open: Summer 11am–1pm and 5–8pm; winter 10am–1pm and 4–7pm; Sunday 10am–2pm. Roman theatre near the entrance. Repair work began in 1990.

Gibralfaro Castle: Above the Alcazaba, commanding magnificent views of city and Mediterranean.

Pablo Picasso Foundation: Located in the house where the painter was born, 16, Plaza de la Merced. Centre for Picasso research, also promotes contemporary art. Organises lectures on various aspects of Picasso's life and work, and "Octubre Picassiano" to celebrate painter's birth, with exhibitions and events. Entry free. Open: 10am–2pm and 5–8pm. Tel: (952) 283 900.

ANTEQUERA

Dolmens – Cueva de Menga: Bronze-age burial site, 1 mile from town centre on Granada road. Open: 10am–1pm and 4–8pm summer, 2–6pm winter.

Cueva de Viera: Nearby. Open: 10am–1pm and 5–7pm summer, 3–5pm winter.

El Chorro: 38 miles (60 km) northwest of Málaga. Dramatic chasm, through which passes the Guadalhorce River.

Cueva de Nerja: Home of prehistoric man, spectacular rock formations. Open: 10am–1.30pm and 4–7pm; May–September 9.30am–9pm.

RONDA

El Tajo (chasm): Spanned by 18th-century bridge Puente Nuevo.

Palacio de Salvatierra, **Casa del Rey Moro** and the **Arab Baths**: Open: 10am–1pm and 4–7pm. Closed: Sunday pm, and Monday.

Plaza de Toros: Oldest bullring in Spain. Open: 10am–6pm.

Cueva de la Pileta: 17 miles (27 km) from Ronda. Prehistoric cave paintings.

SEVILLE

Cathedral and **Giralda Tower**: Colossal 15th-century Gothic building. Many art treasures. Tombs of King Ferdinand the Saint and Pedro the Cruel. Giralda, 12th-century Arab minaret, can be climbed for views. Open: Monday–Friday 11am–6pm, Saturday 11am–4pm, Sunday 2–4pm. School groups 2–4pm. Closed: holidays.

Reales Alcázares: An 11th-century Mudéjar palace. Fine gardens. Open: Saturday 9am–12.45pm and 3–5.30pm, Sunday and holidays 9am–1pm.

Torre del Oro (Tower of Gold): Moorish-built, houses Maritime Museum. Open: 10am–2pm, Sunday and holidays 10am–1pm. Closed: Monday.

Casa Pilatos: Mudéjar-Renaissance mansion. Open: 9am–6pm; upper floor, 10am–1.30pm and 4–6.30pm. Closed: Saturday afternoon, Sunday.

Museo de Bellas Artes (Fine Arts Museum): Plaza del Museo, 9. Works by Murillo and Ribera. Open: 10am–2pm and 4–7pm. Closed: Saturday and Sunday afternoons, Monday.

Parque de los Descubrimientos: This theme park has rescued almost all but the international pavilions of Expo 92 and when entirely completed, the new fairgrounds will also feature an amusement park, a late afternoon parade, a fireworks show on the artificial lake and popular entertainment in the evening. Restaurants, cafeterias and picnic area are available and the monorail, cable cars, scenic train and panoramic towers are also in service. Open: 1 June–17 October Tuesday–Thursday 7pm–2am, Friday and Saturday 10am–4am, Sunday 10am–midnight; 18 October–10 January and 10 February–31 May Friday, Saturday and Sunday 10am–2pm. Closed: 10 January–10 February. Information: Tel: 446 1616.

CARMONA

Girdled by ancient walls, town of fine old buildings, churches.

Roman necropolis: Open: 10am–2pm and 4–6pm. Closed: Monday and holidays.

Ecija: "Town of steeples", many beautiful churches and mansions (Palacio de los Marqueses de Peñaflor, Palacio de los Condes de Valverde), remains of Roman amphitheatre and necropolis.

Itálica: Streets, amphitheatre, mosaics in Roman town, **birthplace of Hadrian**. Open: 9am–6.30pm; October–February 9am–5pm, Sunday 9am–3pm. Closed: Monday.

BULLFIGHTING

Andalusia is the womb of bullfighting, the controversial struggle between man and beast, and the town of Ronda is regarded as the cradle of modern bullfighting. Many of Spain's top *matadors* come from the region and many of the most-respected fighting bulls. There are occasional charity fights in winter, but the season really gets under way at Easter and with the series of *corridas* during the Seville Fair in April.

Seville's Maestranza bullring is the most important arena. Daily fights are held during the fairs in other towns, throughout the summer. Six bulls are killed during a *corrida*, which usually starts at 6pm. Tickets are expensive, particularly if you want to be in the shade ("Sombra") and near the *barrera*, the ringside. Cheaper tickets are sold for "Sol", the seating on the sunny side of the stadium. In a number of communities, bull-runs are held through the streets during local festivities.

CULTURE PLUS

Granada's events guide, *Guía Cultural y de Ocio*, published fortnightly in Spanish and English, gives useful information about cultural events. Seville has two useful entertainment guides, *El Giraldillo*, and the *Guía de Ocio*. On the Costa del Sol, numerous publications, some free, offer information about what's on. *Lookout* magazine has details about theatre, sport, films in English, club events.

Diary of Events: The following is a list of some of the more important or interesting festivals and events in the region. As dates vary each year, it is advisable to check with the organisers or local tourist office for exact details of each year's edition.

CÁDIZ

April: Jerez, World Motorcycling Championship at Jerez race track.

May: Jerez, Jerez Horse Fair. Display of horses and horsemanship. Information: Tel: (956) 347 663.

August: Sanlucar de Barrameda. Horse races along the beach.

Sotogrande, International Polo Competition. Matches throughout the month to dispute three trophies. Jerez, International Flamenco Contest.

September/October: Jerez, Tío Pepe Formula I Grand Prix, Jerez race track.

December: Jerez, National Flamenco Guitar Contest.

CÓRDOBA

May: Córdoba, International Sierra Morena Rally. Gruelling motorcycle race through heart of the

Sierra Morena. Information: Tel: (957) 473 711.
July: Córdoba, Guitar and Dance Courses. Courses in flamènco, classical guitar and dance, organised by the Centro Flamenco Paco Peña, Plaza del Potro, 15, 14002 Córdoba.
July–October: Córdoba, International Guitar Festival. Performances of flamenco and classical guitar. Information from the town hall: Tel: (957) 479 329.

GRANADA

May: Granada, International Drama Festival. Showcase for most innovative international theatre productions. Information from festival office: Palacio de la Madraza, Oficios, 14, Granada 18001. Tel: (958) 228 403.
June/July: Granada, International Festival of Music and Dance. One of Spain's leading festivals offers a varied programme of music and dance by national and international companies. Concerts in the Auditorio Manuel de Falla and the Palacio Carlos V in the Alhambra, dance in the Generalife. Information from the festival office: Gracia, 21–4, 18002 Granada. Tel: (958) 267 442–45.
July: Granada, Romantic Concerts. Classical music concerts in the unusual setting of the Carmen de los Martires, near the Alhambra.
November: Granada, Granada International Jazz Festival. Emphasis on modern jazz. Information from town hall: Tel: (958) 223 573.

SEVILLE

February/March: Seville, Ancient Music Festival. Music from Romantic, Gothic and early baroque periods played on original or replica instruments. Information from town hall: Tel: (954) 218 883.
April: Seville, Spring Fair or Feria. The biggest Andalusian festival and most magnificent.
Seville, Antiques fair. Exhibitors from all over Spain. Information: Palacio de Exposiciones y Congresos, Recinto Ferial, Polígono Aeropuerto, Seville Este. Tel: (954) 675 140.
May/June: Cita en Sevilla. Cultural festival with classic and avant-garde theatre and dance, exhibitions and music from pop, rock, to jazz and blues. Information from the town hall: Tel: (954) 218 883.
July: Italica, International Festival of Theatre and Dance. Contemporary dance and classical ballet by prestigious international companies. Held in the Roman amphitheatre. Information: Fundación Luis Cernuda, Diputación Provincial de Sevilla. Tel: (954) 217 722.
September: Biannual Flamenco Festival. Held every two years (1990, 1992, etc). Lasts throughout the month and represents the best in flamenco. Information from town hall. Tel: (954) 218 883.

NIGHTLIFE

BARS

Seville is justifiably renowned for its bars. They vary from traditional seedy to elegantly modern and offer a vast range of excellent *tapas*. Some examples:
Casa Morales, García de Vinuesa, 11. Old *bodega*, huge barrels, reeking of atmosphere; **El Rinconcillo**, Gerona, 42. Founded 1670. Tiles, beams, wine from the barrel.
Abades, Abades, 13 (Santa Cruz). Elegant *patio* in stylish house, classical music, frequented by upwardly mobile *sevillanos*.
La Carbonería, Levies, 18. Former palace, then coal merchants. Lively hang-out for young artists, musicians.

NIGHTCLUBS

Full-fledged nightclubs are few and far between. If you are looking for a Folies Bergeres-type extravaganza, the Casino Torrequebrada near Málaga is probably the best bet (*see Gambling*). Restaurants and cafés often put on live entertainment. "Sexy shows" usually feature strippers. Remember that a *sala de fiestas* may not be a genuine nightclub. Many establishments use this name when they are in fact brothels, or bars where prostitutes make their contacts. You will often see them on the fringes of towns, signalled with gaudy lighting.

DISCOS

These come in all varieties, for teenagers, the upwardly mobile, jetsetters and just the young-at-heart. This season's "in" place may be "out" by the time you arrive. Entry price is usually from 600 pesetas. Worth investigating are:
CÓRDOBA
Contactos, Eduardo Dato 8.
Saint Cyr, Eduardo Lucena 4.
Zahira, Conde de Robledo 1.
GRANADA
Granada 10, Carcel Baja 13
Oh Granada, Dr Guirao Gea s/n.
Perkussion, Plaza de Gracia 9 (next to Multicines).
Krokis, Santa Barbara 3.
MÁLAGA
Main centres are along the Costa del Sol in Torremolinos/Benalmádena-Costa, Marbella and Puerto Banús.
In Málaga:
Duna, Avda Juan Sebastián Elcano, Pedregalejo.
Extasis, Plaza de Reding, Malagueta.
H2O, Fernando Camino, Malagueta.

In Torremolinos:
Piper's, Avda Palma de Mallorca.
Borsalino Palace, Ctra Cádiz.
No. 1, Avda Carlota Alessandri.

SOUTHERN SPAIN

In Marbella:
Jimmy's, Marbella Club Hotel.
Kiss, Avda Ricardo Soriano.
Olivia Valere, Puerto Banús.
Pepe Moreno, Ctra Cádiz, Km 186.

SEVILLE
Mostly in the Remedios district across the river.
Disco FM, Avda García Morato s/n.
Río, Betis, 67
Groucho, Federico Sánchez Bedoya, 20.
Piruetas, Asunción 3.

FLAMENCO

Flamenco festivals are held throughout Andalusia, sometimes lasting all night. Purists are contemptuous of the shows staged for tourists in the caves of Sacromonte, Granada's gypsy quarter. Visiting one of the caves can be a memorable experience, but you may well feel ripped off.

Places where you can see reasonable-quality commercial flamenco include:
In Granada:
El Corral del Príncipe, Campo de Príncipe s/n.
El Curro, Lavadero de las Tablas.
Tel: (958) 283 537.
La Reina Mora, Mirador de San Cristobal.
In Seville:
Tablao Flamenco de Curro Vélez, Rodo, 7. Tel: (954) 216 492.
El Patio Sevillano, Paseo Colón, 11. Tel: 222 068.
Los Gallos, Plaza Santa Cruz, 11.
Tel: (954) 216 981.

Reservations are recommended for these venues.

GAMBLING

Andalusia has three casinos. Passports or national identity cards must be shown, "correct" dress is expected and an entry fee is payable.
Casino Torrequebrada, Ctra N340, Km 226, Benalmádena Costa, Málaga. Tel: (952) 442 545. Also has restaurant/bar, nightclub, disco and cinema.
Casino Nueva Andalucía, Hotel Andalusia Plaza, Nueva Andalucía, Marbella, Málaga. Tel: (952) 780 800. Jetsetters' favourite.
Casino de Bahía de Cádiz, Ctra Madrid-Cádiz, Km 650,3, Puerto de Santa María, Cádiz. Tel: (956) 862 042. Also has restaurant, disco, cinema, nightclub.

SHOPPING

ALMERÍA
Principal buys are in handicrafts: Ceramics and pottery (from Albox, Níjar, Sorbas and Vera); basketwork (from Almería, Alhabía and Níjar); *jarapas*, rugs made with rags and strips of cotton (from Nijar, Huercal Overa and Berja); bedspreads and blankets from (Albox, Berja and Macael); marble objects from Macael.

CÁDIZ
Sherry from Jerez and Puerto de Santa María (such as Harveys, Williams and Humbert, Pedro Domecq and Osborne, well known to the British market); dolls from doll factory in Chiclana (Fábrica de Muñecas Marín, Rivero, 16. Tel: (956) 400 667); fine leather from Ubrique; carpets from Arcos de la Frontera; capes and ponchos from Grazalema; guitars from Algodonales; wickerwork from Jerez; saddlery from Olvera.

CÓRDOBA
Silver filigree jewellery, for which Córdoba is particularly noted; Montilla wines (*Bodeges* in Montilla, 28 miles/46 km from Córdoba); *anís* liquor from Rute (Anís Machaquito, Anís De Raza); ceramics, Lucena pottery with geometric green and yellow design, and *botijos* (two-spouted drinking pitchers) from La Rambla; leatherwork; decorative metalwork in copper, bronze and brass (from Espejo and Castro del Río).

GRANADA
Foodstuffs – cured mountain hams from the Alpujarras; pottery, most typical is Fajalauza with distinctive blue and green design originally from the Albaicín; leather, especially embossed leatherwork; marquetry (technique of inlaying wood with bone, ivory, mother of pearl and other woods) chests, chess boards, small tables; metal craftwork, lanterns made to traditional Moorish designs; textiles – rugs, cushions, bedspreads from the Alpujarras; handmade guitars, several workshops on the Cuesta de Gomerez leading to the Alhambra; silver filigree jewellery.

HUELVA
Cured hams from Jabugo; white wine from the Condado de Huelva; pottery (from Aracena and Cortejana); rugs from Ecinasola; embroidery (from Aracena, Alonso and Puebla de Guzmán); handmade leather boots (Valverde de Camino).

JAÉN
Glass and ceramics (from Andújar, Bailén and Ubeda); carpets and wickerwork (from Ubeda, Jaén and Los Villares); forged iron objects and lanterns (Ubeda); guitars (Marmolejo).

MÁLAGA
The towns along the Costa del Sol also offer a variety of street markets, colourful though not necessarily the place to find a bargain. Market timings are as follows: Monday Marbella; Tuesday Fuengirola and Nerja; Wednesday Estepona; Thursday Torremolinos and San Pedro de Alcántara; Friday Arroyo de la Miel and Benalmádena *pueblo*; Sunday Estepona port and Málaga (by the football stadium).

SEVILLE
Antiques around the streets Mateos Gago, Placentines and Rodrigo Caro; ceramics and tiles from Santa Ana (factory in Triana) and La Cartuja de Sevilla (factory at Ctra de Mérida, Km 529, tel: 954-392 854); saddlery and leather items, boots and chaps; fashion, Seville's own designers Victorio and Lucchino have showroom at Sierpes, 87; fans and castanets.

USEFUL ADDRESSES

ALMERÍA
Tourist information: Hermanos Machado 4, Edificio Multiple, tel: 234 705; also at Ctra N340, 1 mile (2 km) west of city, tel: 234 859; Airport office: Tel: 221 954.

CÁDIZ
Tourist information: Calderón de la Barca, 1, Cádiz. Tel: 211 053.

Tourist information: Alameda Cristina, 7, Jerez de la Frontera. Tel: 331 150.

Tourist information: Guadalete s/n, Puerto de Santa María. Tel: 863 145. Ferry to Cádiz, summer service from quay.

CÓRDOBA
City Council tourist office: Plaza de Juda Levi, Judería.

Junta de Andalucía tourist information bureau: Torrijos, 10 (Palacio de Congresos). Tel: 471 235.

GRANADA
Municipal tourist office: Libreros, 2, tel: 225 990; also Plaza Mariana Pineda, 10, bajo, tel: 226 688.

Junta de Andalucía tourist office: Casa de los Tiros, Plaza del Padre Suárez. Tel: 221 022.

HUELVA
Tourist office: Vázquez López, 5, Huelva. Tel: 257 403.

JAÉN
Tourist information: Arquitecto Berges, 1, Jaén. Tel: 222 737.

Tourist information: Baeza, Plaza del Pópulo s/n, tel: 740 444; Cazorla, Martínez Delgado, 1, tel: 720 000; Ubeda, Bajos del Ayuntamiento, tel: 750 897.

MÁLAGA
Tourist information: Marqués de Larios, 5, tel: 213 445; also at airport, terminal nacional, tel: 312 044 and terminal internacional, tel: 316 000 ext: 5433. Airport 5 miles (8 km).

Tourist information: Palacio de Najera, Antequera. Tel: 842 180.

Tourist information: Ctra N340, Km 227, Benalmádena Costa; also at Castillo Bil Bil, Ctra N340. Tel: 442 494.

Tourist information: Paseo Marítimo Jorge Manrique s/n, Estepona. Tel: 800 913.

Tourist information: Parque de España, Fuengirola. Tel: 476 166.

Tourist information: Miguel Cano, 1, Marbella. Tel: 771 442.

Tourist information: Puerta del Mar, 4, Nerja. Tel: 521 531.

Tourist information: Plaza de España, 1, Ronda. Tel: 871 272.

Tourist information: Avda de Andalucía, 92-A, Torre del Mar. Tel: 541 104.

Tourist information: Calle Guetaria, La Nogalera, Torremolinos. Tel: 381 578.

Tourist information: Centro Internacional, Bloque 79, Torrox–Costa. Tel: 530 225.

Tourist information: Plaza de España, Vélez–Málaga. Tel: 500 100.

SEVILLE
Tourism office: Avda de la Constitución, 21. Tel: 221 404.

Municipal tourism office: Paseo de las Delicias. Tel: 234 465.

THE CANARY ISLANDS
GETTING THERE

The Canary Island archipelago is situated 71 miles (115 km) off the African coast, while the nearest point on the Spanish Peninsula, Cádiz, is 435 miles (700 km) away. The archipelago is served by the main airlines and direct flights from Madrid take a little over two hours. Most planes land at the international airports of Las Palmas on Gran Canaria or at Santa Cruz on Tenerife. There are regular shipping connections with Cádiz.

GETTING ACQUAINTED

The Canary Islands form an archipelago made up of seven major islands and several small islets, located in the Atlantic Ocean. Their ports are very busy indeed because of their strategic position on the main navigational routes between Europe, Africa and North and South America.

Due to their advantageous location, the major islands of the archipelago – Gran Canaria, Fuerteventura and Lanzarote making up the province of Las Palmas, and Tenerife, La Palma, Gomera and Hierro forming that of Santa Cruz de Tenerife – enjoy a subtropical climate and mild temperatures all year round. There is a mere 43°F (6°C) difference between the average summer temperature and the winter temperature. The more mountainous zones on Tenerife, La Palma and Gran Canaria result in abundant rainfall in winter, which is responsible for the lush, green landscape, in direct contrast to the other drier and more desert-like islands. In view of this eternally pleasant climate and the convenient location, the Canary Islands receive millions of visitors every year.

ACCOMMODATION

Price guide: *5-star = over 20,000 pesetas; 4-star = over 15,000 pesetas; 3-star = 5,000–15,000 pesetas.*

GRAN CANARIA
LAS PALMAS
Meliá Las Palmas ☆☆☆☆☆, Gomera, 6. Tel: 267 600. Modern installations with a pool and an international atmosphere and situated right on Las Canteras beach.

Reina Isabel ☆☆☆☆, Alfredo L. Jones, 40. Tel: 260 100. A modern, comfortable building, with a pool, on Las Canteras beach.

Santa Catalina ☆☆☆☆, León y Castillo 227. Tel: 243 040. A typical Canary-style building, situated in a quiet park area, with a pool, casino and a good restaurant.

Sansofé Palace ☆☆☆☆, Portugal 68 and Playa Canteras, 78. Tel: 224 062. It is located right on the beach and has a restaurant.

OUTSIDE LAS PALMAS
Iberotel Maspalomas Oasis ☆☆☆☆☆, Plaza Las Palmeras, s/n. Maspalomas. Tel: 141 448. A quiet hotel on the beach, surrounded by lovely tropical gardens.

Apolo ☆☆☆☆, Avda Estados Unidos, 28. Playa del Inglés. Tel: 760 058. Swimming pool, tennis and restaurant.

Qrquídea ☆☆☆☆, Plaza del Taralillo, Km 44. Playa del Inglés. Tel: 764 600. A quiet hotel on the beach with restaurant, swimming pool and tennis court.

Ifa Hotel Faro Maspalomas ☆☆☆☆, Plaza del Faro, 1. Maspalomas. Tel: 142 214. Restaurant, swimming pool and gardens.

Buenaventura ☆☆☆, Plaza Ansite, 1. Playa del Inglés. Tel: 761 650. Reasonably priced with restaurant and swimming pool.

TENERIFE
SANTA CRUZ
Mencey ☆☆☆☆☆, Dr José Naveiras, 38. Tel: 276 700. Swimming pool, tennis courts and a good restaurant.

Colón Rambla Hotel-Apartamento ☆☆☆, Vieira y Clavijo, 49. Tel: 272 550. Pool and restaurant.

Diplomático ☆☆☆, Antonio Nebrija, 6. Tel: 223 941. Very reasonably priced and with a pool.

OUTSIDE SANTA CRUZ
Meliá Botánico ☆☆☆☆☆, Richard J. Yeoward, s/n. Puerto de la Cruz. Tel: 381 400. Luxury rooms with magnificent views of the Teide mountain and Puerto de la Cruz.

Meliá San Felipe ☆☆☆☆☆, Avda de Colón, 22. Tel: 383 311. Puerto de la Cruz. One of the best hotels in the city with large rooms and good service.

Meliá Puerto de la Cruz ☆☆☆☆, Avda Marqués Villanueva del Prado, s/n. Puerto de la Cruz. Tel: 384 011. Reasonably priced and backed by the reliability of this important Spanish hotel chain.

Parador Cañadas del Teide ☆☆, Las Cañadas del Teide. Tel: 386 415. Spectacularly located on the Teide peak, with a typical Canary cuisine restaurant.

LANZAROTE
ARRECIFE
Gran Hotel Arrecife Playa ☆☆☆☆, Avda Mancomunidad, s/n. Tel: 811 250. A modern hotel, centrally located, with large rooms and a pool.

Miramar ☆☆☆, Coll, 2. Tel: 810 438. An inexpensive hotel with its own restaurant.

GOMERA

Parador de Turismo Conde de la Gomera ☆☆☆☆, Balcón de la Villa y Puerto. San Sebastián de la Gomera. Tel: 871 100. An old island mansion cum hotel, offering typical Canary cuisine in its restaurant.

LA PALMA

Parador de Turismo de Santa Cruz de La Palma ☆☆☆, Avda Marítima, 34. San Sebastián de la Gomera. Tel: 412 340. A peaceful hotel overlooking the Atlantic.

HIERRO

Parador de Turismo de El Hierro ☆☆☆, Las Playas, s/n. Valverde. Tel: 558 036.

FUERTEVENTURA

Parador de Turismo de Fuerteventura ☆☆☆, Ctra del Aeropuerto, s/n. Puerto del Rosario. Tel: 851 150. In a majestic setting, beside the Playa Blanca beach.

WHAT TO EAT

The local cooking obviously features a lot of fish and seafood dishes, although the local specialties are the *papas arrugadas* (small, tasty, roasted potatoes), served with spicy *mojo* sauce, rabbit in *salmorejo* (another savoury dressing), *sancocho* (stew with meat, yucca and banana), sweet *morcillo* sausage, etc.

The Canary archipelago is a major producer of bananas, although the subtropical climate is also ideal for cultivating other crops, such as tomatoes, avocadoes, papayas, corn and tobacco.

In view of the constant influx of tourists, there is a large sampling of international restaurants in all the major cities.

WHERE TO EAT

GRAN CANARIA

Orangerie (Hotel Palm Beach), Avda Oasis, s/n, Plaza de Maspalomas. Tel: 140 806. Modern cooking, featuring varied salads, very fresh fish, including *carpaccio*, good meat, game in season and excellent desserts. Closed: Sunday lunch and during June and July.

Churchill, León y Castillo, 274, Las Palmas. Tel: 249 192. An original menu which varies greatly according to the quality produce available. Specialities are *carpaccio* fish, patés, salads, duck, tropical fruit desserts and *charlota de chocolate*. Closed: Saturday mid-day and Sunday and holidays.

La Parrilla (Hotel Reina Isabel), Alfredo L. Jones, 40, Las Palmas. Tel: 250 100. Good service and local wines, with such specialties as fish soup, *cherne al cilantro*, hake gratiné with lobster, sirloin, steak, papaya cocktail.

Mesón La Cuadra, General Mas de Gaminde, 32, Las Palmas. Tel: 243 380. Combined Castilian-Canary cooking, specialising in the typical roasts of the mainland. Closed: Monday.

Tenderete II, Avda Tirajana (Edificio Aloe), Playa del Inglés. Tel: 761 400. A typical Canary Island restaurant, with such dishes as fish baked in salt, *sancocho, papas* with *mojo*, *bienmesabe* ice cream, cheese and island wines.

TENERIFE

Café del Príncipe, Plaza del Príncipe, Santa Cruz. Tel: 278 810. Typical Canary Island cooking. Closed: Monday, and Easter week.

La Restaurant (Hotel Mencey), Dr José Naveiras, 38, Santa Cruz. Tel: 276 700. A charming decor and quality food, including avocado with shrimp, baked turbot with saffron and special house desserts. Closed: lunchtime in August.

Taberna del Atlántico (Los Realejos, Hotel Maritim Tenerife), El Burgado, 1-2, Puerto de la Cruz. Tel: 342 012. *Paella*, rabbit in *salmorejo, borrachitos*. Reasonably priced.

LANZAROTE

El Reducto, Fred Olsen, 1, Arrecife. Tel: 816 389. Restaurant specializes in seafood, although it does offer baby goat with *adobo* seasoning and roast baby lamb. Closed: Sunday.

El Diablo, Islote de Hilario, Montaña de Fuego. Tel: 840 057. Magnificent views and typical Canary Island cooking.

THINGS TO DO

TENERIFE

This is the largest island of the archipelago, known as the "island of the eternal spring". Its topography is varied, with an impressive mountain range, including the gigantic natural crater of the Cañadas del Teide, rising over 6,500 ft (2,000 metres) above sea level.

The capital of the island, Santa Cruz de Tenerife, with 220,000 inhabitants, is noted for its endless duty-free shopping possibilities. Worth visiting are the Archaeological and Anthropological Museum; the Church of the Concepción with its Cross of the Conquest, along with the flags taken from the vessels of English Admiral Sir Horace Nelson, when he tired unsuccessfully to conquer the island; and the Museo Municipal de Pintura y Escultura, with works by Ribera, Brueghel, Madrazo and a special section on Canary Island art.

Outside of the capital, an excursion should be made to the city of La Laguna, with its many monuments, including the 15th-century Cathedral, and to the lush La Orotava Valley, with typical island architecture, whose most representative landmark is the famous 17th-century Casa de los Balcones. And then on to the Cañadas del Teide, the highest peak in Spain, rising 12,198 ft (3,718 metres) above sea level. A 15-minute ride in a cable car brings visitors close to the top of the peak for some truly spectacular views.

Puerto de la Cruz is the major touristic centre with its enormous number of top hotels and tourist complexes. Also interesting is the picturesque village of Icod de los Vinos, noted for its wines, as its name implies, and dating back to 1501; and Candelaria, which venerates the image of the Patron Saint of the Canaries, the Virgen de Candelaria, in its Basilica.

GRAN CANARIA

The Grand Canary island is the third largest and offers a varied landscape, including striking mountains, sharp ravines, abrupt cliffs, provocative deserts and tropical forests. For this reason, it has often been referred to as a "miniature continent".

The provincial capital, Las Palmas, is a busy, prosperous city, due to the extensive activity of its port and the major influx of tourists.

In the old part of town is the Gothic Cathedral, constructed in 1497, Columbus' House, which was the home of the island's governors; the Canary Museum with interesting remains of the extinct Guanches; the Nestor Museum, the Home of Pérez Galdós; and the Provincial Fine Arts Museum.

The main tourist areas of the island are the Playa del Inglés and Maspalomas.

LANZAROTE

The volanic island of Lanzarote is one of the most unique places on earth, the result of major eruptions taking place as recently as the 18th and 19th centuries. This mysterious, suggestive landscape is much the way we imagine the moon's surface.

Not to be missed on a tour of the island are the efforts made by the local farmers to raise their crops out of this black, calcined earth and protect them from the low winds sweeping across the terrain.

Excellent full day tours of Lanzarote can be booked from the neighbouring islands and include a visit to the Islote de Hilario on Montaña de Fuego (Fire Mountain), in Timanfaya National Park. Here the 750°F (400°C) temperature at a depth of a mere 33 ft (10 metres) makes it possible to produce on-the-spot geysers or to fry fresh eggs directly on the ground. Also included in the tour is a teetering ride on the back of a dromedary along the mountainous "route of the volcanoes" and a visit to the amazing underground cave of the Jameos del Agua, in which a modern night-club has been installed.

5 January: Parade of the Three Kings in Santa Cruz de Tenerife and Las Palmas de Gran Canaria.
February: The very popular and colourful Carnivals of Santa Cruz de Tenerife and Las Palmas de Gran Canaria.
May: Santa Cruz festivities in Tenerife, including the celebration of the founding of the capital on 3 May, which have been declared of Special Touristic Interest.
20 May: The *Romería* or Pilgrimage of San Isidro the Farmer in Los Realejos (Tenerife), also declared of Special Touristic Interest.
June: Corpus Christi Day. Flower carpets are woven along the streets in Villa de Mazo (La Palma). Processions in Las Palmas de Gran Canaria and La Laguna (Tenerife). Fiestas of Special Touristic Interest.
June: Octava de Corpus. Held eight days after Corpus Christi Day in La Orotava on Tenerife, including a pilgrimage to the San Isidro Sanctuary.
25 July: Fiesta of Santiago Apóstol (St James' Day). Santa Cruz de Tenerife commemorates the heroic defense of the city against Lord Nelson's naval attack.
16 August: San Roque pilgrimage in Garachico (Tenerife), which has been declared of Special Touristic Interest.
25 August: San Ginés *fiestas* celebrated in Arrecife (Lanzarote), also of Special Touristic Interest.
17 September: Fiestas of Special Touristic Interest in honour of Cristo del Calvario in Icod de los Vinos (Tenerife).
October (second Saturday): Pilgrimage of Nuestra Señora de la Luz with a procession of boats. Las Palmas de Gran Canaria.

Due to the excellent climate, the islands are a haven for sports enthusiasts, whose activities may range from all water sports, including diving and sailing, to tennis, golf and horseback riding.

Traditional sport features Canary Island wrestling, cockfights, an original form of fencing with long sticks, and pole-jumping along the steep mountain slopes, particularly on the island of La Palma.

GRAN CANARIA
(Las Palmas). Area code: 928
Tourism Office: Casa del Turismo, Parque Santa Catalina. Tel: 264 623.
Post and Telegraph Office: Primera de Mayo, 62. Tel: 361 320.
Airport: Tel: 254 640.
Trasmediterránea: Muelle Primo de Rivera, s/n. Tel: 273 848.

Police: Edificio de Usos Múltiples. Plaza de los Derechos Humanos. Tel: 361 166 and 362 255.
First Aid: Paseo de Tomás Morales, s/n. Tel: 245 157 and Albareda, 71. Tel: 264 473.
Maspalomas Police Station: Ctra General del Súr, Km 53. Tel: 764 000.

TENERIFE
(Santa Cruz). Area code: 922
Tourism Office: Marina, 57. Tel: 287 516.
Post and Telegraph Office: Plaza de España. Tel: 242 002 and 241 388.
Airport in the North: Tel: 257 940. Reservations: 288 000.
Reina Sofía South International Airport: Tel: 770 050 and 770 100.
Gomera Ferry: Los Cristianos. Tel: 790 215.
Police: Avda Pérez de Ayala, 3. Tel: 212 511 and 212 711.
First Aid: José Murphy, 14. Tel: 241 502.
Tourism Office in Puerto de la Cruz: Plaza de la Iglesia, s/n. Tel: 386 000.

LANZAROTE
(Arrecife). Area code: 928
Tourism Office: Parque Municipal. Tel: 811 860.
Post and Telegraph Office: General Franco, 8. Tel: 811 917.
Airport: Tel: 811 450 and 800 551.
Transmediterránea: José Antonio, 90. Tel: 811 019.
Betancuria Ferry (to Playa Blanca-Corralejo). Tel: 812 534.
Police: Coll, 5. Tel: 812 350 and 812 354.

FUERTEVENTURA
(Puerto del Rosario). Area code: 928
Tourism Office: Avda 1° de Mayo, 33. Tel: 851 024.
Post and Telegraph Office: Avda 1° de Mayo, 58. Tel: 850 412.

Trasmediterránea: León y Castillo, 46. Tel: 850 016.
Airport: Tel: 851 250.
Police: León y Castillo, s/n. Tel: 850 909.

LA PALMA
(Santa Cruz de la Palma). Area code: 922
Tourism Office: Avda Marítima, 3. Tel: 411 642.
Post and Telegraph Office: Plazoleta del Muelle, s/n. Tel: 411 167 and 411 702.
Trasmediterránea: Real, 2. Tel: 411 121.
Airport: Tel: 411 540.
Police: Pérez Galdós, 16. Tel: 411 237.

GOMERA
(San Sebastián). Area code: 922
Tourism Office: Calle del Medio, 20. Tel: 870 103.
Post and Telegraph Office: Calle del Medio, 68. Tel: 871 081.
Trasmediterránea: Terminal Muelle. Tel: 870 802.
Gomera Ferry: Muelle. Tel: 871 007.
Civil Guard: Calvario. Tel: 870 255.

HIERRO
(Valverde). Area code: 922
Tourism Office: Licenciado Bueno, 1. Tel: 550 302.
Post and Telegraph Office: General Franco, 6. Tel: 550 291.
Trasmediterránea: Dr Dorkosky, 3. Tel: 550 129.
Airport: Tel: 550 878 and 550 724.
Civil Guard: Dacio Darias, 87. Tel: 550 105.

OTHER INSIGHT GUIDES

Other *Insight Guides* which highlight destinations in this region are:

Insight Guide: Southern Spain. Your key to Andalusia, the soul of Spain.

Insight Guide: Catalonia. The Costa Brava and Spain's unique Catalan culture.

Insight CityGuide: Barcelona. Trendy, cosmopolitan, and the city of the 1992 Olympics.

Insight CityGuide: Madrid. Spain's big city and its cultural capital, in glorious colour.

Insight Pocket Guides will take you straight to the best of the Spanish cities in day-by-day itineraries specially created by local residents.

Insight Pocket Guides also cover the Spanish islands.

396

ART/PHOTO CREDITS

Photographs by

Page 128/129	Oriol Alamany
200/201, 210, 218, 227, 275	G. Barone
60, 97, 122, 127, 210, 221, 228,	F. Lisa Beebe
237, 253	
22/23	Courtesy of Instituto Geografico Nacional
70, 71, 72, 74, 75, 202/203, 209,	J. D. Dallet
234, 235	
123	Gustave Dore
243, 246	Andrew Eames
62	Efe/José Martin
241, 245	Expo Tenerife
103, 106, 107, 108, 109	Muriel Feiner
84R, 86, 158	Diane Hall
211	Dallas & John Heaton
26, 32R, 33, 36, 63, 67, 329, 333	Imagen 3
1, 115, 278, 314, 332	Veronica Janssen
146/147, 188, 222, 225	Jean Kugler
104, 224, 277, 296	Rita Kummel
131	Alain Le Garsmeur
28, 41, 44, 46	M+W Fine Arts/New York/José Martin
96, 153, 156	Fiona MacGregor
27, 31, 34, 39, 42, 45, 47, 49, 50/51,	José Martin
52, 53, 55, 56, 57, 58, 59, 64, 110/111,	
112, 114, 116, 117, 119, 157R,	
174, 175L, 175R, 176, 187,	
268, 326	
130, 132, 133	Mike Mockler
92/93	Richard Nowitz
7, 30, 84L, 120, 150, 151, 163R, 182	Carl Purcell
244, 247	Jörg Reuther
229	Spanish Institute of New York City
Cover	Spectrum Colour Library
68/69	Topham Picture Source
266L, 266R, 272	Robin Townsend
12/13, 16/17, 20, 32L, 37, 61, 65L,	Joe Viesti
65R, 76/77, 78/79, 83L, 85, 87L, 87R,	
88, 89, 90, 91, 98/99, 100/101, 102,	
105, 124, 125, 136/137, 138/139, 142,	
164/165, 168, 169, 170, 171, 172, 173,	
177, 178, 181, 183, 184, 189, 190,	
192, 193, 194, 195, 196, 197, 199,	
204, 214, 216, 217, 219, 220, 223,	
226, 230, 231, 232, 233, 236, 250/251,	
252, 254L, 254R, 255, 256, 260, 261,	
262L, 262R, 216, 270, 271, 274, 279,	
280, 281, 284, 291, 292/293, 294/295,	
298, 299, 300, 301, 302, 303, 304,	
305, 306, 307, 308, 309, 310, 311,	
312, 315, 316, 317, 318, 321, 322,	
324, 330, 335, 336	
14/15, 18/19, 24/25, 73, 80, 94, 95,	Bill Wassman
134/135, 148, 154, 155, 157L, 159,	
160, 161, 162, 163L, 166/167, 208,	
213, 215, 238/239, 240, 242, 248/249,	
265, 273, 276, 282/283, 286, 288, 289,	
331, 334	

Illustrations Klaus Geisler
Visual Consulting V. Barl

INDEX

Mirador de San Nicolás 228
Mirador del Cable 322
Mirador of San Cristóbal 229
Miramar 288
Miramar Palace 309
Miró Foundation 271, 272
Miró, Joan 114, 118, 152, 261, 267, 315
Mitjorn 290
Moaña 333
Mohammed I 223–224
Moll de Fusta 267
Molló 280
Monasterio de la Encarnación 157
Monasterio de las Descalzas Reales 158
Monasterio de Piedra 305
Monasterio de Santa Maria de las Cuevas 209
Monastery of Guadalupe 191–192
Monastery of La Pedra 306
Monastery of Las Huelgas 186
Monastery of Pedralbes 270
Monastery of San Esteban 184
Monastery of San Francisco 330
Monastery of San Juan de la Peña 306
Monastery of San Martín Pinario 330
Monastery of San Pedro de Arlanza 187
Monastery of San Pedro de Cardeña 186
Monastery of San Telmo 310
Monastery of Sant Pere de Galligants 276
Monastery of Santo Tomás 180
Monastery of Yuste 199
Monfragüe 133
Monjuïc 265, 270–271
Montaner, Domènech i 265, 269
Monte Igueldo 310
Monte Real 335
Montejurra 300
Montijo, Eugenie de 309, 313
Montseny 280
Montserrat 272
Monument to the Fueros 298
Moore, Sir John 327
Moors 25, 33, 35–40, 40, 81, 116, 121, 123, 149,
    169, 170, 177, 179, 181, 184, 185, 185–186, 191,
    192, 194, 195, 195, 196, 198, 205, 206, 208, 210,
    217, 219, 220, 223, 228, 228, 229, 233, 235, 237,
    253, 253, 281, 285, 301, 303, 304, 323, 325,
    328, 329
Mora de Rubielos 307
Morey 287
Morisca 275
moriscos 45, 46, 46, 225, 253, 257, 303
Mount Galatzó 288
Mount Naranco 323
mozarabic style 115, 170, 321, 322
mudéjar style 169, 170, 172, 177, 189, 192, 210, 213,
    219, 303, 304, 305, 307, 320
muleta 103
Murillo, Bartolomé Esteban 113, 117, 118, 207,
    210, 213
museums
    Archeological and Fine Arts (Orense) 331
    Archeological (Badajoz) 195
    Archeological (Barcelona) 271
    Archeological (Córdoba) 220
    Archeological (Mérida) 193
    Archeological (Seville) 212
    Archeology Ethnology and History of Vizcaya, 313
    Archeology (Bilbao) 315
    Archeology (Ibiza) 290
    Army (Madrid) 152
    Basque (San Telmo) 310–311
    Bullfight (Ronda) 233
    Carriage (Madrid) 158
    Casa de las Veletas (Cáceres) 195
    Casa del Mono (Cáceres) 196
    Castillo de San Antón (La Coruña) 327
    Catalan Art (Barcelona) 271
    Ceramic (Barcelona) 270
    City of Barcelona 263
    Clock (Jerez) 232
    Convent of San Vicente (Oviedo) 323
    Crafts (Solsona) 281
    Dalí (Figueres) 276
    Decorative Art (Madrid) 152
    Diocesan (Jaca) 306
    Diocesan (Solsona) 281
    Drassanes Maritime (Barcelona) 267
    Eivissa (Ibiza) 290
    El Greco House and Museum (Toledo) 172
    Fine Arts (Bilbao) 314
    Fine Arts (Córdoba) 220
    Fine Arts (Seville) 213
    Fine Arts (Valencia) 257
    Geology (Barcelona) 265
    Lázaro Galdiano (Madrid) 163
    León Cathedral 185
    Municipal Museum of Fine Arts (Santander) 319
    Municipal (Madrid) 160–161
    Museo de Arte de Cataluña (Barcelona) 116
    Museo de Navarra 298
    Museo de Ricas Telas (Burgos) 186
    Museo del Jamón 153
    Museo Zuloaga (Lequeitio) 312
    Museu d'Art de Catalunya (Montjuïc) 271
    Museu d'Art Modern (Barcelona) 265
    Museu del Vi (Vilafranca) 281
    Museum of the Americas 72
    National Archeological (Madrid) 162
    National Ceramic (Valencia) 257
    Naval (Madrid) 152
    Nuevos (El Escorial) 174
    Picasso (Barcelona) 264
    Prado 48, 113, 116, 117, 118, 143, 149, 151–152
    Provincial Archeological (León) 185
    Provincial Fine Arts (Zaragoza) 304
    Provincial Museum of Fine Arts (Vitoria) 315
    Provincial Museum of Prehistory and Archeology
    (Santander) 320
    Provincial (Lugo) 330
    Romantic (Madrid) 161
    Santo Cruz (Toledo) 171
    Seo Cathedral (Zaragoza) 304
    Sephardic (Toledo) 171
    Theatre (Barcelona) 267
    Valencia Cathedral 256
    Visigothic Culture and Councils (Toledo) 169
    Zoology (Barcelona) 265
Muslims 35, 36
Mussolini, Benito 57

N

Naples 43, 46
Napoleon I 48, 160
Napoleon III 309
Napoleonic Wars 304

Q – R

S

U

V

W – Z